APPLIED
STATISTICS
USING STATA

SAGE was founded in 1965 by Sara Miller McCune to support the dissemination of usable knowledge by publishing innovative and high-quality research and teaching content. Today, we publish over 900 journals, including those of more than 400 learned societies, more than 800 new books per year, and a growing range of library products including archives, data, case studies, reports, and video. SAGE remains majority-owned by our founder, and after Sara's lifetime will become owned by a charitable trust that secures our continued independence.

Los Angeles | London | New Delhi | Singapore | Washington DC | Melbourne

Mehmet Mehmetoglu
Tor Georg Jakobsen

APPLIED
STATISTICS
USING STATA

A Guide for the
Social Sciences

Los Angeles | London | New Delhi
Singapore | Washington DC | Melbourne

Los Angeles | London | New Delhi
Singapore | Washington DC | Melbourne

SAGE Publications Ltd
1 Oliver's Yard
55 City Road
London EC1Y 1SP

SAGE Publications Inc.
2455 Teller Road
Thousand Oaks, California 91320

SAGE Publications India Pvt Ltd
B 1/I 1 Mohan Cooperative Industrial Area
Mathura Road
New Delhi 110 044

SAGE Publications Asia-Pacific Pte Ltd
3 Church Street
#10-04 Samsung Hub
Singapore 049483

Editor: Jai Seaman
Assistant editor: Alysha Owen
Production editor: Ian Antcliff
Copyeditor: Richard Leigh
Proofreader: Kate Campbell
Indexer: Martin Hargreaves
Marketing manager: Sally Ransom
Cover design: Shaun Mercier
Typeset by: C&M Digitals (P) Ltd, Chennai, India
Printed in Great Britain by CPI Group (UK) Ltd,
Croydon, CR0 4YY

Library of Congress Control Number: 2016939501

British Library Cataloguing in Publication data

A catalogue record for this book is available from
the British Library

ISBN 978-1-4739-1322-6
ISBN 978-1-4739-1323-3 (pbk)

CONTENTS

EXTENDED CONTENTS

COMPANION WEBSITE

Applied Statistics Using Stata: A Guide for the Social Sciences is supported by a wealth of online resources to aid study and assist in teaching, which are available at https://study.sagepub.com/mehmetogluandjakobsen

STUDENT RESOURCES

Stata codes and data sets allow you to practice and apply the skills you've learned using real-life examples.

Weblinks direct you to relevant video resources to broaden your understanding of chapter topics and expand your knowledge by linking to real world organizations and conversations on applied statistics.

Multiple choice questions test your statistics knowledge and aid in revision.

Free **SAGE journal articles** reinforce your learning of key topics and provides an ideal starting point for literature reviews, dissertations, or assignments.

INSTRUCTOR RESOURCES

PowerPoint slides cover the key themes and topics of each chapter.

ABOUT THE AUTHORS

Mehmet Mehmetoglu is a Professor of Research Methods in the Department of Psychology at the Norwegian University of Science and Technology (NTNU). His research interests include consumer psychology, evolutionary psychology and statistical methods. Mehmetoglu has publications and co-publications in about 30 different refereed international journals, among them *Scandinavian Journal of Psychology*, *Personality & Individual Differences*, and *Evolutionary Psychological Science*.

Tor Georg Jakobsen is a Professor of Political Science at NTNU Business School at the Norwegian University of Science and Technology. His research interests include political behaviour, peace research and statistical methods. Jakobsen has authored and co-authored articles in, among others, *European Sociological Review*, *Work, Employment & Society* and *Conflict Management & Peace Science*.

PREFACE

Knowing how to use statistics to solve social problems is a crucial competence for students and academics. To gain and develop such a competence requires us to understand the underlying mechanisms of statistical techniques (linear regression, factor analysis, etc.) as well as learning to use flexible and user-friendly software for performing them. We humbly try to help the reader achieve these two salient goals with the current book by elucidating the logic behind each statistical technique and providing actual applications using Stata software. In explaining the different statistical techniques, we use linear regression as our overarching framework based on our motto that 'everything is regression'.

An in-depth knowledge of linear regression lays the foundation for learning any other statistical technique, from apparently simple techniques (e.g., t-test) to more advanced ones (e.g., structural equation modelling). This is also the reason why we choose to treat linear regression and its extensions thoroughly. Having read these chapters, you will observe that linear regression can readily be used as a very flexible substitute for the traditional group comparison techniques of the analysis of variance (ANOVA) family for independent data. The linear regression approach also creates a bridge to the multilevel regression technique that has proved to be a very useful substitute for ANOVA techniques used for analysing repeated measures data.

To get the most from this book the reader will ideally have some background in basic statistics and some experience with inferential statistics. No previous experience of Stata is needed as we provide a detailed introduction to this software before starting to use Stata for the different techniques. As you work through each chapter, we strongly advise you to have Stata open in front of you to replicate the statistical analyses and procedures. Before doing so, you will need to have a look at and download the additional book material (datasets, Stata codes, example journal articles etc.) available on the companion website at https://study.sagepub.com/login?destination=node/30193.

ACKNOWLEDGEMENT

We would like to acknowledge the many useful and encouraging comments from our anonymous reviewers engaged by SAGE. We would also like to thank our StataCorp colleague, Bill Rising, for his thorough review of each chapter and for providing us with lots of valuable comments and suggestions. We further wish to thank another StataCorp colleague, Kristin MacDonald, for her very useful comments on the chapter on structural equation modelling. Both Bill and Kristin are testament to StataCorp's known reputation for professionalism. We also owe thanks to our colleagues Stein Are Sæther, Giovanni Cerulli, Sergio Venturini, Kjell Hines, Arild Blekesaune, Marthe L. Holum, Zan Strabac, Jon Olaf Olaussen, Jonathon W. Moses, Mikael Knutsson, Jo Jakobsen and Morten Blekesaune for their suggestions and comments on different chapters as well as their support throughout this book project. Moreover, we would like to thank our supportive and professional SAGE team consisting of our editor Jai Seaman, Alysha Owen, Ian Antcliff, Sally Ransom, Lily Mehrbod, Vanessa Harwood and copyeditor Richard Leigh. Finally, we thank our respective families (Rannvei and Deniz for Mehmet, and Marthe and Sofie for Tor Georg) for their continued support.

1

RESEARCH AND STATISTICS

learning outcomes

- Understand the methodological foundations of statistical research
- Be able to grasp the logic behind different types of statistical inference

- Understand the importance of sound theory
- Get some hints on how to write quantitative research papers and how to present data

The theory of science and methodology are the pillars on which social scientists stand when conducting research. The researcher's goal when using statistics is to make conclusions that go beyond the collected data. With large-N studies, it is possible to make generalizations about the causal effects of different phenomena, if one has established the direction of causality. In this chapter the reader will be given a summary of the theory of method behind the use of statistics, the statistical method itself, and how to apply it in research.

As this textbook is meant for master's- and PhD-level students, we assume that readers have already taken basic courses in quantitative methods and theory of science. Even so, we will provide some background for the reader when it comes to theory of science and tests of significance. This is to help the student to put the use of statistics into context.

THE METHODOLOGY OF STATISTICAL RESEARCH

There are certain ontological and epistemological presumptions of inferential statistics. Succinctly stated, *ontology* can be said to be the study of reality, or the science or philosophy of being, while *epistemology* is the study of the nature of knowledge. When employing inferential statistics our ontological position is that there exists a real world independent of our perception of it. This point of departure is in line with the positivist tradition, which holds that the world consists of regularities, which implies that everything can – at least in principle – be demarcated, described, measured, compared, explained, and used to make predictions. Following this ontological position, the most important mission of science is to uncover these regularities or laws. This tradition provides us with an epistemological view that these regularities are detectable, and thus, that the researcher can infer knowledge about the real world by observing it. According to the empiricist, knowledge is not congenital; rather, it is grounded on observations and sense impressions. In other words, knowledge consists of empirical data that are aggregated and put in context.

Methodology can be understood as the logic behind the methods we choose, or as Hay (2002: 63) describes it, 'the choice of analytical strategy and research design which underpins substantive research'. When conducting a statistical causal analysis the choice of our ontological and epistemological approach basically implies that we are looking for regularities or correlations in the real world. Our objective is to unveil and explain these regularities.

Positivism in general refers to philosophical positions that emphasize empirical data and scientific methods, and as social scientists we include the belief that the methods of natural science can be applied to all phenomena. Moses and Knutsen (2012) trace the history of modern science back to Galileo Galilei (1564–1642). In his work *Siderius Nuncius* (*The Starry Messenger*) of 1610 he made systematic observations of the Moon, the stars and the moons of Jupiter (Galilei, 1957). His methods stood in contrast to the prevailing approach of that time, namely that advocated by Aristotle and the Church.

In the same century Francis Bacon introduced a combination of induction and experiment into science, as he wished to combine experience with record keeping and thus rejected the deductive method of his time. Francis Bacon, and later John Locke and David Hume, provided the basic framework for the modern positivist tradition. Based on their works, theorists have found fuel for their claim that there exists a real world out there independent of our senses. Modern scientists following this tradition argue that the regularities of this real world can be experienced through systematic sense perceptions. Auguste Comte (1798–1857) is reckoned as one of the founders of modern sociology. His epistemological argument was consistent with that of his positivist predecessors, that is, that scientific knowledge about the real world comes from empirical observation. He also made a distinction between empirical and normative knowledge. Information or knowledge that was not empirical was not considered by Comte to be knowledge about the real world, and thus fell outside the scope of science (Moses and Knutsen, 2012: 35).

The positivist tradition allows for the scientist to choose from a certain 'tool-box' of methods when investigating the real world. This is referred to as the *methodology* of the discipline, and consist of its methods, rules and postulates. One of these methods, the one that is the topic of this book, is the statistical method.

1.2 THE STATISTICAL METHOD

According to King et al. (1994: 8), the goal of scientific research is to make conclusions that go beyond the collected data. With large-N studies it is possible to make generalizations about the causal effects for different phenomena (if one has established the direction of causality). However, this presupposes the availability of data, whether it be a sample of a population, or the whole (or bordering on the whole) population. There are two different types of statistics: descriptive (when we want to describe a distribution) and inferential (when we want to say something about the relationship between two variables). The latter may be used for predictions and hypothesis testing, and is commonplace in the social sciences.

As a tool of the positivist tradition, inferential statistics is a way of identifying patterns and regularities in the observable world. Statistics involves the systematic collection of data with the aim of achieving knowledge by induction, that is, making inferences from observed regularities to general theories. This systematic inductive use of statistics can be traced back to John Graunt, Sir William Petty and Hermann Conring (Moses and Knutsen, 2012). In the seventeenth century they brought the use of descriptive statistics to science. The least-squares method was introduced by Carl Friedrich Gauss at the turn of the eighteenth century. Yet, the phrasing of social science questions in variable terms did not occur until the nineteenth century. Francis Galton introduced the correlation coefficient, the scatter plot, and also regression analysis, the prime tool of modern social science statistics. Karl Pearson carried on Galton's work, and later Émile Durkheim placed statistics centre-stage, finding covariance between suicide and religion, in addition to other variables. Before Durkheim introduced the use of statistics into the social sciences, researchers relied on a more philosophical procedure, based on reasoning and facts of experience (Ellwood, 1931). This can be illustrated by an event that took place in Norway in the seventeenth century.

In 1612 a group of more than 300 mercenaries left Aberdeen in Scotland and sailed across the sea, eventually reaching the coast of Norway. Their plan was to cross the Norwegian interior in order to join their Swedish employers in the Kalmar War.[1] The Scotsmen went through Romsdalen, and after a while they reached the valley of Gudbrandsdalen, located in the heart of the Norwegian interior. When they had reached the narrowest part of the valley, they discovered an unaccompanied, but armed, Norwegian farmer. The Scottish mercenaries, led by Captain George Sinclair, pursued this lone peasant. Suddenly the peasant was out of sight. All the Scotsmen could see was a secluded linden tree. There was no place there to hide, other than in the tree. The Norwegian could not have reached the sides of the valley without being noticed. The only logical explanation was that the farmer was covering himself in between the branches of the linden. Thus, Captain Sinclair concluded that the peasant had climbed up and was hiding in the tree.

The conclusion made by Sinclair was, of course, a valid scientific inference. This is because the Scotsmen's background experience assumed that the farmer had no other means of escape than to climb up the linden tree, taking into account that, as far as the mercenaries knew, no man could fly or disappear into the ground. In the same manner as Captain Sinclair reached this conclusion, the great thinkers of all sciences have reached their conclusions. One has a background experience which one uses as a basis when interpreting the facts. All in all, science involves a large degree of systematized common sense.

Yet, in today's social science tradition many researchers would not have accepted Sinclair's conclusion. They would have demanded further evidence, preferably with 95 per cent certainty. Today's quantitative researcher would probably have insisted on Sinclair's men thrusting pointy sticks or spears through at least nineteen-twentieths of the linden tree, to ensure that one could with enough statistical significance conclude whether the frightened peasant actually was hiding in the tree. One would not have trusted the Captain's experience and common sense alone – one would want numbers and facts on the table before deciding whether or not the farmer was hiding in the tree.

Well, Captain Sinclair was of course right in his conclusion, even though this was not based on numbers or tests of significance. Yet, this was of little help, as about 500 Norwegian farmers came down from above the path, ambushing the mercenaries. The whole incident ended with the defeat of the Scottish troops, the death of George Sinclair, and the tragic fate of the surviving Scotsmen in a barn in the deep interior of Norway. However, this is not what is important about this story. The main point is that the social sciences need to be receptive to all facts, and also to all methods in which one can discover facts that can be useful for understanding social processes.

 THE LOGIC BEHIND STATISTICAL INFERENCE

Using statistical methods, social scientists are able to make generalizations about the empirical world. There are many pitfalls to avoid before making statistical generalizations. One must

---

[1] The Kalmar War (1611–1613) was fought between Sweden and Denmark. The root of the war was the Swedish desire to establish a trade route through northern Norway (Norway was then a part of the Danish kingdom).

define the population correctly, taking into account what the sample should constitute, and which time period to investigate. The researcher needs to be aware of the context and disposition of their data, which are the assumptions that underlie statistical models (John, 2002). Sampling error is not the only source of error encountered in survey data. Other problems include interviewer variability, non-response, and problems connected to the questionnaire (Groves, 1989). According to sample theory the size of our sample greatly influences our ability to generalize results back to the population we are investigating. Still, a couple of questions go unanswered: "Does the population size matter for the level of significance?" and "What if we are examining the whole population?"

1●3●1 Probability theory

However, the most common approach in inferential statistics is to follow the logic of probability theory. As we know, when our sample reaches 1000–1200 it is much easier to obtain significant results than when it is a mere 25. Probability theory centres on the central limit theorem, which briefly states that, as sample size N becomes large, the sampling distribution of the mean becomes approximately normal. Also, the sampling distribution will fall around the variable's population mean. This presupposes that the units are sampled either at random, or with a known probability of being chosen (which later can be adjusted for by the researcher). The latter option is often effected through stratified sampling, where the population is divided into districts with the aim of carrying out a closer examination of subgroups.

It is commonplace to operate with *p-values*, which denote the probability of being mistaken when we reject a null hypothesis (which proposes that there is no relationship between two measured phenomena). The closer a *p*-value is to zero, the more certain we can be that our hypothesis is more likely than the null hypothesis. Even so, one also needs the backing of sound theory to say something about the relationship between variables. Statistical correlations should not be mistaken as being causal explanations. As such, observed relations must be interpreted with a basis in theories about human action (Elster, 1989, 1998). The results from a regression analysis essentially only provide us with correlations between variables, just as Hume (2011) tells us that we can only observe patterns and regularities, not causality. Hume emphatically states that science needs to be careful with regard to causal claims:

> I assert it to be the very same with that betwixt the ideas of cause and effect, and to be an essential part in all our reasonings from that relation. We have no other notion of cause and effect, but that of certain objects, which have been always conjoin'd together, and which in all past instances have been found inseparable. We cannot penetrate into the reason of the conjunction. We only observe the thing itself, and always find that from the constant conjunction the objects acquire a union in the imagination (Hume, 2011: Book I, Part III, Section VI).

The statistical method is suitable for making generalizations that go beyond the collected data, and can thus assist the researcher in identifying patterns and regularities in the observable world. However, there are caveats connected to this choice of method. One of the most pronounced problems is that regression analysis only provides us with *correlation* between variables. Statistical methods exist that can assist in determining causality, but these are not easily applicable and they often presuppose longitudinal data. Therefore, one needs the backing of sound theory to say something about the causal relationship between the variables. When it comes to assessing causal relationships the experimental method is considered the best option available for scientists. This method allows the researcher to manipulate the environment in which causal relationships are tested, thus reassuring us that the relationships discovered are real and not a result of contextual influence (Moses and Knutsen, 2012).

1●3●2 Population size

From sample theory we know that the size of the sample matters when it comes to making inferences beyond the collected data. But what about the size of the population? Do we get better results if we are sampling 1000 Norwegians and generalizing back to the Norwegian population, than if we were sampling 1000 Americans and generalizing to the US population? The short answer is no.

If we look at the mathematics behind probability, we see that the size of the population really does not matter. A given sample size is equally useful in examining the opinions of Icelanders as it is of Chinese. However, there is an exception to this rule. If the size of the sample exceeds a few percent of the population the confidence intervals become smaller. In other words, population size is only likely to be a factor if you are investigating a small and known group of people, such as an organization or sports club. This is illustrated by Table 1.1, showing the sample size needed to get a similar 95 per cent confidence interval for different population sizes.

Table 1.1 Population and the sample size needed for a given confidence interval

Population	Sample
10	10
50	44
100	80
200	132
500	217
1000	278
3000	341
100,000+	385

In essence, once the sample constitutes a small share of the population (as is illustrated in Figure 1.1), the size of the population matters. As the population increases the sample size needed for a given confidence interval increases (proportionally), until it becomes relatively constant at slightly more than 380 cases (Kreijcie and Morgan, 1970).

In essence, what is important for statistical inference is the sample size, and not the population size. However, if the sample size constitutes a large portion of the population

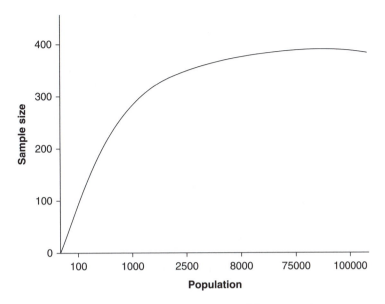

Figure 1.1 Population and the sample size needed for a given confidence interval

(e.g., 30–40 per cent) this can be compensated for by using the *finite population correction factor* (fpc) in Stata. In order to use this command we must declare that the dataset has a survey design (using the svyset command). For example, if we have a sample of 1000 from a population of 2000, the use of fpc might come in handy:

```
. gen fpc=2000
. svyset, fpc(fpc)
. svy: reg Y X X
```

It must be noted that if you are investigating a small and known group of people, you might want to consider a different underlying logic for your use of levels of significance. This leads us on to the next topic.

1●3●3 Why do I need significance levels if I am investigating the whole population?

In many cases a social scientist will be investigating an entire population. It could be within international relations, the study of war and peace, or in international political economy. Or it could be in business, investigating all fast food restaurants in a city. When examining the whole population (or as close as you can get – the important thing is that your aim is to examine the whole population) and not just a sample of it, you are now generalizing within *stochastic model theory* (rather than within sample theory). When following sample theory, we generalize from the sample to the population. According to this logic, when one looks at the entire population, one should get perfect predictions. This is where stochastic model theory becomes useful. In fact, we are generalizing from the observation made, to the process or mechanism that brings about the actual data.

Our starting point is a non-deterministic experiment, which implies that the results of the experiment will vary, even if we try to keep the conditions surrounding it constant. It can be roughly compared to throwing an unloaded dice twice at your desk, without changing the place of your cup, books and pencils between each throw. Thus, the use of confidence intervals and significance levels makes sense, even if we are looking at the entire population. The lack of statistical significance indicates that the association produced by nature is no more probable than that produced by chance. We are thus dealing with a mechanism best described as an unspecified random process (Gold, 1969; Henkel, 1976).

One could argue that for sample data we should then have a double test of significance. In theory this is true, as we have the uncertainty that the sample is a true mirror image of the population, and the uncertainty that the correlations in the population could be produced by chance by the unspecified random process. However, we usually state that our aim is to see if the relationships are present in the population (and not if the relationships in the population are for real), and we thus only have to operate within sample theory.

 GENERAL LAWS AND THEORIES

There are, as already stated, problems with determining causal inference. Hume argued that no finite amount of experimentation can say for certain that X causes Y. This brings us to the question of *falsifiability*. Karl Popper proclaimed that a proposition is scientific only if it is falsifiable, that is, it can be shown to be *not true* by an observation or an experiment. Thus, social scientists should strive towards a less turgid way of justifying causality; the conclusions drawn need to correspond to what common sense and science (or theory) judge as reasonable (Mayo, 1980). Theories provide us with general explanations for social behaviour. A theory must include a statement about constructs, describe causal relations, and be general in its scope, that is, it must apply to people of different settings and time (Smith and Mackie, 2000: 28ff.). We can use statistics to confirm or even to present new *general laws*. Hempel (1942: 35) defines such a law as 'the idea that the statement in question is actually well confirmed or disconfirmed by the relevant evidence available'. He further explains that such a universal hypothesis can be expected to follow a pattern or regularity of the following type: a *cause* will occur at a time and place, and an *effect* will occur at a time and place. The latter will be connected in a specified manner to the time and place of the cause. Yet, he also stresses that, given the theory and logical arguments of the direction of causality, one can in statistical analysis only say with such and such *statistical probability* that the explanation is true. This is what he calls *laws of statistical form*, as opposed to *universal laws*, where all cases satisfying certain conditions will cause a specific event (Hempel, 1959).

Although we as statistical researchers should agree with the positivist assumption that there exist patterns in nature that can be observed, we must also acknowledge the argument that the proxies of what we are measuring are not always optimal. In many cases we do not have direct access to what we are measuring; for example, we could be relying on survey questions that are vulnerable to many types of measurement errors. Therefore, it is essential not to depend on statistics alone, but also have our arguments backed by strong theoretical reasoning. And we want our theories to be causal, non-normative, general, and parsimonious.

1•4•1 Objectivity and critical realism

Hume made a distinction between descriptive and normative statements. A descriptive statement is a portrayal of a course of events, without considering the moral aspect of it. When making a normative statement one says something about not only how things are, but also how things *should* be. One cannot deduce 'ought' from 'is' as morality is not an object of reason (Hume, 2011: Book III; Part I, Section I). Comte followed Hume when making his distinction between empirical and normative knowledge. Weber agreed that science should follow an objective ideal, yet he acknowledged that values and norms play a part in determining the focus of research:

> As we saw, in the domain of the empirical socio-cultural sciences the possibility of meaningful knowledge of what is essential for us in the infinity of events is linked to the consistent use of viewpoints of a specifically particular character, all of which in the last instance are directed by evaluative ideas, which ideas in turn can be registered as elements of all meaningful human action, but which are *not* derived from or validated by the empirical material (Weber 2004: 402–403).

These values are determined by, for example, culture and politics, and are changeable and subjective; they change depending on culture, time-period and place.

Our role as social scientists implies that we seek to achieve objectivity. The underlying assumption is that there is a real and measurable world out there, and it is thus imperative that the researcher himself is objective in his interpretation of data. The conclusions drawn from the data should be based on the actual findings. For example, having stated a hypothesis that is not supported by the results, we as researchers should not carry on arguing in favour of the rejected supposition.

Scientific realism pertains to the belief that our knowledge and scientific theories correspond to reality. The *critical realists* agree that this is the case for some of our sense data. Yet, they acknowledge that some of our impressions and understandings do not accurately represent the real world, as they are influenced by perceptual illusions and cognition. This school of thought within theory of science has its background in the American philosopher Roy Wood Sellars, who wrote the book *Critical Realism* (1916). The central doctrine of critical realism is that our knowledge of external things and of past events is influenced by our interpretation of these. It does not mean the actual presence of these objects in the consciousness of the researcher. One should therefore move away from naïve realism, which has made the mistake of assuming that physical objects can be intuited directly, and instead adopt a view more in keeping with the facts of science (Bode, 1922: 69; Sellars, 1927: 238). The human world differs from the physical world, something that social researchers need to take into account. Human behaviour is stipulated and influenced by social structures, which again are made up of collective human behaviour. In other words, the individuals who are affected by these structures also have the possibility to change the same structures.

1●5 QUANTITATIVE RESEARCH PAPERS

Large parts of the published articles in the social sciences are quantitative. Being able to use statistics increases your chances of writing a good term paper, thesis, or publishing an article in an academic journal. Writing a quantitative research paper means that you must follow many of the standard guidelines for academic writing. You must be able to post a problem which contains one or a few clear points, and shape this into either an interesting research question or a testable hypothesis. As a quantitative researcher you will be concerned with using data you have gathered in order to test your hypothesis (or hypotheses). You also need to be able to summarize previous research, build theoretical arguments leading to your hypothesis (or research question), perform the statistical analysis, present the results in a clear and understandable manner, and describe your own findings, explaining them using the theories presented earlier.

In the research methods section you should describe your sample and population, state your sample size, present your dependent and independent variables and your plan of analysis. You can present your descriptive statistics in a table (including N, mean, standard deviation, and, if relevant, skewness and kurtosis). This can be placed either in the paper itself, in the appendix, or it might be excluded (depending on its importance and size limitations). Then follows the results section, often titled 'analysis'. Here you present your regression tables and give a short presentation of the findings in writing. But save the theoretical interpretation for the discussion or the later part of the analysis section.

There are many different ways of presenting the results. If you only have one or two models you can be thorough and present a detailed table, including both the slope coefficient, standard error, z-score and *p-value* as seen in Table 1.2, which is a regression table explaining the impact of regime type on welfare attitudes.

Table 1.2   Regression model of welfare attitudes

	B	Std. E	*p*
Constant (Liberal)	4.664	0.195	0.000
Social-Democratic	0.216	0.318	0.509
Continental	0.716	0.318	0.042
Southern	0.711	0.364	0.073
Eastern European	0.391	0.292	0.203
Asian	0.631	0.364	0.107
R^2	0.376		
N	19		

You should also present the total N, and measures relevant for the model as a whole (e.g., R-squared, F-statistics, log-likelihood). However, a common way of displaying the results (especially if you are presenting several models) is to include only the slope coefficient, standard error, and an indication of the level of significance, as shown in Table 1.3. Note that Table 1.3 is the same model as in Table 1.2, but contains less information.

It is also a good thing to present figures and graphs illustrating the results. Your job is to communicate your results to the reader, and if graphs can assist in this, it is a good thing to include them. Also, it is common in statistical research to perform what we call a sensitivity

Table 1.3 Regression model of welfare attitudes, slope coefficients and standard errors in parentheses

Constant (Liberal)	4.664***
	(0.195)
Social-Democratic	0.216
	(0.318)
Continental	0.716**
	(0.318)
Southern	0.711*
	(0.364)
Eastern European	0.391
	(0.292)
Asian	0.631
	(0.364)
R^2	0.376
N	19

Note: * significant at 10 per cent, **significant at 5 per cent, and ***significant at 1 per cent.

analysis. This is done by way of running additional models where you make relevant changes to your main analysis. The reason for this is to see if the results change or not (are robust) to different sources of uncertainty. For, example, you could change one explanatory variable for another similar one, you could use a different coding scheme for the dependent variable, or you could test your main model on another sample. The results of your sensitivity analysis could be presented in the appendix or, if there are space limitations, referred to in a footnote.

The term 'replication' or 'reproducibility' is especially important in statistical research. This means that other researchers should be able to reproduce the results of your study. In order to do so, other researchers must know the process by which the data were generated and the analysis produced. As such, when performing your analysis, you must document what you do. In Stata this can be done by writing down all your coding and modelling, with explanations, in a do-file. Not only is this necessary for the sake of others replicating your results, but also if you need to replicate the data. There is a growing tendency for academic journals to require authors of statistical papers to also deliver their datasets along with a do-file, so that any reader can download them, reproduce the results, and build on them.

1.6 CONCLUDING REMARKS

The point of departure for most statistical researchers is the ontological assumption that there exists a real world independent of our perception of it, and that this world consists of patterns. This tradition can be traced back to the works of Galileo Galilei, Francis Bacon and Auguste Comte. Its epistemological view is that the patterns and regularities are detectable, and, thus, the researcher can infer knowledge about the real world by observing it. The statistical method is considered the next best method within this tradition, only surpassed by the experimental method which can control and order causal relationships.

The statistical method is suitable for making generalizations that go beyond the collected data, and can thus assist the researcher in identifying patterns and regularities in the observable world. Mathematics, in the form of statistics, is a great tool that can assist the social scientist in getting access to and explaining the complexities of life. However, the researcher must be aware of the underlying logic of why he or she makes those inferences.

 **key terms**

Positivism A direction within theory of science which argues that knowledge is derived from logical and mathematical treatment of sensory experiences.

Inferential statistics The type of statistics we use when we want to say something about the relationship between two variables and reach conclusions that extend beyond the collected data.

Probability theory A branch of mathematics concerned with the analysis of random phenomena.

Stochastic model theory When generalizing from the observation made, this theory helps explain the process or mechanism that brings about the actual data.

QUESTIONS

1   What is the main advantage of large-N studies compared to small-N studies?
2   In what way does population size matter when it comes to statistical inference?
3   What is the purpose of a sensitivity analysis?

FURTHER READING

Kellstedt, P.M. and Whitten, G.D. (2013) *The Fundamentals of Political Science Research*. Cambridge: Cambridge University Press.

This book gives an introduction to mathematical concepts necessary for starting political science researchers. It focuses on causal claims and includes an introductory treatment of regression models.

King, G. (1995) Replication, replication. *Political Science and Politics*, 28(3): 444–452.

In this article, King highlights the necessity of replication in the social sciences. He also proposes solutions to current problems in political science.

Moses, J.W. and Knutsen, T.L. (2012) *Ways of Knowing: Competing Methodologies in Social and Political Research* (2nd edn). Basingstoke: Palgrave.

A very intuitive and easy-to-grasp introduction to theory of science and the logic behind different research methods.

REFERENCES

Bode, B.H. (1922) Critical realism. *Journal of Philosophy*, 19(3), 68–78.

Ellwood, C.A. (1931) Scientific method in sociology. *Social Forces*, 10(1), 15–21.

Elster, J. (1989) *Nuts and Bolts for the Social Sciences*. Cambridge: Cambridge University Press.

Elster, J. (1998) *A Plea for Mechanisms*. Cambridge: Cambridge University Press.

Galilei, G. (1957) [1610] The starry messenger. In D. Stillman (ed.), *Discoveries and Opinions of Galileo*. Garden City, NY: Doubleday.

Gold, D. (1969) Statistical tests and substantive significance. *American Sociologist*, 4(1): 42–46.

Groves, R.M. (1989) *Survey Errors and Survey Costs*. New York: Wiley.

Hay, C. (2002) *Political Analysis: A Critical Introduction*. Basingstoke: Palgrave.

Hempel, C.G. (1942) The function of general laws in history. *Journal of Philosophy*, 39(2), 35–48.

Hempel, C.G. (1959) The logic of functional analysis. In L. Gross (ed.), *Symposium on Sociological Theory* (pp. 271–307). New York: Harper & Row.

Henkel, R.E. (1976) *Tests of Significance*. Beverly Hills, CA: Sage.

Hume, D. (2011) [1740] *A Treatise of Human Nature* (D.F. Norton and M.J. Norton, eds). Oxford: Oxford University Press.

John, P. (2002) Quantitative methods. In D. Marsh and Stoker, G. (eds), *Theory and Methods in Political Science* (2nd edn). New York: Palgrave.

King, G., Keohane, R.O. and Verba, S. (1994) *Designing Social Inquiry: Scientific Inferences in Qualitative and Quantitative Research*. Princeton, NJ: Princeton University Press.

Kreijcie, R.V. and Morgan, D.W. (1970) Determining sample size for research activities. *Educational and Psychological Measurement*, 30(3), 607–610.

Mayo, D.G. (1980) The philosophical relevance of statistics. *PSA: Proceedings of the Biennial Meeting of the Philosophy of Science Association*, 1980(1), 97–109.

Moses, J.W. and Knutsen, T.L. (2012) *Ways of Knowing: Competing Methodologies in Social and Political Research* (2nd edn). Basingstoke: Palgrave.

Sellars, R.W. (1916) *Critical Realism*. Chicago: Rand-McNally.

Sellars, R.W. (1927) What is the correct interpretation of critical realism? *Journal of Philosophy*, 24(9), 238–241.

Smith, E.R. and Mackie, D.M. (2000) *Social Psychology* (2nd edn). Philadelphia: Psychology Press.

Weber, M. (2004) [1904] The 'objectivity' of knowledge in social science and social policy. In S. Whinster (ed.), *The Essential Weber: A Reader* (pp. 359–404). London: Routledge.

2

INTRODUCTION
TO STATA

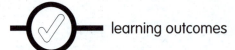

learning outcomes

○ Get accustomed to the Stata interface
○ Enter and import data into Stata
○ Get comfortable with using the Stata command language
○ Learn common data management commands in Stata

○ Obtain basic descriptive statistics and graphs using Stata
○ Do some simple bivariate analyses using Stata

In this chapter we first present the Stata interface along with its components. We then explain how to enter data directly in Stata as well as importing data from sources external to Stata. Following this, we also go through the three main ways of executing commands in Stata. These are the menu system, command system and do-file editor. Furthermore, by using the do-file editor, we execute the most common commands used for data management (recode, generate, etc.) in Stata. We extend our command repertoire by including several other commands used for providing descriptive statistics (frequency, central tendency, etc.) as well as commands for bivariate statistical analyses such as correlation, the t-test, analysis of variance (ANOVA), and chi-squared test.

2●1 WHAT IS STATA?

Stata is statistical software that contains a comprehensive and continuously updated/upgraded list of built-in analytical (linear models, longitudinal data, multiple imputation, etc.) and data management features (importing/exporting data, combining datasets, etc.)[1] as well as a further collection of features[2] developed by users themselves enabled by Stata's programming language. You can, in a way, consider the built-in features of Stata as part of a commercial software suite and view the user-written features/commands[3] made available through Stata as an open-source component. Access to these features requires you to have purchased[4] and installed Stata on your computer.

2●1●1 The Stata interface

Before presenting and explaining how Stata works, it is necessary to get accustomed to its interface which includes several components. Having installed and opened Stata, an interface

---

[1] Stata's built-in features can be found at http://www.stata.com/features/

[2] Type in net from http://fmwww.bc.edu/RePEc/bocode/ to see the list of user-written commands.

[3] The user is required to be connected to the Internet to be able to download these within Stata.

[4] For ordering and pricing, go to http://www.stata.com/order/

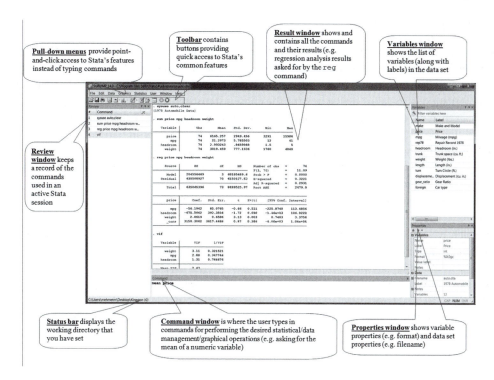

Toolbar contains buttons providing quick access to Stata's common features

Pull-down menus provide point-and-click access to Stata's features instead of typing commands

Result window shows and contains all the commands and their results (e.g. regression analysis results asked for by the reg command)

Variables window shows the list of variables (along with labels) in the data set

Review window keeps a record of the commands used in an active Stata session

Status bar displays the working directory that you have set

Command window is where the user types in commands for performing the desired statistical/data management/graphical operations (e.g. asking for the mean of a numeric variable)

Properties window shows variable properties (e.g. format) and data set properties (e.g. filename)

Figure 2.1 The Stata interface

similar to that depicted in Figure 2.1 appears.[5] Here, we see five main windows (command, review, results, variables and properties) and three additional components on this screen.

In the *command window* we type in the commands[6] that get Stata to perform the desired task. For instance, if we want to compute the mean of a certain variable (price), we would type in here the Stata command (mean) that does this task for us. Also, if we want to regress Y on X1 and X2, we would type in the required command (reg Y X1 X2). The commands that we insert in the command window in a Stata session are all immediately listed in the *review window*. The advantage of this list is that you can at any time in the same session click on any command in the list to rerun it without having to type it in again. Once a command is written in the command window, you just press Enter to run it. The (textual) result of the task performed by the command is then displayed in the *results window*. The variables contained in a dataset that we open (create or import) are listed in the *variables window* along with their labels. The properties of the variables and dataset itself are observed in the *properties window*. These properties can be modified after clicking on the lock icon in the properties window. The Stata windows (results, review, etc.) can be moved to different locations on the screen simply by clicking on and dragging them.

---

[5] This can be customized by right-clicking in the result window and choosing preferences from the menu that appears.

[6] These are also called code, script or syntax, depending on the statistical software.

2•1•2 How to use Stata

We can get Stata to perform different tasks of interest using two main approaches. The first approach is to use the *pull-down menus*. There are, as seen in Figure 2.1, pull-down menus for data management, statistics, and graphics. When you click on one of these menus (e.g., statistics), a so-called dialog box for the chosen statistical task (e.g., regress) pops up. You can then set up your analysis using the options available in the dialog box. The menus and dialog boxes provide access to most of Stata's features. The second approach to using Stata is through *typing commands.*[7] Commands can, as mentioned earlier, be typed in directly in the command window as shown in Figure 2.1. In the command window you can type in one command at a time.

The alternative and far more flexible approach is to use the Stata *do-file editor* shown in Figure 2.2. The do-file editor (accessed by clicking on 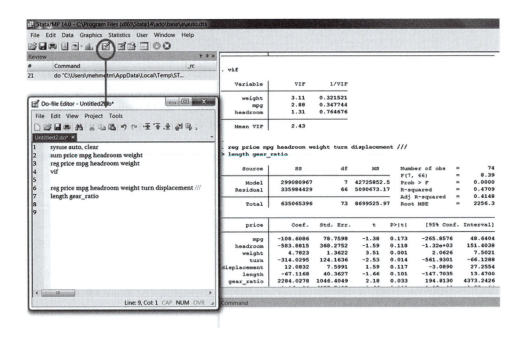) is simply a Stata-integrated text editor in which we can write our commands and run some or all of them at any time. The main advantage of using the do-file editor (over using the command window) is that commands written in a do-file can be saved and easily retrieved on a later occasion, thus facilitating reproducibility. Imagine that you carry out lots of data management (recoding, renaming etc.) and analytical (cross-tabulations, regressions etc.) tasks in a Stata session that you want to keep a record of in order to reproduce the same results later. All you have to do here is save these commands in a do-file and give it a name, and then just open this file from the do-file editor and rerun parts of or all of the commands.

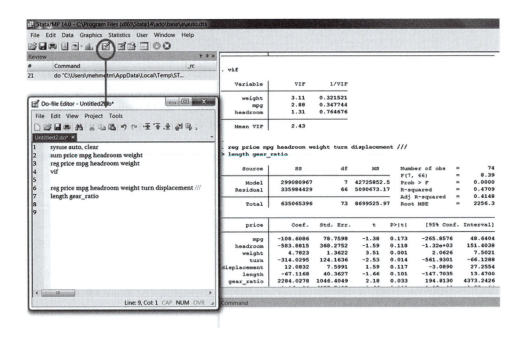

Figure 2.2 Working with the do-file editor

---

[7] Stata was solely a command-driven software until version 8.

In Figure 2.2 a new do-file is opened that shows the same commands as were written in the command window in Figure 2.1. In a do-file long commands can be broken up with three slashes (///) so that the command would still be executed without any problem. To run commands in a do-file, you can either click on 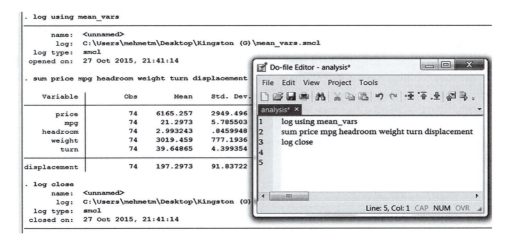 on the toolbar or press Ctrl+D from the keyboard of your PC. Do-files (with a *.do* extension) are saved directly in the do-file editor.

The fact that we can with just one click rerun all the commands in a do-file and get their corresponding results makes it often unnecessary to save these results specifically. However, if needed, the results can be saved in a *log-file* (with a *.smcl* extension[8]). Suppose that you want to compute the means of some variables and save the results. This is done in Figure 2.3 where we first open a log-file by name (say, *mean_vars*), use the sum command to compute the means, and then close the log-file. This log-file is then saved in the working directory.

The *working directory* is shown on the status bar (see Figure 2.1). The default working directory is a path like C:\Users\mydir\Documents. This can easily be changed for any Stata session. For instance, in Figure 2.1, we have changed the working directory to a different location by typing cd "C:\Users\mehmetm\Desktop\Kingston (G)". Specifying the working directory for a session saves you time and accuracy in that any file can be saved or retrieved in Stata without having to write the entire path of the directory in the command itself. For instance, if we want to save a data file in the above directory, since it is specified, we can just write save filename.dta. If the above was not specified as the working directory, then we would have to type in save "C:\Users\mehmetm\Desktop\Kingston (G)\filename. dta". The take-home message is that whenever you work on a project (e.g., article, thesis or dissertation), create a folder for this project and make it your working directory to subsequently keep and save all your Stata files (data, log, do-file, etc.) in.

Stata commands (built-in and user-written) often offer more options than are offered by default. Stata provides *help files* for commands like the ones used above (log, cd, regress, summarize, etc.) which include a description of the command along with the options that

```
. log using mean_vars

       name:  <unnamed>
        log:  C:\Users\mehmetm\Desktop\Kingston (G)\mean_vars.smcl
   log type:  smcl
   opened on: 27 Oct 2015, 21:41:14

. sum price mpg headroom weight turn displacement

    Variable |        Obs        Mean    Std. Dev.
-------------+-----------------------------------
       price |         74    6165.257    2949.496
         mpg |         74     21.2973    5.785503
    headroom |         74    2.993243    .8459948
      weight |         74    3019.459    777.1936
        turn |         74    39.64865    4.399354
-------------+-----------------------------------
displacement |         74    197.2973    91.83722

. log close

       name:  <unnamed>
        log:  C:\Users\mehmetm\Desktop\Kingston (G)
   log type:  smcl
   closed on: 27 Oct 2015, 21:41:14
```

Do-file Editor - analysis*

File   Edit   View   Project   Tools

analysis* ×

```
1      log using mean_vars
2      sum price mpg headroom weight turn displacement
3      log close
4
5
```

Line: 5, Col: 1   CAP   NUM   OVR

Figure 2.3 An example of the use of a log-file

---

[8] Log files can also be saved with the *.log* extension, an alternative making it possible to open and share the log files with a text editor such as Notepad.

can be used with it. A help file can be called by typing `help` and the name of the command, for example, `help reg`. Help files are crucial for learning and understanding the logic of Stata commands. You need to know the name of the command beforehand to call its corresponding help file. However, if you do not know of a specific command, you can still *search* for commands using logical keywords. For instance, if we did not know that there existed the `regress` command in Stata, we would then type `search regression`, which would bring up the `regress` command among the search hits.

In addition to options, many of the commands in help files can also be combined with *if* statements (selection based on group), *in* statements (selection based on observations) and weighting (estimations based on weights). A basic structure of a typical built-in Stata command would look like the following `regress` command:

regress *depvar* [*indepvars*] [*if*] [*in*] [*weight*] [*, options*]

The underlined characters (`reg`) indicate how the complete command (`regress`) can be abbreviated, an example of which is shown in the result window in Figure 2.1.

2 ● 2 ENTERING AND IMPORTING DATA INTO STATA

2●2●1 Entering data

Entering data into Stata means that you create your dataset directly in Stata. This can be done using the data editor (Figure 2.4). You open the data editor by clicking on [icon] on the toolbar or by typing in `edit`. You then start inputting your data in the data editor in the form of rows (representing observations) and columns (representing variables). The first time you enter a value for an observation a variable is automatically created and assigned a name like `var1`, `var2`, `var3`, etc. The variable names (as well as labels, type, format, etc.) can be changed using the properties window located on the right-hand side of the data editor window. After you have entered all your data, you can just exit and come back to the main Stata window. Here, you can save the data file either by using the menu or typing `save filename.dta` or just `save filename`.

In the data editor, you can enter numeric and/or string variables. String variables are entered in the form of textual data or characters. When you input string data (e.g., female or male) for a gender variable, these string data will be shown in red in the data editor. Numeric values are entered by typing in the values. These values can take the form of *byte, int, long, float,* or *double,* ranging from the smallest to largest digit. Stata makes all numeric variables floats by default.

2●2●2 Importing data

There are a few ways of transferring external data files into Stata.[9] These data files come in various formats. Stata can effectively transfer some of the commonly used formats to its own format (*.dta*).[10] Although we recommend the reader to use commands in general, we suggest

---

[9] In most cases, the simplest way of transferring data from other software (Excel, SPSS, etc.) is to copy the data matrix and paste it in directly.

[10] For formats that Stata cannot directly transfer, there is a special program that you can find more information about at http://www.stata.com/products/stat-transfer/.

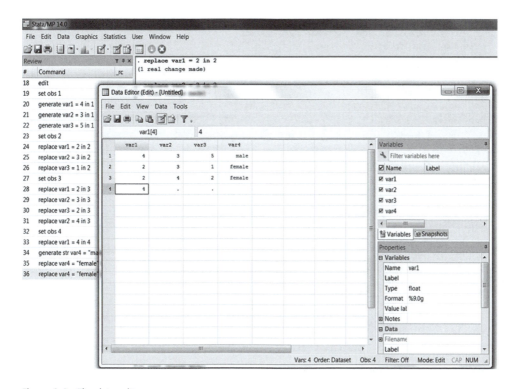

Figure 2.4 The data editor

using the pull-down menu (shown in Figure 2.5) for transferring files from and into Stata.[11] All you have to do is save the file in your directory (preferably in the working directory), choose the corresponding option from the pull-down menu and make any further choices in the dialog box that pops up.

In addition to Stata's official commands and pull-down menu options, there may also exist user-written commands that facilitate transferring a certain type of data file into Stata.[12] An example of this is the user-written command usespss. Type in search usespss in Stata to find out more about this particular command. Moreover, some software may allow its own data files to be saved in Stata's *.dta* format. SPSS is one such program in that you can save a data file as a Stata file in SPSS itself. You can then open this data file directly in Stata.

2●3 DATA MANAGEMENT

In this section, we use a real-life dataset, collected from a sample of members of a training/fitness centre in 2014 in a medium-sized city in Norway. The dataset includes information about motivation and behaviour related to working out as well as socio-demographic data.

---

[11] One other positive side effect of using the pull-down menus is that their command equivalents appear in the results window, which you can use in the command window or in the do-file editor if needed later.

[12] One can also consider purchasing Stat/Transfer, a program used to very easily convert data files that are different formats (from Excel, SPSS, SAS, etc. to Stata and vice versa). Stat/Transfer can be purchased directly from StataCorp.

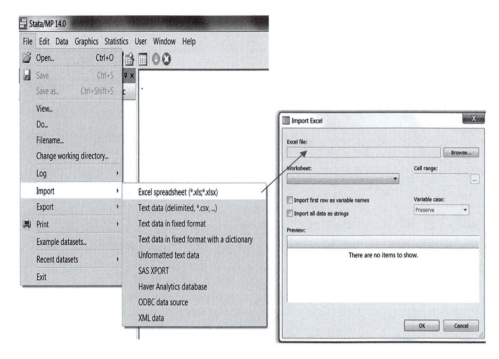

Figure 2.5 Stata's pull-down menu for file transfer

The dataset is called *workout1.dta*, and you should download it into your working directory. It is important to note that we go through a considerable number of commands in this section.[13] To cover these commands with all their options and extensions is not a feasible task to achieve in a single chapter. We recommend therefore that you subsequently explore each of these commands yourself by reading their help files (e.g., type `help codebook`).

2•3•1 Opening data

After launching Stata, we can open the dataset (*workout1.dta*) by typing[14]

```
. use "C:\Users\mehmetm\Desktop\Kingston (G)\workout1.dta"
```

If the dataset is, as suggested, in the working directory, then it should suffice to write

```
. use workout1.dta
```

or

---

[13] We recommend that the reader goes through this section by following the do-file prepared for this chapter that can be downloaded from the companion website of the book.

[14] In the text, when we specify a command to perform a certain task in Stata, we place a dot and a space in front of the command to indicate that all the following text belong to this command. When you type in these commands in the command window or in the do-file editor, you do not have to type in the dot and space. Further, when typing in commands in the do-file editor a command line can be broken with /// whereas in the command window you cannot use /// and thus have to enter all the text belonging to a command as one whole line.

```
. use workout1
```

If there is already a dataset in your Stata session, you should add

```
, clear
```

to the above commands. In other words, the command should then read use workout1, clear. Note, however, that the clear option removes the already active dataset (without saving it) and then brings in the dataset specified in the use command. So it is advised that you save the active dataset before using the clear option.

2•3•2 Examining data

The first command that we might want to use is describe. This command provides us with some compact information about a variable, an example of which is shown below. In this example, we add the variables (v03 v04) after the command (Figure 2.6). If we want the same information about all the variables in the dataset, we type in just describe. The describe command would also work without having to open the dataset. In that case, we type in describe using workout1.

Another useful command to know is codebook. This command gives us some additional information (frequency distribution, label values, etc.) which is very useful to quickly become familiar with and examine all the variables in the dataset and eventually locate possible errors/inconsistencies (e.g., mistyping) in the dataset (Figure 2.7).

```
. describe v03 v04

              storage  display   value
variable name  type    format    label    variable label

v03            byte     %28.0g    labelv03  Educational level
v04            byte     %17.0g    labelv04  What is your personal annual income
```

Figure 2.6 The describe command

```
. codebook v03

v03

              type:  numeric (byte)
             label:  labelv03

             range:  [1,4]                        units:  1
     unique values:  4                          missing .:  1/246

       tabulation:  Freq.   Numeric  Label
                      11        1     Primary/Secondary school
                      74        2     High school
                      65        3     University up to 3 years
                      95        4     University more than 3 years
                       1        .
```

Figure 2.7 The codebook command

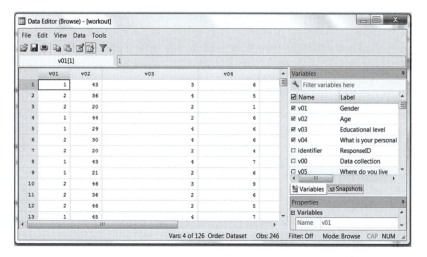

Figure 2.8   Browse window

A third command that you may need for examining the data is browse. It works in the same way as the above two commands, providing an overview of the values inserted for each observation in the data matrix. If we want to see the actual values on one or a set of variables, we would for instance type in browse v01 v02 v03 v04, nolabel. This will open up the browse window shown in Figure 2.8. The nolabel option displays the browse window with numeric values instead of label values (e.g., 2 instead of high school).

Note that we cannot make any changes to these values in the browse window. If we need to do so, we simply replace the browse command with the edit command. Moreover, if you want this overview to appear in the results window, you can just replace the browse command with the list command: list v01 v02 v03 v04, nolabel.

A final command that is useful for examining your data is misstable sum. This command reports the number of missing values contained in each variable. Note that although we type v01 v02 in the example in Figure 2.9, these do not appear in the result. The reason is simply that the command leaves out those variables with complete data from the result and only reports those with missing values. In the example, we see that v03 has one missing value while v04 has four missing values. As you have already observed, missing values are typically represented by a dot (.) which in Stata is considered as a numerical value larger than the largest actual value on a variable. The dot (.) is the default, referred to as the *system missing value*, which is sometimes called *sysmiss* for short.

```
. misstable sum v01 v02 v03 v04
```

				Obs<.		
Variable	Obs=.	Obs>.	Obs<.	Unique values	Min	Max
v03	1		245	4	1	4
v04	4		242	9	1	9

Figure 2.9   The misstable command

In addition to dot (.), we can classify 26 other types of missing values in Stata. For instance, we can insert (.a) representing the missing values of those who refused to answer the question, (.b) for those who thought the question was not relevant, (.c) for those who said the question was not clear enough to answer, and so on. This way of classifying missing values is useful when you particularly want to know the causes of missing values.

2•3•3 Making changes to variables

The `recode` command can be used to change the values of a variable. Suppose that you have imported an external dataset which includes a variable (var1) in which missing values are entered as –999. Since we know that these should be represented by (.) in Stata, we can use the following command to make the change needed:

```
. recode var1 (-999=.)
```

or

```
. recode var1 -999=.
```

If you had a dataset all variables of which contained –999, you could easily apply the following:

```
. recode _all (-999=.)
```

or

```
. recode * (-999=.)
```

Here `_all` and `*` are alternative ways of referring to all the variables in a dataset.

The above can alternatively be done using a command written specifically for this purpose:

```
. mvdecode _all, mv(-999)
```

or

```
. mvdecode *, mv(-999)
```

If you want to do the reverse of this, you can just type:

```
. mvencode _all, mv(-999)
```

or

```
. mvencode *, mv(-999)
```

The `recode` command can be used to make some more complex changes. Suppose we have a distribution of people's annual income (from lowest = 1 to highest = 9), and we want to amalgamate categories 1, 2 and 3 in one group, 4, 5 and 6 in a second group, and 7, 8 and 9 in a third group. This is easily achieved by the command below which produces the distribution on the right-hand side of Figure 2.10. Note, however, that this way of using the recode command replaces the original variable (v04). It is possible, and in fact a better idea, to generate a new variable based on recoding the original variable, an example of which is provided in the next section.

```
. recode v04 (1/3=1) (4/6=2) (7/9=3)
```

Before recoding

v04	Freq.	Percent	Cum.
1	23	9.50	9.50
2	9	3.72	13.22
3	6	2.48	15.70
4	16	6.61	22.31
5	38	15.70	38.02
6	64	26.45	64.46
7	37	15.29	79.75
8	14	5.79	85.54
9	35	14.46	100.00
Total	242	100.00	

After recoding

v04	Freq.	Percent	Cum.
1	38	15.70	15.70
2	118	48.76	64.46
3	86	35.54	100.00
Total	242	100.00	

Figure 2.10 The recode command

The recode command does not work with string variables. Instead, we use the replace command which works with both string and numeric variables. In the example below, we are asking Stata to insert the text 'very good' and 'good' in the variable *exammark* (string) for cases who have received respectively a score above and below 90 on the variable (numeric) *mark*; see Figure 2.11.

```
. replace exammark="very good" if mark>90
. replace exammark="good" if mark<90
```

Before replacing

	exammark	mark
1.		93
2.		92
3.		83
4.		76

After replacing

	exammark	mark
1.	very good	93
2.	very good	92
3.	good	83
4.	good	76

Figure 2.11 The replace command

The rename command can be used in different situations to change the name of a variable. If, for instance, we want to change the name of the above variable v03 to education, then we would just type in rename v03 education. This command is sometimes needed to make variable names appear in lower or upper case. We would then, for instance, type in rename v03, lower or rename v03, upper. If you want to apply this to an entire dataset, then you can just type rename _all, lower or rename _all, upper.

Table 2.1 The three types of mathematical operator used by Stata

Arithmetic		Logical		Relational (numeric and string)	
+	addition	&	and	>	greater than
–	subtraction	|	or	<	less than
*	multiplication	!	not	>=	> or equal
/	division	~	not	<=	< or equal
^	power			==	equal
–	negation			!=	not equal
+	string concatenation			~=	not equal

2•3•4 Generating variables

Before learning about generating new variables, it is a good idea to look at the different mathematical operators that Stata uses.[15] These are classified into three main categories (Table 2.1).

In addition to these operators, Stata also has a large variety of mathematical functions such as log(x), sqrt(x) and exp(x) that can be explored further by typing in help functions.

It is important to distinguish between the single equals sign (=) for assignment, for example generate lnprice = ln(price), and the double equals sign (==) for comparison, for example keep if gender == 2. Using a single equals sign for comparison is one of the most common typos made by new users, so be careful!

There are two convenient and commonly used commands in Stata, namely gen and egen, for generating new variables. The former stands for 'generate', the latter for 'extension to generate'. We will start with the gen command. Here are a few examples of the gen command in use, which can give an idea of how handy this command is to have:

```
. gen age2=age^2            age squared
. gen id=_n                 numbers observations
. gen loghours=log(hours)   log of hours
. gen pdollar=price/6       price (in Norwegian currency) turned into dollars
. gen agecar=2015-year      age of car in 2015
```

It is also quite usual to see gen combined with recode. In the earlier treatment of recode the existing variable is changed. However, here we will see an example that generates a new variable based on recoding an existing variable. The variable v04 is our original/existing variable which is used/changed to create a new variable called inccat (i.e., income categorized):

```
. recode v04 (1/3=1) (4/6=2) (7/9=3), gen(inccat)
```

After the command, we would have both the original and newly generated variable in the dataset.

Another way of getting the same result as above is using the combination of gen and replace. Two points should be commented on here. One is that we exclude the missing

---

[15] Type help operator in Stata to find out more about these operators.

values by adding $(v04< .)^{16}$ in the fourth line below as missing value would be the largest value on this variable. The other point is that gen inccat2=. creates a vector of blanks/ missing values which then are replaced by actual values.

```
.  gen inccat2=.
.  replace inccat2=1 if (v04<=3)
.  replace inccat2=2 if (v04>=4) & (v04<=6)
.  replace inccat2=3 if (v04>=7) & (v04<.)
```

egen is another command that is used for creating variables like gen, but it makes the task of creating new variables (of means, medians, ranges, etc.) a much easier task when compared with gen. We give a few examples based on egen, while noting that it has a lot more features that should be explored in its help file (help egen).

On the left-hand side of Figure 2.12 we create first an average of four variables (var1, ..., var4) by using the gen command. Observe that gen excludes all cases that have a missing value on even one of our four variables. Thus, the newly generated variable (avg) will not have a value for the first two observations. On the right-hand side, we create an average by using the egen command. Here observe that egen calculates an average for the same (first two) observations based on the available values on the other three variables. That is, the average for the first observation is calculated as $(4 + 2 + 1)/3 = 2.33$.

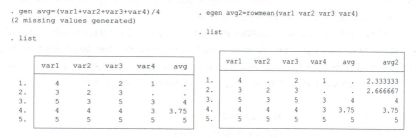

Figure 2.12 Creating an average using the gen and egen command

egen is commonly used to create a standardized version of a variable as follows:

```
.  egen zvar1 = std(var1)
```

It can also be used to create a sum of a set of variables (e.g., var1, ..., var4). The example shown in Figure 2.13, as you can see, treats the missing values as zeros when computing the total values.

If you want to find out the number of observations that have a missing value on one or one set of variables, you can use the commands shown in Figure 2.14. On the left, we see that the first five observations have respectively 2, 3, 1, 3, and 4 non-missing values. On the right, we see the reverse interpretation of this case, the number of missing values, with its own egen command.

---

[16] We could alternatively use (!missing(v04)) instead of (v04<.). The option !missing works with both numeric and string variables.

```
. egen tot = rowtotal(var1 var2 var3 var4)

. list
```

	var1	var2	var3	var4	tot
1.	4	.	2	1	7
2.	3	2	3	.	8
3.	5	3	5	3	16
4.	4	4	4	.	12
5.	5	5	5	5	20

Figure 2.13   Creating a sum using the egen command

```
. egen nonmiss=rownonmiss( var1 var2 var3 var4 )    . egen rmiss= rowmiss( var1 var2 var3 var4 )

. list                                               . list
```

	var1	var2	var3	var4	nonmiss
1.	4	.	.	1	2
2.	3	2	3	.	3
3.	.	3	.	.	1
4.	4	4	4	.	3
5.	5	5	5	5	4

	var1	var2	var3	var4	rmiss
1.	4	.	.	1	2
2.	3	2	3	.	1
3.	.	3	.	.	3
4.	4	4	4	.	1
5.	5	5	5	5	0

Figure 2.14   Finding the number of nonmissing and missing values on a set of variables

The encode command (Figure 2.15) converts a string variable to a numeric one. As seen in the example below, encode assigns a label value to each textual category of var1 in an alphabetical order (economics 1, political science 2, etc.).

```
. encode var1, gen(var1_num)

. list,nol
```

	var1	var1_num
1.	psychology	3
2.	economics	1
3.	sociology	4
4.	political science	2

Figure 2.15   The encode command

There is also another command, namely decode, that does the opposite in that it converts a numeric variable to a string one. This command works in the same way as encode. As an example, you can in fact convert var1_num back to a string variable (var2).

```
. decode var1_num, gen(var2)
```

2•3•5 Subsetting data

We can subset a dataset by keeping or dropping variables or observations. Subsetting can sometimes be necessary or convenient particularly when working with a large dataset. This is easily enabled by Stata's two commands: `keep` and `drop`. Suppose that, for whatever reason, you want only four variables, v01, v02, v03 and v04, present in your dataset rather than the entire dataset. To achieve this, you would type in `keep v01 v02 v03 v04`. On the other hand, if instead you want to remove these four variables from your data, you would type in `drop v01 v02 v03 v04`.

In order to keep and drop observations though, `keep` and `drop` commands need to be used in combination with `if` and `in` statements. Below are some examples of these combinations.

`. drop in 13`	removes observation 13
`. drop in 10/12`	removes observation 10, 11 and 12
`. drop if missing(var5)`	removes observations that have a missing on var5
`. drop if missing(var6, var7)`	removes observations that have a missing value on either var6 or var7
`. keep if !missing(var4)`	keeps observations that have no missing value on var4

2•3•6 Labelling variables

Labelling a variable is done in two steps. In the first step we define the label values, and in the second step we apply these label values to the variables that we want to take on the defined label values. To implement these two steps, we use the commands `label define` and `label values`. Since labelling variables is often used in combination with the `gen` command, we will use our earlier example in the `gen` section here to continue with its labelling.

```
. gen inccat2=.
. replace inccat2=1 if (v04<=3)
. replace inccat2=2 if (v04>=4) & (v04<=6)
. replace inccat2=3 if (v04>=7) & (v04<.)
```

As you can see, there are indeed three categories. Suppose that we want to label these as low-income, medium-income and high-income groups. First we define a label which assigns numbers to these three categories, and this information is stored under the name of `labinc` as follows:

```
. label define labinc 1"low income" 2"medium income" 3"high income"
```

Then we choose the variable (`inccat2`) to apply this labelling to. In other words, `labinc` is applied to `inccat2`:

```
. label values inccat2 labinc
```

In this case, labinc is defined specifically for inccat2 variable, but there are situations in which you may want to define one single label and then apply it to more than one variable. An example of this would be a label lablikert applied to five different variables (var1, ..., var5).

```
. label define lablikert 1"disagree" 6"agree"
. label values var1-var5 lablikert
```

2●4 DESCRIPTIVE STATISTICS AND GRAPHS

Although many readers of this book are most likely to want to use more advanced techniques than simply presenting descriptive statistics, the latter should still be the first step in any substantial quantitative work. Two main types of descriptive statistics are of interest, depending on the measurement level of a variable: the frequency distribution if the measurement level is nominal or ordinal; and the central tendency and variability if the measurement level is interval or ratio.

2●4●1 Frequency distributions

Frequency distributions show the number of observations contained in each category of a variable. In Stata the frequency distribution of a variable is obtained using the tabulate (or just tab) command. Figure 2.16 shows the standard frequency distribution output produced by tab. On the left, we see the percentages of those cases belonging to the 'no' and 'yes' categories after excluding cases with missing values. On the right, where we add the miss option, the cases with missing values are included in the calculation of the percentages.

```
. tab v07_num

  Are you
  divorced  |   Freq.    Percent     Cum.
------------+---------------------------------
        No  |    225      93.36      93.36
       Yes  |     16       6.64     100.00
------------+---------------------------------
     Total  |    241     100.00
```

```
. tab v07_num, miss

  Are you
  divorced  |   Freq.    Percent     Cum.
------------+---------------------------------
        No  |    225      91.46      91.46
       Yes  |     16       6.50      97.97
         .  |      5       2.03     100.00
------------+---------------------------------
     Total  |    246     100.00
```

Figure 2.16 The tabulate command

To see a table with percentages calculated excluding missing values as well as seeing the number of missing values, we can instead of tab use a user-written command called fre.[17] It produces the output in Figure 2.17 which you can compare with the two tables produced by tab in Figure 2.16.

---

[17] Type in ssc install fre to install this command.

```
. fre v07_num
```

v07_num — Are you divorced

		Freq.	Percent	Valid	Cum.
Valid	1 No	225	91.46	93.36	93.36
	2 Yes	16	6.50	6.64	100.00
	Total	241	97.97	100.00	
Missing	.	5	2.03		
Total		246	100.00		

Figure 2.17 The user-written `fre` command

We can support the dissemination of the descriptive statistics further by using graphs. There are two ways of producing graphs in Stata: one way is to use the pull-down menu, and the other is to use the command language. We will go with the latter here, but we will present only the basic graph commands. These standard commands can, however, be further extended. As such, we recommend that the reader go through the help file of each graph command to see and eventually apply the extended features of these commands to their own data.

For frequency distributions, we can use histograms and pie charts. The commands for these two tasks are respectively `histogram` (or just `hist`) and `graph pie`. Let us now produce a histogram of the frequency distribution of our variable v07_num (Figure 2.18). This is done by typing in the following command:

```
. hist v07_num, discrete percent addlabel xlabel(1/2, valuelabel noticks)
```

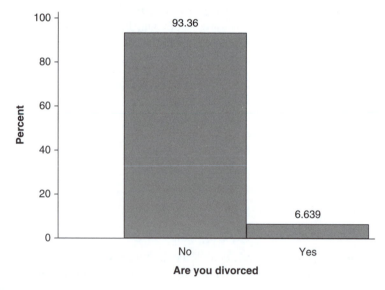

Figure 2.18 The `histogram` command

Alternatively, we can use the following command to produce the pie chart shown in Figure 2.19:

```
. graph pie, over(v07_num) plabel(_all percent)
```

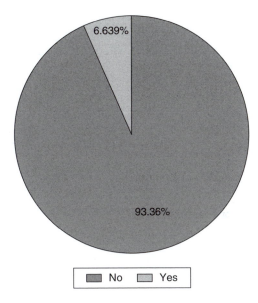

6.639%

93.36%

No ▨ Yes ▨

Figure 2.19 The graph pie command

2•4•2 Summary statistics

When we examine a variable measured at interval or ratio level it is more appropriate to look at the central tendency and variability (i.e., summary statistics) measures rather than the frequency distribution. The central tendency measure that is most commonly examined is the mean (arithmetic average), while the variability measures typically examined are the standard deviation and range. These basic summary statistics can all be computed and provided by the summarize (or just sum) command. In Figure 2.20 we use the price variable from the *auto.dta* file that is installed with Stata to show how the sum command works.

```
. sysuse auto,clear
(1978 Automobile Data)

. sum price
```

Variable	Obs	Mean	Std. Dev.	Min	Max
price	74	6165.257	2949.496	3291	15906

Figure 2.20 The sum command

Several additional central tendency (e.g., median) and variability (variance) measures can also easily be provided by adding the detail (or just d) option to the sum command (Figure 2.21).

If we want to obtain the standard error and confidence interval of the mean, we can use another command for this purpose, namely mean (Figure 2.22).

Although the above two commands can produce summary statistics for more than one variable and conditioned on another variable, an even more effective command that exits for this purpose is tabstat. With this command, we can also customize the summary

```
. sum price, d
```

                                    Price

	Percentiles	Smallest		
1%	3291	3291		
5%	3748	3299		
10%	3895	3667	Obs	74
25%	4195	3748	Sum of Wgt.	74
50%	5006.5		Mean	6165.257
		Largest	Std. Dev.	2949.496
75%	6342	13466		
90%	11385	13594	Variance	8699526
95%	13466	14500	Skewness	1.653434
99%	15906	15906	Kurtosis	4.819188

Figure 2.21 The detailed sum (or sum, d) command

```
. mean price
```

Mean estimation   Number of obs   =   74

	Mean	Std. Err.	[95% Conf. Interval]	
price	6165.2568	342.8719	5481.9140	6848.5995

Figure 2.22 The mean command

statistics to be calculated and displayed. Figure 2.23 shows an example which produces summary statistics[18] for the price, weight and length of domestic and foreign cars. If you want the summary statistics to be displayed horizontally, you can just type in col(stats) at the end of the command below. Moreover, if you want to remove the overall (total) summary statistics overview, you can add nototal at the end of the command.

While tabstat produces a one-way table of summary statistics, another convenient command, tab, combined with the option sum(), can calculate and display a more-than-one-way table of summary statistics. In Figure 2.24 we give an example of this command showing the summary statistics of the variable mpg based on a two-way tabulation of foreign and rep78 which are both categorical variables.

When it comes to the graphical presentation of summary statistics, we can use the histogram and box plot, the commands for which are respectively histogram (or just hist) and graph box. We can illustrate both of these commands using the *nlsw88* dataset installed with Stata. To open this dataset, type in sysuse nlsw88, or sysuse nlsw88,clear if you already have a dataset open (and have made changes to it). Using the following command, we first produce a histogram of wage (measuring people's hourly wage), as shown in Figure 2.25:

```
. hist wage, frequency
```

---

[18] For the full overview of summary statistics and their corresponding Stata codes type in help tabstat.

```
. tabstat price weight length, stats(mean sd range count) by(foreign)

Summary statistics: mean, sd, range, N
  by categories of: foreign (Car type)
```

foreign	price	weight	length
Domestic	6072.423	3317.115	196.1346
	3097.104	695.3637	20.04605
	12615	3040	86
	52	52	52
Foreign	6384.682	2315.909	168.5455
	2621.915	433.0035	13.68255
	9242	1660	51
	22	22	22
Total	6165.257	3019.459	187.9324
	2949.496	777.1936	22.26634
	12615	3080	91
	74	74	74

Figure 2.23 The `tabstat` command

```
. tab rep78 foreign, sum(mpg)
```

Means, Standard Deviations and Frequencies of Mileage (mpg)

Repair Record 1978	Car type Domestic	Foreign	Total
1	21	.	21
	4.2426407	.	4.2426407
	2	0	2
2	19.125	.	19.125
	3.7583241	.	3.7583241
	8	0	8
3	19	23.333333	19.433333
	4.0856221	2.5166115	4.1413252
	27	3	30
4	18.444444	24.888889	21.666667
	4.5856055	2.7131368	4.9348699
	9	9	18
5	32	26.333333	27.363636
	2.8284271	9.367497	8.7323849
	2	9	11
Total	19.541667	25.285714	21.289855
	4.7533116	6.3098562	5.8664085
	48	21	69

Figure 2.24 The `tab, sum` command

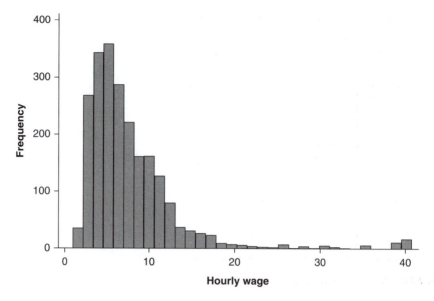

Figure 2.25 The histogram, frequency command

Next, we produce a box plot of the same variable, wage. Box plots are usually used to compare the distribution of a variable for different subsamples. The box plot of the variable wage for two categories of the race variable (Figure 2.26) is produced using the command

```
. graph box wage, by(race)
```

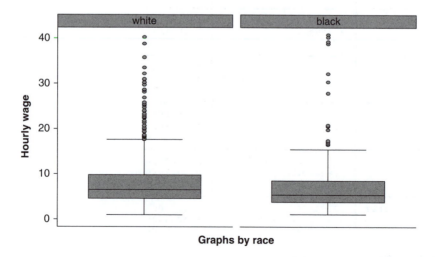

Figure 2.26 The graph box command

2•4•3 Appending data

Appending data means combining two datasets based on observations. This is done by adding the observations of one dataset to another dataset (i.e., *N* increases) which in Stata can be facilitated using the following command:

```
. append using dataset1 dataset2,gen(dataset3)
. save dataset3
```

Dataset1

id	data	var1	var2
1	1	3	2
2	1	4	3
3	1	5	1

Dataset2

id	data	var1	var2
4	2	3	1
5	2	5	3
6	2	5	4

Dataset3
(combined)

dataset3	id	var1	var2
1	1	3	2
1	2	4	3
1	3	5	1
2	4	3	1
2	5	5	3
2	6	5	4

Figure 2.27 Appending data

When we combine `dataset1` and `dataset2` in Figure 2.27, the combined `dataset3` shows which observations belong to which original dataset. This information/variable may be needed for some analytical purposes (e.g., comparing data collected at two different locations).

2•4•4 Merging data

Merging data means combining two datasets based on variables. This is done by adding the variables of one dataset to another dataset (i.e., the number of variables increases). Using the commands below, we first open *data14*, then add the variables of *data15* to *data14*, and finally save the resulting combined dataset as *data1415* (see Figure 2.28):

```
. use data14,clear
. merge 1:1 id using data15
. save data1415
```

Data14

id	v1_14	v2_14
1	3	5
2	4	5
3	2	3
4	1	2
5	1	2

Data15

id	v1_15	v2_15
1	4	5
2	5	5
3	3	4
4	2	3
5	2	3

Data1415
(combined)

id	v1_14	v2_14	v1_15	v2_15
1	3	5	4	5
2	4	5	5	5
3	2	3	3	4
4	1	2	2	3
5	1	2	2	3

Figure 2.28 Merging data

Here too, there are a few observations to make. First, the id numbers in both datasets are identical, whereas the variable names are different. This is because we measure the same observations on two same variables but on two different occasions (2014 and 2015). Second, our 1:1 (one-to-one) merge means that one observation from *data14* is combined with one observation from *data15*. Third, Stata generates a variable named _merge. A value of 1 in _merge means that an observation comes from *data14*, a value of 2 means that it comes from *data15*, and a value of 3 means that it comes from both datasets (*data14* and *data15*), meaning that the merge is performed successfully.

2●4●5 Reshaping data

We may sometimes want to change the structure of our data to be able to facilitate a certain type of analysis (e.g., multilevel modelling). We can change the format from wide to long or from long to wide. In the wide format, data are structured in such a way that there is only one row for each observation, whereas in the long format there is more than one row for each observation (see Figure 2.29). The most common format change made is from wide to long;[19] this is done using the following command:

```
. reshape long v1_ v2_ , i(id) j(year)
```

Wide

id	v1_14	v2_14	v1_15	v2_15
1	3	5	4	5
2	4	5	5	5
3	2	3	3	4
4	1	2	2	3
5	1	2	2	3

Long

id	year	v1_	v2_
1	14	3	5
1	15	4	5
2	14	4	5
2	15	5	5
3	14	2	3
3	15	3	4
4	14	1	2
4	15	2	3
5	14	1	2
5	15	2	3

Figure 2.29 Wide and long formats

The way the reshape command works is that we first specify the desired format (long) to change to. Then, we add v1_ and v2_ which represent the common prefix (i.e., root) of the wide variables (v1_14, v2_14, v1_15 and v2_15). After the comma, in i() we put in id which is the unique identifier of the observations in the dataset. Finally, in j() we insert year to represent the numeric suffix (14 and 15) of the wide variables.

---

[19] In Stata, you can as easily change the format from long to wide. For more information type in help reshape.

2●5 BIVARIATE INFERENTIAL STATISTICS

In this section, we go through some of the most commonly used basic or bivariate inferential statistics using Stata. These include correlation, the *t*-test, ANOVA and chi-squared test. Our purpose here is to show how to obtain these statistics and interpret briefly the resulting output in Stata. Thus, we skip the technical/theoretical treatment of these statistical procedures as we assume that the reader has some knowledge of them from a basic statistics course. We will use the *nlsw88* dataset (installed with Stata) throughout this section. To load this dataset into Stata, type in

```
. sysuse nlsw88, clear
```

2●5●1 Correlation

In Figure 2.30 we carry out a correlation analysis to examine the relationship between hourly wage and work experience. Here, we see that there is a moderate[20] positive correlation between wage and experience that is significant ($r = 0.27$, $N = 2246$, $p < 0.05$).

```
. pwcorr wage ttl_exp, star(0.05) obs

                 |    wage  ttl_exp
        ---------+------------------
            wage |  1.0000
                 |    2246
                 |
         ttl_exp |  0.2655*  1.0000
                 |    2246     2246
                 |
```

Figure 2.30   The pwcorr command

We could alternatively type in corr wage ttl_exp. However, we recommend pwcorr as it uses pairwise deletion with respect to missing values, whereas corr uses listwise deletion. The latter option would then lead to loss of information for a correlation analysis including more than one pair of variables. For complete data, the results of the two commands would be same.

2●5●2 Independent *t*-test

The independent *t*-test is used to test whether the (population) means/averages of a certain variable in two independent samples/groups significantly differ from each other. We perform such a test in Figure 2.31 to find out whether the mean hourly wage of those with a college degree differs significantly from that of those with no college degree. As we apply a

---

[20] *r*-values of 0.1, 0.3 and 0.5 are respectively weak, moderate and strong correlations.

two-tailed test (without any direction), we look at the Stata output obtained based on the hypothesis H_0: diff = 0. This phrase simply says that the mean difference is 0 (i.e., same means). As we see in the output below, this hypothesis should be rejected as p is given as 0.0000. As a result, we can conclude that the difference in the mean wage of those with a college degree and those without a college degree is –3.62 and statistically significant using a two-tailed test ($t(2244) = -13$, $p < 0.001$).

```
. ttest wage, by(collgrad)

Two-sample t test with equal variances

    Group │      Obs        Mean    Std. Err.    Std. Dev.    [95% Conf. Interval]
──────────┼─────────────────────────────────────────────────────────────────────
 not coll │    1,714    6.910561    .1276104     5.283132     6.660273     7.16085
  college │      532    10.52606    .2742596     6.325833     9.987296    11.06483
──────────┼─────────────────────────────────────────────────────────────────────
 combined │    2,246    7.766949    .1214451     5.755523     7.528793    8.005105
──────────┼─────────────────────────────────────────────────────────────────────
     diff │            -3.615502    .2753268                 -4.155424    -3.07558
──────────┴─────────────────────────────────────────────────────────────────────
       diff = mean(not coll) - mean(college)                         t = -13.1317
    Ho: diff = 0                                    degrees of freedom =      2244

     Ha: diff < 0                 Ha: diff != 0                    Ha: diff > 0
  Pr(T < t) = 0.0000      Pr(|T| > |t|) = 0.0000          Pr(T > t) = 1.0000
```

Figure 2.31 The ttest command

Observe in the output in Figure 2.31 that the *t*-test is run based on the assumption of equal variance. However, if we want to run the *t*-test assuming unequal variance, we can add unequal at the end of the above command. Incidentally, to check whether the variances of wage in the two samples are equal or not, just type in sdtest wage, by(collgrad).

2•5•3 Analysis of variance (ANOVA)

ANOVA tests for differences between more than two independent means. Thus, ANOVA can be seen as an extension of the independent *t*-test. In the following example, we are interested in ascertaining whether (population) mean hourly wages of white, black and other groups differ significantly. First, we can obtain the sample means of these three groups using the tab command in Figure 2.32.

```
. tab race, sum(wage)

           │     Summary of hourly wage
      race │        Mean     Std. Dev.        Freq.
───────────┼───────────────────────────────────────
     white │   8.0829994    5.9550691        1,637
     black │   6.8445578    5.0761866          583
     other │   8.5507813    5.2094301           26
───────────┼───────────────────────────────────────
     Total │    7.766949    5.7555229        2,246
```

Figure 2.32 An example of the use of the tab, sum command

According to the output, there appear to be some differences among the means. To find out whether these differences are statistically significant, we perform an ANOVA analysis below. Here, we are testing $H_0: \mu_1 = \mu_2 = \mu_3$, that is, that the (population) means of the three groups are the same. As we can see in the output in Figure 2.33, this hypothesis should be rejected as the overall F-test is significant: $F(2, 2243) = 10.28$, $p < 0.001$.

```
. anova wage race

                      Number of obs =     2,246    R-squared       =   0.0091
                      Root MSE      =  5.73188     Adj R-squared =   0.0082

        Source |  Partial SS        df        MS          F      Prob>F

         Model |  675.51028          2     337.75514    10.28    0.0000

          race |  675.51028          2     337.75514    10.28    0.0000

      Residual |  73692.457      2,243     32.854417

         Total |  74367.967      2,245     33.126043
```

Figure 2.33 The anova command

Consequently, we accept the alternative hypothesis that at least one of the mean differences is significant. To be able to find out which of the groups (white, black and other) differ from each other on the basis of their mean hourly wage, we can next perform pairwise comparisons (Figure 2.34).

```
. pwcompare race, pveffects asobserved

Pairwise comparisons of marginal linear predictions

Margins        : asobserved
```

	Contrast	Std. Err.	Unadjusted t	P>|t|
race				
black vs white	-1.238	0.276	-4.4798	0.000
other vs white	0.468	1.133	0.4129	0.680
other vs black	1.706	1.149	1.4851	0.138

Figure 2.34 The pairwise command

2●5●4 Chi-squared test

The chi-squared test is used to test the relationship between two categorical variables. In the example in Figure 2.35, we use a chi-squared test to find out whether the variable union (0 = non-union and 1 = union) is related to the variable collgrad (0 = no college degree and 1 = college degree). The reason why we want to examine this relationship is that, based on theoretical reasoning, we assume that having a college degree or not would influence the likelihood of being in a union. More typically, we would in this case consider union as dependent variable and collgrad as independent variable.[21]

Looking at the output, we see that the relationship between union and collgrad is statistically significant: $X^2(1, N = 1878) = 17.97, p < 0.001$. More specifically, about 32 per cent of those with a college degree are in a union, compared with about 22 per cent of those without a college degree. This corresponds to a difference of about 10 per cent.

```
. tab union collgrad, col chi2
```

```
  ┌─────────────────────┐
  │ Key                 │
  ├─────────────────────┤
  │       frequency     │
  │  column percentage  │
  └─────────────────────┘
```

union worker	college graduate not colle	college g	Total
non-union	1,101	316	1,417
	77.86	68.10	75.45
union	313	148	461
	22.14	31.90	24.55
Total	1,414	464	1,878
	100.00	100.00	100.00

Pearson chi2(1) = 17.9705   Pr = 0.000

Figure 2.35 The tab, chi2 command

2●6 CONCLUSION

In this chapter, we have provided a basic introduction to Stata encompassing three different areas: Stata's interface, descriptive statistics and graphs, and common bivariate statistics using Stata. Through the presentation of these three areas, we have tried to provide the reader with a sound basis for understanding the way Stata works and learning more of Stata on their own by using the resources internal and external to Stata. The easiest access to these resources through Stata is via the help and search commands. Using the help file of each of the commands presented in this chapter is really the key to becoming an advanced and effective user of Stata. Although the search command is to be used for finding commands available, it can be beneficial to find other Stata-related learning resources (e.g., online tutorials, examples) as well. We would further strongly recommend that the reader goes through the Stata *Getting Started* manual (type in help gsw to bring up this manual in Stata) as well as the video tutorials provided by StataCorp at http://www.stata.com/links/video-tutorials/.

---

[21] An alternative procedure for this example could be prtest union, by(collgrad).

 key terms

Command An instruction to Stata, typed in by the user, to perform some task.

Do-file A file that includes a series of commands.

Log-file A file that includes Stata output.

Working directory The directory that is used for your current Stata session.

Help file For a given Stata command, this provides an explanation of how to use it and a list of further features.

Data editor The window with rows (observations) and columns (variables).

sysuse The command used to open data files installed with Stata.

webuse The command used to open Stata data files over the Internet enabled by Stata.

Appending The operation of extending a dataset row-wise.

Merging The operation of extending a dataset column-wise.

Reshaping The operation of changing the format of a data structure (from wide to long or vice versa).

QUESTIONS

1 What do you think is the best way to learn Stata?
2 Take three variables (continuous) from any dataset and apply all the commands presented in the section on summary statistics.
3 Take three variables (categorical) from any dataset and apply all the commands presented in the section on frequency distributions.
4 Using any dataset, calculate the following basic statistics: correlation, *t*-test, ANOVA, chi-squared test.
5 Using the help file, explore further the anova command.

FURTHER READING

Acock, A.C. (2014) *A Gentle Introduction to Stata*. College Station, TX: Stata Press.

This is a user-friendly book on Stata treating data management, graphs, descriptive statistics, bivariate analysis as well some common advanced topics (logistic regression, structural equation modelling) used in the general social sciences.

StataCorp (2014) *Stata Manual: Release 14*. College Station, TX: Stata Press.

This is the official Stata manual, which includes a most comprehensive and detailed overview and explanations of Stata commands

3

SIMPLE (BIVARIATE) REGRESSION

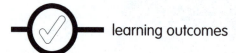

learning outcomes

- Understand the basic concepts of linear regression analysis
- Explain the estimation method of ordinary least squares
- Learn to use linear regression analysis for hypothesis and prediction purposes
- Understand and interpret simple (bivariate) linear regression analysis
- Learn how to develop a simple linear regression model and estimate it using Stata

In this chapter we first explain the mechanics and logic behind regression analysis within the framework of a simple (bivariate) linear regression as several of the regression concepts can easily be presented in this framework and generalized to the multiple regression case that we treat in the next chapter. Detailed conceptual treatment of simple regression is supplemented by a practical session demonstrating how to perform linear regression using Stata based on a real-life dataset. Although some parts of the chapter may seem technical, they are essential in laying down a solid foundation for better understanding and applying regression analysis to your own data.

3.1 WHAT IS REGRESSION ANALYSIS?

Regression analysis is a statistical technique that examines the relationship between one continuous dependent[1] (Y) and one (X_1) or more continuous/categorical independent[2] variables $(X_2, X_3, ..., X_n)$, with the aim mainly being to test one or several hypotheses and/or make predictions. More explicitly, a researcher may readily incorporate these two aims into the same study in an attempt to extract more detailed information from the regression analysis. We can now explain what these aims are actually about.

As far as hypothesis testing is concerned, regression analysis is used to provide quantitative evidence about a relationship between a set of variables measuring different phenomena in a population based upon a random sample of data drawn from the population. The quantitative evidence comes in the form of an estimated regression coefficient showing the strength of the relationship between two variables and an associated statistical test providing evidence for whether or not this relationship is statistically significant. For instance, a researcher may hypothesize a significant positive relationship between people's educational level and their hourly wage level. Such a hypothesis is more typically formulated in the social sciences as a significant positive effect of people's educational level on their hourly wage level. The latter formulation of the researcher's hypothesis is clearly a much stronger statement implying a causal relationship between the two variables which estimations from regression analysis alone cannot support. Frankly speaking, regression analysis cares little

---

[1] Alternative terms used for dependent variable are outcome, response, and endogenous variable.

[2] Alternative terms used for independent variable are predictor, explanatory, and exogenous variable.

about how you formulate your hypothesis! It provides you with the same results regardless. In other words, strictly speaking, causality cannot be established through any statistical techniques including regression analysis. Evidence obtained from regression analysis about a strong and statistically significant relationship between two variables may be attributed to causality through compelling theoretical reasoning and/or common sense. For instance, very few would oppose a research finding saying that educational level affects wage level as it makes sense simply on the basis of logical explanation.

When it comes to the second aim, making predictions, regression analysis is typically used to predict the population mean[3] value of a dependent variable at different values of one or more independent variables based on a random sample of data. Continuing with our previous example, we may, for instance, want to predict the mean hourly wage level of those with 10, 15 and 20 years of education. Predictions from the regression analysis may show that those with 10, 15 and 20 years of education have a mean hourly wage of $22, $40 and $58, respectively. The choice of values of the independent variables (10, 15, and 20 years of education in our example) at which we want to predict the mean value of the dependent variable (hourly wage) will depend on the researcher's analytical purposes. Incidentally, using regression analysis for prediction purposes does not necessarily require that causality should be established between two variables. An independent variable (e.g., number of tables available in a sample of university canteens) can be very useful in predicting a dependent variable (e.g., number of meals sold in these canteens) without having to cause it. If your purpose is solely prediction, you can still use this non-causal independent variable in your regression analysis.

Regardless of the purpose regression analysis is used for, the common first step is to specify a conceptual model and a mathematical function explaining the relationship between the variables of interest (Pedace, 2013). In what follows we show this step by going through simple (bivariate) linear regression analysis. We then transfer these ideas to the multiple regression case in Chapter 4. The reason for this choice is that many regression concepts can more easily be explained and illustrated using simple regression analysis, an approach we think will lay a good foundation for better understanding multiple regression analysis.

3.2 SIMPLE LINEAR REGRESSION ANALYSIS

A simple linear regression analysis examines the relationship between only two variables. Depending on the researcher's conceptual model (i.e., what the researcher thinks the relationship is like in the population), one of these variables will be designated as dependent (Y) and the other as independent (X). This relationship can be phrased mathematically as $Y = f(X)$, which says that changes in Y are a function of changes in X. Having established the reasoning for the relationship, the next step is to decide upon a functional form to apply to this relationship. Unsurprisingly, we typically use a linear function to describe the relationship between Y and X. A linear function simply assumes that a change in X corresponds to a consistent and uniform change in Y.[4] Geometrically, the linear function is represented by a

---

[3] Alternative terms for the population mean of Y are the expected value of Y, the conditional mean of Y, or just mean-Y.

[4] Alternatively, we can also say that a linear function suggests that a one-unit change in the independent variable leads to a certain amount of increase or decrease in the dependent variable.

straight line, also called a regression line, passing through the data cloud showing the relationship between Y and X.

There are several reasons why we almost always choose to apply the linear function by default (Lewis-Beck, 1980; Midtbø, 2007). Firstly, most relationships between different measures (education $\rightarrow$ income, sleeplessness $\rightarrow$ performance, motivation $\rightarrow$ success, etc.) in the social sciences are described in a linear fashion, whether negative or positive. Secondly, there is not always strong theory suggesting a functional form as an alternative to the linear. Thirdly, even some of the nonlinear/curvilinear relationships (age $\rightarrow$ income) can still be examined using a linear regression function. The impetus for investigating nonlinear relationships through linear regression functions is simply that linear regression functions are considered easier to apply and understand. This perception implies simplicity as the fourth reason why linear functions are commonly used in the social sciences.

Having specified the conceptual model and decided upon the linear function, we can mathematically express the hypothesized relationship between Y and X as

$$Y_i = \beta_0 + \beta_1 X_i . \tag{3.1}$$

Equation (3.1) implies that it is the individual Y-values (Y_i) that change linearly with X. This is probably also the reason why we sometimes encounter statements like 'as X increases, so does Y' in social science research articles. More precisely, however, it is rather the mean or expected values of Y (denoted by $E[Y_i]$) that we can assume to change linearly with X in the population.[5] As such, the relationship between Y and X should rather be formulated as[6]

$$E\left[Y_i\right] = \beta_0 + \beta_1 X_i . \tag{3.2}$$

As depicted in Figure 3.1, $E[Y_i]$ is the mean of the Y-values in the population. Typically there will be an $E[Y_i]$ at each level of X. The term β_0 represents the intercept or constant, which is simply the mean-Y value when $X = 0$. In other words, the intercept is the point at which the regression line crosses the Y-axis. Incidentally, the interpretation of the intercept does not generally make sense if the value of zero is not included in the range of X. The term β_1 is the regression coefficient[7] showing the amount of change in mean-Y for every unit increase in X. We could alternatively state that β_1 represents the amount of change in Y (on average) for every unit increase in X. Notice that the first statement uses mean-Y whereas the alternative statement uses just Y. However, both statements mean the same thing. Regardless of these statements, we can simply consider β_1 as the average effect of X on Y. Geometrically, β_1 is represented by the slope/gradient of the regression line, which can be quantified by taking the ratio of the rise ($\uparrow$) to the run ($\rightarrow$) of the slope. More specifically, β_1 is the ratio of the change in mean-Y to the change in X.

---

[5] This assumption is the basis of the so-called population regression function/model expressed in equation (3.2).

[6] $E[Y_i]$ should actually be read as $E[Y_i | X_i]$.

[7] An alternative term for regression coefficient is slope coefficient or just slope.

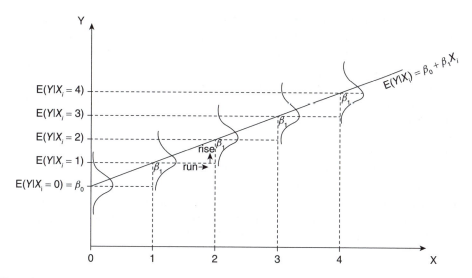

Figure 3.1 Geometric representation of regression

Moreover, there is also an error[8] term causing observed individual Y-values to vary around $E[Y_i]$ or mean-Y at each value of X (see also Figure 3.1). This means that there may be other variables[9] (not included in the regression model) that also influence Y. Suppose that, after estimating a sample regression model (education → wage), we predict that those with 15 years of education earn $40 per hour on average. Not all the individuals with 15 years of education are expected to earn exactly $40 per hour but many of them will do. However, there will also be some earning more/less than $40 as a function of, for instance, number of years of work experience.

Mathematically, the error term represents the difference between the observed individual Y-values (Y_i) and $E[Y_i]$:

$$\varepsilon_i = Y_i - E[Y_i], \text{ where } E[Y_i] = \beta_0 + \beta_1 X_i. \tag{3.3}$$

As such,

$$Y_i = E[Y_i] + \varepsilon_i. \tag{3.4}$$

If we simply substitute $E[Y_i]$, then

$$Y_i = \beta_0 + \beta_1 X_i + \varepsilon_i. \tag{3.5}$$

---

[8] Alternative terms used are noise and disturbance.

[9] Here we do not mean to equate the error term only with independent variables not included. The error term may additionally include measurement error and pure randomness/inconsistency in human behaviour (Gordon, 2010).

Examining (3.5), we observe that a regression model consists of two parts: one deterministic[10] and one random.[11] The deterministic part is represented by $\beta_0 + \beta_1 X_i$ predicting $E[Y_i]$, which is the same for each member of the population with the same value of X. The random part is reflected by ε_i making the population members with the same value of X vary around $E[Y_i]$ (Hamilton, 1992). Furthermore, the deterministic and random parts respectively represent the mean and variance of the distributions of observed individual Y-values at each level of X (Gordon, 2010).

We have so far built up a population regression model. In other words, our treatment has until now been purely theoretical as all we have done is formulate what we think the relationship between Y and X would be like in the population. The next step is to put an estimate on this theoretical idea. As we rarely have access to an entire population in the social science studies, we instead commonly obtain a random sample from the population of interest. We then use this sample information to estimate the population regression model. The estimation method that we typically use to do so is called ordinary least squares (OLS).[12]

3•2•1 Ordinary least squares

The estimation method of OLS is based on the least-squares principle. To estimate the population regression model (equation (3.2)), we first need to express its sample counterpart[13] as follows:

$$\hat{Y}_i = \hat{\beta}_0 + \hat{\beta}_1 X_i ,$$

(3.6)

where $\hat{Y}_i$ is the mean-Y predicted/estimated by the regression line ($\hat{\beta}_0 + \hat{\beta}_1 X_i$) at levels of X.

We can then show that the sample estimate of the error terms (residuals) is equal to the observed individual Y-values minus predicted/estimated mean-Y:

$$\hat{\varepsilon}_i = Y_i - \hat{Y}_i , \text{ where } \hat{Y}_i = \hat{\beta}_0 + \hat{\beta}_1 X_i .$$

(3.7)

As may also have occurred to you, we would naturally want our predicted mean-Y values ($\hat{Y}_i$) to be as close[14] as possible to the actual individual Y-values (Y_i). That is, we would want our residuals ($\hat{\varepsilon}_i$) as small as possible (see Figure 3.2):

$$\min \Sigma \hat{\varepsilon}_i, \text{ where } \hat{\varepsilon}_i = Y_i - \hat{Y}_i .$$

(3.8)

---

[10] Alternative terms used for deterministic are systematic and observed.

[11] Alternative terms used for random are stochastic, non-systematic and latent.

[12] There are several other estimation methods (maximum likelihood, weighted least squares, etc.), some of which we will encounter in some other later chapters of the book.

[13] We put hats (^) over the sample estimates (coefficients and error term) to distinguish them from population parameters.

[14] The closer they are, the better our model may be in predicting the dependent variable in the population.

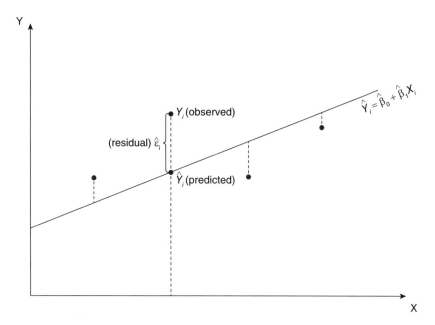

Figure 3.2 The least-squares principle

Although equation (3.8) makes sense conceptually, we encounter a technical problem when trying to minimize the *sum* of the residuals. The sum of the residuals will, as expected, be exactly zero since the positive values (observed *Y*-values above the predicted mean-*Y* values) and negative values (observed *Y*-values below the predicted mean-*Y* values) will cancel each other out. This is where the least-squares principle comes in. The least-squares method remedies this problem by minimizing the sum of the *squared*[15] residuals instead (Dougherty, 2011):

$$\min \Sigma \hat{\varepsilon}_i^2, \text{ where } \hat{\varepsilon}_i^2 = \left(Y_i - \hat{Y}_i \right)^2. \tag{3.9}$$

From equation (3.9), we can also see that the residual sum of squares (RSS)[16] is a function of the values of $\hat{\beta}_0$ (intercept) and $\hat{\beta}_1$ (slope). What the least-squares method does is find those (best) values of the intercept and slope that provide us with the smallest value of the RSS (hence the name least squares!) or the regression line that is on average closest to all the observed individual *Y*-values (thus called line of best fit) than any other line. The least-squares method does some complex calculus to derive the (best) intercept and slope coefficients. We will, however, skip these mathematical details[17] here and instead

---

[15] Squaring makes negative values positive (modulus), so that cancellation is avoided; and it gives larger residuals more weight. For example, if you square –2 you get 4, whereas if you square –4 you get 16.

[16] The sum of the squared residuals is alternatively referred to as the residual sum of squares (RSS) or error sum of squares (SSE or ESS).

[17] Interested readers can find the details of the calculus in any introductory econometrics book (e.g., Dougherty, 2011).

present below the resulting formulae from these calculus, which are relatively easy to apply in the case of a bivariate regression.[18]

The RSS is minimized when

$$\hat{\beta}_1 = \frac{\Sigma(X_i - \bar{X})(Y_i - \bar{Y})}{\Sigma(X_i - \bar{X})(X_i - \bar{X})} \qquad (3.10)$$

and

$$\hat{\beta}_0 = \bar{Y} - \hat{\beta}_1\bar{X} , \qquad (3.11)$$

where $\bar{Y}$ and $\bar{X}$ are the mean values of Y and X, respectively. Equation (3.10) shows a ratio in terms of deviation. We can alternatively present equation (3.10) in terms of variance, which simply will be the ratio of the covariance of Y and X to the variance of X (or covariance of X with itself, if you like), which can be expressed as

$$\hat{\beta}_1 = \frac{\hat{\sigma}_{xy}}{\hat{\sigma}_{xx}} . \qquad (3.12)$$

The regression coefficients obtained through OLS are known to be best linear unbiased estimates (BLUE) of the population regression parameters provided that the Gauss–Markov assumptions are met. These assumptions are treated in detail in Chapter 7. What is meant by unbiasedness is that the mean of the sampling distribution of OLS estimates ($\hat{\beta}$) will approximate the true population parameter (β) value. A second property that makes OLS the best estimator is efficiency. This means that the width (variance) of the sampling distribution of OLS estimates is narrower/less (than that of any other linear estimator).

3•2•2 Goodness of fit

Residual standard deviation

Technically, you can estimate a regression model for any two variables and get a line of best fit. However, we still have to examine how well the line of best fit produced by OLS summarizes/describes the relationship between the two variables. As the aim of OLS is to minimize the residual sum of squares, the starting point would be to quantify the RSS (equation (3.9)). Since the RSS shows the overall deviation from the regression line, it makes sense to average it (i.e., the variance; Gordon, 2010) to be able to compare it across samples of different sizes:

$$\hat{\sigma}_\varepsilon^2 = \frac{\Sigma\hat{\varepsilon}_i^2}{n - K} , \qquad (3.13)$$

where n is the sample size and K is the number of parameters estimated. Now we have an average deviation, but in squared units of Y. It thus makes sense to transform the variance into a more intuitive measure (i.e., the original metric of Y), which is done by simply taking the square root of the variance (Pardoe, 2006):

---

[18] In the case of a multiple regression, we would need to derive the coefficients using complex and time-consuming matrix algebra. Fortunately, we have statistical software like Stata that does this for us very quickly and accurately.

$$\hat{\sigma}_{\varepsilon} = \sqrt{\frac{\sum \hat{\varepsilon}_i^2}{n-K}} \; . \tag{3.14}$$

The resulting quantity is the standard deviation of the residuals,[19] showing us the 'average' distance between the observed individual Y-values (Y_i) and predicted mean-Y values ($\hat{Y}_i$) represented by the regression line (Fox, 1997). So, if you have a Y-value with a range of 180–586 and you estimate the standard deviation of the residuals to be 27, what you can claim is that the observed individual Y-values are, on 'average', 27 units (dollars, metres etc. depending on the metric of Y) away from the regression line.[20] However, there is no general cut-off value for judging whether this distance (27) is a sign of a good model or not, apart from the fact that the closer it gets to zero, the better the model is. That is, out of two competing models, the one with the lowest standard deviation of the residuals ($\hat{\sigma}_{\varepsilon}$) will be favoured.

We can use the arithmetic average of Y as a baseline model to compare our regression model with. After all, in the baseline model we can claim to use the arithmetic average, whereas in the regression model we use the line to predict the dependent variable. As such, the regression line must be, on average, closer to the observed Y-values than the arithmetic average of Y. As a result, we can simply compare the estimated standard deviation of the residuals of the regression model ($\hat{\sigma}_{\varepsilon}$) with the standard deviation of Y ($\hat{\sigma}_Y$) (Hamilton, 1992). Suppose that $\hat{\sigma}_Y$ is 160 and $\hat{\sigma}_{\varepsilon}$ is 27, a finding which clearly indicates that our regression line fits the data better than the baseline model (horizontal line). In a two-variable regression, since we have only one independent variable (X), we can alternatively state that X is a useful variable in predicting Y. In the same manner, by using $\hat{\sigma}_{\varepsilon}$ as a measure, we can compare several competing regression models containing the same Y. Furthermore, we can also complement this numerical approach with a visual approach by examining the scatter plot including the regression line.

Coefficient of determination (R^2)

The coefficient of determination, denoted by R^2, is another measure that is often used to assess the goodness of fit of the regression line.[21] R^2 is obtained by taking the ratio of the explained sum of squares (ESS) to the total sum of squares (TSS) as follows:

$$R^2 = \frac{\text{ESS}}{\text{TSS}} = \frac{\sum(\hat{Y}_i - \bar{Y}_i)^2}{\sum(Y_i - \bar{Y}_i)^2} \; . \tag{3.15}$$

Let us now, in a more intuitive manner, explain what R^2 is about.[22] As we did above, we can consider the arithmetic average of Y as our initial model to predict the value of the dependent

---

[19] Alternative terms used are regression standard error, standard error of estimate, root mean squared error and residual standard error.

[20] Informally, we can consider the regression line as a single unit representing all the predicted mean-Y values.

[21] We use the term 'line' in the case of a simple linear regression, whereas in multiple linear regression we use the term 'plane' or 'surface'. We can alternatively use the term 'model' in both cases.

[22] See also Kahane (2001) for a similar intuitive explanation.

variable. For the sake of simplicity,[23] let us just take a particular observation, say respondent 22. As we see in Figure 3.3, the observed value of respondent 22 (Y_{22}) is far[24] from the average Y model ($\bar{Y}$) represented by the horizontal line. The distance between Y_{22} and $\bar{Y}$ actually shows the amount of variation that is not captured by our average of Y model, which we refer to as the TSS.[25] Next, as an alternative to the average of Y model, we use a two-variable linear regression model ($\hat{Y}_i$) represented by the steep line to predict the dependent variable. As you can again see in Figure 3.3, the Y-value predicted by the regression model ($\hat{Y}_{22}$) is now clearly closer to Y_{22}. Another way of saying this is that our regression model has made an improvement in predicting Y_{22}. We can measure this improvement by quantifying the distance between $\bar{Y}$ and $\hat{Y}_{22}$ which we refer to as the ESS. If we then want to know how much of the total variation (TSS) our regression model (ESS) has managed to capture/explain, we can simply take the ratio of ESS to TSS, as in equation (3.15). Incidentally, there will always be some amount of variation not captured by the regression model (i.e., the RSS) represented by the distance between Y_{22} and $\hat{Y}_{22}$. It follows from this that[26]

$$RSS = TSS - ESS \qquad (3.16)$$
$$TSS = ESS + RSS.$$

If $R^2 = 0$, it simply means that our regression model does not do better than the average of Y model.[27] On the other hand, if $R^2 = 1$, it indicates that the regression line goes through all the data points. However, both of these situations are unrealistic. The more realistic[28] situation in social science applications is that R^2 is often closer to 0 than to 1. As an example, an R^2 value of 0.25 will mean that 25 per cent of the variation in the dependent variable is explained by (attributable to) our regression model. In the case of a two-variable regression,[29] this will mean that our X explains 25 per cent of the variation in Y.

There are, however, no definitive thresholds as to how big R^2 should be. The evaluation of R^2 should be based on substantial considerations rather than a pure statistical quantity. Furthermore, different fields and research questions may perceive a certain value of R^2 differently. One other factor to take into account is the number of predictors included in the model. Generally, a model with few predictors resulting in large R^2 can be asserted to do a better prediction job. A common-sense thing to do is relate the evaluation of R^2 to the tradition in a particular research field. If we have to provide a rule of thumb in the context of a simple linear

---

[23] Although we are here using a single respondent, you should bear in mind that our explanation applies to all data points (respondents). As such, we use notation/equations that apply to the whole sample.

[24] This is usually the case as the average is the simplest model we can use for prediction purposes.

[25] In a way, you could actually look at this as the amount of residual caused by our average of Y model. As this amount cannot be more than it is after fitting the average of Y model, we automatically call it the total sum of squares.

[26] Using the input from equation (3.16), you can also compute R^2 using $1 - RSS/TSS$.

[27] This is the result you would get if you ran a regression with only the intercept (in Stata, regress Y).

[28] Cases where R^2 is unusually high may indicate some problems with your regression model rather than good fit.

[29] Incidentally, in a two-variable regression, the square root of R^2, or R, is equivalent to a simple correlation between Y and X.

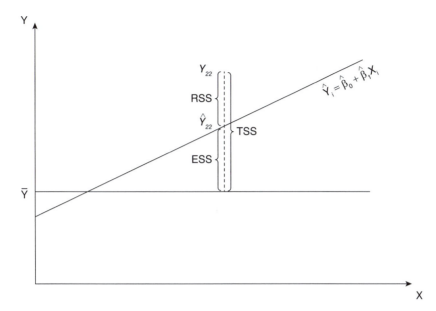

Figure 3.3 Visual representation of R^2

regression, based on our experience we would generally consider $R^2 \leq 0.09$ to be a small effect, R^2 between about 0.1 and 0.3 to be a moderate effect and $R^2 \geq 0.3$ to be a large effect.

When it comes to the decision as to which of the two measures[30] to use, we generally suggest using both $\hat{\sigma}_\varepsilon$ and R^2 (as well as a scatter plot) to assess the goodness of the fit of a regression model on its own, while $\hat{\sigma}_\varepsilon$ is suggested for comparing the goodness of fit of competing models involving the same dependent variable (Pardoe, 2006). Both $\hat{\sigma}_\varepsilon$ and R^2 are omnibus criteria for assessing the goodness of a regression model in that they both measure how well a model is doing in its entirety.[31] An additional procedure that we use to assess a regression model is hypothesis testing for slope coefficients.

3•2•3 Hypothesis test for slope coefficient

The p-value approach

As mentioned at the beginning of this chapter, one common aim of regression analysis is hypothesis testing. Hypothesis testing is about making an inference about a population based on a random sample drawn from that population, a process known as *inferential statistics*. More specifically, as you will remember, we set our regression function ($E[Y_i] = \beta_0 + \beta_1 X_i$) whereby we hypothesize a linear relation between an independent and a dependent variable (i.e., X

---

[30] In the case of a multiple regression, we suggest the use of the adjusted version of R^2, an issue we will return to in the discussion on multiple regression analysis.

[31] In a two-variable regression, since there is only one independent variable, the significance value for R^2 obtained from an F-test will be the same for the coefficient of the independent variable ($\sqrt{F} = t$). However, this is not the case in multiple regression. It is for this reason that we defer consideration of the F-test to Chapter 4.

predicts Y) in the population. As we do not have the population data, we test this hypothesis by assessing a random sample's OLS estimates ($\hat{Y}_i = \hat{\beta}_0 + \hat{\beta}_1 X_i$) of the population parameters.

The fact that we only work with one sample means that we would have only one $\hat{\beta}_1$ (and only one[32] $\hat{\beta}_0$ for that matter), and thus we cannot be sure whether this result[33] has come about due to a sampling error or it really represents the true population parameter (β_1). Thus, we need to know the sampling distribution of $\hat{\beta}_1$ to be able to go ahead with the process of making inferences. Fortunately, under some assumptions,[34] we can derive from the central limit theorem that the sampling distribution of $\hat{\beta}_1$ will be normal with mean β_1 (true/population slope) and standard deviation $\sigma_{\hat{\beta}_1}$.

We also know that we can transform any normally distributed random variable (in this case, $\hat{\beta}_1$) into a *z-score*,

$$z = \frac{\hat{\beta}_1 - \beta_1}{\sigma_{\hat{\beta}_1}},$$ (3.17)

and accordingly use the standard normal distribution to get the associated probability values. One problem that we encounter, however, is that we do not know the denominator ($\sigma_{\hat{\beta}_1}$) in equation (3.17).

Since we do have the sample estimate of the standard error of the slope coefficient, we can simply replace $\sigma_{\hat{\beta}_1}$ with its estimate, $\hat{\sigma}_{\hat{\beta}_1}$. Doing so changes the probability distribution from standard normal to a *t*-distribution with $n - K$ degrees of freedom (Hamilton, 1992):

$$t = \frac{\hat{\beta}_1 - \beta_1}{\hat{\sigma}_{\hat{\beta}_1}}.$$ (3.18)

Further, we can also show that

$$\hat{\sigma}_{\hat{\beta}_1} = \frac{\hat{\sigma}_\varepsilon}{\sqrt{\sum(X_i - \bar{X})^2}}.$$ (3.19)

Now we are ready to test whether this *t*-value comes from the H_0 population.[35] First, we need to set up a null (H_0) and an alternative hypothesis (H_1), put formally as follows:

$$H_0: \beta_1 = 0, \quad H_1: \beta_1 \neq 0.$$

---

[32] Generally in this chapter we do not make any hypothesis about the intercept, thus we will in this section focus solely on the slope coefficient.

[33] If your aim was to use regression analysis only for descriptive purposes, you could simply rely on your estimate without having to do any hypothesis testing. This may, for instance, be the case when you are only interested in finding out what is going on in a specific sample or when you work with census data.

[34] These assumptions are basically (1) independent and (2) normally distributed error. We treat these assumptions separately in detail in Chapter 7. Briefly, since OLS estimates are a linear function of the error term, the error term being normally distributed ensures that the estimates also follow a normal distribution.

[35] Another way of saying this is that we want to find out whether our sample estimate comes from an alternative population (in which there is a relationship between X and Y) to the H_0 population. For reasons it is not necessary to go into here, we start the hypothesis test using H_0 although we are in reality interested in finding out whether there is a relationship.

H_0 assumes that the population parameter is zero, which simply means that mean-Y ($E[Y_i]$) does not change as a result of a change in X (i.e., X does not have an effect on Y). H_1 assumes in contrast that the population parameter is not zero, suggesting that mean-Y ($E[Y_i]$) does change as a result of a change in X (i.e., X does have an effect on Y).

Now that we have the sample estimates ($\hat{\beta}_1$ and $\hat{\sigma}_{\hat{\beta}_1}$) and the population parameter (0) assumed by the null hypothesis, we can plug these values in equation (3.20):

$$t = \frac{\hat{\beta}_1 - 0}{\hat{\sigma}_{\hat{\beta}_1}} = \frac{\hat{\beta}_1}{\hat{\sigma}_{\hat{\beta}_1}},$$ (3.20)

generalized to $t_k = \hat{\beta}_k / \hat{\sigma}_{\hat{\beta}_k}$. Using the theoretical t-distribution table,[36] we find the probability value associated with our resulting t-value/t-statistic (essentially, slope coefficient), which is popularly known as the p-value (also called significance value). The p-value is the probability of obtaining a t-value[37] as large as (or larger than) ours if the null hypothesis were true. We can alternatively define the p-value as the probability of committing a Type I error (falsely rejecting H_0).

We then choose some arbitrary cut-off value to set as the maximum probability that we would accept for committing a Type I error. This probability value (called *alpha*) is typically set at 0.05. If the p-value (e.g., 0.042) associated with our t-statistic is less than the alpha value (0.05) we would reject the null hypothesis (X does not affect Y) and accept the alternative hypothesis (X does have an effect on Y). Incidentally, it is not uncommon to see alpha values of 0.01, 0.001 or even 0.1 being used in the social science applications.

So far we have confined the discussion to a two-sided test. This is because Stata and other statistical programs provide p-values based on two-sided tests in their standard output. However, it is not uncommon to see one-sided tests being presented in publications. A one-sided test is used when you specify the direction of your hypothesis. So, if you have a strong theory suggesting that X has a positive effect on Y then you would *a priori* state your alternative hypothesis and its counterpart formally as:

$$H_0: \beta_1 = 0, \quad H_1: \beta_1 > 0.$$

Or if your theory implies that X has a negative effect on Y then you would again *a priori* state the required hypotheses formally as:

$$H_0: \beta_1 = 0, \quad H_1: \beta_1 < 0.$$

In both cases, to test the significance of the slope coefficients, you simply divide the two-sided p-value (provided by default in Stata output) by 2. If the sign of your estimated slope proves to be in the expected direction and the associated p-value is less than 0.05, you would

---

[36] You can alternatively use Stata to compute the probability associated with a t-value using `display 2*(ttail(df, abs(t-value)))`. None of the options is necessary, however, as by default you get the p-value for a slope coefficient in the standard output of Stata.

[37] The t-value simply shows how far our estimated slope is from the true parameter of zero (mean) in terms of the standard deviation in the sampling distribution of the estimated slope.

accept the alternative hypothesis. If your estimated slope is not shown to be in the expected direction, then you would fail to reject the null hypothesis regardless of the *p*-value.

The confidence interval approach

Another (more informative) way of testing a slope hypothesis is the confidence interval approach. The first step is to construct a 95 per cent confidence interval[38] (two-sided) around the estimated coefficient using

$$\text{lower bound } \hat{\beta}_1 - t_{n-K}\left(\hat{\sigma}_{\hat{\beta}_1}\right), \text{ upper bound } \hat{\beta}_1 + t_{n-K}\left(\hat{\sigma}_{\hat{\beta}_1}\right), \tag{3.21}$$

where $\hat{\beta}_1$ is our point estimate, $t_{n-K}\left(\hat{\sigma}_{\hat{\beta}_1}\right)$ represents the *margin of error*, and t_{n-K} is obtained from the theoretical *t*-distribution.[39]

Suppose that in a regression analysis (*Y* regressed on *X*) run on a random sample of 95 individuals we obtain a slope coefficient of 31,644 (with a standard error of 2685). The 95 per cent confidence interval for the slope will then have lower bound

$$31{,}644 - t_{95-2}(2685) = 31{,}644 - 1.986 \times 2685 = 26{,}312$$

and upper bound

$$31{,}644 + t_{95-2}(2685) = 31{,}644 + 1.986 \times 2685 = 36{,}976.$$

Now that we have calculated the boundaries, the second step is to contrast this result against the claim made by the null hypothesis. Since the null hypothesis assumes no effect ($\beta_1 = 0$), we should check if the value of zero is included in the confidence interval. As we can see, the interval (26,312–36,976) does not include zero, which means that our estimated slope is very unlikely to have come from the null hypothesis population. Thus, we would reject the null hypothesis and accept the alternative which assumes an effect.

3•2•4 Prediction in linear regression

As stated previously, the second common aim of regression analysis is prediction. Prediction is about estimating mean-*Y* and *Y* for a specific individual. Since the former is more typical in social science applications, we will here focus on that. We now know that the expression that we would use to predict mean-*Y* is simply $\hat{\beta}_0 + \hat{\beta}_1 X_i$ (see equation (3.6)). All we have to do here is plug in the estimated values for $\hat{\beta}_0$ and $\hat{\beta}_1$, and choose the level of *X* at which we want to predict the mean-*Y* ($\hat{Y}_i$). Suppose that we have the following estimated equation based on a random sample of 82 observations:

---

[38] We can alternatively construct intervals at different values (90 per cent, 95 per cent or 99 per cent).

[39] The *t*-distribution approximates the standard normal distribution when *n* gets large (greater than 100), so t_{n-K} will be approximately equal to the *z*-value, which (for an alpha of 0.05) is 1.96. If *n* is small, then it is necessary to find t_{n-K} in *t*-distribution tables (or using software) as we do in our example below, thus we use 1.986 and not 1.96 in the formula.

$$\hat{\beta}_0 + \hat{\beta}_1 X_i = 2{,}674{,}274 + 151{,}855 X_i .$$

Let us assume that X ranges from 1 to 6. Then:

when $X=1$, mean-$Y = 2{,}674{,}274 + 151{,}855 \times 1 = 2{,}826{,}129$;

when $X=2$, mean-$Y = 2{,}674{,}274 + 151{,}855 \times 2 = 2{,}977{,}984$;

when $X=3$, mean-$Y = 2{,}674{,}274 + 151{,}855 \times 3 = 3{,}129{,}839$;

when $X=4$, mean-$Y = 2{,}674{,}274 + 151{,}855 \times 4 = 3{,}281{,}694$;

when $X=5$, mean-$Y = 2{,}674{,}274 + 151{,}855 \times 5 = 3{,}433{,}549$;

when $X=6$, mean-$Y = 2{,}674{,}274 + 151{,}855 \times 6 = 3{,}585{,}404.$

As we did with the slope coefficients, we can also construct[40] confidence intervals around the predicted mean-Y using the formulas below:

$$\text{lower bound } \hat{Y}_i - t_{n-K}\left(\hat{\sigma}_{\hat{Y}_i}\right), \text{ upper bound } \hat{Y}_i + t_{n-K}\left(\hat{\sigma}_{\hat{Y}_i}\right), \tag{3.22}$$

$$\hat{\sigma}_{\hat{Y}_i} = \hat{\sigma}_\varepsilon \sqrt{\frac{1}{n} + \frac{\left(X_P - \bar{X}\right)^2}{\sum\left(X_i - \bar{X}\right)^2}} . \tag{3.23}$$

3●3 EXAMPLE IN STATA

In this section we will make use of a real-life dataset called *flat.dta*, containing information about 95 flats (apartments) that were put up for sale in the first half of 2013 in a medium-sized city in Norway. The dataset includes information about the price, floor size, location, year built, and energy efficiency of the flats. The price was originally set in Norwegian kroner but is converted into US dollars in the following analysis. Since we present a simple linear regression here, let us for now use the flat price as the dependent variable (Y) and floor size as the independent variable (X) from our dataset. We further assume that flat prices in the population will on average change (increase) with changes (increase) in floor size, which we can express in terms of a population regression function as

$$E[flat\_price_i] = \beta_0 + \beta_1 floor\_size_i .$$

Next, we will OLS estimate this function using Stata based on our sample data using

$$\widehat{flat\_price}_i = \hat{\beta}_0 + \hat{\beta}_1 floor\_size_i .$$

Stata has a command called `regress` (or just `reg`) to estimate a regression model and OLS is the default estimation method of this command. The command `reg` is followed first by a dependent variable and then one or more independent variables: `reg Y X`. This is applied to our

---

[40] Although you can try doing this manually, we will in the following section present the powerful `margins` command in Stata to do this easily for us, along with several other related features.

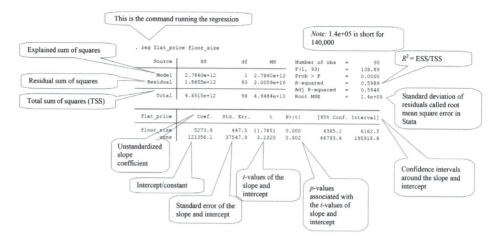

Figure 3.4 Stata output for a simple regression

example study in Figure 3.4 in which we have regressed `flat_price` on `floor_size`, the results of which we can start interpreting. Incidentally, we also briefly show the different concepts of simple linear regression that we have so far covered using the Stata output in Figure 3.4.

We can start examining the regression output first by assessing the goodness of fit of the regression model. As you will remember, we have two measures to help us with this task, namely the standard deviation of the residuals (called root MSE in Stata) and R^2. Starting with the root MSE, we see that it is 1.4e+05 (140,000) meaning that the observed flat price values are on average 140,000 units (dollars) away from our regression line. When we compare the standard deviation of the residuals of the regression model ($\hat{\sigma}_\varepsilon = 140,000$) with the standard deviation[41] of the baseline/average model ($\hat{\sigma}_Y = 222,450$), we see that $\hat{\sigma}_\varepsilon$ is clearly much less than $\hat{\sigma}_Y$, a finding suggesting that our regression model makes a considerable contribution to predicting flat prices. We can further support this finding with an examination of a scatter plot that we can obtain using `graph twoway (scatter flat_price floor_size)` `(lfit flat_price floor_size)`, the outcome of which is shown in Figure 3.5.

Figure 3.5 shows that the observed flat price values are indeed relatively closely scattered around the regression line. We can also look at the R^2 value of the model which is almost 0.6, which simply indicates that our model (consisting of only the variable `floor_size`) explains 60 per cent of the variation in flat prices. Again, although we do not have any clear cut-off values, 60 per cent sounds relatively high and suggests that our regression model fits the data quite well and is thus deemed useful in predicting flat prices. However, in many real-life studies, we may not have such obvious strong relationships between a dependent and an independent variable, thus such high R^2 values are less commonly seen in social science research publications. Generally, an R^2 value of 0.20–0.30 is considered satisfactory in many social science disciplines.

Having assessed the goodness-of-fit measures, we can next apply what we call the 3S criterion to examine other salient components of our estimated regression model. 3S stands

---

[41] We obtain the standard deviation of Y using the following syntax in Stata: `sum flat_price`

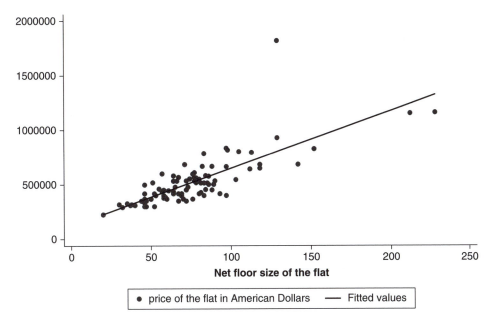

Figure 3.5 Regression line fitted to flat prices

simply for sign, size and significance of slope coefficient(s). As far as the sign of the slope is concerned, it is positive.[42] When it comes to the size of slope, it is almost 5274 dollars. Finally, we observe also that the *p*-value for our slope is 0.0000.[43] If we put all these three components together, the interpretation would be that floor size has a statistically significant positive effect on flat price. Furthermore, we can state that for every additional square metre, the flat price on average (or mean flat price) increases by about 5274 dollars. Incidentally, although the assessment of both $\hat{\sigma}_\varepsilon$ and R^2 has already confirmed the good fit of our regression model, we can also see that this is the case through judging the size of the slope. Moreover, as it is hard to imagine a flat with zero floor size, it does not make any sense to interpret the intercept/constant in this case.

We can extend the interpretation of the regression analysis by also presenting the predicted/estimated average flat prices at different values of floor size. Earlier in this chapter we showed how we could do this by hand. However, this time we will obtain the predicted values using a very useful command of Stata named `margins`. This command, with its extensions, can calculate not only the predicted values but also confidence intervals (CI) around these values, as well as providing a visual plot. Prior to using `margins`, we will as usual decide on the values of the independent variable at which we want the predicted average flat prices.

---

[42] We are in this example using a two-sided test for the sake of our presentation since that is the most common procedure used. In practice, though, a researcher could justify the use of a one-sided test prior to data collection and stick to it throughout the analysis.

[43] The *p*-value can never be exactly 0. Here it is very close to 0, and this is indicated by 0.0000.

```
. margins, at(floor_size=(60(20)220))
```

Adjusted predictions   Number of obs   =   95
Model VCE   : OLS

Expression   : Linear prediction, predict()

1._at   : floor_size   =   60

2._at   : floor_size   =   80

3._at   : floor_size   =   100

4._at   : floor_size   =   120

5._at   : floor_size   =   140

6._at   : floor_size   =   160

7._at   : floor_size   =   180

8._at   : floor_size   =   200

9._at   : floor_size   =   220

		Delta-method			
	Margin	Std. Err.	t	P>|t|	[95% Conf. Interval]
_at					
1	437784.7	16479	26.57	0.000	405060.7 470508.7
2	543260.9	14578.59	37.26	0.000	514310.7 572211.1
3	648737.1	17712.04	36.63	0.000	613564.5 683909.7
4	754213.3	23981.26	31.45	0.000	706591.3 801835.4
5	859689.5	31570.38	27.23	0.000	796997 922382.1
6	965165.8	39730.1	24.29	0.000	886269.7 1044062
7	1070642	48171.32	22.23	0.000	974983.3 1166301
8	1176118	56768.6	20.72	0.000	1063387 1288849
9	1281594	65460.49	19.58	0.000	1151603 1411586

Figure 3.6 Predicted flat prices using `margins`

Since floor size is a continuous variable ranging from 20 to 228, it is not sensible to just calculate the predicted values at every level. Suppose we are for some reason (theoretical and/or practical) interested in flats from 60 to 220 square metres, in 20-unit increments (60, 80, 100, …). We calculate the predicted flat prices for these floor sizes in Stata in Figure 3.6. We can see that flats 60 square metres in size are predicted to be for sale on average at a price of 437,785 dollars (CI: 405,061–470,509).

We can, moreover, plot these predicted values along with their 95 per cent CIs on a graph (as shown in Figure 3.7) by just typing `marginsplot` after `margins`.

So far, we have exclusively discussed simple linear regression analysis. Although this has served us well in our purpose of conveying difficult concepts of regression in an easy manner, it is not very often used in the social sciences which generally depend on and use non-experimental data. This means that we need to give a detailed treatment of multiple regression analysis, and it is to this that we turn in the next chapter.

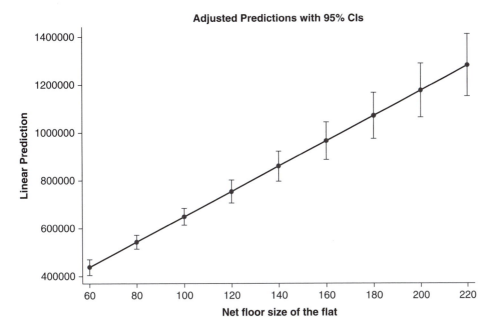

Figure 3.7 Predicted mean-*Y* values depicted using `marginsplot`

3 4 CONCLUSION

Regression analysis is an easy and a flexible statistical approach that can (with its extensions) tackle various complex research problems in the social sciences. Understanding regression at a deeper level would indeed provide a sound basis for comprehending statistical modelling in general. In other words, regression analysis should be seen not just as a statistical technique but as a way of thinking. This is why we have spent time in this chapter explaining many of the regression concepts in detail within the context of simple regression. We have in this chapter also presented basic regression-related commands in Stata. However, Stata offers many more features that can be explored by typing `help regress`.

 key terms

Expected value The mean value of a distribution.

Population regression function How we think variables are related in the population.

Sample regression function The estimated version of the population regression function.

OLS Abbreviation for the estimation technique of ordinary least squares.

RSS Residual sum of squares.

ESS Explained sum of squares.

TSS Total sum of squares.

(Continued)

(Continued)

Root MSE The root mean squared error or residual standard deviation.

R^2 The share of variation explained.

Regression coefficient The ratio of the change in mean-Y to the change in X.

Simple regression One independent variable predicting one dependent variable.

Multiple regression More than one independent variable predicting one dependent variable.

QUESTIONS

1 What is regression analysis?
2 Explain how OLS works through an example.
3 How would you evaluate the goodness of fit of a simple regression model?
4 Estimate a regression model and interpret the resulting table.

FURTHER READING

Dougherty, C. (2011) *Introduction to Econometrics* (4th edn). Oxford: Oxford University Press.

This is a technical book on econometrics explaining the mechanics of linear regression in detail. The book covers several other advanced topics related to regression analysis.

Gordon, R.A. (2010) *Regression Analysis for the Social Sciences* (4th edn). Abingdon: Routledge.

This is a comprehensive book on linear regression analysis from an applied perspective with various kinds of examples provided, along with Stata codes and output in the appendix.

Hamilton, L.C. (1992) *Regression with Graphics: A Second Course in Applied Statistics*. Belmont, CA: Duxbury Press.

This is a technical but still accessible text on linear regression analysis for social science students. Some Stata output is also provided.

REFERENCES

Dougherty, C. (2011) *Introduction to Econometrics* (4th edn). Oxford: Oxford University Press.
Fox, J. (1997) *Applied Regression Analysis, Linear Models, and Related Methods*. Thousand Oaks, CA: Sage.
Gordon, R.A. (2010) *Regression Analysis for the Social Sciences* (4th edn). Abingdon: Routledge.
Hamilton, L.C. (1992) *Regression with Graphics: A Second Course in Applied Statistics*. Belmont, CA: Duxbury Press.
Kahane, L.H. (2001) *Regression Basics*. London: Sage.
Lewis-Beck, M.S. (1980) *Applied Regression: An Introduction*, Quantitative Applications in the Social Sciences, Vol. 07-022. Newbury Park, CA: Sage.

Midtbø, T. (2007) *Regresjonsanalyse for samfunnsvitere* [*Regression Analysis for Social Scientists*]. Oslo: Universitetsforlaget.

Pardoe, I. (2006) *Applied Regression Modeling: A Business Approach*. Hoboken, NJ: John Wiley & Sons.

Pedace, R. (2013) *Econometrics for Dummies*. Hoboken, NJ: John Wiley & Sons.

4

MULTIPLE REGRESSION

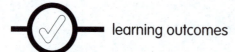

learning outcomes

o   Understand the reasoning behind multiple regression

o   Apply and extend the simple regression concepts to multiple regression

o   Learn to evaluate the quality of a multiple regression model

o   Understand and interpret multiple linear regression analysis

o   Develop a multiple regression model and estimate it using Stata

Building on our knowledge from the previous chapter on simple (bivariate) regression we extend the scope of linear regression analysis by explaining multiple regression. Thus, we recommend that the reader goes through the previous chapter prior to working with the current chapter. In this chapter we provide the main reasons for the popularity of multiple regression analysis in the social sciences, and explain how to build, estimate and evaluate a multiple regression model. In doing so, we put emphasis on the typical multiple regression concepts of adjusted R-squared, partial slope coefficients, and the relative importance of regression coefficients. After these conceptual treatments, we illustrate how to use Stata to estimate a multiple regression model as well as interpreting the resulting Stata output.

4 1 MULTIPLE LINEAR REGRESSION ANALYSIS

Multiple linear regression analysis is an extension of simple linear regression analysis. While simple regression is used to examine the relationship between a dependent and an independent variable, multiple regression analysis is a technique used to examine the relationship between a continuous dependent and two or more continuous or/and categorical independent variables. One reason why we may want to include more than one independent variable in our conceptual model is that human behaviour is a complex phenomenon influenced by various factors that we need to consider in order to get a more complete picture of the phenomenon under study. The second and a more salient reason is to be able to estimate the effect of a factor (e.g., gender) on a phenomenon (e.g., annual salary) by taking into account or controlling for other relevant factors (e.g., experience, educational level) that may also influence the phenomenon (Keith, 2006).

The regression concepts that we treated in the simple regression framework in the previous chapter are (only with some slight adjustments) directly transferable to a multiple regression situation. Here, too, we first develop a theory-driven conceptual model and state it mathematically as follows:

$$Y_i = \beta_0 + \beta_1 X_{1i} + \beta_2 X_{2i} + \ldots + \beta_k X_{ki} .$$

(4.1)

As in the simple regression situation, what we more realistically can claim is that[1]

$$E[Y_i] = \beta_0 + \beta_1 X_{1i} + \beta_2 X_{2i} + ... + \beta_k X_{ki}. \tag{4.2}$$

The term β_0 (intercept/constant) is the mean-Y value when all the independent variables in the model are equal to zero $(X_1, X_2,..., X_k = 0)$. β_1 is the regression coefficient showing the amount of change in mean-Y for every unit increase in X_1, while holding the value of all other independent variables in the model constant. This applies also to the interpretation of the coefficients $(\beta_1, \beta_2, ..., \beta_k)$ on the remaining independent variables in the regression model.

Again, as there will still be an error term (though less than that in simple regression) causing observed individual Y-values to vary around $E[Y_i]$, we introduce an error term

$$\varepsilon_i = Y_i - E[Y_i], \text{ where } E[Y_i] = \beta_0 + \beta_1 X_{1i} + \beta_2 X_{2i} + ... + \beta_k X_{ki}. \tag{4.3}$$

As such,

$$Y_i = E[Y_i] + \varepsilon_i. \tag{4.4}$$

If we simply substitute $E[Y_i]$, then

$$Y_i = \beta_0 + \beta_1 X_{1i} + \beta_2 X_{2i} + ... + \beta_k X_{ki} + \varepsilon_i. \tag{4.5}$$

4•1•1 Estimation

The least-squares principle that we explained in Chapter 3 on simple linear regression can readily be used to estimate multiple regression models. As the estimation and visualization get quite cumbersome in multiple regression models including several independent variables, we will from here on discuss the multiple regression concepts within the framework of a multiple regression including not more than two independent variables. The sample regression function of such a model would look like this:

$$\hat{Y}_i = \hat{\beta}_0 + \hat{\beta}_1 X_{1i} + \hat{\beta}_2 X_{2i}. \tag{4.6}$$

Here, too, the least-squares method chooses those (best) values of the intercept and slopes that provide us with the smallest value of the residual sum of squares, or the regression plane[2] (see Figure 4.1) that is on average closest to all the observed individual Y-values.

---

[1] $E[Y_i]$ should actually be read $E[Y_i | X_{1i},..., X_{ki}]$.

[2] In a regression model with one, two and more than two independent variables, geometrically the regression model is represented by a line, a plane and a surface, respectively.

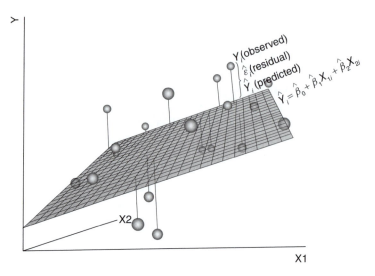

Figure 4.1 The least-squares principle in multiple regression

$$\min \Sigma \hat{\varepsilon}_i^2, \text{ where } \hat{\varepsilon}_i^2 = \left(Y_i - \hat{Y}_i\right)^2. \tag{4.7}$$

In the simple regression case, we provided two formulas calculating the regression coefficients that provide us with the smallest RSS. As you might also guess, we cannot apply those formulas directly to multiple regression situations. The idea behind the derivation of the regression coefficients is, however, the same in both cases, apart from the fact that it gets mathematically harder to calculate the regression coefficients by hand as the number of independent variables increases. This is a task that statistical software handles easily by applying matrix algebra. We will thus skip the mathematical details and rely on the output from the software instead.

4•1•2 Goodness of fit and the F-test

The goodness of fit of a multiple regression model can also be assessed using the residual standard deviation ($\hat{\sigma}_\varepsilon$) and coefficient of determination (R^2) measures. The explanation that we provided about these two measures in the simple regression chapter is directly transferable to the multiple regression case. Briefly put, the lower $\hat{\sigma}_\varepsilon$ or the higher R^2 is, the better the model can be claimed to fit the data.

In the multiple regression case, it makes further sense to specifically examine the omnibus F-test associated with the R^2 of a model. Intuitively, the F-test tests whether the amount of explained variation (coefficient of determination, R^2) is statistically significantly different from zero. More precisely, this means that the F-test tests whether the regression coefficients on all of the independent variables in a model are equal to zero (Gordon, 2010). Formally, we would apply the F-test to a three-variable regression model to test

$$H_0: \beta_1 = \beta_2 = 0,$$

(i.e., none of the independent variables is useful in predicting the dependent variable) against

$$H_1: \text{at least one of the two coefficients} \neq 0$$

(i.e., at least one of the independent variables is useful in predicting the dependent variable). The F-statistic for our test is obtained using one of the formulas[3] below:

$$F_{df_2}^{df_1} = \frac{R^2/(K-1)}{(1-R^2)/(n-K)} \quad \text{or} \quad \frac{\text{Mean square (model)}}{\text{Mean square (residual)}} \tag{4.8}$$

where $df_1 = K-1$ and $df_2 = n-K$. As seen in these formulas, we are calculating a ratio of one variance to another. This ratio would follow an F-distribution with df_1 and df_2 degrees of freedom. We can then use[4] the F-distribution to find the probability value[5] associated with our resulting F-statistic. If the p-value associated with the F-statistic is less than the chosen alpha value (most commonly 0.05), we would reject the null hypothesis that none of the independent variables has any effect, and accept the alternative hypothesis that at least one of our independent variables has an effect on the dependent variable. In order to pinpoint exactly which independent variable(s) has an effect, we would examine the individual t-tests for the estimated coefficients in the model. Needless to say, if the p-value is above the chosen alpha value, we would fail to reject the null hypothesis. In this case there would be in general no reason to examine the estimated regression coefficients individually.

4•1•3 Adjusted R^2

The adjusted R^2 (denoted R_a^2), as its name implies, is an adjusted/corrected version of the ordinary R^2. When you increase the number of independent variables in a regression model, regardless of the relevance or usefulness of the added variables, the ordinary R^2 will always increase, that is, never decrease (Pedace, 2013). Such artificial upward shifts in R^2 may then lead to misjudgement of the explanatory power of regression models. The adjusted R^2 remedies this situation by imposing a penalty for increasing the number of independent variables, as seen in the following equation:

$$R_a^2 = R^2 - \frac{K-1}{n-K}(1-R^2). \tag{4.9}$$

---

[3] Although not apparent in the formulas, the F-test actually tests the full (unrestricted) model against the (restricted) model with no independent variable (arithmetic average of Y). The F-test thus tests whether the unrestricted model is making a statistically significant prediction improvement as compared to the restricted model. You can easily extend this idea to also testing the joint significance of a subset of independent variables in a regression model.

[4] This assumes that the assumption of normally distributed error terms is met. See Chapter 7 on the assumptions of regression for more details.

[5] Although Stata gives you the p-value by default in the output, you can also compute p-values for any F-statistic using the following command: di Ftail(df1,df2,F-value).

In other words, R_a^2 (as opposed to R^2) will indeed decrease if an added independent variable does not contribute significantly to the explanatory power of the regression model (Pardoe, 2006). This is the reason why R_a^2 is often used to judge the goodness of fit of multiple regression models. However, we think that the gap between R_a^2 and R^2 will be trivial in multiple regression models developed using a sound theoretical foundation. Further, R_a^2 only remedies a possible problem with R^2; it does not solve any other possible problems (e.g., mis-specification) with the regression model (Dougherty, 2011).

4•1•4 Partial slope coefficients

Earlier we mentioned that the major reason for the popularity of multiple regression analysis is that it is a technique allowing for statistical control or adjustment. What do we actually mean by 'statistical control'?

Briefly put, strict experimental research ensures comparability. For instance, if the purpose of a piece of research is to ascertain the effect of a coaching programme on speech performance, in an experiment both the conditions (room temperature, audience, etc.) the speech is taking place in (through careful design) and all the remaining characteristics (gender, age, etc.) of those in the treatment and control group (using random assignment) are on average kept the same/equal. The two groups can then be said to be comparable. We can in fact use just simple regression to compare the two groups based on their speech performance. A resulting significant difference between the two groups can then be attributed directly to the coaching programme, and no other factor. In this case, what we have done is really identify the effect of the coaching programme on speech performance after having removed the effect of all other possible factors *by design*.

However, if we are to tackle the exact same research problem using a survey (non-experimental design) we would first have to gather information about the conditions (room temperature, audience, etc.) the speech is taking place in as well as the remaining characteristics (gender, age, etc.) of all the respondents, which we think may influence the speech performance. We would then use a multiple regression analysis[6] to compare the two groups by also including all the additional information (typically called control variables or covariates) in the regression model (Hamilton, 1992). A resulting significant difference between the two groups in this case can only through theoretical/logical reasoning be attributed to the coaching programme. What we have done here is again ascertain the effect of the coaching programme on speech performance after having removed the effect of all other possible factors *by analysis*.

In other words, setting the values of control variables (say X_2) constant enables us to identify the pure effect of an independent variable (X_1) on a dependent variable (Y). Mathematically, this is the same as saying that the differences between the predicted mean-Y at any two values of X_1 (say, 14 and 15) using two different values of X_2 in the prediction equation will be exactly the same. Note that when calculating the predicted mean-Y we are

---

[6] It is important to note that multiple regression analysis cannot substitute an experimental design. One reason is that although we gather the extra information, there will always be some measurement error involved. Second, for practical reasons we cannot gather information about all the possible influential factors. Third, we still need theory and/or common sense to establish causality for relations discovered by multiple regression analysis. We can, however, still consider it a pragmatic approach to statistical control or adjustment.

keeping X_2 constant at a certain value[7] in both equations below. Incidentally, the difference between the predicted mean-Y value is, as you know, the slope coefficients.

$$\hat{Y}_i = \hat{\beta}_0 + \hat{\beta}_1 X_{1i} + \hat{\beta}_2 X_{2i}$$

$\hat{Y}_i = -90.3 + 16.8 \times 14 + 2.23 \times 37.15 = 228$ $\hat{Y}_i = -90.3 + 16.8 \times 14 + 2.23 \times 44 = 243$

$\hat{Y}_i = -90.3 + 16.8 \times 15 + 2.23 \times 37.15 = 245$ $\hat{Y}_i = -90.3 + 16.8 \times 15 + 2.23 \times 44 = 260$

Difference = 17   Difference = 17

These equations work out fine, as expected, since the regression coefficients on X_1 and X_2 are estimated having removed the effects of X_1 and X_2 on each other as well as on Y. To remove the effect of X_2 on Y, we regress Y on X_2 and obtain the residuals quantified by $Y_i - \hat{Y}_i$. To remove the effect of X_2 on X_1, we regress X_1 on X_2 and obtain the residuals by $X_i - \hat{X}_i$. Finally, we regress $Y_i - \hat{Y}_i$ on $X_i - \hat{X}_i$ to obtain the regression coefficient on X_1, referred to as the 'partial slope coefficient' (Hamilton, 1992). We would apply the exact same procedure for estimating the partial slope coefficient on X_2. However, as mentioned before, the derivations of the regression coefficients are done by statistical software using matrix algebra.

The resulting regression coefficients are now partial/controlled/adjusted values, and should be interpreted accordingly. We would typically say that $\hat{\beta}_1$ is the amount by which the predicted mean-Y changes for every unit increase in X_1, having controlled for X_2, and in the same manner $\hat{\beta}_2$ is the amount by which the predicted mean-Y changes for every unit increase in X_2, having controlled for X_1. These regressions coefficients, estimated using multiple regression analysis, can be claimed to be less biased (over- or underestimated) as compared to their counterparts from simple regression due to the statistical control/adjustment.

When it comes to significance testing of the partial regression coefficients, we would follow the same procedure[8] (equation (3.17)) that we explained for the simple linear regression. We also use an identical approach (equation (3.19)) to that in simple regression to construct confidence intervals around the partial regression coefficients. In both cases, as implied by the equations, the only change in the multiple regression case is the reduction in degrees of freedom as a result of there being more than one independent variable.

4●1●5 Prediction in multiple regression

As with simple regression, one of the two main aims of using multiple regression analysis is to predict future values of the dependent variable. In simple regression we try to predict the mean-Y given a specific value of an independent variable (X_1), whereas in multiple regression we want to predict the mean-Y for a combination of independent variables (X_1, X_2, etc.). For instance, in a three-variable multiple regression, what we have to do is plug in the estimated

---

[7] We usually keep the control variables constant at their mean values. In this example, we have inserted the mean of X_2 in the equation to the left and another random value in the equation to the right.

[8] Note that in equation (3.18), the $\sum(X_i - \bar{X})^2$ in the denominator reflects the RSS (as X is the only variable, RSS = TSS). The corresponding equation in the multiple regression case would include the RSS obtained from a regression of an independent variable on all the other variables in the model.

values for $\hat{\beta}_0$, $\hat{\beta}_1$ and $\hat{\beta}_2$ as well as the levels of X_1 and X_2. Suppose that we have the following estimated equation:

$$\hat{Y}_i = \hat{\beta}_0 + \hat{\beta}_1 X_{1i} + \hat{\beta}_2 X_{2i} = 2{,}674{,}274 + 151{,}855 X_{1i} + 100{,}000 X_{2i}.$$

Suppose also that you want to predict the mean-Y when $X_1 = 3$ and $X_2 = 5$ then,

$$\text{mean-}Y = 2{,}674{,}274 + 151{,}855 \times 3 + 100{,}000 \times 5 = 3{,}629{,}839.$$

Using the procedure above, as you might guess, we can predict the mean-Y for any combination of values contained in the range of the concerned independent variables. Furthermore, as we did with simple regression, we can also construct[9] confidence intervals around the predicted mean-Y. However, in the multiple regression case, two minor adjustments are made. One is the reduction in the number of degrees of freedom when quantifying the t-value. The other adjustment is that equation (3.21) is generalized using matrix algebra to estimate the standard error of the predicted mean-Y. This is easily done by a Stata command that we will show applications of later in the chapter.

4•1•6 Standardization and relative importance

When all the independent variables in a multiple regression model are measured using the same metric (e.g., a seven-point scale), we can directly compare the magnitude of their associated partial slope coefficients (unstandardized/raw) and identify the relative importance of each of the independent variables. However, it is common in the social science studies for independent variables in multiple regression models to be expressed either in different measurement units or using unintuitive measures. In such cases, we can use standardized coefficients (also called beta coefficients) to determine the relative importance of the independent variables (Allison, 1999). Standardized coefficients would basically be the default coefficients obtained from a multiple regression run on z-scores $((X_i - \bar{X})/\hat{\sigma}_X)$ of both dependent and independent variables.[10] Alternatively, standardized coefficients ($\hat{b}_k$) can be obtained directly using the unstandardized coefficients:

$$\hat{b}_k = \hat{\beta}_k \left(\frac{\hat{\sigma}_{X_k}}{\hat{\sigma}_Y} \right). \tag{4.10}$$

What equation (4.10) does is turn the interpretation of effects from the original metric into standard deviations. We would then say that 'the mean-Y changes by $\hat{b}_k$ standard deviations for every standard deviation increase in X_k, having controlled for the other variables'. Unless the independent variables are highly correlated, the standardized coefficients do vary between -1 and $+1$. The closer the standardized coefficient is to ± 1, the stronger the relationship is between an independent and a dependent variable. Generally, based on our empirical

---

[9] Although you can try doing this manually, we will later present the powerful `margins` command in Stata which can do this easily for us, along with several other related features.

[10] In this case, the intercept of the regression equation will be zero.

experience, we consider $\hat{b}_k \leq 0.09$ to be a small effect, $\hat{b}_k$ between 0.1 and 0.2 to be a moderate effect and $\hat{b}_k \geq 0.2$ to be a large effect.

We should add two additional measures that are also used to assess the relative importance of independent variables in a multiple regression. These are partial and semi-partial/part correlation (see Warner, 2008: 447). In a partial correlation, the variation that control variables share with both the dependent and independent is removed, whereas in a semi-partial/part correlation the variation that control variables share only with the independent variable is removed. Squaring any of these two correlations will provide us with a different share of variation that an independent variable alone explains. Squared semi-partial correlations are generally preferred since the dependent variable stays the same for all the independent variables. The squared semi-partial correlation shows the amount of R^2 to be decreased if the variable of interest is removed from the model, thus reflecting its unique contribution.

Although standardized coefficients, partial correlations and semi-partial correlations appear to make the assessment of relative importance easy, we recommend that researchers first examine the unstandardized coefficients in relation to their natural measurement units in order to decide the relative importance of variables in a multiple equation. This suggestion will avoid researchers being completely dependent on using the standardized measures which in fact may lead to wrong conclusions on some occasions.[11]

4.2 EXAMPLE IN STATA

In this section we will use a hypothetical dataset (*present.dta*) to illustrate multiple regression using Stata. Let us now assume that we have estimated a multiple regression model whereby we have regressed a variable called present_value (amount in dollars one has spent on a birthday present for one's partner) on two attitudinal variables (one measuring how *attractive* a person views her/his partner to be and the other measuring how *kind* the person considers her/his partner on a 1–7 scale) and age. We assume that the money spent on a present in the population will on average change (increase) the more attractive and the more kind one considers one's partner and with age. We can express this as

$$E[Present\_Value_i] = \beta_0 + \beta_1 \, Attractiveness_i + \beta_2 \, Kindness_i + \beta_3 \, Age_i \, .$$

Next, we will OLS-estimate this population function using Stata from our sample data using

$$\overline{Present\_Value}_i = \hat{\beta}_0 + \hat{\beta}_1 \, Attractiveness_i + \hat{\beta}_2 \, Kindness_i + \hat{\beta}_3 \, Age_i \, .$$

To do so, we simply use the same command as in simple regression by adding the additional independent variables to the command (see Figure 4.2). By adding beta after the comma, we are asking Stata to estimate and show the standardized regression coefficients[12] (see Figure 4.3).

---

[11] For instance, standardized coefficients can be very misleading when making cross-population comparisons as variables get standardized differently in each population.

[12] These are also called complete standardized coefficients. If you type listcoef after reg, you can also obtain the semi-standardized coefficients. First, type net install sg152, from (http://www.stata.com/stb/stb57)

. reg Present_Value Attractiveness Kindness Age

Source	SS	df	MS
Model	698034.608	3	232678.203
Residual	258623.592	16	16163.9745
Total	956658.2	19	50350.4316

Number of obs = 20
F(3, 16) = 14.39
Prob > F = 0.0001
R-squared = 0.7297
Adj R-squared = 0.6790
Root MSE = 127.14

Present_Value	Coef.	Std. Err.	t	P>|t|	[95% Conf. Interval]	
Attractiveness	49.48174	19.41294	2.55	0.021	8.328152	90.63532
Kindness	33.93441	14.94049	2.27	0.037	2.26198	65.60683
Age	5.595464	2.58597	2.16	0.046	.1134516	11.07748
_cons	-66.95579	84.62477	-0.79	0.440	-246.3523	112.4407

Figure 4.2 Stata output for a multiple regression

. reg Present_Value Attractiveness Kindness Age, beta

Source	SS	df	MS
Model	698034.608	3	232678.203
Residual	258623.592	16	16163.9745
Total	956658.2	19	50350.4316

Number of obs = 20
F(3, 16) = 14.39
Prob > F = 0.0001
R-squared = 0.7297
Adj R-squared = 0.6790
Root MSE = 127.14

Present_Value	Coef.	Std. Err.	t	P>|t|	Beta
Attractiveness	49.48174	19.41294	2.55	0.021	.3949602
Kindness	33.93441	14.94049	2.27	0.037	.3534765
Age	5.595464	2.58597	2.16	0.046	.3236054
_cons	-66.95579	84.62477	-0.79	0.440	.

Figure 4.3 Stata output for a multiple regression with beta values

As shown in Figures 4.2 and 4.3, when we add beta we lose the confidence intervals in the output. Unless we are interested in the confidence intervals, this is just fine. Otherwise, we need to run both commands as shown in Figures 4.2 and 4.3. Sometimes a researcher may also be interested in constructing confidence intervals around the beta values as well. The way you can go about doing so in Stata is simply by standardizing all the variables in the regression equation by typing egen z_Age = std(Age), egen z_Kindness = std(Kindness), etc., first and then estimating the regression model based on these standardized variables using the usual reg command for multiple regression. The resulting default coefficients are the same as the beta values that you got in Figure 4.3. You would also get confidence intervals for these coefficients in the output.

Let us continue with the output section by examining the goodness of fit of our multiple regression model. As we see in Figure 4.3, the root MSE (standard deviation of residuals) is about 127, indicating that the observed *Present_Value* is on average 127 dollars, far from the estimated/predicted *Present_Value*. We also see that 127 is much less than the standard deviation of *Present_Value* (224), indicating that our multiple regression model (as opposed to the baseline/average model) makes a considerable contribution to predicting *Present_Value*. The relatively high values of both R^2 (0.73) and R_a^2 (0.68) confirm further that our model fits the data well. We would consider these values a sign of a large effect. Notice that R^2 dropped by 5 percentage points when adjusted. Had we incidentally included several irrelevant independent variables in the model, R_a^2 would certainly have been much less than 0.68.

Next, we observe that the F-test associated with the R^2 of our model is statistically significant as the p-value is clearly below the chosen alpha value (0.05). This means that we would reject the null hypothesis that none of the independent variables has an effect, and accept the alternative hypothesis that at least one of our independent variables has an effect on the dependent variable. As a result of the significant F-test, we can proceed to examining the individual components of our model by applying the 3S criterion as we did with the simple regression.

The signs of the three coefficients indicate a positive relationship between each of the independent variables and the dependent variable. We further observe that all of the coefficients are statistically significant (i.e., different from 0) as their respective p-values are below our chosen alpha value of 0.05. Briefly, we can state that as *Attractiveness*, *Kindness*, or *Age* increases by one unit, so does *Present_Value* on average by as much as their respective coefficients, *ceteris paribus*.[13] If we want to identify and compare the importance of these three variables, we explained earlier that in addition to interpreting the effects based on their unstandardized coefficients, we can make use of two standardized measures.

The first option is to examine the magnitudes of the standardized (beta) coefficients. The beta coefficients on *Attractiveness*, *Kindness*, and *Age* are about 0.39, 0.35 and 0.32 respectively. According to the general guideline we provided earlier, these are all above 0.20 indicating that each of the independent variables has a large effect. As far as the comparison is concerned, we could indeed construct a test statistic for the difference between the standardized coefficients and test its significance using the `test` command in Stata. Prior to doing so, however, we need to re-estimate the entire model using the standardized versions of our variables. The resulting coefficients are now, as you know, the standardized one. We could test equality of the standardized coefficients[14] as shown in Figure 4.4. As we can see from these results, there is no statistically significant difference between any pair of standardized coefficients. This indicates that *Attractiveness*, *Kindness* and *Age* exert equal impact on the dependent variable.

The second measure that we could also use is the squared semi-partial correlation which we obtain as shown in Figure 4.5.[15] As we can see, *Attractiveness*, *Kindness* and *Age* uniquely explain about 11, 9 and 8 per cent of the variation in the dependent variable, respectively. Incidentally, the squared semi-partial correlations do not sum up to the R^2 value of the entire model due to correlation between the three independent variables. That is, the difference (73 per cent – 28 per cent) represents the same part of the variance (thus not unique) explained by two or more independent variables.

Moreover, we can also test the significance of the coefficients using the confidence interval approach that we explained previously. Figure 4.2 shows the 95 per cent confidence intervals for the coefficients. As we can see, none of the confidence intervals includes the value of zero,

---

[13] Everything else kept constant.

[14] The reason why we compare the standardized coefficients is that *Age* is measured using a different metric than *Attractiveness* and *Kindness*. Otherwise, we could simply use the `test` command to test the equality of *Attractiveness* and *Kindness* as follows: `test Attractiveness = Kindness`. Alternatively, we could type `lincom Attractiveness – Kindness`. This command can also be used for comparing the standardized coefficients.

[15] This command produces the squared partial correlations as well. To get the squared partial correlations you can alternatively type `estat esize` after estimating the model using regress.

```
· test z_Attractiveness = z_Kindness

( 1)   z_Attractiveness - z_Kindness = 0

       F(  1,    16) =     0.03
              Prob > F =    0.8742

· test z_Attractiveness = z_Age

( 1)   z_Attractiveness - z_Age = 0

       F(  1,    16) =     0.09
              Prob > F =    0.7724

· test z_Kindness = z_Age

( 1)   z_Kindness - z_Age = 0

       F(  1,    16) =     0.01
              Prob > F =    0.9043
```

Figure 4.4   Testing equality of standardized coefficients

```
. pcorr   Present_Value Attractiveness Kindness Age
(obs=20)

Partial and semipartial correlations of Present_Value with
```

Variable	Partial Corr.	Semipartial Corr.	Partial Corr.^2	Semipartial Corr.^2	Significance Value
Attractiv~s	0.5374	0.3313	0.2888	0.1098	0.0215
Kindness	0.4938	0.2952	0.2438	0.0872	0.0373
Age	0.4758	0.2813	0.2264	0.0791	0.0460

Figure 4.5   Squared semi-partial correlation

indicating that all the coefficients are statistically different from zero. This result is in line with that from the *p*-value approach. By the way, if we for some reason wish to obtain, say, 90 per cent confidence intervals for the coefficients, we can simply type reg Present_Value Attractiveness Kindness Age, level(90).

In addition to conveying information regarding the effects of the independent variables from our regression model, we can further use our regression estimates to predict the dependent variable. As in the case of simple regression, here too we will make use of the margins and marginsplot commands. Suppose we want to obtain the average money spent on a present (predicted mean-*Y*) by those who give their partners an attractiveness rating of 7, a kindness rating of 7 and are 50 years old; we can use the margins command as below. You can generalize this idea to more complex prediction purposes. One additional advantage of the margins command is that it also provides us with standard errors (see Figure 4.6).

We might for some reason be interested in calculating the predicted mean-*Y* values at specific values of an independent variable, holding the remaining independent variables constant (at their mean values). This is also done using the margins command with the atmeans option as shown in Figure 4.7.

Right after the margins command, by typing marginsplot, we can get the predicted values and their confidence intervals visualized in a graph as we did in the chapter on simple regression. The resulting graph can easily be exported to Microsoft Word or any other application; simply copy and paste it.

```
. margins, at(Attractiveness=7 Kindness=7 Age=50)

Adjusted predictions                                Number of obs   =        20
Model VCE     : OLS

Expression    : Linear prediction, predict()
at            : Attractive~s    =         7
                Kindness        =         7
                Age             =        50
```

	Margin	Delta-method Std. Err.	t	P>|t|	[95% Conf. Interval]
_cons	796.7304	65.64376	12.14	0.000	657.5719 935.889

Figure 4.6 The `margins` command

```
. margins, at(Attractiveness=(1(1)7)) atmeans

Adjusted predictions                                Number of obs   =        20
Model VCE     : OLS

Expression    : Linear prediction, predict()

1._at         : Attractive~s    =         1
                Kindness        =       3.9  (mean)
                Age             =     32.75  (mean)

2._at         : Attractive~s    =         2
                Kindness        =       3.9  (mean)
                Age             =     32.75  (mean)

3._at         : Attractive~s    =         3
                Kindness        =       3.9  (mean)
                Age             =     32.75  (mean)

4._at         : Attractive~s    =         4
                Kindness        =       3.9  (mean)
                Age             =     32.75  (mean)

5._at         : Attractive~s    =         5
                Kindness        =       3.9  (mean)
                Age             =     32.75  (mean)

6._at         : Attractive~s    =         6
                Kindness        =       3.9  (mean)
                Age             =     32.75  (mean)

7._at         : Attractive~s    =         7
                Kindness        =       3.9  (mean)
                Age             =     32.75  (mean)
```

	Margin	Delta-method Std. Err.	t	P>|t|	[95% Conf. Interval]
_at					
1	298.1216	57.08541	5.22	0.000	177.1059 419.1372
2	347.6033	41.39577	8.40	0.000	259.8482 435.3584
3	397.085	30.36774	13.08	0.000	332.7083 461.4618
4	446.5668	29.74077	15.02	0.000	383.5192 509.6144
5	496.0485	40.00689	12.40	0.000	411.2377 580.8593
6	545.5303	55.41041	9.85	0.000	428.0654 662.9951
7	595.012	72.7585	8.18	0.000	440.7709 749.2531

Figure 4.7 The `margins` command with the `atmeans` option

Speaking of exporting output from Stata, there are several user-developed commands that allow one to easily export output of a regression analysis from Stata to, for instance, Microsoft Word. Using any of these commands, you can generate publication-ready tables, saving you a considerable amount of time as well as providing complete presentation accuracy. Out of these commands, esttab, is part of the estout package. You should first install this overarching package by typing ssc install estout, replace. Then we can start using it to produce a publication-ready table of the regression output shown in Figure 4.2 and 4.3 using the following syntax:

```
. reg Present_Value Attractiveness Kindness Age
. estimates store my_regression
. estadd beta
. esttab my_regression, title (Regression Model) nonumber ///
mlabel (Results) ///
cells (b (star fmt (2)) ci (par) beta (par)) ///
stats (N p r2 r2_a rmse, ///
labels ("Number of observations" ///
"Model significance" "R-square" ///
"Adjusted R-square" "Residual standard deviation")) ///
varwidth (30) legend
```

After copying and pasting the above code into a do-file, you can run it to get the results in a table in a Stata output window as shown in Figure 4.8. You can also export[16] this table as it is to Microsoft Word by simply inserting using my_regression.rtf before the first comma in the above code.[17] You will find a Word file named *my_regression* in the directory you are currently working in that contains the table you have just generated in Stata.

Regression Model

	Results b/ci95/beta
Attractiveness	42.39***
	[29.10,55.68]
	(0.42)
Kindness	36.46***
	[24.65,48.28]
	(0.40)
Age	5.52***
	[3.69,7.34]
	(0.33)
_cons	-90.06*
	[-171.28,-8.84]
Number of observations	126.00
Model significance	0.00
R-square	0.63
Adjusted R-square	0.62
Residual standard deviation	124.27

* p<0.05, ** p<0.01, *** p<0.001

Figure 4.8 Stata output showing regression model

---

[16] In this example we show how the output can be exported to Microsoft Word. You can easily export the output to several other applications as well. To see the complete options type help esttab.

[17] Alternatively, you can simply continue the syntax above by a comma and then type using my_regression.rtf.

4 ● 3 CONCLUSION

Multiple regression analysis is a flexible statistical technique that can address an array of social science research problems. We have learnt that the main feature that has made multiple regression analysis popular among scholars is the fact that it allows for estimating the effect of an independent variable on a dependent variable by taking into account or controlling for other variables. Several of the concepts (e.g., partial slope coefficients, F-test) that we have learnt in this chapter will certainly help the reader to understand more complicated topics like dummy-variable regression and interaction/moderation effects which are respectively the topics of the next two chapters. We have in this chapter also presented some more regression-related commands (test, esttab, etc.) in Stata. To explore further regression-related commands type help regress, and to learn more about how to create publication-ready regression tables type help esttab.

 key terms

Multiple regression Includes one dependent and two or more independent variables.

F-test Tests whether regression coefficients in a model are all equal to zero.

Adjusted R^2 Adjusted/corrected version of the ordinary R^2 of a multiple regression model.

Partial slope coefficients Effect of an independent variable on a dependent variable, having removed the effect of all other factors in the model.

Statistical control or adjustment Keeping the values of the controlled variables at a constant value.

Standardized coefficients Used to determine the relative importance of the independent variables.

Squared semi-partial correlation Reflects the unique contribution of an independent variable.

QUESTIONS

1 What do we gain from using multiple regression as compared to simple regression?
2 How would you evaluate the goodness of fit of a multiple regression model?
3 Estimate a multiple regression model and interpret the resulting table.
4 How would you evaluate the relative importance of your independent variables?
5 Using the command esttab, create your own publication-ready table of your regression output from Stata.

FURTHER READING

Allison, P.D. (1999) *Multiple Regression: A Primer*. Thousand Oaks, CA: Pine Forge Press.

This book is specifically about multiple regression analysis from an applied perspective, with various kinds of multiple regression models drawn from scholarly works published in international journals.

Dougherty, C. (2011) *Introduction to Econometrics* (4th edn). Oxford: Oxford University Press.

This is a technical book on econometrics explaining the mechanics of linear regression in detail. The book covers several other advanced topics related to regression analysis.

Keith, T.Z. (2006) *Multiple Regression and Beyond*. Boston: Pearson Education.

This is an applied text on linear regression analysis treating a large number of issues/ concepts related to linear regression using different types of examples. The book also covers structural equation modelling.

REFERENCES

Allison, P.D. (1999) *Multiple Regression: A Primer*. Thousand Oaks, CA: Pine Forge Press.
Dougherty, C. (2011) *Introduction to Econometrics* (4th edn). Oxford: Oxford University Press.
Gordon, R.A. (2010) *Regression Analysis for the Social Sciences* (4th edn). Abingdon: Routledge.
Hamilton, L.C. (1992) *Regression with Graphics: A Second Course in Applied Statistics*. Belmont, CA: Duxbury Press.
Keith, T.Z. (2006) *Multiple Regression and Beyond*. Boston: Pearson Education.
Pardoe, I. (2006) *Applied Regression Modeling: A Business Approach*. Hoboken, NJ: John Wiley & Sons.
Pedace, R. (2013) *Econometrics for Dummies*. Hoboken, NJ: John Wiley & Sons.
Warner, R.M. (2008) *Applied Statistics: From Bivariate through Multivariate Techniques*. London: Sage.

5

DUMMY-VARIABLE REGRESSION

Independent *t*-test, ANOVA, ANCOVA and two-way ANOVA

learning outcomes

o Understand the logic behind dummy-variable regression

o Learn how to compare group means using dummy-variable regression

o Explain the link between regression and ANOVA

o Understand the use of the *F*-test to test the significance of a set of coefficients

o Learn how to develop a dummy-variable regression model and estimate it using Stata

In this chapter we explain the logic and equations behind linear regression analysis with categorical independent variables, an approach which is commonly referred to as dummy-variable regression in the social science literature. It is important to emphasize that in dummy-variable regression, as in the previous two chapters, our dependent variable is still continuous and the models we build are still linear. Following our theoretical treatment of different types of dummy-variable regression models, we show some analyses using real-life data with the help of Stata. In so doing, we also explicitly show how dummy-variable regression equates with the independent *t*-test, ANOVA and ANCOVA.[1]

 WHY DUMMY-VARIABLE REGRESSION?

In the previous chapter, we presented linear regression applied to models including only continuous independent variables (e.g., price, income). However, in social science inquiries we often wish to estimate models including not only continuous but also categorical independent variables. In principle, we can estimate regression models including only categorical independent variables. In non-experimental investigations, we commonly combine continuous and categorical independent variables to facilitate statistical control. For instance, we may be interested in examining the effect of gender (categorical) on personal annual income by controlling for educational level (continuous) and vice versa. This three-variable regression can be extended to include several other categorical and/or continuous variables. Models including only categorical or a combination of categorical and continuous independent variables can readily be estimated using the so-called dummy-variable regression technique.

5●1●1 Creating dummy variables

Categorical variables on the right-hand side of the regression equations can be dichotomous (two categories/values) or polytomous (more than two categories/values). In order for a categorical variable to be included in a linear regression model, it must first be transformed into a dummy variable. A dummy variable (also called indicator variable) takes on the values 0 and 1 to represent two different attributes respectively (e.g., male and female, unsuccessful and

---

[1] A similar approach is also followed elsewhere (Hamilton, 1992; Hardy, 1993; Gordon, 2010).

successful, private and public). If not already coded as 0 and 1 in the data collection phase, the two categories of a dichotomous variable can easily be converted into a dummy variable through simple recoding.

Transforming a polytomous variable into dummy variables, on the other hand, is less straightforward but follows the same principle. Since a polytomous variable has more than two categories, we must initially create as many dummy variables as there are categories. However, we always omit one of the resulting dummy variables when estimating the regression model. Suppose that we want to generate dummy variables out of a categorical variable (e.g., *location*) in our dataset called *flat2.dta* including four categories: flats located in the *centre* (1), *south* (2), *west* (3), and *east* (4) of the city.

What we would do to create the four dummy variables is to code each of these categories one by one as 1 and the remaining categories as 0. For instance, if you code the first category (originally labelled *centre*) as 1 and the rest as 0, this provides you with the first dummy variable indicating respectively the flats located in the city centre and the flats located in the south, west or east of the city. Next, you would code the second category (originally labelled *south*) as 1 and the rest as 0, indicating respectively the flats in the south of the city and the flats in the other three areas of the city. You continue in the same manner to create the remaining dummy variables. When creating the dummy variables, you simply label them in a way to easily recollect what each of them represents. We would in our example label the resulting four dummy variables as *centre*, *south*, *west* and *east* (see Table 5.1).

Table 5.1 Creating dummy variables for a polytomous variable

Polytomous variable	Dummy variables			
Location	centre	south	west	east
1=centre	1	0	0	0
2=south	0	1	0	0
3=west	0	0	1	0
4=east	0	0	0	1

Using Stata, let us now create the above four dummy variables (from *location* in our dataset called *flat2.dta*). One way of doing this is to use the generate[2] command as follows:

```
. generate centre = 0
. replace centre=1 if location==1
. generate south = 0
. replace south=1 if location==2
. generate west = 0
. replace west=1 if location==3
. generate east= 0
. replace east=1 if location==4
```

[2] generate centre=0 gives the value 0 to all observations first, and then, with the replace command, we simply give the value 1 to those in the category of *centre* while keeping the rest still at 0. This then results in a vector 1 and 0 values.

An alternative and, in fact, more effective way of creating a set of dummy variables in Stata is to use the `tabulate` command:

`. tabulate location, generate(d_location)`

Although each of the above approaches to creating dummy variables is useful to know, Stata allows one to even more effectively create a set of dummy variables in the regression estimation command[3] (regress) itself as well. Stata facilitates this using the so-called factor variables. By way of illustration, suppose we want to regress *flat price* on *location*. The command[4] for this estimation would then look like:

`. reg flat_price i.location`

In this case `i.location` is our factor variable creating dummy (indicator) variables from our original categorical variable *location*. By default, Stata creates four dummy variables and uses the first dummy as the reference group in the estimation. In our example, since the first category of *location* is *centre*, it will be used as the reference group. If we want to change the reference group, however, this can be done easily by modifying the base operator as follows:

`. reg flat_price ib(2).location`

or just

`. reg flat_price b2.location`

Here we have changed the base operator from `i` to `ib(2)`. This has changed the reference group from the default (first) category to our choice (second) category. We could alternatively choose the third or fourth category as the reference group simply by typing `ib(3)` or `ib(4)`, or just `b3` or `b4`, respectively.

5•1•2 The logic behind dummy-variable regression

Linear regression analysis is basically a technique used to examine the association between a continuous dependent (Y) and a continuous independent variable (X). We also learnt in the previous two chapters that we calculate a regression coefficient quantifying the strength of the relationship between Y and X. We know that the resulting regression coefficient (β) shows the amount of change in mean of Y or $E[Y_i]$ for every unit increase in X. This would then imply that when we move by one unit (from 0 to 1) on the X-scale, β shows simply the difference between the mean of Y at two different values (0 and 1) of X.

Let us further imagine that X is not a continuous but a dummy variable, with values of 0 and 1 representing, for instance, males and females respectively. The regression coefficient

---

[3] In fact, this applies to most of the estimation commands (`logit`, `mixed`, etc.) in Stata.

[4] We could alternatively use the `xi` command, typing `xi: reg flat_price i.location`.

would then indicate the difference between the mean scores, on any variable we want (income, weight, height, etc.), of males and females. The fact that regression coefficients reflect simply mean differences (Hardy, 1993) makes linear regression a readily available and a flexible technique for comparing group means as well.

5●2 REGRESSION WITH ONE DUMMY VARIABLE

Regression with one dummy variable (predictor) corresponds directly to an independent *t*-test, a case which soon will become clear (if not already so) from our explanation provided above. Suppose that we hypothesize an association between geographical location (non-centre versus centre flats) and flat prices and accordingly develop the following population regression function:

$$E[Y_i] = \beta_0 + \beta_1 X_i . \tag{5.1}$$

Here Y represents flat prices measured in dollars (continuous), whereas X denotes the geographical location of the flats (dummy), whereby we have coded flats outside the city centre 0 and flats in the city centre 1. Furthermore, we also know that $E[Y_i]$ shows the mean of Y at each value of X. Then, using the prediction approach, we can easily obtain $E[Y_i]$ when X is 0 (non-centre flats)[5] and 1 (centre flats) . When $X = 0$, we have that

$$E[Y_i] = \beta_0 + \beta_1(0) = \beta_0 \tag{5.2}$$

is the mean price of non-centre flats.[6] When $X = 1$,

$$E[Y_i] = \beta_0 + \beta_1(1) = \beta_0 + \beta_1 . \tag{5.3}$$

is the mean price of centre flats.

Equation (5.2) shows that β_0 (the intercept/constant) is the mean value of non-centre flats, whereas equation (5.3) shows that $\beta_0 + \beta_1$ is the mean value of centre flats. So the difference between the two mean values is simply β_1, as shown geometrically in Figure 5.1.

We use the same hypothesis testing procedure that we learnt in the chapter on simple linear regression to test whether or not β_1 is statistically significant from zero. In this case, our null hypothesis would be H_0: $\beta_1 = 0$, suggesting that the difference between the two means is zero (the two means are the same) and the alternative hypothesis would be H_1: $\beta_1 \neq 0$, proposing that the difference between the two means is not equal to zero (the two means are different). This formal set-up of hypotheses applies to the other variants of dummy-based regression that we treat in the following as well.

---

[5] The category coded 0 is typically referred to as the reference category or baseline category.

[6] $\beta_1(0)$ should be interpreted by the reader as $\beta_1 \times 0$.

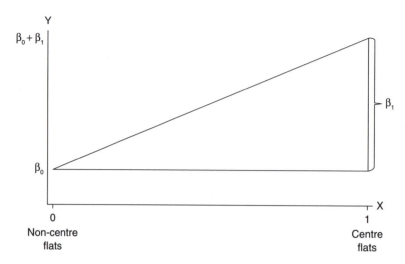

Figure 5.1 Geometrical representation of regression with a dummy variable

5•2•1 Example in Stata

In our example model shown in equation (5.1) we wanted to compare the mean price of flats in the city centre with that of flats outside the city centre. This is simply comparing two independent means. The regression approach to tackling this matter is regressing the *flat price* on the dummy variable indicating flats in the city centre and those outside the city centre. Before estimating the model, we should create this dummy variable from our original categorical variable *location* in our dataset *flat2.dta*. This is done easily, as follows:

```
. generate centre = 0
. replace centre=1 if location==1
```

We then use this dummy variable as an independent variable predicting *flat price* which is expressed by the following command:

```
. reg flat_price centre          `
```

We can also do the above two-stage procedure with a single command:

```
. reg flat_price i(1).location or reg flat_price i1.location
```

The estimated regression function and values are shown below (see the Stata output in Figure 5.2):

$$\widehat{flat\_price}_i = \hat{\beta}_0 + \hat{\beta}_1 centre_i = 491{,}292 + 106{,}428 centre_i. \tag{5.4}$$

The mean price of flats outside city centre is about 491,292 dollars, as reflected by the intercept/constant ($\hat{\beta}_0$). We also observe that the difference between the mean price of flats in the city centre and outside the city centre is about 106,428 dollars, as represented by the regression coefficient ($\hat{\beta}_1$). Adding the regression coefficient and the intercept/constant together, $\hat{\beta}_0 + \hat{\beta}_1$, gives the mean price of the flats in the city centre. We further note that the slope coefficient (mean difference) is statistically significant, suggesting that flats located in the city centre cost on average more than those outside the city centre. The rest of the output in Figure 5.2 can be interpreted following the same procedures described in the chapter on simple linear regression.

```
. reg flat_price centre

     Source  |       SS         df        MS              Number of obs =      95
-------------+------------------------------              F(  1,     93) =    5.22
      Model  |  2.4729e+11       1    2.4729e+11          Prob > F       =  0.0246
   Residual  |  4.4042e+12      93    4.7357e+10          R-squared      =  0.0532
-------------+------------------------------              Adj R-squared  =  0.0430
      Total  |  4.6515e+12      94    4.9484e+10          Root MSE       =  2.2e+05

------------------------------------------------------------------------------
  flat_price |      Coef.   Std. Err.      t    P>|t|     [95% Conf. Interval]
-------------+----------------------------------------------------------------
      centre |   106428.2    46574.6     2.29   0.025      13940.3    198916.2
       _cons |   491292.4   27862.93    17.63   0.000     435962.1    546622.6
------------------------------------------------------------------------------
```

Figure 5.2   Stata output of regression with one dummy variable

5 ● 3   REGRESSION WITH ONE DUMMY VARIABLE AND A COVARIATE

Let us extend our previous regression by including a covariate[7] in our population regression model, which will be expressed as

$$E[Y_i] = \beta_0 + \beta_1 X_{1i} + \beta_2 X_{2i}. \tag{5.5}$$

In equation (5.5) Y again represents flat prices and X_1 indicates the geographical location of the flats (dummy). In addition, X_2 represents our covariate, floor size, measured in square metres. Here, too, we can readily obtain $E[Y_i]$ when X_1 is 0 (non-centre flats, the reference or baseline category) and 1 (centre flats), but now we must also take X_2 into account (holding it constant). When $X_1 = 0$, we have that

$$E[Y_i] = \beta_0 + \beta_1(0) + \beta_2 X_{2i} = \beta_0 + \beta_2 X_{2i} \tag{5.6}$$

is the mean price of non-centre flats. When $X_1 = 1$,

$$E[Y_i] = \beta_0 + \beta_1(1) + \beta_2 X_{2i} = \beta_0 + \beta_1 + \beta_2 X_{2i}. \tag{5.7}$$

---

[7] Including one or more covariates or control variables in a model makes dummy-variable regression superior to the independent t-test.

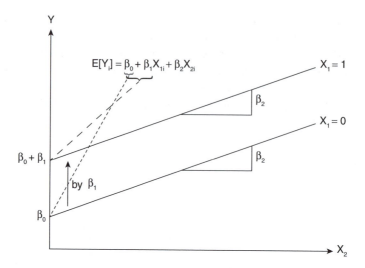

Figure 5.3 Dummy-regression with a covariate

is the mean price of centre flats. The only difference between (5.6) and (5.7) is β_1, which is simply the difference between the adjusted means[8] of group 0 and 1. This difference[9] indicates at the same time differing intercepts in the equations for the two groups: in (5.6) an intercept equal to β_0 and in (5.7) an intercept equal to $\beta_0 + \beta_1$. While (5.6) and (5.7) have different intercepts, they do have the same slope coefficient (β_2) on X_2 as implied by our initial regression model, a situation which is depicted geometrically in Figure 5.3.

Here, we can use the same approach to hypothesis testing (as well as other procedures, such as R^2, root MSE and confidence intervals) that we learnt in the chapter on multiple regression to test whether β_1 and β_2 are jointly (*F*-test) and individually (*t*-test) statistically different from zero. A joint significance of β_1 and β_2 would suggest that at least one of these coefficients is statistically significant. A significant β_1 would indicate that there is a difference between the means of the two groups of X_1, having controlled for X_2. A significant β_2 would indicate the change in mean-Y for every additional unit in X_2, having controlled for X_1. Although, in this particular example, we would particularly be interested in the significance of β_1 (since our primary aim is to compare two means), in some other cases we may want to examine the effect of X_2 on Y, having controlled for a dummy variable like X_1.

---

[8] The adjusted mean is the predicted mean after having controlled for one/several covariates.

[9] The coefficient on the dummy variable is also referred to as a differential intercept coefficient (see Hamilton, 1992, for more details). It shows both the intercept difference and predicted mean difference. However, this does not mean that intercepts are equal to the means we want to predict. The predicted means can result in any number depending on the value of X_2 we choose to plug into the equation, whereas the intercept is by definition the predicted mean when all the X variables are set to zero. However, the difference between the means we predict for two groups of X_1 at any level of X_2 will always be equal to the intercept difference.

5●3●1 Example in Stata

We will estimate our example model shown in equation (5.5) with Stata using the dataset *flat2.dta*. We want to compare the mean price of flats in the city centre and outside the city centre by also controlling for the floor size of the flats. To do so, we will simply extend our earlier command by adding the variable *floor_size*:

. reg flat_price centre floor_size

The estimated regression function and values are shown below (see the Stata output in Figure 5.4):

$$\widehat{flat\_price_i} = \hat{\beta}_0 + \hat{\beta}_1 centre_i + \hat{\beta}_2 floor\_size_i \qquad (5.8)$$
$$= 103{,}227 + 72{,}920\ centre_i + 5{,}170\ floor\_size_i$$

We see that the adjusted (having controlled for floor size) mean price difference between flats in the city centre and outside the city centre as represented by $\hat{\beta}_1$, is equal to about 72,920 dollars. Incidentally, note that the mean difference in the bivariate case (without controlling for floor size) in equation (5.4) was 106,428 dollars. Since we have *floor_size* as an additional independent variable in (5.8), $\hat{\beta}_0$ no longer represents[10] the mean price of flats outside the city centre. To be able, however, to find the mean price of flats outside the city centre, we could indeed use the margins command that we learnt in Chapter 4 on multiple regression as follows:

. margins, at(centre=(0))

This command gives 503,285 as the adjusted mean[11] price of flats outside the city centre. Adding 503,285 and 72,920 ($\hat{\beta}_1$) will then naturally give us the adjusted mean price of flats in the city centre: 576,205. We can check this outcome by also asking for the mean price of flats in the city centre by using the same margins command:

. margins, at(centre=(1))

As you might already have guessed, you can shorten the above two margins commands to a single one by typing margins, at(centre=(0 1)).

We further observe in Figure 5.4 that the slope coefficient (mean difference) found is statistically significant, suggesting again that flats in the city centre on average still cost more than those outside the city centre. Incidentally, we observe also that our covariate (floor size) is also statistically significant. The covariate and the rest of the output in Figure 5.4 can be interpreted following the same procedures described in the chapter on multiple regression analysis. This same rule applies equally well to the remaining example models that we will treat in the following sections of this chapter. After all, any model with more than one independent variable (be it continuous or dummy) is technically a multiple regression.

---

[10] $\hat{\beta}_0$ now represents the mean price of flats outside the city centre with floor size 0 square metres.

[11] margins leaves all unmentioned covariates at their individual values, computes predicted values and then averages.

```
. reg flat_price centre floor_size
```

Source	SS	df	MS
Model	2.9010e+12	2	1.4505e+12
Residual	1.7505e+12	92	1.9027e+10
Total	4.6515e+12	94	4.9484e+10

```
Number of obs =      95
F(  2,    92) =   76.23
Prob > F      =  0.0000
R-squared     =  0.6237
Adj R-squared =  0.6155
Root MSE      =  1.4e+05
```

flat_price	Coef.	Std. Err.	t	P>|t|	[95% Conf. Interval]
centre	72920.12	29657.72	2.46	0.016	14017.33 131822.9
floor_size	5170.821	437.8402	11.81	0.000	4301.233 6040.409
_cons	103226.5	37305.04	2.77	0.007	29135.45 177317.5

Figure 5.4   Stata output of regression with one dummy variable with a covariate

5.4 REGRESSION WITH MORE THAN ONE DUMMY VARIABLE

Regression with more than one dummy variable (predictor) corresponds directly to an independent analysis of variance (ANOVA). In this section we extend the idea of regression with a dummy variable. In the regression case with a dummy variable earlier, we compared the difference between mean prices of the flats in the city centre with those of flats outside the city centre. Suppose that we want to compare the mean prices of flats in four different parts (centre, south, west and east) of the city this time. The population regression function for this model would then be

$$E[Y_i] = \beta_0 + \beta_1 X_{1i} + \beta_2 X_{2i} + \beta_3 X_{3i}. \tag{5.9}$$

Here we have three dummy variables included in the model, with one excluded. The included dummy variables are X_1 (*south*), X_2 (*west*) and X_3 (*east*), and the excluded dummy variable is X_4 (*centre*). The choice of the excluded[12] variable is a matter of convenience. The reason why we always exclude one of the dummy variables[13] generated from the regression model is to avoid the situation of perfect multicollinearity,[14] a condition which hinders the estimation of regression coefficients.[15] In our regression equation in (5.9), the intercept is calculated as the mean of the excluded group. Let us further, again by using

---

[12] The choice of excluded variable depends on which group (reference group) you want to compare the remaining groups with. In principle, you can use any of the dummy variables as the excluded/reference group. Whichever dummy you use as the reference group, you will at the end be able to get the exact same information (mean differences) from the estimation of the model.

[13] The number of dummy variables to be entered into the regression model is always equal to $g - 1$, where g is the number of groups.

[14] We will treat the topic of multicollinearity in more depth in Chapter 7 on regression assumptions.

[15] The linear combination of all of the dummies included will be equal to 1 for all the observations, which will be perfectly collinear with the constant which also has the value 1 for all the observations. Excluding one of the dummy variables avoids this situation (see Dougherty, 2011: 236).

the prediction approach, find what the remaining coefficients in (5.9) actually represent. When X_1, X_2, $X_3 = 0$,

$$E[Y_i] = \beta_0 + \beta_1(0) + \beta_2(0) + \beta_3(0) = \beta_0 \tag{5.10}$$

is the mean price of flats in the city centre. When $X_1 = 1$ and X_2, $X_3 = 0$,

$$E[Y_i] = \beta_0 + \beta_1(1) + \beta_2(0) + \beta_3(0) = \beta_0 + \beta_1 \tag{5.11}$$

is the mean price of flats in the south. When $X_2 = 1$ and X_1, $X_3 = 0$,

$$E[Y_i] = \beta_0 + \beta_1(0) + \beta_2(1) + \beta_3(0) = \beta_0 + \beta_2 \tag{5.12}$$

is the mean price of flats in the west. When $X_3 = 1$, and X_1, $X_2 = 0$

$$E[Y_i] = \beta_0 + \beta_1(0) + \beta_2(0) + \beta_3(1) = \beta_0 + \beta_3 \tag{5.13}$$

is the mean price of flats in the east. We now can read the means of all the four groups in equations (5.10)–(5.13). Since the mean of the reference group (*centre*) is β_0, by subtracting the means of the three included groups from β_0 we easily obtain the difference between the mean of the reference group and each of the included categories:

Groups to compare	Mean difference
South versus centre	$(\beta_0 + \beta_1) - \beta_0 = \beta_1$
West versus centre	$(\beta_0 + \beta_2) - \beta_0 = \beta_2$
East versus centre	$(\beta_0 + \beta_3) - \beta_0 = \beta_3$

As the calculations above also confirm, in a regression model estimated with constant/intercept,[16] the coefficient on each dummy variable indicates the difference between the mean of cases for which that dummy equals 1 and the reference group. In our case β_1 indicates the difference between the mean of south and centre flats, β_2 the difference between the mean of west and centre flats, and β_3 the difference between the mean of east and centre flats. Furthermore, when the coefficient is positive, this shows that the mean of the included group (south, west or east) is higher than that of the reference group (centre) and vice versa.

We show the idea of regression with more than one dummy variable geometrically in Figure 5.5. As you see in the figure, each coefficient in theory represents a slope which we interpret in dummy-variable regression as a mean difference rather than slope. As the three different graphs imply, although we estimate the regression model (with all three included dummy variables) in one go, the resulting coefficients can still be considered bivariate regressions where we separately compare the mean of the reference group (centre) with the mean of the cases for which each dummy equals 1 (south, west, and east). Incidentally, since the prices of flats in the city centre are on average in our example (and everywhere else, we would assume) higher

---

[16] The only case in which you can include all of the four dummy variables is when you estimate the regression model without the constant. However, in such a case, the resulting coefficients would simply provide the means of each group. Thus, we would still have to perform a further test comparing the differences between these means.

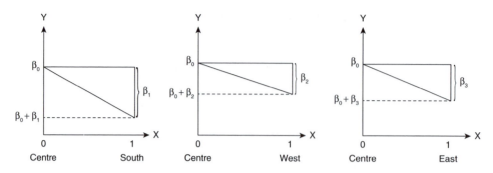

Figure 5.5 Geometrical representation of regression with more than one dummy variable

than those in the remaining three locations, the sign of the regression coefficients (β_1, β_2 and β_3) would naturally be negative, resulting in downward-sloping straight lines.

Since regression coefficients reflect mean differences, the next step is then to test whether these mean differences (β_1, β_2 and β_3) are statistically different from zero. Here, too, we use the same approach to hypothesis testing (as well as other procedures) that we learnt in Chapter 4 on multiple regression to test whether β_1, β_2, β_3 are jointly (F-test) and individually (t-test) statistically different from zero. Joint significance of β_1, β_2 and β_3 would suggest that at least one of these coefficients is statistically significant (i.e., there is a mean difference between the centre and one of the other locations). A significant coefficient will eventually show which pair of group means significantly differ.

5•4•1 Example in Stata

We will now estimate our example model shown in equation (5.9) with Stata using the dataset *flat2.dta*. We will compare the mean price of flats in the four different locations. This means that we need to create four dummy variables from *location* and leave one out in the estimation. We know now that we can do this more effectively using a factor variable in the regression estimation as follows:

```
. reg flat_price i.location
```

The estimated regression function and values are shown below (see the Stata output in Figure 5.6):

$$\widehat{flat\_price_i} = \hat{\beta}_0 + \hat{\beta}_1 \, south_i + \hat{\beta}_2 \, west_i + \hat{\beta}_3 \, east_i \tag{5.14}$$
$$= 597{,}721 - 172{,}350 \, south_i - 83{,}933 \, west_i - 97{,}993 \, east_i$$

We know that Stata uses the first category[17] of the variable *location* as the reference group in the estimation. $\hat{\beta}_0$ represents the mean price of the reference group (flats in the city centre). $\hat{\beta}_1$, $\hat{\beta}_2$ and $\hat{\beta}_3$ reflect the mean difference between the flats in the city centre and flats in

---

[17] If you want to see what the reference category is instead of having to remember it each time, you can type `set showbaselevels on, permanently` and then run your estimations.

south, west and east, respectively. More specifically, then, flats in the *south* cost on average about 172,350 dollars less than those in the city centre. We also observe that this difference is statistically significant. Further, flats in the *west* cost on average about 83,933 dollars less than those in the city centre. However, this difference is statistically not significant. Finally, flats in the *east* cost on average about 97,933 dollars less than those in the city centre. This difference is only just non-significant, a fact we will choose to ignore for our present purposes.

```
. reg flat_price i.location
```

Source	SS	df	MS		Number of obs =	95
					F(3, 91) =	2.05
Model	2.9488e+11	3	9.8294e+10		Prob > F =	0.1120
Residual	4.3566e+12	91	4.7875e+10		R-squared =	0.0634
					Adj R-squared =	0.0325
Total	4.6515e+12	94	4.9484e+10		Root MSE =	2.2e+05

flat_price	Coef.	Std. Err.	t	P>|t|	[95% Conf. Interval]	
location						
south	-172350.2	82021.29	-2.10	0.038	-335275.4	-9424.993
west	-83932.71	75896.81	-1.11	0.272	-234692.4	66826.99
east	-97992.95	50751.9	-1.93	0.057	-198805.4	2819.474
_cons	597720.6	37524.39	15.93	0.000	523183	672258.2

Figure 5.6 Stata output of regression with more than one dummy variable

5●4●2 Comparing the included groups

So far, using the standard regression estimation, we have been able to compare[18] the means of the included groups (south, west and east) with that of the reference group (centre). However, in some cases we may also be interested in comparing the means of the included groups themselves. The standard regression estimation/output does not provide us with this information. There are however two main procedures that we can apply to compare the means of the included groups: changing the reference group and linear combination (see also Gordon, 2010).

Changing the reference group

The first option, as you might guess, is to re-estimate the same regression model by simply changing the reference group each time. Using *centre* as the reference group yields tests of the differences between the means of *centre* and the remaining groups (*south* versus *centre, west* versus *centre,* and *east* versus *centre*). Then using *south* as the reference group yields two new mean comparisons (*west* versus *south,* and *east* versus *south*) that we could not directly get from the first estimation. Finally, using *west* as the reference group yields one more mean difference (*east* versus *west*) which we could not obtain from either of the two preceding estimations.

---

[18] What we mean by 'comparing means' is that we statistically test the mean difference.

Estimation 1	Estimation 2	Estimation 3
Reference group	Reference group	Reference group
centre	south	west
Included groups	Included groups	Included groups
south	centre	centre
west	west	south
east	east	east

Let us now run these estimations using Stata. We can do this by simply changing the base operator of the factor variable as follows:[19]

```
. reg flat_price ib(2).location, noheader
. reg flat_price ib(3).location, noheader
```

Here ib(2) uses the second category (*south*) while ib(3) uses the third category (*west*) as the reference group. The results of the two re-estimations are shown in Figure 5.7.

```
. reg flat_price ib(2).location, noheader
```

flat_price	Coef.	Std. Err.	t	P>|t|	[95% Conf. Interval]	
location						
centre	172350.2	82021.29	2.10	0.038	9424.993	335275.4
west	88417.5	98344.59	0.90	0.371	-106932	283767
east	74357.26	80542.46	0.92	0.358	-85630.44	234345
_cons	425370.4	72934.3	5.83	0.000	280495.3	570245.4

```
. reg flat_price ib(3).location, noheader
```

flat_price	Coef.	Std. Err.	t	P>|t|	[95% Conf. Interval]	
location						
centre	83932.71	75896.81	1.11	0.272	-66826.99	234692.4
south	-88417.5	98344.59	-0.90	0.371	-283767	106932
east	-14060.24	74296.18	-0.19	0.850	-161640.5	133520
_cons	513787.9	65971.56	7.79	0.000	382743.5	644832.3

Figure 5.7 Stata output of re-estimated regressions (with more than one dummy variable)

Incidentally, there is no reason to re-estimate the model by using the fourth category as the reference group. These two re-estimations, together with the default estimation, provide us with all possible pairwise comparisons (of which there are six). The coefficients in Figure 5.7 are interpreted in the same manner as those in Figure 5.6. The coefficients are simply the mean difference between the group chosen as the reference group and the included dummy groups.

---

[19] The noheader option suppresses the first part (ANOVA-like table) of the regression estimation from the output. We do so because re-estimation will not change any of this information.

Linear combination

The second option to use for testing the mean differences among the included groups is a t-test for a linear combination of coefficients. A linear combination is most commonly about adding or subtracting regression coefficients. In equation (5.9) the differences between any pair of regression coefficients would provide us with the mean difference of the chosen two groups: $\beta_1 - \beta_2 = \Delta_1$ is the difference between the means of south and west; $\beta_1 - \beta_3 = \Delta_2$ is the difference between the means of south and east; and $\beta_2 - \beta_3 = \Delta_3$ is the difference between the means of west and east. Note that each of these delta (Δ) measures is a linear combination (subtracting two coefficients). We then use a t-test to test the significance of the three delta measures. In so doing, as we did in the previous chapters, we need to construct a t-statistic. As you will recall, the shortened formula for constructing a t-statistic is simply $t_k = \beta_k / \sigma_{\beta_k}$. We will, however, have to extend this formula to include two regression coefficients and their associated standard errors due to linear combinations involving more than one coefficient. Thus, our extended formula is

$$t_\Delta = \frac{\beta_j - \beta_k}{\sigma_{(\beta_j - \beta_k)}}$$

which follows a t-distribution with $n - K$ degrees of freedom, and where

$$\sigma_{(\beta_j - \beta_k)} = \sqrt{\sigma_{\beta_j}^2 + \sigma_{\beta_k}^2 - 2\,\mathrm{cov}\left(\beta_j, \beta_k\right)}\ .$$

Using the theoretical t-distribution table, we find the probability value associated with our resulting t-statistic to decide whether the difference between the two chosen regression coefficients is significantly different from zero. If so, then we can claim that the means of the chosen two groups are significantly different.

This is done easily using the lincom command in Stata. With four groups we have at most six pairwise comparisons, three of whose results would already have been provided by the first estimation using the first category (*centre*) as the reference group. These comparisons are naturally south vs. centre, west vs. centre, and east vs. centre. As for the three remaining pairwise comparisons (west vs. south, east vs. south and east vs. west), we can test the following linear combinations:[20]

```
. lincom _b[3.location]- _b[2.location]
. lincom _b[4.location]- _b[2.location]
. lincom _b[4.location]- _b[3.location]
```

As shown in Figure 5.8, the above three commands provide us with the mean differences among the included groups as well as standard errors and confidence intervals for these differences, which in some case may prove to be additionally useful information. If you like, you can check the mean differences (Figure 5.8) that we obtain using the lincom command

---

[20] Each of the dummy variables included is represented by a legend in the estimation (for instance, *2.location* represents *south*). To obtain these we need to type reg, coeflegend.

```
. lincom _b[3.location]- _b[2.location]

( 1)   - 2.location + 3.location = 0
```

flat_price	Coef.	Std. Err.	t	P>|t|	[95% Conf. Interval]
(1)	88417.5	98344.59	0.90	0.371	-106932	283767

```
. lincom _b[4.location]- _b[2.location]

( 1)   - 2.location + 4.location = 0
```

flat_price	Coef.	Std. Err.	t	P>|t|	[95% Conf. Interval]
(1)	74357.26	80542.46	0.92	0.358	-85630.44	234345

```
. lincom _b[4.location]- _b[3.location]

( 1)   - 3.location + 4.location = 0
```

flat_price	Coef.	Std. Err.	t	P>|t|	[95% Conf. Interval]
(1)	-14060.24	74296.18	-0.19	0.850	-161640.5	133520

Figure 5.8 Results from the linear combination tests

with those obtained by re-estimation (Figure 5.7) by changing the reference category.[21] For instance, the first lincom estimation computes the difference between the mean price of flats in the *west* and *south* as about 88,418 dollars and statistically non-significant. This is exactly the same result that we got in our re-estimation using the *south* reference group in Figure 5.7.

5●5 REGRESSION WITH MORE THAN ONE DUMMY VARIABLE AND A COVARIATE

Regression with more than one dummy variable and a covariate[22] corresponds directly to an independent analysis of covariance (ANCOVA). Let us carry on with our example from the previous section in which we regress flat prices on the geographical location (centre, south, west and east) of the flats. This time, however, we will extend our regression model with an additional covariate which we call *floor_size*, measuring the size of the flats in square metres. The resulting regression model would then be

$$E[Y_i] = \beta_0 + \beta_1 X_{1i} + \beta_2 X_{2i} + \beta_3 X_{3i} + \beta_5 X_{5i}. \tag{5.15}$$

---

[21] As an alternative procedure to re-estimation and linear combination approaches, we could get the exact same information by just typing pwcompare location, effects. The advantage of the pwcompare procedure is that you can also adjust for the multiple comparisons by simply adding mcompare(scheffe).

[22] Both continuous and dummy variables can be covariates in a model.

As in equation (5.9), we have in (5.15) included the dummy variables X_1 (*south*), X_2 (*west*) and X_3 (*east*) but excluded the dummy variable X_4 (*centre*). Additionally, we have the covariate X_5 (*floor_size*) included in the model. Let us now ascertain what the coefficients on the dummy variables in (5.15) would indicate by also taking X_5 into account (holding it constant). When $X_1, X_2, X_3 = 0$,

$$E[Y_i] = \beta_0 + \beta_1(0) + \beta_2(0) + \beta_3(0) + \beta_5 X_{5i} = \beta_0 + \beta_5 X_{5i}. \qquad (5.16)$$

When $X_1=1$ and $X_2, X_3 = 0$,

$$E[Y_i] = \beta_0 + \beta_1(1) + \beta_2(0) + \beta_3(0) + \beta_5 X_{5i} = \beta_0 + \beta_1 + \beta_5 X_{5i}. \qquad (5.17)$$

When $X_2=1$ and $X_1, X_3 = 0$,

$$E[Y_i] = \beta_0 + \beta_1(0) + \beta_2(1) + \beta_3(0) + \beta_5 X_{5i} = \beta_0 + \beta_2 + \beta_5 X_{5i}. \qquad (5.18)$$

When $X_3=1$ and $X_1, X_2 = 0$,

$$E[Y_i] = \beta_0 + \beta_1(0) + \beta_2(0) + \beta_3(1) + \beta_5 X_{5i} = \beta_0 + \beta_3 + \beta_5 X_{5i}. \qquad (5.19)$$

As we can see, in equations (5.17)–(5.19) the coefficients on the dummy variables still reflect the difference between the mean of each included group and the reference group. These means are, however, now the adjusted means arrived at after controlling for the covariate X_5. We again have different intercepts in the equations for the four groups: (5.16) with an intercept equal to β_0, (5.17) with an intercept equal to $\beta_0 + \beta_1$, (5.18) with an intercept equal to $\beta_0 + \beta_2$ and (5.19) with an intercept equal to $\beta_0 + \beta_3$. But these four equations still have the same slope coefficient (β_5) on X_5 as indicated by our regression model.

If we wished to show a geometrical representation of a regression model with more than one dummy variable including a covariate, we would simply add two additional parallel lines to Figure 5.3. All the regression lines would incidentally show a negative relationship. The reason is simply that we have used *centre* as the reference group, which we expect to have a higher mean price than the other three groups included in the model. Furthermore, for hypothesis testing (F-test and t-test), here too we can directly use the procedures that we learnt in the chapter on multiple regression.

5•5•1 Example in Stata

Let us now estimate (5.15) comparing the mean prices of flats in four different locations by controlling for an additional covariate, *floor_size*. To do this in Stata we simply add the covariate to the command as follows:

```
. reg flat_price i.location floor_size
```

The estimated regression function and values are shown below (see the Stata output in Figure 5.9):

$$\overline{flat\_price}_i = \hat{\beta}_0 + \hat{\beta}_1\,south_i + \hat{\beta}_2\,west_i + \hat{\beta}_3\,east_i + \hat{\beta}_4\,floor\_size_i \qquad (5.20)$$
$$= 165{,}997 - 182{,}491\,south_i - 79{,}204\,west_i - 45{,}982\,east_i +$$
$$5295\,floor\_size_i$$

. reg flat_price i.location floor_size

Source	SS	df	MS		Number of obs =	95
					F(4, 90) =	42.35
Model	3.0377e+12	4	7.5942e+11		Prob > F =	0.0000
Residual	1.6138e+12	90	1.7931e+10		R-squared =	0.6531
					Adj R-squared =	0.6376
Total	4.6515e+12	94	4.9484e+10		Root MSE =	1.3e+05

flat_price	Coef.	Std. Err.	t	P>|t|	[95% Conf.	Interval]
location						
south	-182490.9	50203.81	-3.64	0.000	-282229.5	-82752.28
west	-79203.74	46450.5	-1.71	0.092	-171485.8	13078.29
east	-45981.88	31343.61	-1.47	0.146	-108251.4	16287.69
floor_size	5295.314	428.1549	12.37	0.000	4444.709	6145.918
_cons	165996.8	41784.01	3.97	0.000	82985.57	249008

Figure 5.9 Stata output of a regression with more than one dummy variable and a covariate

In Figure 5.9, we observe directly the adjusted (having controlled for floor size) mean price difference between the flats in three different locations (south, west and east) and those in the city centre. These mean differences are respectively represented by $\hat{\beta}_1$, $\hat{\beta}_2$ and $\hat{\beta}_3$. Since in (5.20) we have *floor_size* as an additional independent variable, in Figure 5.9, $\hat{\beta}_0$ no longer represents[23] the mean price of the reference group (centre). To be able to find out the mean price of flats in the city centre (and in the remaining locations), however, we can easily use the margins command that we learnt about earlier in this chapter:

. margins, at(location=(1 2 3 4)) noatlegend[24]

or more effectively just,

. margins location, noatlegend

This command will provide us with the estimated mean prices of flats in all four locations of the city (see Figure 5.10).

As we did in the previous section, we can also use the re-estimation procedure or lincom command to test the mean difference among the variables included in the regression model.

---

[23] $\hat{\beta}_0$ now represents the mean price of flats outside the city centre with floor size 0 square metres.

[24] The noatlegend option suppresses the first part of the results from the output.

```
. margins, at(location=(1 2 3 4)) noatlegend
```

Predictive margins   Number of obs =   95
Model VCE   : OLS

Expression   : Linear prediction, predict()

	Margin	Delta-method Std. Err.	t	P>|t|	[95% Conf. Interval]	
_at						
1	575686.8	23033.96	24.99	0.000	529925.9	621447.8
2	393195.9	44711.61	8.79	0.000	304368.5	482023.4
3	496483.1	40398.9	12.29	0.000	416223.6	576742.6
4	529705	21052.85	25.16	0.000	487879.8	571530.1

Figure 5.10 Estimated means provided by the `margins` command

5.6 REGRESSION WITH TWO SEPARATE SETS OF DUMMY VARIABLES

Regression with two different sets of dummy variables (i.e., two categorical variables) corresponds directly to an independent two-way ANOVA.[25] Suppose that we want to extend equation (5.9) where we regress flat prices on geographical location (centre, south, west and east) with an additional categorical variable (*energy efficiency*) consisting of three categories (1 = best, 2 = mediocre and 3 = poor). In this case, since we have two categorical variables we would have to create two separate sets of dummy variables, one for *geographical location* and another for our additional categorical variable *energy efficiency*. Our new regression model would then be:

$$E[Y_i] = \beta_0 + \beta_1 X_{1i} + \beta_2 X_{2i} + \beta_3 X_{3i} + \beta_6 X_{6i} + \beta_7 X_{7i}. \quad (5.21)$$

Here we have X_1 (*south*), X_2 (*west*) and X_3 (*east*) included in the model, while the dummy variable X_4 (*centre*) is excluded. Additionally, we include two of the three dummy variables that we created for the variable *energy efficiency*, namely X_6 (*mediocre*) and X_7 (*poor*); we designate X_8 (*best*) as the reference group and exclude it from the model.

Let us show what the coefficients on the dummy variables in (5.21) represent in this case. When $X_1, X_2, X_3, X_6, X_7 = 0$,

$$E[Y_i] = \beta_0 + \beta_1(0) + \beta_2(0) + \beta_3(0) + \beta_6(0) + \beta_7(0) = \beta_0 \quad (5.22)$$

is the mean price of flats in the city *centre* with *best* energy efficiency. When $X_1 = 1$ and $X_2, X_3, X_6, X_7 = 0$,

$$E[Y_i] = \beta_0 + \beta_1(1) + \beta_2(0) + \beta_3(0) + \beta_6(0) + \beta_7(0) = \beta_0 + \beta_1 \quad (5.23)$$

---

[25] The reason why it is called two-way ANOVA is that we have two categorical independent variables.

is the mean price of flats in the *south* with *best* energy efficiency. When $X_2 = 1$ and X_1, X_3, X_6, $X_7 = 0$,

$$E[Y_i] = \beta_0 + \beta_1(0) + \beta_2(1) + \beta_3(0) + \beta_6(0) + \beta_7(0) = \beta_0 + \beta_2 \qquad (5.24)$$

is the mean price of flats in the *west* with *best* energy efficiency. When $X_3 = 1$ and X_1, X_2, X_6, $X_7 = 0$,

$$E[Y_i] = \beta_0 + \beta_1(0) + \beta_2(0) + \beta_3(1) + \beta_6(0) + \beta_7(0) = \beta_0 + \beta_3 \qquad (5.25)$$

is the mean price of flats in the *east* with *best* energy efficiency. When $X_6 = 1$ and X_1, X_2, X_3, $X_7 = 0$,

$$E[Y_i] = \beta_0 + \beta_1(0) + \beta_2(0) + \beta_3(0) + \beta_6(1) + \beta_7(0) = \beta_0 + \beta_6 \qquad (5.26)$$

is the mean price of flats in the *centre* with *mediocre* energy efficiency. When $X_7 = 1$ and X_1, X_2, X_3, $X_6 = 0$,

$$E[Y_i] = \beta_0 + \beta_1(0) + \beta_2(0) + \beta_3(0) + \beta_6(0) + \beta_7(1) = \beta_0 + \beta_7 \qquad (5.27)$$

is the mean price of flats in the *centre* with *poor* energy efficiency.

As we can see in equations (5.23)–(5.27), the coefficients on each dummy variable represent the difference between the intercept and mean of cases for which that dummy equals 1. For instance, $\beta_1 = (\beta_0 - (\beta_0 + \beta_1))$ represents the difference between the mean price of flats in the city centre with best energy efficiency and flats in the south with best energy efficiency. We interpret the remaining coefficients in a similar manner.

Again we follow the procedures (*F*-test, *t*-test) used in the chapter on multiple regression to test the overall significance of the above model as well as the significance of the individual coefficients. We can also, as mentioned in the chapter on multiple regression, generalize the idea of the *F*-test to test the significance of a set of coefficients in a regression model. Such an approach would indeed be more relevant in a dummy-based regression model including more than one categorical variable, as in our example. Suppose that we are not only interested in the overall significance of our complete model but we also want to test whether the variable *energy efficiency* or *geographical location* is individually significant. Since these two variables are represented by two different sets of dummy variables, we would need to test whether each of these sets of coefficients is jointly significant by controlling for each other. To do so, we construct an *F*-statistic,

$$F = \frac{(\text{RSS}_R - \text{RSS}_{UR})/P}{\text{RSS}_{UR}/(n-K)} \qquad (5.28)$$

which follows an *F*-distribution with $df_1 = p$ and $df_2 = n - K$ degrees of freedom, and where RSS_R and RSS_{UR} are the residual sum of squares of the restricted and the unrestricted model, P is the number of restrictions, n is the number of observations, and K is the number of parameters.

If we test the significance of the variable *energy efficiency*, the unrestricted model would represent our complete model including all five dummy variables while the restricted model would be the one including only the three dummy variables from the variable *geographical location*. The reason why we call this a restricted model is that we here implicitly assume that the variable *energy efficiency* does not have any effect (H_0: $\beta_6 = \beta_7 = 0$). Since we restrict these two coefficients to be zero, the number of restrictions is naturally 2. If the resulting *F*-test proves to be significant, we would favour the alternative hypothesis that *energy efficiency* does have an effect, having controlled for *geographical location*.

Moreover, we can also use the linear combination approach (which we used to test differences between the included dummy groups) to test the difference between the means of different groups in a regression model with two categorical variables.

Although we have so far confined our regression model (two-way ANOVA) to only two categorical variables, we could easily extend it by including additional covariates. This same idea applies when we have a dummy variable with a covariate and more than one dummy variable with a covariate. After all, any model including more than one independent variable, continuous or categorical, is a multiple regression one. Thus, we can simply use the knowledge from the chapter on multiple regression to further assess several aspects of these dummy-based models, as we partly have done in this chapter.

5•6•1 Example in Stata

The model shown in equation (5.21) includes two independent categorical variables, namely *location* and *energy_efficiency*. Once again *location* includes four categories (*centre*, *south*, *west* and *east*) and *energy_efficiency* includes three categories (*best*, *mediocre* and *poor*). Now we want to regress *flat_price* on *location* and *energy_efficiency*. Since both the independent variables are categorical, we will have two factor variables in our Stata command:

```
. reg flat_price i.location i.energy_efficiency
```

The estimated regression function and values are shown below (see the Stata output in Figure 5.11):

$$
\begin{aligned}
\widehat{flat\_price}_i &= \hat{\beta}_0 + \hat{\beta}_1\, south_i + \hat{\beta}_2\, west_i + \hat{\beta}_3\, east_i + \hat{\beta}_6\, mediocre_i + \hat{\beta}_7\, poor_i &\text{(5.29)}\\
&= 743{,}601 - 199{,}209\ south_i - 102{,}148\ west_i - 133{,}096\ east_i - \\
&\quad 112{,}341\ mediocre_i - 198{,}577\ poor_i
\end{aligned}
$$

In Figure 5.11, the coefficient on each dummy variable represents the difference between the intercept and mean of cases for which that dummy equals 1. For instance, 199,209 dollars would represent the difference between the mean price of flats in the city centre with best energy efficiency and flats in the south with best energy efficiency. We interpret the remaining coefficients in a similar manner.

Furthermore, using *F*-test procedure explained earlier, we can also test the joint significance of the coefficients on the dummy variables created from each of the two categorical variables. Such a test would simply tell us whether a categorical variable does have a significant effect or not. This is done readily in Stata as follows:

```
. testparm i.location
. testparm i.energy_efficiency
```

. reg flat_price i.location i.energy_efficiency

Source	SS	df	MS		Number of obs	=	82
					F(5, 76)	=	2.16
Model	5.1228e+11	5	1.0246e+11		Prob > F	=	0.0669
Residual	3.5993e+12	76	4.7360e+10		R-squared	=	0.1246
					Adj R-squared	=	0.0670
Total	4.1116e+12	81	5.0761e+10		Root MSE	=	2.2e+05

flat_price	Coef.	Std. Err.	t	P>|t|	[95% Conf. Interval]	
location						
south	-199208.5	85099.86	-2.34	0.022	-368699.6	-29717.43
west	-102147.8	82903.83	-1.23	0.222	-267265	62969.53
east	-133096	57940.96	-2.30	0.024	-248495.4	-17696.59
energy_efficiency						
mediocre	-112340.8	77756.19	-1.44	0.153	-267205.7	42524.08
poor	-198576.9	85724.61	-2.32	0.023	-369312.3	-27841.56
_cons	743600.9	87636.03	8.49	0.000	569058.7	918143.2

Figure 5.11 Stata output of a regression with two polytomous categorical variables

. testparm i.location

(1) 2.location = 0
(2) 3.location = 0
(3) 4.location = 0

    F(3,   76) =   2.55
       Prob > F =   0.0620

. testparm i.energy_efficiency

(1) 2.energy_efficiency = 0
(2) 3.energy_efficiency = 0

    F(2,   76) =   2.84
       Prob > F =   0.0644

Figure 5.12 *F*-test results

Figure 5.12 shows the results of the *F*-tests telling us that both of the categorical variables (after controlling for each other) may be considered to have a significant effect on *flat_price* given an alpha level of 0.1.

Here, too, we can also make use of the re-estimation procedure or `lincom` command to test mean differences other than the default ones in Figure 5.11.

5.7 CONCLUSION

In this chapter we have shown in detail that the dummy-variable regression approach to comparing means, particularly with the help of Stata, is identical to if not more flexible and powerful than the traditional analysis of variance approach to comparing means. We believe that understanding the dummy-based regression approach provides a sound foundation for better understanding statistical modelling involving combinations of continuous and categorical variables. As far as Stata is concerned, we recommend that readers look for further features in the commands `lincom`, `test`, `testparm`, `margins` and `pwcompare`.

 key terms

Dichotomous A categorical variable including two groups.

Polytomous A categorical variable including more than two groups.

Dummy variable A dichotomous variable taking on the value of 0 and 1.

Independent *t*-test A test of two independent group means.

ANOVA A test of more than two independent group means.

ANCOVA A test of more than two independent group means by controlling a covariate.

Reference group A group that is excluded from the regression model.

Included groups Groups compared to the reference group.

Mean difference A group mean difference represented by a regression coefficient.

F-test Tests the significance of a set of coefficients in a regression model.

pwcompare Pairwise comparison command in Stata.

lincom Linear combination command in Stata.

QUESTIONS

1 What is a dummy variable?
2 What is the dummy-variable regression technique?
3 Why can we use regression to compare means?
4 Set up a dummy-variable regression model that includes two categorical variables each containing three categories/groups and a continuous variable?
5 Explain with examples what the `margins` command is used for.

FURTHER READING

Hardy, M.A. (1993) *Regression with Dummy Variables*. London: Sage.

As its title indicates, this book provides a brief but a detailed treatment of dummy-variable regression that will supplement the current chapter.

Williams, R. (2012) Using the margins command to estimate and interpret adjusted predictions and marginal effects. *Stata Journal*, 12(2), 308–331.

This is a very good article showing different applications (including dummy variable regression) of the `margins` command that we make use of in several chapters in this book.

REFERENCES

Dougherty, C. (2011) *Introduction to Econometrics* (4th edn). Oxford: Oxford University Press.
Gordon, R.A. (2010) *Regression Analysis for the Social Sciences* (4th edn). Abingdon: Routledge.
Hamilton, L.C. (1992) *Regression with Graphics: A Second Course in Applied Statistics*. Belmont, CA: Duxbury Press.
Hardy, M.A. (1993) *Regression with Dummy Variables*. London: Sage.

6

INTERACTION/ MODERATION EFFECTS USING REGRESSION

Factorial ANOVA and factorial ANCOVA

learning outcomes

- Understand what a statistical interaction/moderation effect is
- Understand the technical details behind interaction models
- Understand the link between regression and factorial ANOVA
- Understand the use of centred, standardized and raw data in interaction models
- Learn how to develop an interaction model and estimate it using Stata

In this chapter we first explain what an interaction/moderation effect is. Subsequently, we present the product-term approach that is most commonly used to examine two-way interaction models. To facilitate an even deeper understanding of interactions, we go through the details of different kinds of interaction models: interaction between a continuous predictor and a continuous moderator; interaction between a continuous predictor and a dummy moderator; interaction between a dummy predictor and a dummy moderator; and finally, interaction between a continuous predictor and a polytomous moderator.[1] We then show how exactly we can estimate these interaction models using Stata. As also implied in the title of the chapter, the interaction approach we present here can readily be used to examine factorial ANOVA/ANCOVA models.

6.1 INTERACTION/MODERATION EFFECT

Social scientists typically specify a statistical model based on the assumption that the effect of an independent variable on a dependent variable is invariant of any other independent variable in the model. More precisely, the coefficient of an independent variable is assumed to be exactly the same at every level of another independent variable in the model. Such linear additive models may not hold in some situations, however, leading at best to less nuanced or even incorrect information. Thus, the importance of non-additive statistical models (also called interaction models) has been continuously stressed in the methodology literature. In linear additive models we examine main effects, whereas in non-additive models we are often interested in testing interaction/moderation effects (see Figure 6.1). Incidentally, we refer to interaction and moderation effects interchangeably. An interaction effect is said to occur when a third variable (moderator, X_1) affects the relation between an independent variable (X_2) and a dependent variable (Y). The interaction/moderation effect is demonstrated through a significant change in the size and/or direction of the coefficient of the independent variable at different values of the moderator. The concept of interaction/moderation effect can best be explained through some real-life examples.

---

[1] A similar approach is also followed elsewhere (Gordon, 2010; Jaccard and Turrisi, 2003; Mitchell, 2012; Pardoe, 2006).

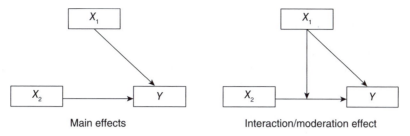

Figure 6.1 Illustration of additive and non-additive models

For instance, an organizational psychologist finds out that the effect of an authoritarian leadership style on employee effectiveness differs between inexperienced and experienced employees: authoritarian leadership has a stronger and a positive effect on effectiveness among inexperienced employees than among experienced employees. In this case, authoritarian leadership is the predictor,[2] effectiveness is the dependent variable and employee status (inexperienced/experienced) is the moderator. In another example, we may have a political scientist discovering in her research that the effect of attitude towards immigrants on opinions about right-wing politics differs from a low-unemployment year (1990) to a high-unemployment year (1991). More specifically, attitude towards immigrants has a stronger negative effect on opinions about right-wing politics in the low-unemployment year than it has in the high-unemployment year. Here, year of employment rate (1990 versus 1991) is the moderator variable. The researcher can thus claim that year moderates the effect of attitude towards immigrants on opinions about right-wing politics. In a third example, we have a marketing scholar discovering that a company's image moderates the effect of media coverage on willingness to buy a product. In other words, as people have a more favourable image of a company, the effect of media coverage of the company on people's willingness to buy a product from that company increases.

Bear in mind that in the first example, we have a categorical moderator (inexperienced/experienced employee). We have a categorical moderator in the second example as well. However, the moderator in this case includes two time points. In the third example, we have a continuous moderator variable (image, measured using a scale). These examples imply that we can readily use both categorical and continuous variables as moderators in interaction models.

In the following, we present the product-term approach that is most commonly used in the social sciences to examine statistical interaction/moderation effects using linear regression (Jaccard and Turrisi, 2003).[3]

---

[2] We will call the variable whose effect is moderated a predictor/independent variable, and the variable moderating the effect a moderator. In practice, as you might imagine, both of these variables are simply predictors/independent variables in the regression model.

[3] This is also the source that we have benefited most from in the writing of this chapter.

6●2 PRODUCT-TERM APPROACH

The product-term approach is about creating a new variable (X_3) by multiplying two variables ($X_1 \times X_2$) that we assume interact with each other and then entering this new variable[4] (X_3) into the regression model together with its component terms X_1 and X_2 which results in:

$$E[Y_i] = \beta_0 + \beta_1 X_{1i} + \beta_2 X_{2i} + \beta_3 X_{1i} X_{2i} \,. \tag{6.1}$$

The product-term approach is visualized in Figure 6.2. For pedagogical reasons, in Figure 6.2, we denote X_1 as the moderator variable and X_2 as the predictor. However, we can readily reverse this situation and still apply the same product-term equation. In other words, the product term $X_1 X_2$ can equally be interpreted as if either X_1 or X_2 is the moderator variable. In practice, though, the researcher's hypothesis decides what variable is to be treated as the moderator.

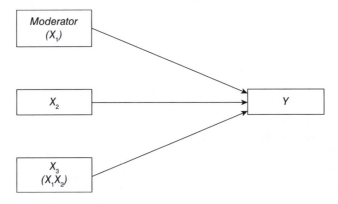

Figure 6.2 Depiction of the product-term approach

In order to better understand the interpretation of the results from a non-additive model estimated with a product term, we first recall how one interprets the coefficients in an additive model (i.e., with no product term). An additive version of the model depicted in Figure 6.2 would be

$$E[Y_i] = \beta_0 + \beta_1 X_{1i} + \beta_2 X_{2i} \,. \tag{6.2}$$

In equation (6.2) we are purely interested in examining the main effects of X_1 and X_2 on Y. Intuitively put, β_1 reflects the 'average' effect of X_1 (to be precise, the effect of a change of X_1) on Y at all levels of X_2. β_1 is subsequently assumed to be constant across X_2. More formally, β_1 represents the number of units that mean-Y changes by as a result of one-unit increase in X_1 while holding X_2 constant, while β_2 represents the number of units that mean-Y changes by as a result of one-unit increase in X_2 while holding X_1 constant.

---

[4] This is usually referred to as the product or interaction term.

However, in the non-additive model shown in (6.1), β_1 and β_2 no longer represent main (unconditional) effects. They now reflect the so-called simple main (conditional) effects. Specifically, β_1 represents the effect of X_1 on Y when X_2 is equal to 0, and β_2 represents the effect of X_2 on Y when X_1 is equal to 0. More importantly, β_3 represents the change in the slope coefficient of Y on X_2 as a result of a one-unit increase in X_1. Had we chosen X_2 as the moderator variable instead, β_3 would then represent the change in the slope of Y on X_1 as a result of a one-unit increase in X_2. Mathematically, these two interpretations are equally legitimate.

Model (6.1) illustrates one further important point that, in our opinion, is often neglected or left implicit in the dissemination of results from interaction analysis in research publications. That is, in the case of interaction between two continuous variables the form of the interaction effect is assumed to be linear. However, in some situations the effect of an independent variable on a dependent variable may not necessarily follow a linear pattern. For instance, a researcher may hypothesize that the effect of coffee intake of employees in a factory on productivity increases linearly with the number of hours of sleep the employees have had before the shift. However, this appears to be the case for up to 8 hours of sleep, beyond which we may have the reverse situation. The interaction effect in this case may take a nonlinear form, which is beyond the scope of this book.

In interaction models, the coefficient on the product/interaction term is used to test the linear form of interaction effects. We use the same hypothesis testing procedure that we learnt in the chapters on linear regression to test whether or not the coefficient on the product term is statistically significant from zero. For instance in (6.1), the null hypothesis would be that $\beta_3 = 0$, so if β_3 proves to be significantly different from 0, then we can claim that X_1 indeed moderates the relation between X_2 and Y. As such, a non-significant β_3 is a sign of no linear interaction effect; however, it should not be seen as a sign of no form of interaction at all. Thus, researchers should be cautious about making hasty conclusions in such cases. This procedure of testing the coefficient on the product term applies in the same manner to all the interaction models we discuss in the following sections.

Let us now show, by using Stata, how we can create a product/interaction term between two variables (*health* and *age*) in our dataset called *workout.dta* and include this interaction term in a regression model. One way of doing this is to use the generate command as follows:

```
. gen healthage=health*age
```

We then use the newly generated variable healthage, representing the interaction between *health* and *age* variables, in a regression model:

```
. reg whours health age healthage
```

Although this is a convenient enough way of creating an interaction term and estimating an interaction model, Stata has some further features that make this task even more convenient. In Stata, without having to actually generate a variable (*healthage*) as we did above, we can estimate the interaction model by using the following command:

```
. reg whours c.health c.age c.health#c.age
```

We think it is good practice to insert the factor-variable operator c. in front of the two predictors to indicate that these are continuous variables, although we do not actually have to. We further create a so-called virtual interaction variable (not seen in the dataset) by combining (mathematically multiplying) the two predictors (with c. in front, of course) with the binary operator # to specify simple interaction between them. The above command can further be reduced to the following command in which the binary operator ## specifies full factorial interaction:

```
. reg whours c.health##c.age
```

When we have categorical variables (dummy or polytomous) to include in the interaction models we then insert the factor-variable operator i. in front of them. Estimation of interaction models using the binary operators (instead of generating a product term) further allows for post-estimation procedures that make the interpretation of interaction models easier and more accurate. We will see some evidence for this statement in the following sections.

6●2●1 Interaction between a continuous predictor and a continuous moderator

We will now expand our discussion by explaining the logic behind the statistical interaction between a continuous predictor and a continuous moderator variable. Suppose that we hypothesize that the effect of health motivation (to avoid health problems) on the number of hours spent working out will increase as age increases. The population regression function for this model would be

$$E[Y_i] = \beta_0 + \beta_1 X_{1i} + \beta_2 X_{2i} + \beta_3 X_{3i} \qquad (6.3)$$
$$= \beta_0 + \beta_1 X_{1i} + \beta_2 X_{2i} + \beta_3 X_{1i} X_{2i}.$$

Here X_1 represents our predictor (*health*), X_2 represents our moderator (*age*) and $E[Y_i]$ represents the mean-*Y*. *Y* measures the number of hours spent working out in a month. While *age* is measured in number of years, *health* is measured using a six-point scale (1=not important to 6=important). β_1 represents the coefficient on *health* when *age* is equal to zero,[5] and β_2 the coefficient on *age* when *health* is equal to zero. Finally, β_3 shows the amount by which the coefficient on *health* changes as a result of a one-unit increase in *age*.

By using the prediction approach based on (6.3), we can further calculate simple main (conditional) effects[6] of *health* at different values of the moderator variable *age*, which may be of interest for practical and/or theoretical reasons. Suppose that we are interested in calculating the simple main effect of *health* for people aged 20, 30, 40, 50, and 60. When $X_2 = 20$,

---

[5] It may bother you that we do not have the value of 0 in the range of *age*. In this case, it does not naturally make sense to interpret the coefficient on *health*. However, with *age* centred, β_1 is the coefficient on *health* at the mean of *age*. This idea applies to β_2 as well. Centring is treated later in the chapter.

[6] If you have any difficulty understanding these equations, just hypothetically insert the value 1 for all of the coefficients (β), and then reread the text following these equations.

$$E[Y_i] = \beta_0 + \beta_1 X_{1i} + \beta_2(20) + \beta_3(X_{1i} \times 20) \tag{6.4}$$
$$= (\beta_0 + 20\beta_2) + (\beta_1 + 20\beta_3) X_{1i}.$$

When $X_2 = 30$,

$$E[Y_i] = \beta_0 + \beta_1 X_{1i} + \beta_2(30) + \beta_3(X_{1i} \times 30) \tag{6.5}$$
$$= (\beta_0 + 30\beta_2) + (\beta_1 + 30\beta_3) X_{1i}.$$

When $X_2 = 40$,

$$E[Y_i] = \beta_0 + \beta_1 X_{1i} + \beta_2(40) + \beta_3(X_{1i} \times 40) \tag{6.6}$$
$$= (\beta_0 + 40\beta_2) + (\beta_1 + 40\beta_3) X_{1i}.$$

When $X_2 = 50$,

$$E[Y_i] = \beta_0 + \beta_1 X_{1i} + \beta_2(50) + \beta_3(X_{1i} \times 50) \tag{6.7}$$
$$= (\beta_0 + 50\beta_2) + (\beta_1 + 50\beta_3) X_{1i}.$$

When $X_2 = 60$,

$$E[Y_i] = \beta_0 + \beta_1 X_{1i} + \beta_2(60) + \beta_3(X_{1i} \times 60) \tag{6.8}$$
$$= (\beta_0 + 60\beta_2) + (\beta_1 + 60\beta_3) X_{1i}.$$

Essentially, each of equations (6.4)–(6.8) corresponds to a simple linear regression. In (6.4), for instance, $(\beta_0 + 20\beta_2)$ represents the intercept while $(\beta_1 + 20\beta_3)$ represents the simple main (conditional) effect of *health* (X_1) for those aged 20. In the same manner, we can observe the intercepts and simple main effects for those at the other age values selected. What is also important to notice here is that the simple main effect of *health* changes by $10\beta_3$ for every 10-unit increase in *age*. Had we increased *age* by one unit, the simple main effect of health would have changed by β_3. This confirms the notion of the linear interaction effect that we mentioned earlier in the chapter.

Example in Stata

Let us now estimate our example model formulated in equation (6.3) with Stata using the dataset *workout.dta*. We want to test whether the effect of *health* on *whours* (workout hours) varies depending on *age*. This test has come about as a result of our hypothesis that as people grow older they will work out more often to keep themselves healthy. To estimate our model including the dependent variable (*whours*), component terms (*health* and *age*) and the product term (*health* × *age*) using the regression approach, we could type the following in Stata:

```
. reg whours c.health c.age c.health#c.age
```

The estimated regression function and values are shown below (see the Stata output in Figure 6.3):

$$\widehat{whours_i} = \hat{\beta}_0 + \hat{\beta}_1\, health_i + \hat{\beta}_2\, age_i + \hat{\beta}_3(health \times age)_i \tag{6.9}$$
$$= 27.6 - 1.8\, health_i - 0.48\, age_i + 0.06(health \times age)_i$$

As we can see in Figure 6.3 and equation (6.9), $\hat{\beta}_1$ represents the coefficient on *health* when *age* is equal to zero, and $\hat{\beta}_2$ shows the coefficient on *age* when *health* is equal to zero. However, unless we centre these two variables before the estimation, interpreting these coefficients would not make any sense. We should after all mainly be interested in testing $\hat{\beta}_3$ in our interaction model. $\hat{\beta}_3$ shows that for each unit increase in *age*, the effect (coefficient) of *health* on *whours* increases by 0.06. The associated *p*-value shows additionally that this change (increase) is statistically significant ($p < 0.1$).

```
. reg whours c.health c.age c.health#c.age
```

Source	SS	df	MS		Number of obs =	210
					F(3, 206) =	5.48
Model	808.220699	3	269.4069		Prob > F =	0.0012
Residual	10119.7031	206	49.1247724		R-squared =	0.0740
					Adj R-squared =	0.0605
Total	10927.9238	209	52.2867168		Root MSE =	7.0089

whours	Coef.	Std. Err.	t	P>|t|	[95% Conf. Interval]	
health	-1.796974	1.361392	-1.32	0.188	-4.481022	.8870748
age	-.4756232	.191777	-2.48	0.014	-.8537204	-.097526
c.health#c.age	.0639482	.0368331	1.74	0.084	-.00867	.1365665
_cons	27.6244	6.912041	4.00	0.000	13.99699	41.25181

Figure 6.3 Stata output for an interaction model with two continuous variables

Suppose that, for some practical/theoretical reasons, we are interested in calculating the simple main (conditional) effect of *health* on *whours* for those aged 16, 26, 36, 46, 56, 66 and 76. To do so, we could type the following in Stata:

```
. margins, dydx(health) at(age=(16(10)76))
```

Here dydx refers to change-in-*Y*/change-in-*X* ratio. The (10) between 16 and 76 shows the increment chosen. You could insert any other value that serves your analytical purpose.[7] We can see the results of the above command in Figure 6.4. The effect of *health* on *whours* for those at *age* 16, 26 and 36 is statistically non-significant, meaning that the health motive does not influence the number of hours they work out. However, the effect is statistically significant ($p < 0.1$) for the remaining age groups. Furthermore, we can clearly see that the magnitude of this effect is indeed increasing for every 10-unit increase in *age*. For instance, for those at the age of 76, for every unit increase in *health* people on average work out about 3 hours more in a month.

---

[7] Here you could also insert the mean of *age* so that you can get the simple main effect of *health* at the mean of *age*. Thinking this way makes centring even less necessary before the estimation.

```
. margins, dydx(health) at(age=(16(10)76))
```

Average marginal effects   Number of obs   =   210
Model VCE   : OLS

```
Expression   : Linear prediction, predict()
dy/dx w.r.t. : health
```

```
1._at        : age              =           16

2._at        : age              =           26

3._at        : age              =           36

4._at        : age              =           46

5._at        : age              =           56

6._at        : age              =           66

7._at        : age              =           76
```

	dy/dx	Delta-method Std. Err.	t	P>|t|	[95% Conf. Interval]	
health						
_at						
1	-.7738018	.8284528	-0.93	0.351	-2.407135	.8595316
2	-.1343195	.5564723	-0.24	0.810	-1.231431	.9627917
3	.5051629	.452023	1.12	0.265	-.3860216	1.396347
4	1.144645	.6085426	1.88	0.061	-.0551248	2.344415
5	1.784128	.8986986	1.99	0.048	.0123013	3.555954
6	2.42361	1.231394	1.97	0.050	-.0041401	4.85136
7	3.063092	1.57998	1.94	0.054	-.0519124	6.178097

Figure 6.4   Stata output of simple main effects

We can further visualize the interaction effect using the following command which yields the more intuitive result in Figure 6.5:

```
. margins, at(health=(1(1)6) age=(16(10)76))
```

[output omitted]

```
. marginsplot, noci x(health) recast(line)
```

What the `margins` command above does is calculate the mean-Y at all six values of *health* for each age 16, 26, 36, 46, 56, 66 and 76. There will then be six mean-Y values calculated for each age. The `marginsplot` command simply draws a line through the six mean-Ys for each age group. For instance, the line for age 76 is the steepest and shows a positive relation. More explicitly, this line confirms our numerical finding that *health* has the strongest and positive effect on *whours* for age 76. We interpret the remaining lines in the same manner.

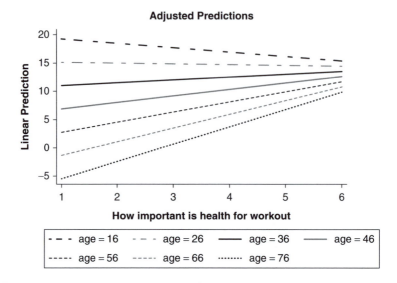

Figure 6.5 Graphical representation of an interaction using `marginsplot`

6•2•2 Interaction between a continuous predictor and a dummy moderator

We now explain another type of interaction model, including a continuous predictor and a dummy-variable moderator. For this particular case, we will assume that the effect of age on the number of hours spent working out is dependent on gender. The population regression function would again be

$$E[Y_i] = \beta_0 + \beta_1 X_{1i} + \beta_2 X_{2i} + \beta_3 X_{3i} \tag{6.10}$$
$$= \beta_0 + \beta_1 X_{1i} + \beta_2 X_{2i} + \beta_3 X_{1i} X_{2i}.$$

Here X_1 represents our predictor (*age*), X_2 represents our dummy-variable moderator (*gender*) and $E[Y_i]$ represents the mean-Y. Y measures the number of hours spent working out in a month. While *age* is measured in years, *gender* contains the categories of women (coded 0) and men (coded 1). β_1 represents the coefficient on *age* for women, and β_2 the coefficient on *gender* when *age* is equal to zero.[8] Finally, β_3 represents the difference between the slope coefficient on *age* for men and women. Alternatively, as we go up by one unit on the X_2 scale, 0 (women) to 1 (men), you can think of it in terms of the slope coefficient on *age* changing by β_3. Whether this change is an increase or decrease is decided by the sign of β_3.

As we did earlier, by using the prediction approach this time based on (6.10), we can calculate simple main (conditional) effects of *age* for women (0) and men (1) as follows. When $X_2 = 0$,

$$E[Y_i] = \beta_0 + \beta_1 X_{1i} + \beta_2(0) + \beta_3(X_{1i} \times 0) \tag{6.11}$$
$$= \beta_0 + \beta_1 X_{1i}.$$

---

[8] Here too, you may consider centring *age* to get a meaningful interpretation of β_2.

When $X_2 = 1$,

$$E[Y_i] = \beta_0 + \beta_1 X_{1i} + \beta_2(1) + \beta_3(X_{1i} \times 1) \tag{6.12}$$
$$= (\beta_0 + \beta_2) + (\beta_1 + \beta_3)X_{1i}.$$

Here too, we have reduced (6.10) to two simple regression equations. In (6.11), β_1 represents the coefficient on *age* for women and in (6.12) $\beta_1 + \beta_3$ is the coefficient on *age* for men. These are basically the simple main effects of age for two genders.

You might suggest that we could test the above interaction effect using the multi-group/sample approach which is about regressing Y on *age* in samples of women and men, which essentially will be the same as (6.11) and (6.12). However, although we can observe the difference between the coefficients in the samples of women and men, we would not directly obtain a significance test for this difference.[9] On the other hand, when estimating interaction models using the product-term approach, not only do we observe the difference between the coefficients, but also we directly obtain a significance test for this difference (β_3). A stronger argument for using the product-term approach is its flexibility in that it allows for estimation of more complex interaction models. Having said that, for pedagogical purposes, you can still also make use of the multi-sample approach to assist you in interpreting the results from the product-term approach which, to many, could seem complicated. This suggestion does apply to other types of interaction models treated later in the chapter as well.

Example in Stata

In our second example model shown in equation (6.10), we want to explicitly test whether the effect of *age* on *whours* is different for women and men. To estimate our model in Stata (using the dataset *workout.dta*), we could simply type

```
. reg whours c.age i.gender c.age#i.gender
```

The estimated regression function (see the Stata output in Figure 6.6) is as follows:

$$\widehat{whours}_i = \hat{\beta}_0 + \hat{\beta}_1 \, age_i + \hat{\beta}_2 \, gender_i + \hat{\beta}_3 \, (age \times gender)_i \tag{6.13}$$
$$= 13.1 - 0.03 \, age_i + 10.6 \, gender_i - 0.21(age \times gender)_i \, .$$

As we can see in Figure 6.6 and equation (6.13), $\hat{\beta}_1$ represents the coefficient on *age* when *gender* is equal to zero. Since women are coded 0, we would say that the coefficient (effect) of *age* on *whours* decreases by 0.03 for women. $\hat{\beta}_2$ is the coefficient on *gender* when *age* is equal to zero. However, unless we centre *age* before the estimation, interpreting its coefficient would not make sense. $\hat{\beta}_3$ represents the difference between the slope coefficients on *age* for men and women, meaning that the coefficient (effect) of *age* on *whours* for men is about 0.21 more than that for women. The associated *p*-value shows that this difference is statistically significant. Note that the coefficients on *age* for both women and men are negative, confirming that the effect of *age* on *whours* for both groups is decreasing. However, it does so to a greater extent for men.

---

[9] Actually, we can do this easily with Stata as well using a post-estimation command. It will, however, be more cumbersome (or even impossible) to do this with other standard statistical software packages.

```
. reg whours c.age i.gender c.age#i.gender
```

Source	SS	df	MS		Number of obs =	210
					F(3, 206) =	8.49
Model	1202.50438	3	400.834794		Prob > F =	0.0000
Residual	9725.41943	206	47.2107739		R-squared =	0.1100
					Adj R-squared =	0.0971
Total	10927.9238	209	52.2867168		Root MSE =	6.871

whours	Coef.	Std. Err.	t	P>|t|	[95% Conf. Interval]	
age	-.0317262	.0546461	-0.58	0.562	-.1394635	.0760111
gender						
men	10.61049	3.25435	3.26	0.001	4.19439	17.02659
gender#c.age						
men	-.2135282	.0789673	-2.70	0.007	-.3692158	-.0578406
_cons	13.09677	2.290885	5.72	0.000	8.580188	17.61336

Figure 6.6 Stata output for an interaction model with a continuous and a dummy variable

From the information displayed in Figure 6.6 we could directly calculate the simple main effect of *age* for men. We can also use the following margins command to do so, which yields Figure 6.7:

```
. margins, dydx(age) at(gender=(0 1))
```

or

```
. margins gender, dydx(age)
```

As we can see in Figure 6.7, the coefficient (effect) of *age* on *whours* for men is about −0.25 and statistically significant. We also observe the corresponding coefficient (−0.03 and non-significant) for women, which we already knew from Figure 6.6. As you might expect, the difference between these two coefficients is simply the size of $\hat{\beta}_3$.

```
. margins, dydx(age) at(gender=(0 1))
```

Average marginal effects		Number of obs =	210
Model VCE : OLS			

Expression : Linear prediction, predict()
dy/dx w.r.t. : age

1._at	: gender	=	0
2._at	: gender	=	1

		Delta-method				
	dy/dx	Std. Err.	t	P>|t|	[95% Conf. Interval]	
age						
_at						
1	-.0317262	.0546461	-0.58	0.562	-.1394635	.0760111
2	-.2452544	.0570056	-4.30	0.000	-.3576435	-.1328652

Figure 6.7 Stata output of simple main effects

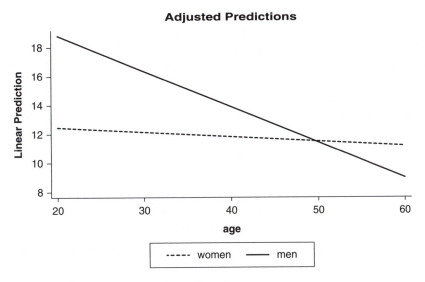

Figure 6.8 Graphical representation of an interaction using `marginsplot`

As we did earlier, here too we can visualize the interaction effect using the following command which will generate Figure 6.8:

```
. margins, at(age=(20(10)60) gender=(0 1))
```

[output omitted]

```
. marginsplot, noci x(age) recast(line)
```

Having previously explained the logic behind the above command, we focus now on the graphical representation of the interaction depicted in Figure 6.8. As we can see, the lines for both women and men are negative. However, the line for men is much steeper, indicating once again the stronger effect of *age* on *whours* for men.

6●2●3 Interaction between a dummy predictor and a dummy moderator

We now explain the mechanics behind the statistical interaction between a dummy predictor and a dummy-variable moderator. We will hypothesize that the effect of gender on the number of hours spent working out is dependent on marital status. The population regression function would then be

$$E[Y_i] = \beta_0 + \beta_1 X_{1i} + \beta_2 X_{2i} + \beta_3 X_{3i} \tag{6.14}$$
$$= \beta_0 + \beta_1 X_{1i} + \beta_2 X_{2i} + \beta_3 X_{1i} X_{2i}.$$

Here X_1 represents our dummy predictor (*gender*), X_2 represents our dummy variable moderator (*marital status*) and $E[Y_i]$ represents the mean-Y. Y measures the number of hours spent working out in a month. While *gender* contains the categories of women (coded 0) and men (coded 1), *marital status* includes the categories of married (0) and single (1). β_1 represents the coefficient on *gender* for those who are married, and β_2 the coefficient on *marital status* for women. Finally, β_3 represents the difference between the coefficients on *gender* for married and single people.

Here, too, by using the prediction approach based on [6.14], we can calculate simple main (conditional) effects of *gender* for married (0) and single (1) as follows. When $X_2 = 0$,

$$E[Y_i] = \beta_0 + \beta_1 X_{1i} + \beta_2(0) + \beta_3(X_{1i} \times 0) \tag{6.15}$$
$$= \beta_0 + \beta_1 X_{1i}.$$

When $X_2 = 1$,

$$E[Y_i] = \beta_0 + \beta_1 X_{1i} + \beta_2(1) + \beta_3(X_{1i} \times 1) \tag{6.16}$$
$$= (\beta_0 + \beta_2) + (\beta_1 + \beta_3) X_{1i}.$$

As such, in (6.15), β_1 represents the coefficient on *gender* for married, and in (6.16), $\beta_1 + \beta_3$ represents the coefficient on *gender* for single.

Example in Stata

In our third example model represented by equation (6.14), we examine the interaction between a dummy predictor (*gender*) and a dummy moderator (*marital status*). Our purpose this time is to test whether the effect of *gender* on *whours* is different for married and single people. To estimate this interaction model in Stata (using *workout.dta*), we can use the command

```
. reg whours i.gender i.marital i.gender#i.marital
```

The estimated regression function (see the Stata output in Figure 6.9) is as follows:

$$\widehat{whours}_i = \hat{\beta}_0 + \hat{\beta}_1 \, gender_i + \hat{\beta}_2 \, marital_i + \hat{\beta}_3 \, (gender \times marital)_i \tag{6.17}$$
$$= 11.5 + 0.56 \, gender_i + 0.70 \, marital_i + 3.47 \, (gender \times marital)_i \,.$$

As we can see in Figure 6.9 and equation (6.17), $\hat{\beta}_1$ represents the coefficient on *gender* when *marital* is equal to zero. Since married people are coded 0, we would then say that men work out 0.56 hours more than women do among those who are married. This coefficient (difference) is unsurprisingly non-significant though. $\hat{\beta}_2$ shows the coefficient on *marital* when *gender* is equal to zero. Since women are coded 0, we would also assert that single people work out 0.70 hours more than married people do among women. This coefficient (difference) is non-significant, too. $\hat{\beta}_3$ shows, however, that men work out 3.47 hours more than women do among singles. This coefficient (difference) is statistically significant ($p < 0.1$).

Note that, by using the following command, we can directly obtain the coefficient on gender for singles as well as for married people (which we already know, by the way):

```
. margins, dydx(gender) at(marital=(0 1))
```

This yields the results displayed in Figure 6.10.

. reg whours i.gender i.marital i.gender#i.marital

Source	SS	df	MS
Model	678.978763	3	226.326254
Residual	10248.945	206	49.7521604
Total	10927.9238	209	52.2867168

```
Number of obs =     210
F(  3,    206) =    4.55
Prob > F       =  0.0041
R-squared      =  0.0621
Adj R-squared  =  0.0485
Root MSE       =  7.0535
```

whours	Coef.	Std. Err.	t	P>|t|	[95% Conf. Interval]	
gender men	.5609594	1.392495	0.40	0.687	-2.184409	3.306328
marital single	.6956962	1.274683	0.55	0.586	-1.817401	3.208794
gender#marital men#single	3.47811	2.02265	1.72	0.087	-.5096378	7.465859
_cons	11.5443	.7935831	14.55	0.000	9.979718	13.10889

Figure 6.9 Stata output for an interaction model with two dummy variables

. margins, dydx(gender) at(marital=(0 1))

```
Conditional marginal effects                    Number of obs   =        210
Model VCE    : OLS

Expression   : Linear prediction, predict()
dy/dx w.r.t. : 1.gender

1._at        : marital         =             0

2._at        : marital         =             1
```

	dy/dx	Delta-method Std. Err.	t	P>|t|	[95% Conf. Interval]	
1.gender _at						
1	.5609594	1.392495	0.40	0.687	-2.184409	3.306328
2	4.03907	1.466994	2.75	0.006	1.146823	6.931316

Figure 6.10 Stata output of simple main effects

Here, too, we can try visualizing the interaction effect using similar commands to those we have used so far, namely:

. margins, at(gender=(0 1) marital=(0 1))

[output omitted]

. marginsplot, noci x(gender) recast(line)

These commands will produce Figure 6.11. As we can see, the top line representing singles is much steeper than the bottom line for married people, emphasizing our numerical results that the difference between the mean-Y of men and women is larger among singles than it is among those who are married.

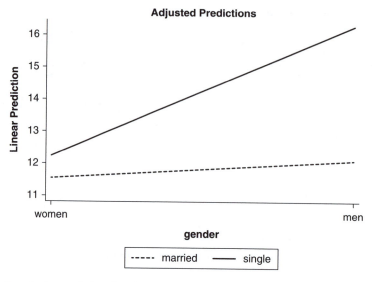

Figure 6.11 Graphical presentation of an interaction using marginsplot

6•2•4 Interaction between a continuous predictor and a polytomous moderator

In this section we will examine a rather complex type of interaction model including a continuous predictor and a polytomous moderator that contains three categories. As an example, we will assume that the effect of *age* on the number of hours spent working out is dependent on education level. Since education level contains three categories (secondary/high school, university, more than university), we will create three[10] dummy variables, two of which we will interact with *age* and one of which will be the reference category. We will then include all the component and interaction terms in the regression model, which we can write as follows:

$$E[Y_i] = \beta_0 + \beta_1 X_{1i} + \beta_2 X_{2i} + \beta_3 X_{3i} + \beta_4 X_{4i} + \beta_5 X_{5i} \qquad (6.18)$$
$$= \beta_0 + \beta_1 X_{1i} + \beta_2 X_{2i} + \beta_3 X_{3i} + \beta_4 X_{1i} X_{2i} + \beta_5 X_{1i} X_{3i}.$$

Here X_1 represents our continuous predictor (*age*), X_2 represents our first dummy-variable moderator (*university*), X_3 represents our second dummy-variable moderator (*more than university*) and $E[Y_i]$ represents the mean-*Y*. *Y* measures the number of hours spent working out in a month. β_1 is the coefficient on *age* for those with secondary/high school education. β_2 is the difference between the mean-*Y* for those with *university* and *secondary/high school* education when *age* is zero.[11] β_3 is the difference between mean-*Y* for those with *more than university* and *secondary/high school* education when age is zero. β_4 is the difference between the coefficients on *age* for those with *university education* and those with *secondary/high school* education.

---

[10] As we learned in the chapter on dummy-variable regression, the dummy variable that is not included in the interaction model is the reference group (those with secondary/high school education).

[11] We could centre *age* here to get a more meaningful interpretation of the coefficient.

β_5 reflects the difference between the coefficients on *age* for those with *more than university* education and those with *secondary/high school* education.

Let us also calculate simple main (conditional) effects of *age* for the three educational groups (*secondary/high school, university* and *more than university*). When $X_2 = 0$ and $X_3 = 0$,

$$E[Y_i] = \beta_0 + \beta_1 X_{1i} + \beta_2(0) + \beta_3(0) + \beta_4(X_{1i} \times 0) + \beta_5(X_{1i} \times 0) \qquad (6.19)$$
$$= \beta_0 + \beta_1 X_{1i}.$$

When $X_2 = 1$ and $X_3 = 0$,

$$E[Y_i] = \beta_0 + \beta_1 X_{1i} + \beta_2(1) + \beta_3(0) + \beta_4(X_{1i} \times 1) + \beta_5(X_{1i} \times 0) \qquad (6.20)$$
$$= (\beta_0 + \beta_2) + (\beta_1 + \beta_4)X_{1i}.$$

When $X_2 = 0$ and $X_3 = 1$,

$$E[Y_i] = \beta_0 + \beta_1 X_{1i} + \beta_2(0) + \beta_3(1) + \beta_4(X_{1i} \times 0) + \beta_5(X_{1i} \times 1) \qquad (6.21)$$
$$= (\beta_0 + \beta_3) + (\beta_1 + \beta_5)X_{1i}.$$

In (6.19), and as already stated, β_1 represents the coefficient on *age* for those with *secondary/ high school* education. In (6.20), $\beta_1 + \beta_4$ represents the coefficient on *age* for those with *university* education. Finally, in (6.21), $(\beta_1 + \beta_5)$ represents the coefficient on *age* for those with *more than university* education.

Although the significance test of the coefficients of β_4 and β_5 in (6.18) tells us about individual interaction effects, we need to test the significance of the overall interaction effect. We can do this by simply generalizing the idea of the *F*-test to test the significance of a set of coefficients. Since we have two interaction coefficients (β_4 and β_5) in our model, we need to test whether these two coefficients are jointly significantly different from zero. To do so, we construct an *F*-statistic (see equation (5.28) in Chapter 5), which follows an *F*-distribution with $df_1 = p$ and $df_2 = n - K$ degrees of freedom, and where $\mathrm{RSS_R}$ and $\mathrm{RSS_{UR}}$ are the residual sum of squares of the restricted and the unrestricted model, p is the number of restrictions, n is the number of observations, and K is the number of parameters.

The unrestricted model represents our complete model including all the component terms (X_1, X_2 and X_3) and product terms (X_4 and X_5), while the restricted model would include only the component terms (X_1, X_2 and X_3). The reason why we call this a restricted model is that we here implicitly assume that the product/interaction terms have coefficients of zero (H_0: $\beta_4 = \beta_5 = 0$). Since we restrict these two coefficients to be zero, the number of restrictions is naturally 2. If the resulting *F*-test[12] proves to be significant, we would favour the alternative hypothesis that there is an overall interaction effect.

Example in Stata

In our final model shown in equation (6.18), we examine whether the effect of *age* on *whours* is dependent on educational level. This example is quite similar to the one in which we had a dummy variable representing our categorical moderator (*gender*). In the current example

---

[12] Instead of running two separate regressions, obtaining an *F*-statistic and then finding the associated *p*-value, we usually employ a hierarchical regression to yield the *F*-statistic and associated *p*-value automatically. The hierarchical regression involves one block including the component terms and a second block including both the component and product terms.

we would, however, have a set of dummy variables representing our categorical variable which this time is education level with three levels. We will estimate this model in Stata (using *workout.dta*) with the command

. reg whours c.age i.educ c.age#i.educ

The estimated regression function (see the Stata output in Figure 6.12) is as follows:

$$\widehat{whours_i} = \hat{\beta}_0 + \hat{\beta}_1 age_i + \hat{\beta}_2 univ_i + \hat{\beta}_3 m\_univ_i + \hat{\beta}_4 (age \times univ)_i + \hat{\beta}_5 (age \times m\_univ)_i \quad (6.22)$$
$$= 23 - 0.22\, age_i - 10.46\, univ_i - 13.36\, m\_univ_i + 0.20\, (age \times univ)_i + 0.26 (age \times m\_univ)_i$$

As we can see in Figure 6.12 and equation (6.22), β_1 represents the coefficient on *age* for those with secondary/high school education. That is, among those with secondary/high school education, each unit increase in *age* will on average lead to a 0.22 decrease in *whours*. β_2 and β_3 represent respectively the difference between the mean-Y for those with *university* and *secondary/high school* education and the difference between the mean-Y of those with *more than university* and *secondary/high school* education when *age* is zero. However, unless we centre *age* here, it does not make sense to interpret these coefficients.

Let us now focus on interpreting the interaction term coefficients. As we know, β_4 represents the difference between the coefficients on age for those with university education and those with secondary/high school education. Explicitly put, each unit increase in age will on average lead to 0.20 more *whours* for those with university education than it will for those with secondary/high school education. This difference is indeed statistically different. We also remember that β_5 reflects the difference between the coefficients on age for those with more than university education and those with secondary/high school education. This would mean that, each unit increase in age will on average lead to 0.26 more *whours* for those with more than university education than it will for those with secondary/high school education. This difference is also statistically different. Here if we want to test the difference between the coefficient on age for those with *university* and those with *more than university* education, we then suggest simply change the reference category (*secondary/high school*) to any of the other two categories.

. reg whours c.age i.educ c.age#i.educ

Source	SS	df	MS		
Model	1455.73963	5	291.147926		
Residual	9472.18418	204	46.4322754		
Total	10927.9238	209	52.2867168		

Number of obs = 210
F(5, 204) = 6.27
Prob > F = 0.0000
R-squared = 0.1332
Adj R-squared = 0.1120
Root MSE = 6.8141

whours	Coef.	Std. Err.	t	P>|t|	[95% Conf. Interval]
age	-.2190014	.0579104	-3.78	0.000	-.3331811 -.1048217
educ					
university	-10.46198	4.363082	-2.40	0.017	-19.06449 -1.859459
more than university	-13.36174	4.018536	-3.33	0.001	-21.28493 -5.438548
educ#c.age					
university	.2014475	.102947	1.96	0.052	-.001529 .404424
more than university	.2564962	.0985739	2.60	0.010	.062142 .4508504
_cons	23.00372	2.148345	10.71	0.000	18.76791 27.23953

Figure 6.12 Stata output for an interaction model with a continuous and a polytomous variable

```
. margins, dydx(age) at(educ=(1 2 3))
```

```
Average marginal effects                          Number of obs   =         210
Model VCE      : OLS

Expression     : Linear prediction, predict()
dy/dx w.r.t.   : age

1._at          : educ            =          1

2._at          : educ            =          2

3._at          : educ            =          3
```

		Delta-method			
	dy/dx	Std. Err.	t	P>|t|	[95% Conf. Interval]
age					
_at					
1	-.2190014	.0579104	-3.78	0.000	-.3331811 -.1048217
2	-.0175539	.0851144	-0.21	0.837	-.1853707 .1502629
3	.0374948	.0797696	0.47	0.639	-.1197838 .1947734

Figure 6.13 Stata output of simple main effects

Let us also calculate simple main (conditional) effects of *age* for the three educational groups (*secondary/high school, university* and *more than university*) using Stata. These results (Figure 6.13) will further validate the interpretations of the interaction term coefficients as well.

```
. margins, dydx(age) at(educ=(1 2 3))
```

or

```
. margins educ, dydx(age)
```

We can further visualize the interaction effects using the following commands in Stata which yield the results in Figure 6.14.

```
. margins, at(age=(20(10)60) educ=(1 2 3))
```

[output omitted]

```
. marginsplot, noci x(age) recast(line)
```

As we can see, the line for those with *secondary/high school* is the steepest and shows a negative association. This simply supports the numerical finding in Figure 6.13 suggesting that as these people grow older, they work out less. The lines for those with *university* and with *more than university* education show simply that the importance of age for workout hours is indeed higher for these groups.

The final (but in practice, the first) thing we need to do is test whether the overall interaction effect is statistically significant. To do so, in Stata we would type after the regression estimation:

```
. test (2.educ#c.age 3.educ#c.age)
```

or

```
. testparm i.educ#c.age
```

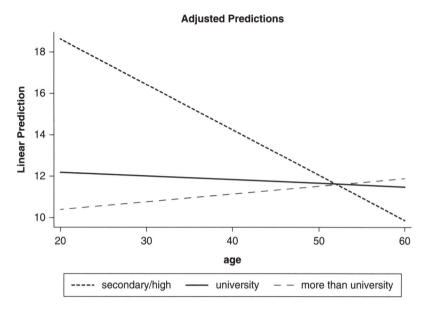

Figure 6.14 Graphical presentation of an interaction using marginsplot

This command yields Figure 6.15. The resulting *F*-test is statistically significant, suggesting that there is an overall interaction effect. This result incidentally justifies the interpretation of the individual coefficients of our interaction model.

It is worth mentioning again that in all of the above interaction models, we could if necessary treat the moderator variables as predictors and the predictors as moderator variables. We would then proceed much as we have previously, trying to interpret the resulting coefficients as well as calculating the simple effects that are of interest to us. Furthermore, in the above interaction model including more than one dummy variable, we could if necessary simply change[13] the reference category (as we did in Chapter 5 on dummy-variable regression) and re-estimate the model to obtain other information/comparisons that we may be interested in. Until now, in all of the above interaction models, we have deliberately not included any covariates to keep the focus solely on the interpretation of the interaction effects. However, including covariates in interaction models does not do anything different to interaction

```
. test (2.educ#c.age 3.educ#c.age)

( 1)   2.educ#c.age = 0
( 2)   3.educ#c.age = 0

    F(  2,   204) =     4.06
         Prob > F =   0.0186
```

Figure 6.15 Significance test of an overall interaction effect

---

[13] We could alternatively use the linear combinations approach here as well. However, for simplicity, we do not go into the theoretical details of this approach here. It is, after all, treated in Chapter 5 on dummy-variable regression.

models than it does to additive (non-interaction) models. That is, the estimated coefficients are basically adjusted as a result of taking into account the covariate(s).[14]

Significant versus non-significant interaction

Up to now, we have implicitly assumed that product/interaction terms are statistically significant. What if an interaction is statistically non-significant? The answer to this question should actually be no different than when it comes to inclusion/exclusion of a predictor in a regression model in general. So, if you *a priori* (before data collection) hypothesized a significant interaction, then the interaction should still be included in your model even if it proves to be a non-significant one. However, as most will agree, interactions are usually examined *a posteriori* (after data collection) in the social sciences (particularly in non-experimental) research. In this case, exclusion of non-significant interactions is recommended in order to estimate a statistically parsimonious and a less complex regression model. Furthermore, in interaction models we generally recommend focusing on the interpretation of the interaction terms and simple (conditional) effects instead of main effects[15] of the variables constituting the interaction terms.

Centring and standardization

We have so far deliberately only worked with raw data (i.e., untransformed) data to get a deeper understanding of interactions. Recall that a coefficient on a predictor in an interaction model reflects the slope (effect) when the moderator is zero, and vice versa. Such an interpretation, however, makes no sense when the moderator/predictor variable does not have zero in its scale range. One way to address this issue is to centre the moderator/predictor variable. You can in theory centre the variable at any point, but the most common procedure is to centre it at its mean. That is, we simply subtract the mean value of the moderator/predictor from the score of each observation. When we then estimate the interaction model with the centred data, the coefficient on the predictor will reflect the slope for those having the mean score. Thus, the main advantage of centring is ease of interpretation. Incidentally, the coefficient on the interaction term will not be influenced by this transformation. As an alternative to mean centring, you can still use the equation, based on the raw data, to obtain the slopes at any value of interest (including the mean) of the moderator/predictor as done in the interaction models. After all, the coefficient estimated at the mean itself is a simple effect.

Another transformation procedure that is sometimes used is the z-score transformation. This transformation is quite similar to centring, but when standardizing a variable we subtract the mean from the values of the variable and divide by the standard deviation. As in an interaction model with centred data, the coefficients on the moderator/predictor will still reflect the slope at the value of 0. Since 0 is the mean of a z-transformed variable, the coefficient will reflect the slope at the mean of the moderator/predictor. As opposed to raw scales used for the interpretation in the centred solution, the coefficients in the standardized solution will be

---

[14] Adding a covariate to interaction models with a categorical variable with regression is equivalent to factorial ANCOVAs.

[15] Incidentally, interaction models estimated using ANOVA still provide main effects (of the component terms) due to effect coding, whereas regression provides them as simple main effects due to dummy coding.

interpreted in terms of standard deviations. The interpretation of the standardized solution is similar to that in multiple regression analysis.

Our answer to the question whether one should work with raw, centred or standardized solutions is that unless you have a specific reason for choosing centring[16] or standardization, we in general recommend working with raw data and interpreting the resulting coefficients in the original metric of the variables. This approach gives the researcher flexibility (i.e., working with prediction equations) as well as a basis for making more substantial interpretations. This makes even more sense when the moderator/predictor is a categorical variable, as then there is no sensible reason to either centre or standardize the variables.

6 ● 3 CONCLUSION

In this chapter we have shown in detail how we can build up, estimate and interpret interaction models. The examples that we have examined in this chapter are confined to two-way interaction models. However, the ideas of two-way interaction models provide a solid foundation for figuring out three-way interaction models. Although we have examined interaction effects using linear regression, the same ideas apply (with some minor adjustments) to logistic regression, structural equation models and other techniques (Poisson regression, survival analysis, etc.) that we do not treat in this book. Furthermore, interaction models provide a springboard to understanding multilevel modelling. We have also shown how readily we can estimate and understand these rather complex models with appealing features of Stata.

 key terms

Interaction effect A third variable changes the relationship between two variables.

Factorial ANOVA ANOVA with full interactions.

Factorial ANCOVA ANCOVA with full interactions.

Additive model A model in which we assume constant coefficient.

Non-additive model A model in which coefficient changing depending on the moderator.

Two-way interaction An interaction occurring between two predictors.

Product-term A multiplication of two predictors.

Multi-sample approach Effect of X on Y is estimated in more than one sample.

Moderator The variable that changes the relationship between two other variables.

Predictor Independent variable.

Centring The mean of a variable is transformed to 0.

Simple main effects Effect of X on Y at certain values of the moderator.

---

[16] As also mentioned in Jaccard and Turrisi (2003), whether *centred* or *raw*, the results of the significance test of and confidence intervals for the coefficient on the interaction terms are identical. Multicollinearity occurring between the interaction/product term and the component terms is not a problem. What is more problematic is multicollinearity between the component terms, which is treated in Chapter 7 on regression assumptions.

QUESTIONS

1 Explain when/why we use interaction models.
2 Explain with an example what a statistical interaction/moderation is.
3 Build and estimate an interaction model including a dummy predictor and a continuous moderator.

FURTHER READING

Jaccard, J. and Turrisi, R. (2003) *Interaction Effects in Multiple Regression* (2nd edn). London: Sage.

As its title indicates, this is a detailed book on interaction effects using multiple regression, with more details and examples.

REFERENCES

Gordon, R.A. (2010) *Regression Analysis for the Social Sciences* (4th edn). Abingdon: Routledge.

Jaccard, J. and Turrisi, R. (2003) *Interaction Effects in Multiple Regression* (2nd edn). London: Sage.

Mitchell, M.N. (2012) *Interpreting and Visualizing Regression Models Using Stata*. College Station, TX: Stata Press.

Pardoe, I. (2006) *Applied Regression Modeling: A Business Approach*. Hoboken, NJ: John Wiley & Sons.

7

LINEAR REGRESSION ASSUMPTIONS AND DIAGNOSTICS

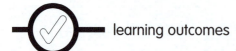

learning outcomes

- o understand the assumptions of OLS regression
- o Learn how to test for nonlinearity, heteroscedasticity, distribution of error
- terms and other assumptions using Stata
- o Understand how to deal with breaches of assumptions

In all forms of regression analysis there are certain assumptions that must be met. If they are not, then we cannot trust that the estimates from our models are correct. Ordinary least-squares regression is our central method of estimation, and when its assumptions are met, it cannot be improved upon. However, in many cases its assumptions are not met. Our data could for example be nested, or we could have a dependent variable that is not continuous. The main questions asked when it comes to regression diagnostics are whether we have simplified too much and whether our assumptions are plausible. In this chapter we will guide the reader through the assumptions of OLS regression, show how to detect these using Stata and how to deal with breaches of these assumptions.

The least-squares method is usually attributed to the German mathematician Karl Friedrich Gauss. In 1821 he presented his theorem on the ordinary least-squares estimator which gives the best linear unbiased estimator if certain assumptions are met. This theorem was rediscovered in 1900 by Andrei Markov, and is today known as the Gauss–Markov theorem. The Gauss–Markov conditions are that the error term has a conditional mean of zero, that the error term has constant variance and that the errors are uncorrelated for different observations and with the X-variables.

In addition to the Gauss–Markov conditions there are some other assumptions that should be met. These include that the model is correctly specified, that the explanatory variables should not be too correlated with each other and that the residuals should be normally distributed. In this chapter, we will guide you through all of these assumptions, and show methods in Stata to test whether or not the model adheres to these. In addition, we will look into influential cases.

We should always start by running frequency distributions for our Y- and X-variables. Here we can identify potential problems, such as skewed, flat or pointy variable distributions.

ORIGINAL GAUSS–MARKOV ASSUMPTIONS

1. Error term has a conditional mean of zero (see Section 7.2.1)
2. Error term has constant variance (see Section 7.2.2)
3. Errors are uncorrelated (see Section 7.2.3)

ADDITIONAL ASSUMPTIONS

4. Model is correctly specified (see Sections 7.1.1, 7.1.2 and 7.1.3)
5. Absence of multicollinearity (see Section 7.1.4)
6. Normally distributed residuals (see Section 7.2.4)

Normally distributed variables often give normally distributed error terms and fewer influential cases. So, in order to prevent problems when it comes to regression assumptions, it is wise to start working with the variables through recoding and transformations (for more on this, see Chapter 13). Also, if the dependent variable is not continuous (or approximately continuous), we have to look into other types of regression analysis than least squares (see Chapter 8).

7●1 CORRECT SPECIFICATION OF THE MODEL

We can divide regression assumptions in to two parts: one part deals with the specification of the least-squares model, the other with assumptions about the residuals. What we call model specification error can occur when we fail to include theoretically relevant variables, include irrelevant variables, or model linear relationships when the true effect is not linear. If we improve our model by including new variables we should test whether the improvement constitutes a significant improvement of the model. If the difference between the two models is one explanatory variable, we can use a *t*-test (and look at the *p*-value for the new variable). However, if we include more than one variable (or an interaction or squared term) we should conduct an *F*-test (for more on this, see Chapter 4, p. 70f). This is done by first running the restricted (small) model, saving the estimates, then running the unrestricted (large) model, saving the estimates, and seeing if the F-test is significant:

```
. reg Y X1 X2 X3 X4 X5
. test X4 X5
```

7●1●1 All *X*-variables relevant, and none irrelevant

The first assumption we present is that all relevant *X*-variables and no irrelevant *X*-variables should be included. This is first and foremost a theoretical question. That is, you should take care to identify the variables that should be expected to influence your dependent variable. Ideally, all of these should be included in your model. However, data limitations can make this assumption difficult to accommodate. You should not include *X*-variables that you have no theoretical or logical reason to include. One reason for this is that we are operating with some uncertainty when it comes to our tests of significance. For example, if we accept 5 per cent uncertainty in our results (95 per cent confidence intervals), we increase the risk of producing false significant results by including explanatory variables at random, as well as having the other coefficients 'controlled for' by unnecessary variables.

The linktest command in Stata can be run after any single-equation estimation (we also use this in Chapter 8). This test is used to see whether our model suffers from a misspecification problem, that is, whether or not the wrong forms of the variables have been used or whether some additional independent variables should have been included. In short, the test gives us a regression with two variables: _hat (the linear predicted value), which, if we have a good model, should be a good predictor of *Y*; and _hatsq (the squared linear predicted value), which should not be significant if the model has been properly specified. It is the latter variable that composes the test: if _hatsq is significant, then the linktest is significant (which means that we have omitted relevant variables and/or the model is not correctly specified). We use the dataset *ESSGBdiagnostics.dta* and run a regression where we want to explain the causes of trust in the legal system (0–10) using the explanatory variables *age*, *woman* (0–1), *political_interest* (1–4) and *religious* (0–10):

```
. quietly regress trstlgl age woman political_interest religious
. linktest
```

Source	SS	df	MS		
Model	535.277594	2	267.638797		
Residual	10020.7077	1899	5.27683396		
Total	10555.9853	1901	5.55285917		

				Number of obs =	1902
				F(2, 1899) =	50.72
				Prob > F =	0.0000
				R-squared =	0.0507
				Adj R-squared =	0.0497
				Root MSE =	2.2971

trstlgl	Coef.	Std. Err.	t	P>|t|	[95% Conf. Interval]	
_hat	2.224391	1.591641	1.40	0.162	-.8971575	5.34594
_hatsq	-.1155341	.1498937	-0.77	0.441	-.4095077	.1784395
_cons	-3.211569	4.200487	-0.76	0.445	-11.44962	5.026485

Figure 7.1 Stata output for `linktest`

The output from the test is shown in Figure 7.1. It is evident that we do not have a very good model (as _hat is not significant); however, we cannot say that we have a misspecification problem (as _hatsq is also not significant).

When it comes to the problem of omitted variables, we can use Stata's `ovtest` command. This carries out two versions of Ramsey's (1969) regression specification error test for omitted variables:

```
. quietly regress trstlgl age woman political_interest religious

. estat ovtest

Ramsey RESET test using powers of the fitted values of trstlgl
       Ho:  model has no omitted variables
             F(3, 1894) =      0.98
             Prob > F =      0.4000
```

A non-significant test means that we keep our null hypothesis of no omitted variables, that is, our model is fine according to this test.

However, passing a diagnostic test like `ovtest` or `linktest` does not mean that we have specified the best possible model, either statistically or substantively. We should only interpret this to mean that our model has passed some minimal statistical threshold of data fitting. Our `ovtest` should be interpreted not as a test for unused omitted variables, but rather as a test for misspecified used variables. And `linktest` is also not a miracle test that can detect bias from omitted variables. In the following sections we will look at how to improve our model, despite passing the above-mentioned diagnostic tests.

In addition, there is the assumption that the X-variables should be measured without error. This concerns the reliability of our data. Measurement error causes relationships to be underestimated for the variable in question, and the possible overestimation of other explanatory variables in our model. Standard regression models assume that the variables in the equation have been measured without error.

7•1•2 Linearity

The assumption of linearity means that a one-unit increase in X_i is associated with a constant amount of change in mean-Y, holding all other X-variables constant. This change in Y (either positive or negative) is the same regardless of the level of X_i (i.e., if you move from 3 to 4 or from 7 to 8 on X_i, the change in Y is the same). However, in the real world this is often not the case. For example, the change in Y could be dependent on the level of X_i (e.g., that the change in Y is positive for a 3–4 step, but negative for a 45–46 step). In this case we say that the relationship is nonlinear. In other words, the relationship between our independent and dependent varies according to context, namely the level of that specific X-variable (see Figure 7.2). If a model is functionally misspecified its slope coefficients may give the wrong picture of the reality.

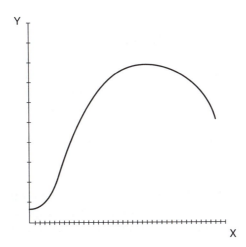

Figure 7.2 A nonlinear (curvilinear) relationship

If we model a nonlinear relationship as linear we risk getting incorrect slope coefficients, biased standard errors, and thus invalid t- and F-statistics. The possibility of a nonlinear relationship should first occur to us in the theoretical work on the effects of our variable. Is it reasonable to assume that the X–Y relationship is linear, or could it be curvilinear? We can assess nonlinearity by, for example, examining a scatter plot of our Y- and X-variables.

Curvilinearity with one bend

In order to model a nonlinear relationship with one curve, we can include the square of the variable in the regression. For example, if we were investigating the association between *age* (*X*) and *length of education* (*Y*) we could expect the relationship to be curvilinear. The reason is that in general we should expect people to have spent more years in education the older they get, except for older generations who have often had less schooling. To model this we include both *age* and *age* multiplied by *age* (age × age) in our analysis. We call this latter variable *age²*.

Table 7.1 *Age* and *age squared*

age	age²	increase in *age*	increase in *age²*
20	400	–	–
30	900	10	500
40	1600	10	700
50	2500	10	900
60	3600	10	1100
70	4900	10	1300
80	6400	10	1500

In Table 7.1 the increase in *age* is the same from 20 to 30 years as it is from 30 to 40 and so on. However, *age squared* increases more and more for each year, so the effect becomes larger the older you are. Therefore, the effect of the squared term will be larger the higher your value on the original variable is. Consider the regression where we want to predict years of education as a function of age, and we model the effect to be curvilinear. Suppose we obtain

$$Y = 8.712 + 0.274X - 0.003X^2, \tag{7.1}$$

where Y is *length of education* and X is *age*.

First, we notice that the positive *age* coefficient is much larger than the *age²* coefficient, which is quite small. That is, for young people there will be a large positive effect of *age*, and a small negative effect of *age²*. However, as age increases, the effect of *age²* increases even more, and will, after a certain age is reached, be stronger than the age effect. This can be shown through some simple predictions. Let us predict three values, one for a 20-year-old, one for a 40-year-old and one for a 70-year-old. For age $X = 20$,

$$Y = 8.712 + 0.274X - 0.003X^2 = 8.712 + 0.247 \times 20 - 0.003 \times 20^2 = 12.45 \text{ years.}$$

For age 40,

$$Y = 8.712 + 0.274X - 0.003X^2 = 8.712 + 0.247 \times 40 - 0.003 \times 40^2 = 13.79 \text{ years.}$$

For age 70,

$$Y = 8.712 + 0.274X - 0.003X^2 = 8.712 + 0.247 \times 70 - 0.003 \times 70^2 = 11.30 \text{ years.}$$

We can use derivation to find the exact top or bottom point of a graph (where the effect of *age* changes direction). Here, we would be interested in the top point, but the same equation can be used to find the bottom point. For

$$f(x) = ax^2 + bx + c \tag{7.2}$$

where ax^2 is the squared term, bx is the original variable and c is the constant (intercept), the top point occurs at

$$x = \frac{-b}{2a}.$$ (7.3)

Substituting the numbers from our regression (equation (7.1)), we get

$$x = \frac{-0.247}{-0.006} = 41.16.$$

The top point of the graph is 41.16. This is the age where *length of education* is at its highest.

Modelling curvilinearity in Stata

Returning to our dataset *ESS5GBdiagnostics.dta*, we want to explain the causes of trust in the legal system:

```
. regress trstlgl age woman political_interest religious
```

Source	SS	df	MS
Model	532.142701	4	133.035675
Residual	10023.8426	1897	5.28404986
Total	10555.9853	1901	5.55285917

```
Number of obs =    1902
F(  4,  1897) =   25.18
Prob > F      =  0.0000
R-squared     =  0.0504
Adj R-squared =  0.0484
Root MSE      =  2.2987
```

trstlgl	Coef.	Std. Err.	t	P>|t|	[95% Conf. Interval]
age	-.0045918	.0028796	-1.59	0.111	-.0102393 .0010557
woman	-.3239065	.108797	-2.98	0.003	-.5372809 -.1105321
political_interest	.4534565	.0581223	7.80	0.000	.3394662 .5674468
religious	.0892736	.0217054	4.11	0.000	.0467046 .1318426
_cons	4.172909	.2254221	18.51	0.000	3.730808 4.615011

Figure 7.3 Stata output exploring trust in the legal system

The results in Figure 7.3 show a negative and not significant effect of *age*. However, we are not sure if this is modelled correctly, as we might have breached the assumption of linearity. If we suspect that the effect of age is not linear, then we should check this out. We can start by assessing the shape of the bivariate relationship between *age* and *trust* by using the lowess command. This enables us to create a variable that predicts the value based on a locally weighted regression of *age* on *trust*. The lowess command is desirable as it gives us a good representation of the data.[1] We use it primarily to explore the data. We obtain the graph in Figure 7.4.

```
. lowess trstlgl age, nograph gen(yhatlowess)
. line yhatlowess age, sort
```

[1] An alternative to lowess is lpoly which performs a local polynomial regression and displays smoothed values.

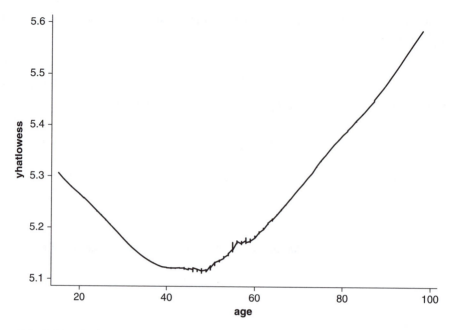

Figure 7.4 Relationship between *age* and *trust*

We see from the graph that there is a convex curvilinear relationship, and we should model this in our regression. With a continuous measure like *age* (which has many values), the best way of doing this is by including a quadratic (squared) term in our model. This can be done by using the interaction operator ##, which multiplies *age* with *age*.[2] Also, we need to specify that *age* is a continuous variable (instead of categorical, which is the default) by writing c.age. We could also have done this by generating a new variable called age2 (generate age2 = age*age) and included this in the regression, which would have yielded the exact same results. However, this would have prevented us from using the margins post-estimation command to graph the relationship. Instead we use the interaction operator and include the other explanatory variables:

```
. regress trstlgl c.age##c.age woman political_interest religious
```

We see from the output in Figure 7.5 that both age terms are significant, showing a convex (U-shaped) curvilinear relationship. If the original variable is negative and the squared term is positive, then we most likely have a convex relationship. If it is the other way around, we most likely are dealing with a concave (inverted U-shaped) relationship. The exceptions are if the form is more like an inverted J or an inverse J (if both terms have the same sign). Now we can use the margins command to plot the effect and obtain Figure 7.6:

```
. margins, at(age=(15(1)98))
. marginsplot
```

---

[2] ## gives us the factorial interaction of (age + age*age), while a single # will produce a single interaction (age*age). In most cases we are interested in the former.

Source	SS	df	MS
Model	574.94511	5	114.989022
Residual	9981.04017	1896	5.26426169
Total	10555.9853	1901	5.55285917

Number of obs = 1902
F(5, 1896) = 21.84
Prob > F = 0.0000
R-squared = 0.0545
Adj R-squared = 0.0520
Root MSE = 2.2944

Effect of age

Effect of age × age

trstlgl	Coef.	Std. Err.	t	P>|t|	[95% Conf. Interval]	
age	-.0467456	.0150601	-3.10	0.002	-.0762818	-.0172095
c.age#c.age	.0004126	.0001447	2.85	0.004	.0001288	.0006964
woman	-.3257212	.108595	-3.00	0.003	-.5386995	-.112743
political_interest	.4723812	.0583918	8.09	0.000	.3578623	.5869
religious	.0864412	.0216875	3.99	0.000	.0439074	.1289751
_cons	5.074485	.3880667	13.08	0.000	4.313403	5.835568

Figure 7.5 Stata output incorporating *age* squared

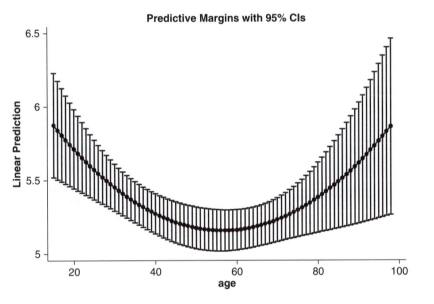

Figure 7.6 Marginsplot of *age* and *trust*

The most common curvilinear relationship encountered in the social sciences can be addressed by the inclusion of a squared term, as done in the example above. Even though the squared term is not significant, we can think of both terms as one substantial variable and thus carry out an F-test comparing one model without *age* and *age²*, and one including both terms. If this shows a significant improvement of the model, we can choose to include the squared term. Also, the reader should remember that including too many polynomial terms (e.g., *age × age × age*) will lead to higher multicollinearity and lower standard errors. It is therefore standard to limit oneself to one polynomial term in a social science model.

We can also model curvilinear relationships when there is statistical interaction. Here we can include both the interaction terms as well as squared interaction terms. For our example, we will test if there is a conditional effect of age and gender on trust, as well as a curvilinear effect of age.

To do this, we need to include both *age × woman*, but also *age × age* and *age × age × woman*. We could have generated these variables and included them in a regression model:

```
. generate woman_age = age*woman
. generate age2 = age*age
. generate age2_woman = age*age*woman
. regress trstlg woman age woman_age age2 age2_woman political_interest
religious
```

However, we will stick to using the `margins` command (the results are exactly the same and are shown in Figure 7.7):

```
regress trstlgl c.age##c.age##i.woman political_interest religious
```

Source	SS	df	MS		Number of obs =	1902
					F(7, 1894) =	15.64
Model	576.785799	7	82.3979713		Prob > F =	0.0000
Residual	9979.19948	1894	5.26884872		R-squared =	0.0546
					Adj R-squared =	0.0511
Total	10555.9853	1901	5.55285917		Root MSE =	2.2954

trstlgl	Coef.	Std. Err.	t	P>|t|	[95% Conf. Interval]	
age	-.0373657	.0236285	-1.58	0.114	-.0837259	.0089946
c.age#c.age	.0003313	.0002306	1.44	0.151	-.0001209	.0007836
1.woman	.0910325	.7326664	0.12	0.901	-1.345885	1.52795
woman#c.age						
1	-.0161969	.0305791	-0.53	0.596	-.0761692	.0437754
woman#c.age#c.age						
1	.0001389	.0002951	0.47	0.638	-.0004399	.0007178
political_interest	.4723383	.0584197	8.09	0.000	.3577645	.5869122
religious	.0870871	.0217246	4.01	0.000	.0444804	.1296938
_cons	4.831897	.577209	8.37	0.000	3.699865	5.963929

Effect of *age*

Effect of *age × age*

Effect of *woman*

Effect of *woman × age*

Effect of *woman × age × age*

Figure 7.7 Regression output using margins, interaction and squared effect

Notice that we have written `c.age` (as it is continuous) and `i.woman` (as it is categorical). The output is somewhat complicated to read, but you must use the same principles as when interpreting a simple interaction between a continuous and categorical variable (see Chapter 6, p. 118). Both men and women get the effect of `age` and `c.age##c.age`, but only women get the effect of `woman`, `woman##c.age` and `woman##c.age##c.age`. The table shows that the proposed interaction is not significant, but we can still graph the effect (see Figure 7.8):

```
. margins, at (age=(15(1)98) woman=(0 1))
. marginsplot
```

Curvilinearity with two bends

We may encounter data where there are two bends in the relationship. In such a case, we can include *age*, *age × age* and *age × age × age*. We will now explore the relationship between age

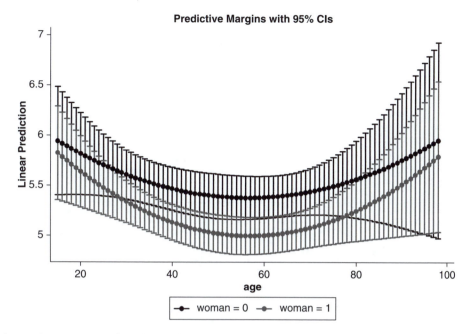

Figure 7.8 Interaction and curvilinear effect

and how happy the respondent is. Our dependent variable *happy* ranges from 0 to 10. We follow the same procedure as earlier, using the lowess command:

```
. lowess happy age, nograph gen(yhatlowess2)
. line yhatlowess2 age, sort
```

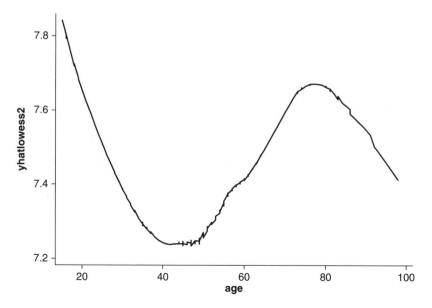

Figure 7.9 Curvilinear effect with two bends

Figure 7.9 shows that there are two bends in the bivariate relationship between how old and how happy the respondent is. Using the `margins` commands we can now model (Figure 7.10) and graph (Figure 7.11) the relationship:

. regress happy c.age##c.age##c.age woman political_interest religious

Source	SS	df	MS		Number of obs	=	1,968
					F(6, 1961)	=	10.45
Model	210.540198	6	35.0900329		Prob > F	=	0.0000
Residual	6583.70167	1,961	3.35731855		R-squared	=	0.0310
					Adj R-squared	=	0.0280
Total	6794.24187	1,967	3.45411381		Root MSE	=	1.8323

happy	Coef.	Std. Err.	t	P>|t|	[95% Conf. Interval]	
age	-.2012868	.0417848	-4.82	0.000	-.2832341	-.1193395
c.age#c.age	.0038114	.0008525	4.47	0.000	.0021396	.0054832
c.age#c.age#c.age	-.000022	5.39e-06	-4.08	0.000	-.0000326	-.0000114
woman	.0022172	.0857334	0.03	0.979	-.1659208	.1703553
political_interest	.0661554	.0456159	1.45	0.147	-.0233053	.1556161
religious	.0921023	.0170106	5.41	0.000	.0587415	.125463
_cons	9.961683	.6295115	15.82	0.000	8.727102	11.19627

Figure 7.10 Regression output using margins, squared effect

. margins, at(age=(15(1)98))
. marginsplot

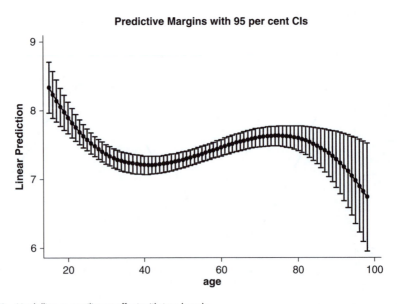

Predictive Margins with 95 per cent CIs

Figure 7.11 Modelling a curvilinear effect with two bends

Using dummy variables to model nonlinearity

In order to square a variable it needs to be continuous with several values. Sometimes we are dealing with variables where there is a curvilinear effect, but the explanatory variable has few values, so it might be an idea to model the relationship through dummy variables. For example, if we are investigating the relationship between self-placement on a political left–right scale (*lrscale*, 0–10), where high values denote a rightist respondent) and age when the respondent completed full-time education, we might find that there is no significant linear effect:

```
. regress edagegb woman religious lrscale
```

Source	SS	df	MS		Number of obs	=	1,616
					F(3, 1612)	=	1.34
Model	45.6492119	3	15.216404		Prob > F	=	0.2585
Residual	18252.4789	1,612	11.3228777		R-squared	=	0.0025
					Adj R-squared	=	0.0006
Total	18298.1281	1,615	11.3301103		Root MSE	=	3.3649

edagegb	Coef.	Std. Err.	t	P>|t|	[95% Conf. Interval]	
woman	-.0430257	.1704685	-0.25	0.801	-.377389	.2913375
religious	.0568193	.0343665	1.65	0.098	-.0105884	.124227
lrscale	-.0567907	.0447401	-1.27	0.205	-.1445455	.0309641
_cons	17.50897	.2981823	58.72	0.000	16.9241	18.09383

Figure 7.12   Effect of left–right attitudes on education

Figure 7.12 shows that the more rightist the respondent is, the lower his/her age was on leaving education, but the relationship is not significant. A reasonable assumption here would be that persons defining themselves as belonging to the political centre would have more education than those situated at the political extremes – in other words, a curvilinear effect. We can model this either by including the square of lrscale or by introducing dummy variables for belonging to the political extremes:[3]

```
. regress edagegb woman religious c.lrscale##c.lrscale
. margins, at(lrscale=(0(1)10))
. marginsplot, noci

. generate Dleft = (lrscale < 3) if !missing(lrscale)
. generate Dcentre = (lrscale > 2 & lrscale < 8) if !missing(lrscale)
. generate Dright = (lrscale > 7) if !missing(lrscale)
. regress edagegb woman religious Dleft Dright
```

---

[3] If the number of categories is reasonable we can test for nonlinearity with: `regress edagegb woman religious i.lrscale`

7●1●3 Additivity

We briefly touched upon the subject of additivity in the previous section (and Chapter 6), as we modelled a nonlinear interaction effect. The assumption on additivity means that the change in Y for a one-unit increase in X_i is the same regardless of the values of the other X-variables. This assumption is breached if the slope for one X-variable differs depending on your value on another X-variable (as shown in Figure 7.13). It can be addressed by including an interaction term composed of the two relevant X-variables. Statistical interaction is thoroughly explained in Chapter 6.

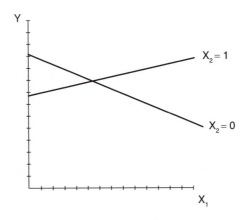

Figure 7.13 Interaction effect

7●1●4 Absence of multicollinearity

This assumption implies that two X-variables in the same model cannot be perfectly correlated, and that one X-variable cannot be perfectly explained by a linear combination of other X-variables in our model. Problems can also arise if correlations are over about 0.8, for example that the coefficients cannot be easily interpreted and the variables will steal explanatory power from each other. This can result in standard errors that are too low and difficulties in assessing the relative importance of the different explanatory variables. The essence here is that you should not include X-variables that measure the same phenomenon (either statistical or theoretical). The best solution to the problem of multicollinearity is to understand the cause of it and remove it. You should either exclude one of the variables (if they measure the same phenomenon, this is no great loss to the model), or, if possible, collapse the variables into a scale or index. The latter option is especially relevant for individual social science data in which batteries of questions are hinting at the same underlying phenomenon. One can test the possibility of scale construction by means of reliability analysis (Cronbach's alpha[4] and factor analysis; see Chapter 11).

---

[4] The command for Cronbach's alpha is `alpha v1 v2 v3`. If the scale reliability coefficient is > 0.7 it is considered acceptable to construct a scale of the included variables (given that they measure the same underlying factor; see Chapter 11).

We can test this by letting each X-variable be a dependent variable in a regression including all the other X-variables. By taking $1 - R^2$ in such a regression we get what is called the tolerance value. If the tolerance value is below about 0.2, then we have a problem with multicollinearity. There is no clear rule on what constitutes too much multicollinearity (e.g., we accept lower tolerance values for interaction terms, squared terms, and the variables that constitute them). Yet, multicollinearity could be a symptom of a model problem, for example if you include per capita GDP and the Human Development Index (HDI) in the same model (since the HDI includes per capita gross national income). If this is the case, we clearly have to remove one of the variables. In other cases, one could argue that since multicollinearity mainly gives the effect of having a lower sample size (meaning that it produces larger standard errors) you could go ahead with the regression. Nevertheless, the general rule is to try to avoid tolerance values below 0.2 (except for models including interactions or polynomials).

We get the variance inflation factor (VIF) and tolerance values by running the command `estat vif` after a regression. If the VIF value is more than 5 for any variable, we may have a multicollinearity problem. The VIF and tolerance measure the same thing (as tolerance = 1/VIF), and we will focus on the latter as its interpretation is more intuitive. The `vif` command can only be run after a linear regression, so in the case of a logistic regression (or any other model) you can just run the model as a linear model and then test for multicollinearity (see Figure 7.14):

```
. quietly regress trstlgl age woman political_interest religious
. estat vif
```

Variable	VIF	1/VIF
religious	1.07	0.935108
woman	1.04	0.959921
political_~t	1.04	0.962326
age	1.03	0.968541
Mean VIF	1.05	

Figure 7.14 Tolerance values

For a more detailed examination of multicollinearity we could examine the variance–covariance matrix after running the regression:[5]

```
. estat vce
```

If we include a squared term or an interaction term we will naturally get multicollinearity. This is something we might have to accept, as it leads to a better model (due to the assumptions of linearity and additivity). However, we should be careful about accepting multicollinearity in other instances.

---

[5] It is also possible to graph the matrix for visual identification: `graph matrix trstlgl age woman political_interest religious`

7●2 ASSUMPTIONS ABOUT RESIDUALS

This part of our discussion on regression assumptions includes the classic Gauss–Markov assumptions in addition to the assumption about normally distributed errors. As in Section 7.1, we will guide you through each assumption, explaining the logic behind it and how to test for it.

7●2●1 That the error term has a conditional mean of zero

The error term ε_i has a mean of zero given any values of the independent variables, or

$$E(\varepsilon_i \mid X_1, \ldots, X_n) = 0. \tag{7.4}$$

This assumption means that the distances between the actual data points and the regression line are random (some are over and some are under the line), and that the mean/expected value is zero. In other words, the total distance from the data points above the line to the line should be the same as the total distance from the data points below the line to the line (see Figure 7.15).

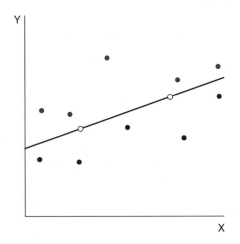

Figure 7.15 The error term has zero mean

This will always be the case in the sample due to the qualities of the least-squares method. It is therefore not necessary to test directly for this. If we have a non-zero mean of the errors and fit a least-squares model, the non-zero mean will be absorbed by the constant term and the residuals will be zero in our model. However, in that case OLS would no longer necessarily be the best estimator. That is, our parameters would not be representative of the population parameters (even though our model has $E(\varepsilon_i \mid X_1, \ldots, X_n) = 0$). This could be due to X-variables being not strictly exogenous, as the explanatory variables should be uncorrelated with the errors, and can be discovered when testing for homoscedasticity or autocorrelation (see Sections 7.2.2 and 7.2.3).

7•2•2 Homoscedasticity

Homoscedasticity is the assumption that the error term has constant variance, or

$$\mathrm{var}(\varepsilon_i \mid X_1,\ldots,X_n) = \sigma_u^2, \quad 0 < \sigma_u^2 < \infty. \tag{7.5}$$

This is important for valid statistical generalization of the results from the sample to the population. Homoscedasticity means that variance in the residuals must be the same for units regardless of their predicted values (see Figure 7.16). For example, if the model predicts values better for those with low values than for those with high values on Y (or vice versa), this assumption is breached and we have a situation of heteroscedasticity. In other words, the variance of the outcome variable should be stable at all levels of the predictor variable. The presence of heteroscedasticity (which means the absence of homoscedasticity) will create a bias in the estimates of standard errors in your model.

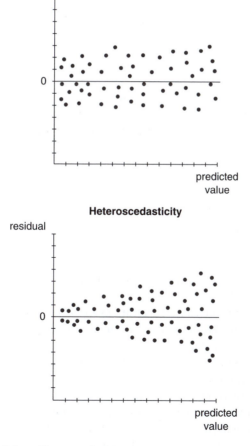

Figure 7.16 Homoscedasticity and heteroscedasticity

There are two ways we can check for heteroscedasticity in Stata. First, we can examine a plot of the predicted values versus the residuals:

```
. quietly regress trstlgl age woman political_interest religious
. rvfplot
```

Ideally such a plot should not show any pattern. Often we will have a degree of heteroscedasticity associated with our model, but the question is whether we consider this problematic. To get a numerical measure of the degree of heteroscedasticity (and whether we can call it significant or not) we can run the Breusch and Pagan (1979) or Cook and Weisberg (1983) test for heteroscedasticity. This test estimates the variance of Y from the average of squared values of the residuals. It is a chi-squared test of the null hypothesis that we have homoscedastic residuals in our model, so if the p-value is less than 0.05 it means that we have a problem with heteroscedasticity:

```
. estat hettest

        Breusch-Pagan / Cook-Weisberg test for heteroskedasticity
                Ho: Constant variance
                Variables: fitted values of trstlgl

                chi2(1)      =      0.00
                Prob > chi2  =    0.9707
```

We see that the Prob > chi2 value is much greater than 0.05, and we can conclude that we do not have a problem with heteroscedasticity in our model. If we should have a problem with heteroscedasticity one solution is to use robust standard errors (as described in Chapter 10, p. 235).

7●2●3 Uncorrelated errors

This assumption states that the errors should be uncorrelated for different observations and with the X-variables:

$$E(\varepsilon_i \varepsilon_j \,|\, X_1,...,X_n) = 0, \quad i \neq j. \tag{7.6}$$

This assumption can be breached if the observations are dependent on each other, for example if we are dealing with nested data (multilevel, panel, time series). If the errors are correlated we call this autocorrelation (which reflects connections among cases). This should not be a problem if we are dealing with cross-sectional data that are a random sample of a population. But it can occur with time series or with geographical data, as the observations are not always independent (last year's value influences today's value, or the value for Mississippi value is related to that for Alabama). If we have either a time or geographical nesting of the data, we can use the Durbin–Watson (Durbin and Watson, 1950, 1951) test. In order to carry out this test, we need to 'time-set' (tsset) the data according to a time variable (if we have time series data) or a geographical variable. We now open the dataset called *Durbin_Watson. dta* where the observations are yearly observations from the USA. Then we run a regression explaining foreign direct investment as a function of per capita GDP, GDP growth and presence of conflict:

```
. tsset year
. quietly regress FDI GDPperCapita GDPGrowth incidence
. estat dwatson
```

The third line produces the following output:

```
. estat dwatson

Durbin-Watson d-statistic(  4,    27) =  .8928362
```

The test statistic *d* is a function of 27 observations and four parameters in our model. We operate with two critical values, d_L (lower) and d_U (upper). If we look in a table of critical values for the Durbin–Watson test, we find that $d_L = 1.18$ and $d_U = 1.65$. Our critical value of 0.893 is smaller than both critical values and thus we can reject the null hypothesis of no positive autocorrelation (i.e., we do have a problem with correlated errors). If our test observation should be between d_L and d_U the test is inconclusive. For more discussion on tests for serial correlation, see Chapter 10.

7•2•4 Normally distributed errors

The assumption of normally distributed errors is necessary for valid statistical generalization in small samples:

$$\varepsilon_i \sim N(0,\sigma^2), \quad \text{for all } i. \tag{7.7}$$

However, highly skewed distributions of either the dependent variable or the residuals will most often be problematic. Normally distributed errors are not necessary for OLS regression to be the best linear unbiased estimate, but it can lead to invalid *t*- and *F*-statistics (especially with small samples) and reduce the efficiency of OLS regression.

In order to check the residuals, we must first save them after running a regression. We open the dataset *ESSGBdiagnostics.dta*:

```
. quietly regress trstlgl age woman political_interest religious
. predict res, residual
```

We have saved the residuals as a variable. First we can run a histogram, displaying the normal curve (Figure 7.17):

```
. histogram res, normal
```

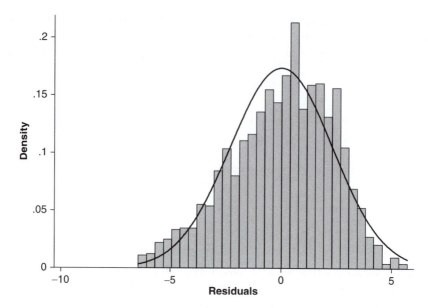

Figure 7.17 Histogram of residuals

We can also look at the skewness and kurtosis values. In a perfectly normal distribution the skewness should be 0 and kurtosis should be 3 (for more on this, see Chapter 13):

```
. summarize res, detail
```

```
                              Residuals

            Percentiles        Smallest
  1%         -5.638871         -6.445363
  5%         -4.200909         -6.307609
 10%         -3.121597         -6.266284        Obs                  1902
 25%         -1.515425         -6.258616        Sum of Wgt.          1902

 50%          .2627242                          Mean            2.05e-09
                                 Largest        Std. Dev.       2.296286
 75%          1.704694          5.242521
 90%          2.778896           5.42769        Variance        5.272931
 95%          3.397863          5.627698        Skewness       -.3750581
 99%          4.379029          5.714409        Kurtosis        2.677971
```

Figure 7.18 Summary statistics of residuals

We can see from both the graph in Figure 7.17 and the statistics in Figure 7.18 that the residuals of our model are approximately normally distributed. Using the sktest we can test if the skewness and kurtosis values are significantly different from what they would be had they been normally distributed:[6]

---
[6] sktest implements a test that compares the skewness and kurtosis values against a normal distribution using a chi-square distribution.

					joint	
		Skewness/Kurtosis tests for Normality				
Variable		Obs	Pr(Skewness)	Pr(Kurtosis)	adj chi2(2)	Prob>chi2
res		1,902	0.0000	0.0008	45.19	0.0000

The test is significant (which means that our residuals are significantly different from a normal distribution). However, there are two reasons why we should not set too much store by this test. First, our large sample ($N = 1902$) contributes to the test being significant. Second, our large N makes it less critical to have normally distributed errors. Here, we should rather look at the plot in Figure 7.17 and the skewness and kurtosis values and conclude that we do not have a problem with non-normally distributed errors.

Alternatives to sktest are the Shapiro–Wilk normality test swilk (if $N < 2000$) and the Shapiro–Wilk test sfrancia (if $N < 5000$).

 7.3 INFLUENTIAL OBSERVATIONS

Many influential observations are what we can call 'outliers', that is, observations that have either unusual values on one or more variables (possibly both on X and Y), or unusual combinations on several variables. We can distinguish between observations with unusual values and observations that have great influence on the result of a model (but in many cases we are talking about the same observations). An observation can be described as being influential if its exclusion alters the results of the regression substantially. Such outliers can affect the calculation of the slope coefficients, standard errors and R^2.

We will look at three different measures of influential units: the leverage (unusual combinations of values on different explanatory variables), DFBETA (each observation's influence on each X-variable) and Cook's distance (each observation's influence on the model as a whole).

7.3.1 Leverage

Leverage tells us the *potential* for influence which is the result of unusual combinations of values on X-variables. We use the *hat statistic* to calculate the leverage of a covariate pattern. This ranges from $1/N$ to 1. A large value on the hat statistic indicates a pattern of X-variables that is far from the average covariance pattern. The influence of an observation with a given leverage value on the regression line depends on its Y-value (as leverage is a measure of the X-variables and the potential influence on the model). If the Y-value is consistent with the pattern of the rest of the sample, deleting this observation does not substantially change the regression line. However, if the Y-value is much lower or higher than the general pattern, the regression line can shift substantially when deleting the observation (see also Hamilton, 1992: 131).

We now open the dataset *Influential_units.dta* which is a cross-section of countries in 2011. First we run a regression explaining the log-transformed foreign direct investment in a country as a function of per capita GDP, GDP growth, incidence of war and ethnic fractionalization. Then we predict the hat statistic, and produce a box plot labelling the outliers according to their country name:

```
. quietly regress lnFDI GDPperCapita GDPGrowth incidence ethfrac
. predict h if e(sample), hat
. graph box h, mark (1, mlab(ccode))
```

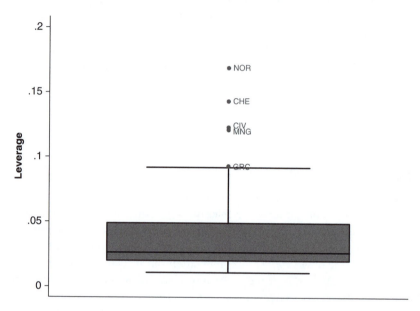

Figure 7.19 Leverage plot

We can see from Figure 7.19 that Norway is the country that is potentially most influential in our model. According to Huber (1981), leverage values larger than 0.5 should be avoided, and values between 0.2 and 0.5 are risky. The reason is that too much of the sample's information comes from that observation. Values below 0.2 are considered safe. In our example no countries are considered risky. We can anyways check if removing Norway has any substantial influence on our model (which it should not, as the leverage value was less than 0.2):

```
. regress lnFDI GDPperCapita GDPGrowth incidence ethfrac
. regress lnFDI GDPperCapita GDPGrowth incidence ethfrac if ccode!="NOR"
```

7●3●2 DFBETA

The dfbeta command calculates the DFBETA for the variables we choose after running a regression. This is a measure of each observation's effect on each regression coefficient. More specifically, it tells us the difference between the regression coefficient when a given observation is included/excluded in/from the model. Even more specifically, it tells us by how many standard errors of the coefficient the slope differs. If the reported value for an observation is positive the unit pulls the coefficient upwards, if the value is negative it pulls it downwards. The larger the absolute value the greater the influence of a particular observation. We run the regression, save the DFBETA values for each of the four explanatory variables, and produce a box plot for each variable labelling the observations after a relevant identifier variable:

```
. quietly regress lnFDI GDPperCapita GDPGrowth incidence ethfrac
. dfbeta GDPperCapita GDPGrowth incidence ethfrac
. graph box _dfbeta_1 _dfbeta_2 _dfbeta_3 _dfbeta_4, marker(1, mlab(ccode))
marker(2, mlab(ccode)) marker(3, mlab(ccode)) marker(4, mlab(ccode))
```

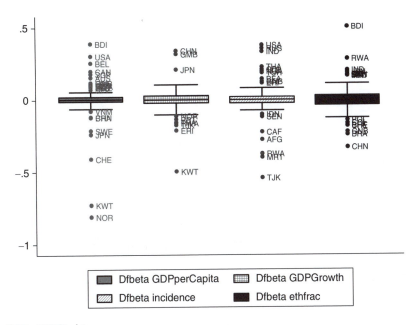

Figure 7.20 DFBETA plot

We see from Figure 7.20 that different observations are outliers on the different X-variables. According to Belsley et al. (1980) there some criteria for whether we can consider the DFBETA value to be too large. First, they suggest that if a unit has a larger value than 2 it has too much influence on that particular variable. However, a good strategy is to produce a box plot (like the one in Figure 7.20) and see if any observations stand out, perhaps on more than one explanatory variable (like BDI, which stands for Bangladesh). Then we can try to run a new model with strange cases removed and see if the results change substantially.

7•3•3 Cook's distance

To measure an observation's influence on our model as a whole we employ Cook's distance. This increases with the size of the standardized residual and the leverage. According to

Hamilton (1992), there are two ways of identifying unusually influential cases. First, we can use an absolute cut-off if Cook's distance is greater than 1. Second, we can use a size-adjusted cut-off, that is, influential cases will have a Cook's distance greater than 4/N. In our regression 4/N = 4/137 = 0.029:

```
. quietly regress lnFDI GDPperCapita GDPGrowth incidence ethfrac
. predict cooksd if e(sample), cooksd
. graph box cooksd, mark(1, mlab(ccode))
```

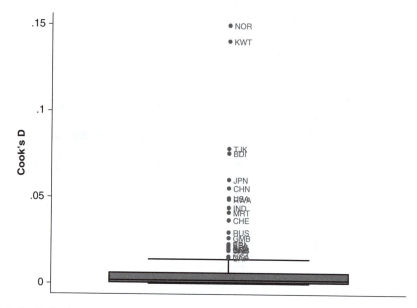

Figure 7.21 Cook's distance plot

We see that our box plot in Figure 7.21 identifies Norway (NOR) and Kuwait (KWT) as being the observations that exert most influence on our regression model. To identify which observations fall above our size-adjusted cut-off we run the following commands, which yield Figure 7.22:

```
. gsort -cooksd
. list ccode cooksd if cooksd >4/_N & e(sample)
```

Our suggestion is to follow the absolute cut-off of 1 rather than the size-adjusted cut-off. You could, however, try to run the regression again with the one or two most influential cases removed. A common strategy in research is to run two separate models, and present one in the appendix (which one should be your main model is also a theoretical question). Even though some observations exert too much influence on the model, they are also a part of the data material (for more on influential units, see also Chapter 13). If the outliers are due to bad

	ccode	cooksd
1.	NOR	.1497058
2.	KWT	.1403551
3.	TJK	.078076
4.	BDI	.0755098
5.	JPN	.0602023
6.	CHN	.0553728
7.	USA	.0495966
8.	RWA	.0488876
9.	IND	.0439449
10.	MRT	.0412257
11.	CHE	.0367208
12.	RUS	.0296731
13.	GMB	.0265119
14.	ERI	.0229048
15.	BFA	.0224502
16.	AFG	.0213804

Figure 7.22 Influential cases

data (punching errors or outright wrong data) then they can be removed; in other instances, the separate models option makes more sense.

7 ● 4 CONCLUSION

In this chapter we have explained the assumptions of ordinary least-squares regression, and how to test these using Stata. We looked at the assumptions concerning the model specification, the assumptions concerning the residuals, and how to detect influential observations. We have given special attention to the assumption on linearity in the parameters and how to model nonlinear relationships.

We have also created a package called `regcheck`, which examines all the regression assumptions with one easy command (including influential units, treated in Section 7.3). This package can be installed by writing:

```
. ssc install regcheck
```

Running `regcheck` after a regression produces output on how your model adheres to the assumptions of homoscedasticity, multicollinearity, normally distributed residuals, correctly specified model, appropriate functional form and influential cases. We open the dataset ESS5 GBdiagnostics.dta and:

```
. quietly regress trstlgl age woman political_interest religious
. regcheck
```

key terms

Gauss–Markov conditions A set of regression assumptions presented attributed to Karl F. Gauss and Andrei Markov.

Curvilinearity This is a type of relationship where the effect of a one-unit increase in X_i differs depending on the value of X_r

Homoscedasticity This means that the error term has constant variance, regardless of the predicted values.

Autocorrelation This refers to correlations between values of the same variables across different units, which is often associated with autocorrelated residuals.

Cook's distance This is a measure of the influence of a given observation on our last run regression model.

QUESTIONS

1   What are the assumptions of ordinary least-squares regression?
2   Name two ways of modelling nonlinear relationships.
3   What measure do we use to test for an observations influence on a given explanatory variable?

FURTHER READING

Berry, W.D. (1993) *Understanding Regression Assumptions*. Newbury Park, CA: Sage.

Part of the Sage series on quantitative applications in the social sciences, this book both presents the regression assumptions and goes into detail about the substantive meaning of each assumption.

Fox, J. (1991) *Regression Diagnostics*. Newbury Park, CA: Sage.

Part of the Sage series on quantitative applications in the social sciences, this book covers the different tests of regression diagnostics.

Hamilton, L.C. (1992) *Regression with Graphics: A Second Course in Applied Statistics*. Belmont, CA: Duxbury.

The chapter on 'Regression Criticism' gives a good explanation of the assumptions, above the level of an introductory text, yet still accessible for those without a mathematical background.

REFERENCES

Belsley, D.A., Kuh, E. and Welsh, R.E. (1980) *Regression Diagnostics: Identifying Influential Data and Sources of Collinearity*. New York: John Wiley & Sons.
Breusch, T.S. and Pagan, A.R. (1979) A simple test for heteroskedasticity and random coefficient variation. *Econometrica*, 47(5), 1287–1294.

Cook, R.D. and Weisberg, S. (1983) Diagnostics for heteroskedasticity in regression. *Biometrika*, 70(1), 1–10.

Durbin, J. and Watson, G.S. (1950) Testing for serial correlation in least squares regression, I. *Biometrika*, 37(3–4), 409–428.

Durbin, J. and Watson, G.S. (1951) Testing for serial correlation in least squares regression, II. *Biometrika*, 38(1–2), 159–179.

Hamilton, L.C. (1992) *Regression with Graphics: A Second Course in Applied Statistics*. Belmont, CA: Duxbury Press.

Huber, P.J. (1981) *Robust Statistics*. New York: John Wiley & Sons.

Ramsey, J.B. (1969) Tests for specification errors in classical linear least squares regression analysis. *Journal of the Royal Statistical Society, Series B*, 31(2), 350–371.

8

LOGISTIC REGRESSION

 learning outcomes

- o Understand the logic behind logistic regression
- o Interpret logistic regression output correctly, including conditional effects
- o Understand how to model categorical variables with more than two categories
- o Understand how to model ordinal dependent variables

A prerequisite of OLS regression is that the dependent variable is continuous. However, sometimes researchers wish to investigate whether a certain phenomenon is present or not, which means that the dependent variable only has two values. This means that we face several problems when using ordinary least squares. First, we cannot have a linear association between X and Y. Second, there will be heteroscedasticity present. Third, we risk predicting values that fall outside the 0–1 interval. Therefore, if we are investigating a dichotomous dependent variable, the method of choice is logistic regression. In this chapter we guide the reader through the basics of logistic regression and how to perform and interpret it in Stata. We also take a look at how to treat dependent variables with more than two categories as well as ordinal variables.

This method can be traced to Pierre-François Verhulst's (1838) demonstration of growth curves in France, Belgium, Essex and Russia, which he later named the logistic function (Verhulst, 1845). Today researchers employ this function to investigate dependent variables with only two values. It is also possible to do regression analysis on categorical variables with more than two values (multinomial regression) or with categorical variables with more than two values that can be ordered logically (ordered logit regression). Both of these methods are variants of logistic regression and are described later in this chapter.

The logistic (or logit) regression model gives the calculated probability of the dependent variable having the value 1 (and not 0), given the values on the explanatory variables.[1] This logit model is estimated by maximum likelihood rather than by least squares.[2] This maximum likelihood estimation gives the estimates for the model's parameters. In other words, we estimate the parameters as those which would make our data most likely.

---

[1] The numerical values are arbitrary and not intrinsically of interest. The important matter is which of the two categories the units fall into. Logistic models are similar to probit models. The main difference between these methods lies in the assumption about the distribution of error terms in the model. In practice, both models work fine and often lead to the same conclusions.

[2] Maximum likelihood estimation (MLE) was developed by Sir Ronald Fischer (1912, 1922). Fisher presented the numerical procedure in 1912 with his 'absolute criterion' and ended up with the method of maximum likelihood in 1922. Some years earlier Francis Edgeworth (1908) had presented similar ideas. The maximum likelihood estimate can be described as the hypothetical population value that maximizes the likelihood of the observed sample. In an OLS regression model it is identical to OLS; however, for categorical dependent variables it becomes helpful in order to calculate how the likelihood of having $Y=1$ varies with the different values of our explanatory variables. For an introduction to the logic behind MLE, see Wonnacott and Wonnacott (1990: 564–578). The reason why MLE is preferred to OLS is that as we are dealing with a dichotomous dependent variable the assumptions of homoscedasticity, linearity and normality are violated, and the least-squares estimates will be inefficient and will often produce estimates outside the 0–1 range.

8.1 WHAT IS LOGISTIC REGRESSION?

In linear regression, the parameter estimate tells us how much the dependent variable changes for a one-unit change in X. In logit regression, on the other hand, one estimates how much the *natural logarithm* of the *odds* for $Y = 1$ changes for each one-unit change in X.[3] $P(Y = 1)$ tells us the probability that the dependent variable (which is dichotomous, 0–1) equals 1. The probability that Y does not equal 1 is $P(Y \neq 1) = P(Y = 0) = 1 - P(Y = 1)$.

However, we have to go through certain steps before we reach the intuitive concept of probability. If we had used OLS regression to model the probability of $Y = 1$ we would have ended up with predicted values that could be less than 0 or greater than 1. In order to achieve a linear function we use the natural logarithm of the odds for $Y = 1$. Odds are another (less intuitive) way of expressing probability.[4] The odds (ϕ) favouring $Y = 1$ are

$$\varphi(Y = 1) = \frac{P(Y = 1)}{1 - P(Y = 1)}. \tag{8.1}$$

The odds range from 0 (when $P(Y = 1) = 0$) to ∞ (infinity, when $P(Y = 1) = 1$). Since this will not produce a linear function in the model, we get a *logit* by calculating the natural logarithm of the odds:

$$L = \ln\varphi = \ln\left(\frac{P}{1 - P}\right). \tag{8.2}$$

The logit ranges from $-\infty$ (when $P(Y = 1) = 0$) to ∞ (when $P(Y = 1) = 1$). When we make it linear in the axiomatic definition of the logit model, it will still be linear in its parameters (see Figure 8.1).

In OLS regression we know that the coefficient tells us how much the dependent variable changes for a one-unit increase in the independent variable. However, in logistic regression the direct interpretation is not as intuitive, as the logit (L)[5] shows us the change in the natural logarithm of the odds for $(Y = 1)$ for a one-step change in the independent variable. Also, the effect of a change in the probability will differ depending on where you are situated on the total predicted logit (calculated from the intercept and all the logits of all X-variables). In other words, the effect of one X-variable is conditioned on the scores of the other X-variables. The equation for a logistic model can be written as

$$L_i = \beta_0 + \beta_1 X_{1i} + \beta_2 X_{2i} + \beta_3 X_{3i} + \ldots + \beta_{k-1} X_{k-1,i}, \tag{8.3}$$

where the logit (the total logit) is a linear function of the X-variables. k is the number of parameters in the model (the constant and all X-variables). As illustrated in Figure 8.1, the logit ranges from $-\infty$ to ∞. We use this logit as it is not possible to predict probabilities directly. We can, however, calculate the total logit and transform it to probabilities. Since probability has an S-shape and the logit has a linear shape, a change in the logit (e.g., in the effect of one X-variable) has a different effect on the probability depending on where we are on the logit scale (see Figure 8.2).

---

[3] The natural logarithm of a number is its logarithm to the mathematical constant e (2.71828…). For example, the natural logarithm of 10 is 2.3026 because $10 = e^{2.3026} = 2.71828^{2.3026}$.

[4] The odds that $Y = 1$ is the ratio of the probability that $Y = 1$ to the probability that $Y = 0$.

[5] Keep in mind that we use the term logit (L) for two things: the logit for each X-variable and the total logit when predicting a unit's total score on the logit from a regression.

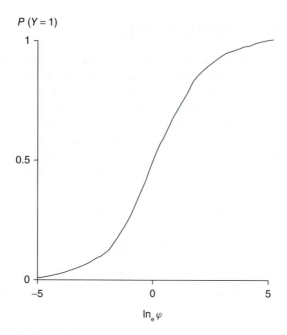

Figure 8.1 Probability and the logit function

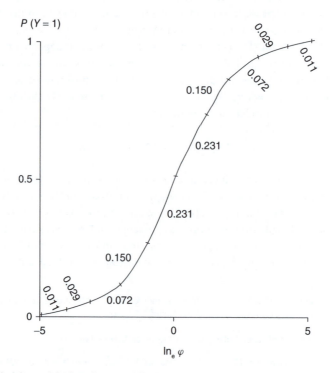

Figure 8.2 Probability and the logit function, differences in effects

Table 8.1 Logits and probabilities

Logit	Probability
5	0.993
4	0.982
3	0.953
2	0.881
1	0.731
0	0.500
−1	0.269
−2	0.119
−3	0.047
−4	0.018
−5	0.007

This is also illustrated by calculating a table of different total logit values and the corresponding probabilities (of $Y = 1$; see Table 8.1). We see that if $L = 0$ then $p = 0.5$, if $L > 0$ then $p > 0.5$, and if $L < 0$ then $p < 0.5$. It is also relatively easy to convert the calculated logit (from a regression equation with given values) back to odds, and then to the more intuitive probabilities. First, we transform from logit (L) to odds:

$$\varphi(Y = 1) = e^L = e^{\beta_0 + \beta_1 X_{1i} + \beta_2 X_{2i} + \beta_3 X_{3i} + \ldots + \beta_{k-1} X_{k-1,i}}. \tag{8.4}$$

Then we can transform the odds to probability (p):

$$p = \frac{\varphi}{1 + \varphi}. \tag{8.5}$$

We can also skip a step and calculate directly from logit to probability:

$$p = \frac{1}{1 + e^{-L}}. \tag{8.6}$$

So, for example, for a logit of −2.4, we would have

$$p = \frac{1}{1 + e^{-(-2.4)}} = 0.083;$$

for a logit of 3.1,

$$p = \frac{1}{1 + e^{-3.1}} = 0.957.$$

In the Stata output we can also ask for the *odds ratio* (OR) instead of the logit coefficient in the output. This is the exponential of the logit and tells us the change in odds (for $Y = 1$) if we move one step up on the X-variable (whether it is a categorical or a continuous measure):

$$OR = \frac{\text{odds after a unit change in } X}{\text{original odds}}. \tag{8.7}$$

An OR of 1.000 means that there is no change (i.e., no effect of that variable). If the OR is 1.240 it means that the odds for $Y = 1$ increases by 24 per cent for each step up on the independent variable. If the OR is 0.83 it means that it decreases by 17 per cent. Thus, the stronger the relation the farther the OR will be from 1.

8•1•1 Tests of significance

The probability of being mistaken when we reject a null hypothesis (which states that there is no relationship between two measured phenomena) is shown as a *p*-value in the coefficient table. The closer a *p*-value is to 0, the more certain we can be of not rejecting a true null hypothesis when accepting our own alternative hypothesis. There are several methods for testing the null hypothesis in logistic regression.[6] One is the likelihood ratio test (for comparing two models), which is regarded as best for evaluating the significance of individual variables (Menard, 2002). In this test, we compare two logistic regression models, one with and one without the variable being tested. A drawback with the likelihood ratio test is that it requires more time to calculate.

However, Stata provides us with the *z*-statistics for the individual coefficients in the output:

$$z = \left(\frac{b_1}{SE(b_1)} \right). \tag{8.8}$$

This *z*-statistic is the ratio of the parameter estimate and its standard error;[7] it is also known as the Wald statistic (Wald, 1943). It is similar in form to the *t*-statistic in linear regression (Hosmer et al., 2013), but follows a standard normal distribution, while its square follows a chi-squared (χ^2) distribution. A drawback of the Wald test is that if b is large the standard error is inflated, thus increasing the chance of committing a Type II error.[8]

The *log-likelihood* (LL) is parallel to the *F*-test in least-squares regression (see Chapter 4). The LL is the criterion for selecting parameters in our logistic model. Stata presents the *log-likelihood* in the logistic regression output. It is a negative value, and the smaller this negative value is, the better our prediction of our dependent variable. In order to carry out the test we have to multiply the log-likelihood by −2. This −2LL is positive, and the larger the value, the worse the prediction of our dependent variable. We can use the

---

[6] In the statistical package SPSS, the Wald statistic is reported as z^2, which has a chi-square distribution.

[7] The distribution of the test statistic is approximated by a normal distribution if $n > 30$, as opposed to the *t*-statistic which is assumed to have a *t*-distribution.

[8] Failure of rejecting a false null hypothesis.

likelihood ratio test to compare two logistic models.[9] Here we look at the difference in log-likelihood between two models estimated on the same data material (i.e., ideally the two models should have the same N):

$$\chi_h^2 = -2\left(LL_{k-h} - LL_k\right).$$ (8.9)

Here LL_{k-h} is the LL value for the model with fewer parameters (restricted) and LL_k is the LL value for the larger model (unrestricted). h is the difference in number of parameters between the two models. The calculated test statistic will, if the null hypothesis of no difference between the models is correct, approximately follow a chi-squared (χ^2) distribution with h degrees of freedom. If the number is larger than the corresponding number in the chi-squared table, the larger model is a significant improvement over the smaller model. An easy way to see if one model is a significant improvement over another is to use the `logtest` command:

```
. ssc install logtest
. logtest, m1(Y X1 X2) m2(Y X1 X2 X3)
```

In OLS regression R^2 measures the overall fit of our model (see Chapter 4). We can calculate the R^2 in logistic regression. However, as this is dependent on the Wald statistic it is not a precise measure. There is an ongoing discussion over what would make a good analogue to the R^2 in logistic regression, and several measures have been proposed. However, we should treat these with some caution, as R^2 is not recommended for comparing non-nested models. There is no general agreement as to which R^2 measure is best for logistic regression. Stata presents McFadden's (1974) *pseudo R^2*. This measure treats the log-likelihood of the intercept model as a total sum of squares, and the log-likelihood of the full model as the sum of squared errors. The ratio of likelihoods tells us the improvement of our model over the empty model. For two models with the same data, the R^2 is higher for the model with the higher likelihood.

8 2 ASSUMPTIONS OF LOGISTIC REGRESSION

In logistic regression, four assumptions have to be met. If they are, the maximum likelihood estimates of logit parameters should be unbiased and sufficient. The assumptions are as follows:

o The model must be correctly specified; that is, the logit of Y is a *linear* function of the X-variables. This will in some instances call for the transformation of X-variables that do not exhibit a linear relationship with the logit (more precisely, where the dependent variable is not a linear function of the logit of the explanatory variable). An example of this is if we expect a relationship to be *curvilinear*, where a squared X-variable, in addition to the original one, would be appropriate in order to secure linearity.

---

[9] We can use this to test the significance of single variables. This can be done if only one variable constitutes the difference between our two models. The likelihood ratio test is especially advised for this purpose if N is small or if the logit is large.

o No important variables must be left out of the model, and no unnecessary variables should be included. This is more a question of theory: the model and the causal relationships need to be grounded in strong theoretical arguments.

o Each observation needs to be independent of the other observations. For how to treat data that are nested, see Chapters 9 and 10.

o None of the explanatory variables must be linear functions of the other X-variables, as this will result in multicollinearity. This latter point is not a model assumption, but it is an important estimability requirement. To test this, we can obtain the tolerance value of each X-variable (see Chapter 7).

In addition to these assumptions, influential cases also lead to problems for logit regression. The same is relevant for cases with unusual combinations of X-variable values. In large-N samples, this is usually not a major concern. Potentially influential cases can be tested for in logistic regression using the Pregibon (1981) $\Delta \hat{\beta}$ influence statistic. This measures the standardized change in estimated parameters that results from deleting the observation along with the other observations that share the same covariate pattern. A large value of $\Delta \hat{\beta}$ indicates that the given pattern exerts substantial influence (values over 1 are considered large).

Discrimination is also a problem associated with logistic regression. It refers to our ability to predict the dependent variable. It appears when, for a given X-value, we get a perfect or an almost perfect prediction of the value of Y. This can occur when we have a zero cell count (complete separation), that is, when all or close to all with a given X-value have the same value on Y. If we were investigating the effect of political ideology on the likelihood on being in favour of revolution, we might be faced with the data shown in Table 8.2.

Table 8.2 Discrimination

	For revolution	Against revolution
Conservative	0	28
Liberal	11	30
Socialist	22	11

Here we see that the odds of being revolutionary if you are liberal are $11/30 = 0.367$. The corresponding odds if you are conservative are $0/28 = 0$. If being liberal serves as the reference category, the odds ratio of being conservative will become $0/0.367 = 0$. This implies that the coefficient becomes $-\infty$; we would get a warning message in Stata and the conservatives would be dropped from the model. We would still have the problem of discrimination if only one of the conservatives had been for revolution. This would result in large standard errors and uncertain estimates.

If we have a problem with discrimination, one solution is to recode the independent variable in a meaningful way (in this example we could code into socialist and non-socialist). Discrimination applies to categorical variables and not continuous or ordinal variables.

Related to the problem of discrimination is the question of the distribution on the dependent variable. As we have seen, the correctness of the logit estimates is dependent not only on sample size, but also on the number of cases with a particular combination of values on the X- and Y-variables. A skewed distribution of the dependent variable can easily lead to problems. It is better to have a 50/50 distribution on the dependent than a 95/5. In analysis of rare events data (e.g., with a more skewed distribution than 1/99) the coefficients are biased if there are fewer than 200 observations with $Y = 1$. This can be countered by using the *ReLogit* software (King and Zeng, 2001) or the exact logistic regression command `exlogistic`.

8●2●1 Example in Stata

For our example, we will use data from the *European Social Survey*, and open the dataset called *Logistic_ESS5.dta*. Our dataset includes 2422 respondents from the United Kingdom. The dependent variable in our example is called *vote*, denoting whether the respondent voted (1) or not (0) in the last national election. First, we can check the distribution of our Y-variable:

```
. tabulate vote
```

vote	Freq.	Percent	Cum.
0	650	28.01	28.01
1	1,671	71.99	100.00
Total	2,321	100.00	

Figure 8.3 Frequency of vote

Figure 8.3 shows that our variable is dichotomous with values 0 and 1,[10] has a solid N (2321 respondents) and a good distribution (28/72 per cent).

The next step is to run a logistic regression model in Stata including the three independent variables *woman* (0–1), *age* and *political interest* (1–4) where high values indicates that the respondent is very interested in politics. We can first run our model using the `logit` command:

```
. logit vote woman age political_interest
```

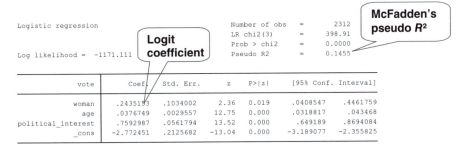

vote	Coef.	Std. Err.	z	P>|z|	[95% Conf. Interval]
woman	.2435193	.1034002	2.36	0.019	.0408547 .4461759
age	.0376749	.0029557	12.75	0.000	.0318817 .043468
political_interest	.7592987	.0561794	13.52	0.000	.649189 .8694084
_cons	-2.772451	.2125682	-13.04	0.000	-3.189077 -2.355825

Figure 8.4 Logistic regression on likelihood of voting

[10] As far as Stata is concerned, it is more important that the variable is 0/1 than that it has two categories. A 0/1/2/3 variable would still work in logistic regression as 0/(1 2 3), but a 1/2 variable would not work, as it would be interpreted as 0/(1 2) and all the outcomes would be positive.

Figure 8.4 tells us that we have 2312 units in our analysis (listwise deletion) and a log-likelihood of –1171.111. The latter can be used to compare different models using the –2LL test (see equation (8.9)). We also get the coefficients (logits), standard errors, standardized coefficients, *p*-values and 95 per cent confidence intervals of the logits presented in the output. Unlike OLS regression, we cannot directly interpret the logits (as they represent how the natural logarithm of the odds for $Y = 1$ changes for each one-step increase in X). Even so, we are able to interpret a few things directly from the output. We can see the direction of the effects (positive or negative) and whether or not they are statistically significant. From our results we see that women, older people and those that are interested in politics are more likely to vote than men, younger people and those with little interest in politics. We can also compare the significance of the relationships by looking at the *p*-values or the *z*-scores (larger means more significant), and conclude that *political interest* is the most statistically significant variable in our model. If the 95 per cent confidence interval does not cross zero it means that the effect is significant at the 5 per cent level (in other words, that the *p*-value is less than 0.05).

In OLS regression, the coefficient tells us how much a unit increases or decreases on the *Y*-variable for each one-unit change in the *X*-variable. To get a similar substantive interpretation of the logit we have to predict values of the logit and transform them from logits to probabilities. However, we should bear in mind that each step on the logit has a different effect on the probability depending on where we are on the logit scale. In other words, the effect of one *X*-variable is dependent on the values of the other *X*-variables (this is illustrated in Figure 8.2).

We can start by looking at the effect of *woman* by predicting the total logit for a woman and a man when all other variables are set at their mean. Inputting

```
. estat summarize
```

yields the descriptive statistics for those units included in our last model (Figure 8.5).

```
Estimation sample logit                    Number of obs =    2312
```

Variable	Mean	Std. Dev.	Min	Max
vote	.7201557	.4490197	0	1
woman	.5635813	.4960482	0	1
age	51.08478	18.41821	15	98
political_~t	2.447232	.9486063	1	4

Figure 8.5 Descriptive statistics

For a woman (with value 1 on *woman*) the calculation is

$$L_i = -\beta_0 + \beta_1 X_{1i} + \beta_2 X_{2i} + \beta_3 X_{3i}$$
$$= cons + \beta_1 woman + \beta_2 mean\_age + \beta_3 mean\_polit$$
$$= -2.772451 + (0.2435153 \times 1) + (0.0376749 \times 51.08478) + (0.7592987 \times 2.447232)$$
$$= 1.254.$$

For a man the calculation is

$$L_i = -2.772451 + (0.2435153 \times 0) + (0.0376749 \times 51.08478) + (0.7592987 \times 2.447232)$$
$$= 1.010.$$

Now we have the predicted logits for women and men when all other variables are set at their means. The formula for transforming the logits to probabilities is:

$$p = \frac{1}{1+e^{-L}}.$$ (8.10)

For women the probability is

$$p = \frac{1}{1+e^{-1.254}} = 0.778.$$

For men the probability is

$$p = \frac{1}{1+e^{-1.010}} = 0.733.$$

In other words, one step up on the *woman* variable means that the probability of having voted increases by 4.5 per cent.

This calculation can be done more easily in Stata, and we can also include the effect for X_2 and X_3 with the other variables set at their mean (including *women*):

```
. quietly logit vote woman age political_interest
. margins, dydx(*) atmeans
```

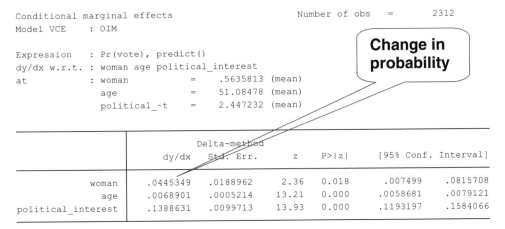

```
Conditional marginal effects              Number of obs    =     2312
Model VCE     : OIM

Expression    : Pr(vote), predict()
dy/dx w.r.t.  : woman age political_interest
at            : woman            =     .5635813  (mean)
                age              =     51.08478  (mean)
                political_~t     =     2.447232  (mean)
```

Change in probability

	dy/dx	Delta-method Std. Err.	z	P>|z|	[95% Conf. Interval]	
woman	.0445349	.0188962	2.36	0.018	.007499	.0815708
age	.0068901	.0005214	13.21	0.000	.0058681	.0079121
political_interest	.1388631	.0099713	13.93	0.000	.1193197	.1584066

Figure 8.6 Logistic regression using margins

In Figure 8.6 we get the change in probability for each one-step change in X for all variables in our model, with the other variables set at their mean. This can also be illustrated graphically with the command

```
marginsplot
```

Figure 8.7 shows that the effect of all three variables is positive and that the confidence interval does not cross the zero line.

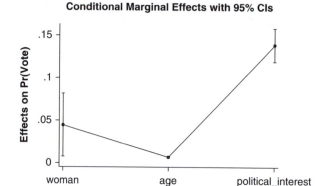

Figure 8.7 Change in probability for a one-step change in X

We can do the same analysis, only changing the values of the other variables to their minimum and maximum values respectively (which we get by writing estat summarize, as shown on p. 170).

```
. quietly logit vote woman age political_interest
. margins, dydx(*) at(woman=(0) age=(15) political_interest=(1))
. marginsplot
```

and

```
. quietly logit vote woman age political_interest
. margins, dydx(*) at(woman=(1) age=(98) political_interest=(4))
. marginsplot
```

We read from the output (not shown) that the jump in probability for all variables is greater when the other variables are set at their mean then when they are set at their minimum and maximum values.

It is also possible to use the logistic command in Stata. Both logit and logistic use maximum likelihood estimation, and they produce the same result. However, logistic yields the odds ratios rather than the coefficients (see Figure 8.8):

```
. logistic vote woman age political_interest
```

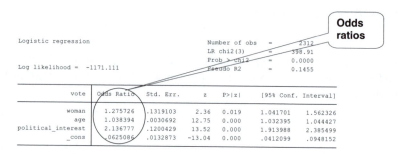

Figure 8.8 Logistic regression, showing odds ratios

We can think of 1.000 as equivalent to a coefficient of 0, and an odds ratio greater than 1.000 means that the effect is positive, while an odds ratio less than 1.000 means that the effect is negative. If the 95 per cent confidence interval does not cross 1.000 it means that the effect is significant at the 5 per cent level, similar to the `logit` output). The odds ratio tells us by how many per cent the odds for $Y = 1$ increase for a one-unit increase in X. For the variable *age* we see that the odds increase by 3.8 per cent for each year older a person is (1.038 − 1.000). We get the odds ratio by raising the mathematical constant e to the power of the coefficient. So, for the coefficient for women (which is 0.2435153, as we saw in Figure 8.4) we get $e^{0.24352} = 1.2757$. The odds ratio is not as intuitive as probabilities, so in order to get a substantial interpretation it is recommended to transform the logits into probabilities. We can alternatively use the `listcoef` command to help us interpret the odds ratios. First, we must install a package called spost13 which contains the `listcoef` command:

. net install spost13_ado, from (http://www.indiana.edu/~jslsoc/stata)

After we have used the `logit` or `logistic` command, we can type:

. listcoef, help

The help option will provide us with a description of the estimates (Figure 8.9).

```
logit (N=2312): Factor change in odds

    Odds of: 1 vs 0
```

	b	z	P>|z|	e^b	e^bStdX	SDofX
woman	0.2435	2.355	0.019	1.276	1.128	0.496
age	0.0377	12.746	0.000	1.038	2.002	18.418
political_~t	0.7593	13.516	0.000	2.137	2.055	0.949
constant	-2.7725	-13.043	0.000	.	.	.

```
        b = raw coefficient
        z = z-score for test of b=0
    P>|z| = p-value for z-test
      e^b = exp(b) = factor change in odds for unit increase in X
  e^bStdX = exp(b*SD of X) = change in odds for SD increase in X
    SDofX = standard deviation of X
```

Figure 8.9 `Listcoef` output

Alternatively, we could choose to produce the change in percentage in the odds ratios:

. listcoef, help percent

After running a logistic model we can also view the goodness of fit by typing `estat class`:

. quietly logit vote woman age political_interest
. estat class

```
Logistic model for vote
```

Classified	True D	~D	Total
+	1541	430	1971
-	124	217	341
Total	1665	647	2312

```
Classified + if predicted Pr(D) >= .5
True D defined as vote != 0
```

Sensitivity	Pr(+| D)	92.55%
Specificity	Pr(-|~D)	33.54%
Positive predictive value	Pr(D| +)	78.18%
Negative predictive value	Pr(~D| -)	63.64%
False + rate for true ~D	Pr(+|~D)	66.46%
False - rate for true D	Pr(-| D)	7.45%
False + rate for classified +	Pr(~D| +)	21.82%
False - rate for classified -	Pr(D| -)	36.36%
Correctly classified		76.04%

Figure 8.10 Goodness of fit

In Figure 8.10 the observations that, from our latest run model, get a probability of at least 0.50 are predicted as having the event (in our case, that they voted), and the others are predicted as not having the event (did not vote). We see that of the 1665 that voted, 1541 were correctly predicted, and 124 were wrongly predicted. Of the 647 that did not vote, 217 were correctly predicted and 430 were wrongly predicted. From this we can get a picture of how great the errors in our model are.

We can also produce an effect plot for the variables. In this example, we will make a plot for *age*, keeping *woman* and *political interest* at their minimum, mean and maximum values (Figure 8.11):

```
. quietly logit vote woman age political_interest
. generate L1 = _b[_cons] + _b[woman]*0 + _b[age]*age + _b[political_
interest]*1
. generate Phat1 = 1/(1+exp(-L1))
. generate L2 = _b[_cons] + _b[woman]*0.5635813 + _b[age]*age +
_b[political_interest]*2.447232
. generate Phat2 = 1/(1+exp(-L2))
. generate L3 = _b[_cons] + _b[woman]*1 + _b[age]*age + _b[political_
interest]*4
. generate Phat3 = 1/(1+exp(-L3))
. graph twoway mspline Phat1 age || mspline Phat2 age || mspline Phat3 age
```

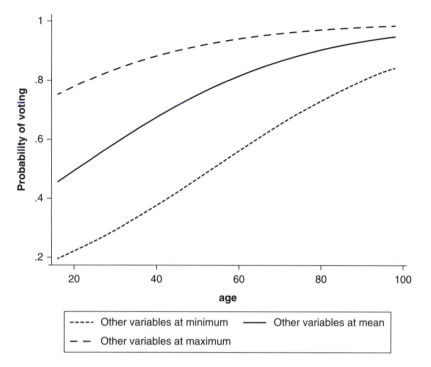

Figure 8.11 Effect of *age* on *vote*

An easy way to predict a given individual's probability of voting is to use the `margins` command after running a logit model:

```
. quietly logit vote woman age political_interest
. margins, atmeans
```

In the output (not shown) we get `Pr(vote)=.759`. This is the probability for a person with mean value on all *X*-variables on the last run model. We can also define the values, for example if we wanted to predict the values for a 27-year-old woman who is quite interested in politics:

```
. margins, at(woman=1 age=27 political_interest=3)
```

This yields 0.683 as her predicted probability of having $Y = 1$.[11]

8●3 CONDITIONAL EFFECTS

Conditional effects in logistic regression have many similarities to those in OLS regression. However, the interpretation is rather more complex. In order to interpret the results we

---

[11] We can use the `margins` command to illustrate one of the reasons why we should not use OLS on dichotomous dependent variables. If we run the regression `regress vote woman age political_interest` and then predict the following person: `margins, at(woman=1 age=75 political_interest=4)` we get a prediction of 1.105, outside of the 0–1 range of our dependent variable.

should transform the logits to probabilities, and the conditional effects are thus also dependent on the values of the *X*-variables that are not part of the interaction. In some cases this can lead to substantive results that differ from the sign and strength shown in the logistic regression table (Berry et al., 2010). Therefore, it is good practice to test (and possibly graph) the interaction for different starting points of the logit scale (e.g., set the other variables at their minimum, mean and maximum values) as we should expect values to differ for each observation.

We can use the `margins` command to produce a conditional effect plot expressed in probabilities (Figure 8.12):

```
. quietly logit vote i.woman##c.age political_interest
. margins, at(age=(15(1)98) woman=( 0 1))
. marginsplot
```

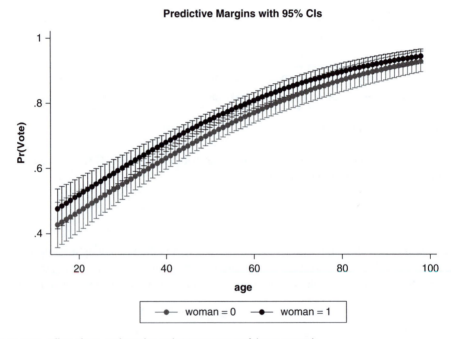

Predictive Margins with 95% CIs

Figure 8.12 Effect of age and gender, with 96 per cent confidence intervals

To check whether this relationship (though not significant) holds, we can graph the effect when *political interest* is set at its minimum (1) and maximum (4) values:

```
. quietly logit vote i.woman##c.age political_interest
. quietly margins, at(age=(15(1)98) woman=( 0 1) political_interest=(1))
. marginsplot, noci recast(line)
. quietly margins, at(age=(15(1)98) woman=( 0 1) political_interest=(4))
. marginsplot, noci recast(line)
```

Inspection of the graphs (Figures 8.13 and 8.14) shows that the interaction effect is somewhat dependent on the value of the variable that is not included in the interaction.

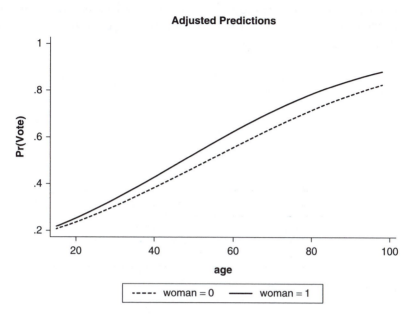

Figure 8.13   Conditional effect of *woman* and *age* with *political interest* at minimum value

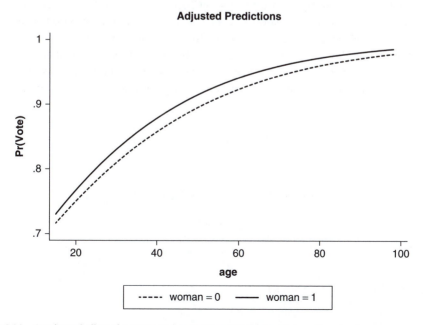

Figure 8.14   Conditional effect of *woman* and *age* with *political interest* at maximum value

8●4 DIAGNOSTICS

The assumptions that the model should be correctly specified is first and foremost a theoretical question. However, Stata provides a test for model specification called the link test (Pregibon, 1980). The `linktest` command works for any single-equation estimation command, including `logit` and `logistic`:

```
. quietly logit vote woman age political_interest
. linktest, nolog
```

```
Logistic regression                             Number of obs   =        2312
                                                LR chi2(2)      =      400.08
                                                Prob > chi2     =      0.0000
Log likelihood = -1170.5297                     Pseudo R2       =      0.1460
```

vote	Coef.	Std. Err.	z	P>|z|	[95% Conf. Interval]	
_hat	1.086406	.0985975	11.02	0.000	.8931587	1.279654
_hatsq	-.0518307	.0478049	-1.08	0.278	-.1455265	.0418651
_cons	.0071204	.0681802	0.10	0.917	-.1265103	.1407511

Figure 8.15 Stata output for `linktest`

The test includes two variables, _hat and _hatsquared (see Figure 8.15). Ideally, the variable _hat should be significant if it is a good model and _hatsq should not be significant if the model is correctly specified (see also Chapter 7, pp. 135–136). This is the case for our model. Yet, there is strong reason to believe that we could find some other significant explanatory variable predicting *vote*, something that is not tested for with `linktest`. For this purpose we can employ `estat gof` after running the model. This tests whether the observed 0/1 values on the dependent variable match the expected 0/1 values, either for the number of covariate patterns in our data or for a set number of groups (which we get by typing `estat gof, group(10)`):[12]

```
. quietly logit vote woman age political_interest
. estat gof
```

```
            Logistic model for vote, goodness-of-fit test

                 number of observations =        2312
           number of covariate patterns =         546
                      Pearson chi2(542) =      556.92
                           Prob > chi2 =      0.3195
```

Figure 8.16 The `estat gof` command

---

[12] This option is recommended if the number of covariate patterns is close to the number of observations, as this makes the test questionable (Hosmer, Lemeshow and Sturdivant, 2013: 157–160).

A significant value means that we have to reject our model, while $p > 0.05$ means that our model fits reasonably well (Figure 8.16). We should only view this as a sign that we have chosen good predictors in our model. This test can assist us in detecting incorrectly specified models, but we should also use our own theoretical judgement.

We can easily test for multicollinearity, using the `vif` command. Multicollinearity indicates high interrelations between the X-variables. The tolerance value (1/VIF) of each X-variable is the proportion of its variance that is not shared with the other X-variables. If tolerance values are lower than 0.2, the estimated coefficients become less stable. The inclusion of interaction or squared terms in a model will result in multicollinearity which we will have to accept if it makes the model substantially better.[13] We cannot run the `estat vif` option after a `logit` or `logistic` model, so instead we run a linear regression followed by the command

```
. quietly regress vote woman age political_interest
. estat vif
```

Variable	VIF	1/VIF
political_~t	1.02	0.980265
woman	1.02	0.983888
age	1.00	0.995168
Mean VIF	1.01	

Figure 8.17 The `estat vif` command

In our model the tolerance values (1/VIF) are greater than 0.2 (see Figure 8.17), so we conclude that we have no problem with multicollinearity.

We can test for influential cases by using Pregibon's (1981) $\Delta\hat{\beta}$ influence statistic `dbeta`. First, we predict the probability of $Y=1$ for each unit:

```
. quietly logit vote woman age political_interest
. predict p
. predict db, dbeta
. scatter db p
```

Figure 8.18 shows us the change in the estimated parameters that results from deleting all cases with a specific pattern. We can identify the units with the highest influence on the model as a whole by browsing the identification number and $\Delta\hat{\beta}$ -value (alternatively, this can be done by writing `scatter db p, mlabel(idno)`):

```
. sort db
. browse idno db
```

---

[13] If we include squared terms for mean-centred variables we do not add to the problem of multicollinearity.

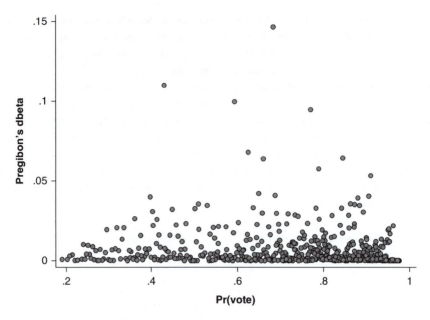

Figure 8.18 Pregibon's measure of influential observations

We scroll down and find the cases with the most influential pattern (Figure 8.19), which could merit further examination.

	idno	db
2301	16713322	.1098591
2302	18516919	.1098591
2303	18817596	.1098591
2304	10500950	.1098591
2305	18617107	.1098591
2306	15410655	.1466112
2307	18617123	.1466112
2308	10200372	.1466112
2309	13206225	.1466112
2310	12104108	.1466112
2311	22424773	.1466112
2312	27534892	.1466112
2313	10400780	.
2314	17615148	.

Figure 8.19 Stata output of influential cases

8.5 MULTINOMIAL LOGISTIC REGRESSION

Multinomial regression builds on ordinary binary logistic regression but allows the researcher to explore dependent variables that have more than two categories, where the categories have no natural ordering. This makes it possible to examine a categorical dependent variable with more than two outcomes in the same model. Suppose we wish to investigate the variable *party voted* denoting whether the respondent voted Conservative, Liberal Democrat, Labour or for another party (grouped into one category). We thus have a nominal dependent variable with four values. Figure 8.20 shows its frequency distribution.

As this variable has four categories, three of these will be compared separately to the one we choose as the reference category. In a binary model, the base outcome $Y = 1$ is the same as $1 - P(Y = 0)$. But in a model with three or more possible outcomes, the results $Y = 1$ and $1 - P(Y = 0)$ are different. The equation for a multinomial model with a dependent variable with four categories is as follows:

$$L_1 = \ln\left(\frac{P(Y = 1)}{P(Y = 0)}\right) = \beta_{01} + \beta_{11}X_1 + \beta_{21}X_2 + \beta_{31}X_3 + \varepsilon_1, \tag{8.11}$$

$$L_2 = \ln\left(\frac{P(Y = 2)}{P(Y = 0)}\right) = \beta_{02} + \beta_{12}X_1 + \beta_{22}X_2 + \beta_{32}X_3 + \varepsilon_2,$$

$$L_3 = \ln\left(\frac{P(Y = 3)}{P(Y = 0)}\right) = \beta_{03} + \beta_{13}X_1 + \beta_{23}X_2 + \beta_{31}X_3 + \varepsilon_3.$$

As we can see from equation (8.11), we now have different logit coefficients for three of the four categories. If we look at our dependent variable we get three sets of coefficients explaining the relationship between: the probability of voting Liberal Democrat and the probability of voting Conservative; the probability of voting Labour and the probability of voting Conservative; and the probability of voting for another party and the probability of voting Conservative.

```
. tab party_voted
```

party_voted	Freq.	Percent	Cum.
Conservative	583	37.40	37.40
Liberal Democrat	342	21.94	59.33
Labour	490	31.43	90.76
Other	144	9.24	100.00
Total	1,559	100.00	

Figure 8.20 Frequency distribution of dependent variable

To run the multinomial logistic regression model we use the `mlogit` command. We can decide which category should function as a reference by inserting its value as the base outcome. If we do not use this option, the lowest value on the dependent will be used as default. We choose Conservative (0), as it is a well-defined category with a large N:

```
. mlogit party_voted woman age political_interest, base(0)
```

The output is in Figure 8.21.

```
Multinomial logistic regression                      Number of obs   =       1556
                                                     LR chi2(9)      =      51.43
                                                     Prob > chi2     =     0.0000
Log likelihood = -1973.3684                          Pseudo R2       =     0.0129
```

party_voted	Coef.	Std. Err.	z	P>|z|	[95% Conf. Interval]
Conservative	(base outcome)				
Liberal_Democrat					
woman	-.0275363	.1406261	-0.20	0.845	-.3031585 .2480858
age	-.019776	.0039771	-4.97	0.000	-.0275709 -.0119811
political_interest	-.072617	.0799505	-0.91	0.364	-.2293171 .0840831
_cons	.7542039	.3344822	2.25	0.024	.0986309 1.409777
Labour					
woman	-.0251884	.1266712	-0.20	0.842	-.2734595 .2230826
age	-.0127739	.0035614	-3.59	0.000	-.0197541 -.0057936
political_interest	-.1955991	.0710975	-2.75	0.006	-.3349475 -.0562506
_cons	1.065986	.3021007	3.53	0.000	.4738791 1.658092
Other					
woman	-.4468886	.1902763	-2.35	0.019	-.8198233 -.0739539
age	-.013044	.0053657	-2.43	0.015	-.0235606 -.0025274
political_interest	-.4292863	.1046578	-4.10	0.000	-.6344117 -.2241609
_cons	.6725144	.4304668	1.56	0.118	-.171185 1.516214

> **Results for Liberal Democrat vs. Conservative**
>
> **Results for Labour vs. Conservative**
>
> **Results for Other vs. Conservative**

Figure 8.21 Multinomial logistic regression

By including a *Y*-variable with four categories, three of them (Liberal Democrat, Labour and Other) are compared separately with the reference category (Conservative). For example, women have a smaller probability of voting Liberal Democrat, Labour or Other than they have of voting Conservative. However, only the difference between Other and Conservative is statistically significant. It is also possible here to use the `mfx` command to predict the probability of $Y = 0$, $Y = 1$, $Y = 2$ or $Y = 3$ for a given person:

```
. margins, predict(outcome(0))
. margins, predict(outcome(1))
. margins, predict(outcome(2))
. margins, predict(outcome(3))
```

Here, the *X*-variables are set at their mean values. We can also predict a person with specific characteristics:

```
. margins, predict(outcome(0)) at (woman=1 age=27 political_interest=3)
. margins, predict(outcome(1)) at (woman=1 age=27 political_interest=3)
. margins, predict(outcome(2)) at (woman=1 age=27 political_interest=3)
. margins, predict(outcome(3)) at (woman=1 age=27 political_interest=3)
```

We can graph our results, but remember that the effects will differ depending on the values on the other *X*-variables (as in binary logistic regression). In the example we will graph the effect of *age* on voting for each of the four alternatives, keeping the other variables at their mean (Figure 8.22). To find the means we type:

```
. quietly mlogit party_voted woman age political_interest, base(0)
. summarize woman political_interest if e(sample)
```

```
. generate L1m = [1]_b[_cons] + [1]_b[woman]*0.5694087 + [1]_b[age]*age +
[1]_b[political_interest]*2.647815
. generate L2m = [2]_b[_cons] + [2]_b[woman]*0.5694087 + [2]_b[age]*age
+ [2]_b[political_interest]*2.647815
. generate L3m = [3]_b[_cons] + [3]_b[woman]*0.5694087 + [3]_b[age]*age
+ [3]_b[political_interest]*2.647815
. generate P0m = 1/(1+exp(L1m) + exp(L2m) + exp(L3m))
. generate P1m = exp(L1m) / (1+exp(L1m) + exp(L2m) + exp(L3m))
. generate P2m = exp(L2m) / (1+exp(L1m) + exp(L2m) + exp(L3m))
. generate P3m = exp(L3m) / (1+exp(L1m) + exp(L2m) + exp(L3m))
. graph twoway mspline P0m age || mspline P1m age || mspline P2m age ||
mspline P3m age
```

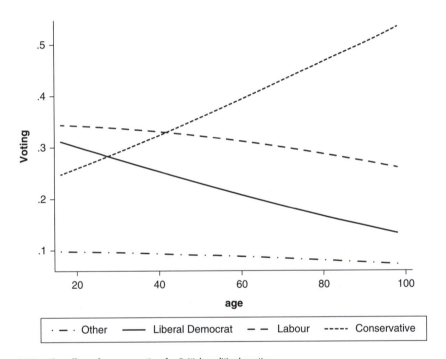

Figure 8.22 The effect of *age* on voting for British political parties

If we specify `rrr`, we get the results as relative-risk ratios and the corresponding standard errors and confidence intervals (similar to using `logistic` in logistic regression):

```
. mlogit party_voted woman age political_interest, base(0) rrr
```

An important assumption associated with multinomial logistic regression is the *independence of irrelevant alternatives* (IIA). The logic is that if *A* is preferred to *B* out of a choice set of *A* and *B*, the introduction of a third alternative *C* must not make *B* preferable to *A*. In essence, this means that our dependent categorical variable must be exhaustive (in addition to being mutually exclusive), that is, it should include all possible alternatives as values. This also includes if one category can be divided into subcategories that could alter the results (as, in theory could be the case with our "Other" alternative).

To test for this we could use the Hausman test for IIA, via the `mlogtest` command. This works by first fitting a full model with all alternatives on Y. Next, it fits a restricted model by eliminating one or more of the alternatives on Y. Then the test is calculated using the coefficients from the first two steps (Long and Freese, 2014). If the Hausman test statistic H is significant it means that the IIA assumption has been violated. After running our model we type:

```
. mlogtest, hausman
```

```
Hausman tests of IIA assumption (N=1556)

Ho: Odds (Outcome-J vs Outcome-K) are independent of other alternatives

                     chi2      df    P>chi2

      Conserva        0.346      8    1.000
       Liberal       -0.041      8       .
        Labour        0.608      8    1.000
         Other       -0.141      8       .

Note: A significant test is evidence against Ho.
Note: If chi2<0, the estimated model does not meet asymptotic assumptions.
```

Figure 8.23 Stata output for Hausman test

Figure 8.23 shows that two of our values are negative, and thus do not meet the assumptions of the test. However, because of the difficulties associated with the Hausman test, it is recommended to use the *seemingly unrelated estimation* (suest) version of the Hausman test when evaluating the IIA assumption.[14]

To use the `suest` test we fit our multinomial model including all four alternatives, as well as fitting three restricted multinomial modes in which one alternative is excluded. Then we run the test; if the IIA assumption holds, the coefficients of all the four equations should be equal (Hausman and McFadden, 1984). We can then see if this is the case by running the `suest` test.

As `suest` stores the estimations using the labels as names, we first need to make sure there are no blank spaces in the value labels (in our case, the label 'Liberal Democrat' has a blank space):

```
. label define partynames 0 Conservative 1 LiberalDemocrat 2 Labour 3 Other
. label value party_voted partynames
. tab party_voted
```

---

[14] For more on this test, see www.stata.com/manuals13/rsuest.pdf

Then we estimate our four models:

```
. quietly mlogit party_voted woman age political_interest
. estimates store m1, title(all categories)
. quietly mlogit party_voted woman age political_interest if party_voted !=1
. estimates store m2, title(party_voted != "LiberalDemocrat":party_voted)
. quietly mlogit party_voted woman age political_interest if party_voted !=2
. estimates store m3, title(party_voted != "Labour":party_voted)
. quietly mlogit party_voted woman age political_interest if party_voted !=3
. estimates store m4, title(party_voted != "Other":party_voted)
```

Now we can run the test:

```
. suest m*, noomitted
```

From the table (too large to reproduce and therefore omitted) we see that there are no substantial differences between coefficients from the different equations. In order to test if the assumption holds for the different estimations, we run the different alternatives:

```
. test [m1_LiberalDemocrat = m3_LiberalDemocrat], cons
. test [m1_LiberalDemocrat = m4_LiberalDemocrat], cons
. test [m1_Labour = m2_Labour], cons
. test [m1_Labour = m4_Labour], cons
. test [m1_Other = m2_Other], cons
. test [m1_Other = m3_Other], cons


 ( 1)   [m1_LiberalDemocrat]woman - [m3_LiberalDemocrat]woman = 0
 ( 2)   [m1_LiberalDemocrat]age - [m3_LiberalDemocrat]age = 0
 ( 3)   [m1_LiberalDemocrat]political_interest - [m3_LiberalDemocrat]political_interest = 0
 ( 4)   [m1_LiberalDemocrat]_cons - [m3_LiberalDemocrat]_cons = 0

            chi2(  4) =     5.24
          Prob > chi2 =   0.2632
```

Figure 8.24 Testing the IIA assumption

From the output (note that we have only reported one of the six tests in Figure 8.24) we see from the Prob > chi2 value (which is greater than 0.05) that we cannot reject the equality of the coefficients across the models, which means that our model is unproblematic (this is the case for all six tests).

8●6 ORDERED LOGISTIC REGRESSION

Although it is common to use OLS regression on ordinal variables with several values, the correct way of modelling a dependent variable when the real distance between categories is unknown is *ordinal logistic regression*. Unlike multinomial regression, the values can now be ranked from low to high. Here, we only get one estimate for each independent variable. The reason is that we assume that the transition from one value to another on the dependent variable follows the same processes. The assumption is that we have a latent variable Y^* ranging from $-\infty$ to ∞ which is expressed through our observed variable Y. Our observed variable is thought of as providing incomplete information about the latent variable (Long and Freese, 2014).

Suppose we wish to investigate the dependent variable *political interest*. This is an ordinal variable ranging from 1 to 4.[15] The command

```
. tab political_interest
```

political_interest	Freq.	Percent	Cum.
Not at all interested	522	21.57	21.57
Hardly interested	604	24.96	46.53
Quite interested	1,018	42.07	88.60
Very interested	276	11.40	100.00
Total	2,420	100.00	

Figure 8.25 Frequency distribution of dependent variable

produces the output in Figure 8.25. So, we assume that there is a latent variable Y^* ($-\infty$ to ∞), which is represented by our ordinal variable Y. In other words, our latent variable is divided into j ordinal categories where $Y_i = m$ if $\tau_{m-1} \leq Y_i^* < \tau_m$ for $m = 1, ..., j$. In our example $j = 4$:

$$Y_i = \begin{cases} 1 & \text{if } \tau_0 = -\infty \leq Y_i^* < \tau_1, \\ 2 & \text{if } \tau_1 \leq Y_i^* < \tau_2, \\ 3 & \text{if } \tau_2 \leq Y_i^* < \tau_3, \\ 4 & \text{if } \tau_3 \leq Y_i^* < \tau_4 = \infty. \end{cases} \tag{8.12}$$

So, when our latent Y^* crosses a cut-point the observed category changes (Long and Freese, 2014). We thus end up with the following regression equation:

$$L = 1n\{P(Y \leq m)\} = \tau_m + \beta_1 X_1 + \beta_2 X_2 + \varepsilon . \tag{8.13}$$

To run this model in Stata we use the `ologit` command, which yields the output in Figure 8.26:

```
. ologit political_interest woman age
```

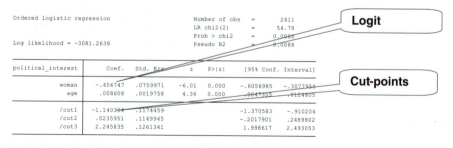

Figure 8.26 Stata output for ordered logistic regression

---

[15] By typing `numlabel, add` (and then pressing Enter), we can add numbers (in addition to the labels) to our output.

The cut-points can be compared to intercepts and are used as a starting point to calculate probabilities.[16] We get logits (coefficients) instead of odds ratios. The probabilities are calculated in the same manner as in logistic regression, but we must choose the correct cut-point for our prediction. We can predict probabilities in the same way as we did for multinomial regression:

```
. margins, predict(outcome(1))
. margins, predict(outcome(2))
. margins, predict(outcome(3))
. margins, predict(outcome(4))
```

Also here, the X-variables are set at their mean values. And we can also predict a person with specific characteristics:

```
. margins, predict(outcome(1)) at (woman=1 age=27)
. margins, predict(outcome(2)) at (woman=1 age=27)
. margins, predict(outcome(3)) at (woman=1 age=27)
. margins, predict(outcome(4)) at (woman=1 age=27)
```

We can look at the effect of explanatory variables for the different outcomes of our dependent:

```
. quietly ologit political_interest woman age
. margins, predict(outcome(1)) at(age=(15(1)98))
. marginsplot
. margins, predict(outcome(2)) at(age=(15(1)98))
. marginsplot
. margins, predict(outcome(3)) at(age=(15(1)98))
. marginsplot
. margins, predict(outcome(4)) at(age=(15(1)98))
. marginsplot
```

As *age* is positive and significant in our model, it has a negative impact on the likelihood of having small values (1 and 2) on our dependent variable, and a positive impact on the likelihood of having large values (3 and 4); see Figure 8.27.

Ordered logistic regression needs to adhere to the *parallel regression assumption*. This assumption states that the relationship between each pair of outcome groups is the same. Because of this, we can have only one set of coefficients (otherwise we would need different models for the relationship between each pair of outcome groups). To test this we can use the Brant test of the parallel regression assumption after running our model (Long and Freese, 2014). This tests both whether any variable violates this assumption, as well as testing the assumption for each variable separately. The detail option provides us with a series of binary logistic regressions:

```
. quietly ologit political_interest woman age
. brant, detail
```

---

[16] For a short explanation of cut-points, see http://www.stata.com/support/faqs/statistics/cut-points/

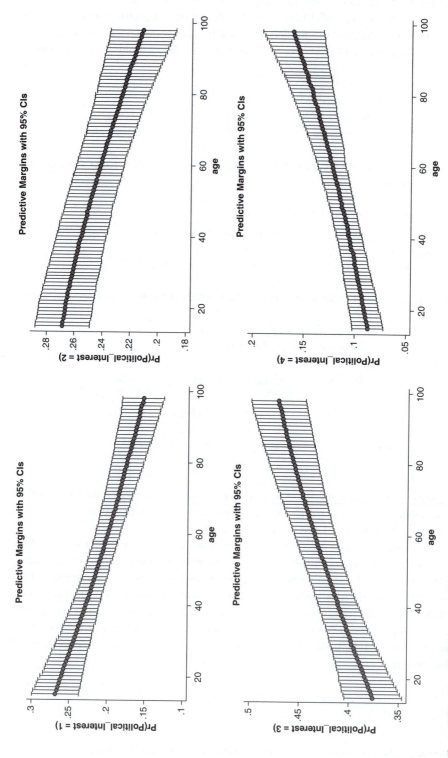

Figure 8.27 The effect of *age* on *political interest*

Estimated coefficients from binary logits

Variable	y_gt_1	y_gt_2	y_gt_3
woman	-0.330	-0.438	-0.696
	-3.24	-5.25	-5.36
age	0.009	0.009	0.006
	3.47	4.29	1.80
_cons	1.033	-0.076	-2.011
	6.94	-0.61	-10.37

legend: b/t

Brant test of parallel regression assumption

	chi2	p>chi2	df
All	7.01	0.136	4
woman	5.98	0.050	2
age	0.89	0.639	2

A significant test statistic provides evidence that the parallel regression assumption has been violated.

Figure 8.28 Parallel regression assumption

If the test is significant, it shows that the parallel regression assumption is violated. The logistic regressions presented show first category 1 versus the 2, 3 and 4; then categories 1 and 2 versus 3 and 4; and last categories 1, 2 and 3 versus 4. These coefficients (not the intercepts) should be the same except for sampling variability (Williams, 2006). Figure 8.28 shows that our model and variables are fine (though *woman* is close to significant). If this assumption is violated, we risk getting incorrect or misleading results. One option then is to use multinomial logistic regression instead.

8.7 CONCLUSION

In this chapter we have shown how to treat dependent variables that are not continuous. We have introduced the concepts of logit, odds and probabilities, and we have given special attention to the latter concept. Interpreting logistic output is more challenging than interpreting OLS regression output, thus a large part of this chapter has been dedicated to the graphical presentation of results. We have also discussed multinomial and ordinal logistic regression.

key terms

Binary logistic regression This is an estimation method for a dichotomous dependent variable, showing how much the natural logarithm of the odds for $Y = 1$ changes for each unit's change in X.

Logit This is the natural logarithm of the odds for $Y = 1$.

Odds ratio The odds ratio is the exponential of the logit, which tells us the change in odds for $Y = 1$ if we move one step up on X.

Multinomial logistic regression This method is a generalization of logistic regression to categorical dependent variables with more than two non-ordered values.

Ordered logistic regression This is a regression model for ordinal dependent variables.

QUESTIONS

1   What are the problems associated with running a linear regression on a dichotomous dependent variable?
2   What are the assumptions of logistic regression?
3   Which method should be chosen for a categorical dependent variable with more than two values?

FURTHER READING

Hilbe, J.M. (2009) *Logistic Regression Models*. Boca Raton, FL: CRC Press.

This book provides an overview and understanding of terminology and concepts for the full range of logistic models, including binary, proportional, ordered and categorical response regression.

Long, J.S. and Freese, J. (2014) *Regression Models for Categorical Dependent Variables using Stata* (3rd edn). College Station, TX: Stata Press.

Here, the authors provide the reader both with an introduction to Stata and how to use the program to treat categorical dependent variables. It includes a special focus on how to estimate and interpret such models.

Menard, S. (2002) *Applied Logistic Regression Analysis* (2nd edn). Thousand Oaks, CA: Sage.

Part of the Sage series on quantitative applications in the Social Sciences, this book gives the reader a basic understanding of the logic behind logistic modelling.

REFERENCES

Berry, W.D., DeMerrit, J.H.R. and Esarey, J. (2010) Testing for interaction in binary logit and probit models: Is a product term essential? *American Journal of Political Science*, 54(1), 248–266.

Edgeworth, F.Y. (1908) On the probable errors of frequency-constants. *Journal of the Royal Statistical Society*, 71(3), 499–512.

Fisher, R.A. (1912) On an absolute criterion for fitting frequency curves. *Messenger of Mathematics*, 41, 155–160.

Fisher, R.A. (1922) On the mathematical foundations of theoretical statistics. *Philosophical Transactions of the Royal Society of London, Series A*, 222, 309–368.

Hausman, J.A. and McFadden, D.L. (1984) Specification tests for the multinomial logit model. *Econometrica*, 52, 1219–1240.

Hosmer, D.W., Lemeshow, S. and Sturdivant, R.X. (2013) *Applied Logistic Regression*. Hoboken, NJ: Wiley.

King, G. and Zeng, L. (2001) Logistic regression in rare events data. *Political Analysis*, 9(2), 137–163.

Long, J.S. and Freese, J. (2014) *Regression Models for Categorical Dependent Variables using Stata* (3rd edn). College Station, TX: Stata Press.

McFadden, D.L. (1974) Conditional logit analysis of qualitative choice behavior. In P. Zarembka (ed.), *Frontiers in Econometrics* (pp. 105–142). New York: Academic Press.

Menard, S. (2002) *Applied Logistic Regression Analysis* (2nd edn). Thousand Oaks, CA: Sage.

Pregibon, D. (1980) Goodness of link tests for generalized linear models. *Applied Statistics*, 29(1), 15–24.

Pregibon, D. (1981) Logistic regression diagnostics. *Annals of Statistics*, 9(4), 705–724.

Verhulst, P.F. (1838) Notice sur la loi que la population suit dans son accroissement [Instructions on the law of growth in populations]. *Correspondance Mathématique et Physique, publiée par A. Quetelet*, 10, 113–121.

Verhulst, P.F. (1845) Recherches mathématiques sur la soi d'accroissement de la population [Mathematical research into the law of population growth increase]. *Nouveaux Mémoires de l'Académie Royale des Sciences et Belles-Lettres de Bruxelles*, 18, 1–42.

Wald, A. (1943) Tests of statistical hypotheses concerning several parameters when the number of observations is large. *Transactions of the American Mathematical Society*, 54, 426–482.

Williams, R. (2006) Generalized ordered logit/partial proportional odds models for ordinal dependent variables. *Stata Journal*, 6(1), 58–82.

Wonnacott, T.H. and Wonnacott, R.J. (1990) *Introductory Statistics* (5th edn). New York: John Wiley & Sons.

9

MULTILEVEL ANALYSIS

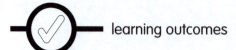

learning outcomes

- o Understand the structure of nested data and why we apply multilevel modelling
- o Use Stata to run different types of multilevel models, including logistic and three-level models

- o Understand the concept of intraclass correlation and how to calculate variance at the different levels
- o Model interaction effects between variables at different levels

Regression models are considered the workhorse of the social sciences. Numerous researchers have investigated thoroughly how individual-level characteristics influence other individual-level characteristics, and how country-level characteristics influence other country-level characteristics. In this chapter we discuss how to treat hierarchical data and run two-level and three-level regression models. We give examples of both linear and logistic multilevel modelling, and of weighting the data.

Harvey Goldstein (1986) is considered to be one of the founders of multilevel modelling. In 1991 he developed software that allowed the user to run so-called two- and three-level models. The assumption of multilevel modelling is that a unit at the lowest level (level 1) was nested within a higher-level unit, such as a region, country or school (level 2); see Figure 9.1. This type of modelling was brought to prominence by Bryk and Raudenbush (2002) with the development of the HLM software for the estimation of hierarchical linear models with two levels.

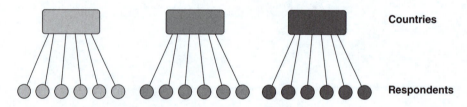

Figure 9.1 **Hierarchical data:** some units are nested within other units

Multilevel modelling soon became popular within educational research, where students were nested within school classes, which again were nested within schools. Ordinary regression models assume the independence of units, and this assumption is breached in such data because of the nesting. This is taken into account when running hierarchical models (another name for multilevel). The object of a multilevel analysis is to account for variance in a dependent variable measured at the lowest level, by investigating information from all levels of analysis. These models are also known as hierarchical linear models, random effects models and random coefficient models.

There are both theoretical and statistical reasons for using a multilevel approach. One theoretical reason for making use of multilevel analysis is that when we are investigating hierarchical data we are often interested in the effects of variables located at different levels. For example, if we are investigating individual behaviour, we could be interested in the

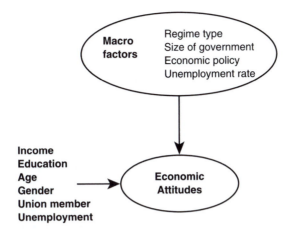

Figure 9.2 Multilevel nature of social phenomena

explanatory power of both characteristics of the individual and with his or her school (or country, or any other level-2 unit), as is illustrated in Figure 9.2. From a theoretical point of view, the researcher would then be concerned with the relationship between the individual and their surroundings, for example arguing that the individual is influenced by the features of his or her country, region, or school. Observations that are close in space are likely to be more similar than observations far apart. Thus, respondents from the same country may be more similar than respondents from different countries due to shared history, experiences, environment, etc. Many of these relationships are unexplored, and pave the way for the up-and-coming social scientist trying to gather new knowledge that can lead to better policy or teaching.

This nesting of units also implies a statistical reason for using multilevel modelling. Such a shared context is a cause of dependency among observations. If the individual-level dependent variable is influenced, for example, by country-level variables, the observations at the lowest level are not independent.

An additional feature is that multilevel modelling is a good statistical reply to the criticism made by several proponents of the qualitative method, namely that one needs to take into account the context of the individuals when studying them. In traditional survey research the individual is often seen in isolation from the context. This is actually one of the advantages of multilevel analysis. By including level-2 factors in the regression equation one allows for the context surrounding the individuals to be accounted for.

9.1 MULTILEVEL DATA

Multilevel analysis presupposes that the data are hierarchically structured. The data could initially be presented in different formats, but to perform the analysis it needs to be presented in long format as in Figure 9.3 (as opposed to a wide format; see Figure 9.4).[1]

---

[1] Long format means that each observation at the lowest level is represented by its own line in the data matrix. For more on wide and long format, see Chapter 2, p. 38.

country	id	woman	age	GDPcapi~1000
1	1	0	31	43.848
1	2	1	46	43.848
1	3	0	37	43.848
2	1	0	56	6.40315
2	2	0	17	6.40315
2	3	1	40	6.40315
3	1	1	67	65.79007
3	2	1	61	65.79007
3	3	0	31	65.79007
4	1	1	66	29.42791
4	2	0	81	29.42791
4	3	0	80	29.42791
5	1	1	47	18.80566
5	2	1	62	18.80566
5	3	0	59	18.80566
6	1	0	23	40.27525
6	2	1	40	40.27525
6	3	1	28	40.27525
7	1	0	70	56.22658
7	2	1	51	56.22658
7	3	0	33	56.22658

Figure 9.3 Long data format

country	woman1	woman2	woman3	age1	age2	age3	GDPcap~10001	GDPcap~10002	GDPcap~10003
1	0	1	0	31	46	37	43.848	43.848	43.848
2	0	0	1	56	17	40	6.40315	6.40315	6.40315
3	1	1	0	67	61	31	65.79007	65.79007	65.79007
4	1	0	0	66	81	80	29.42791	29.42791	29.42791
5	1	1	0	47	62	59	18.80566	18.80566	18.80566
6	0	1	1	23	40	28	40.27525	40.27525	40.27525
7	0	1	0	70	51	33	56.22658	56.22658	56.22658
8	1	0	1	57	20	73	14.26401	14.26401	14.26401
9	1	0	1	40	41	30	31.71424	31.71424	31.71424
10	0	0	0	65	36	36	44.83771	44.83771	44.83771
11	1	1	1	54	77	33	40.47706	40.47706	40.47706
12	0	1	0	42	59	63	35.33128	35.33128	35.33128
13	0	1	0	28	.	55	25.83221	25.83221	25.83221
14	0	0	1	45	25	33	13.4614	13.4614	13.4614
15	0	1	0	17	38	54	12.63455	12.63455	12.63455

Figure 9.4 Wide data format

Multilevel analysis can be seen as a generalization of OLS regression to accommodate the complexities of estimating regression models with two or more levels. One example could be students who are grouped into school classes, and where these classes are nested within schools. Other examples are individuals who are grouped within countries, departments within faculties, or even test results grouped within students.

In Figure 9.5, pupils are nested within classes, which are nested within schools. Data on the students' individual characteristics are called level-1 data, while data on the classes and on the schools are called level-2 and level-3 data, respectively. There is no theoretical limit for the number of levels in a multilevel model. However, the models become increasingly complex with increased numbers of levels. The simplest model is one with two levels.

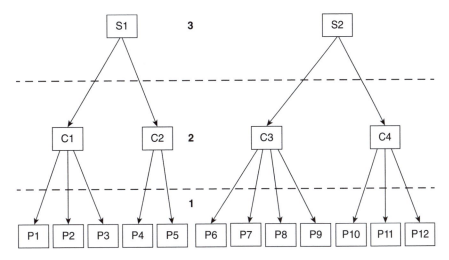

Figure 9.5 Schools, classes and pupils

Table 9.1 Example of multilevel data where students are nested within classes

Class (level 2)	Student (level 1)	Y (level 1)	X_1 (level 1)	X_2 (level 2)
1	1	12	33	1
1	2	16	25	1
1	3	14	35	1
1	4	15	40	1
2	1	22	93	0
2	2	23	64	0
2	3	26	86	0
2	4	26	86	0
3	1	18	58	1
3	2	20	53	1

Table 9.1 gives an example where we have a dependent variable (Y) situated at level 1 (students' test score), one X-variable at the student level (level 1), and one that varies at the class level (level 2). In Table 9.2 we add a third level (school) to the data structure.

A level is a variable that identifies units sampled from a population (where statistical tests based on sampling theory are used), or which constitutes the whole population (i.e., all OECD countries). For example, students can be thought of as a random sample of students within each school, and the schools can be thought of as a random sample from a larger population of schools. We call this variable an *identifier* variable. There needs to be an identifier at each level of the model except the first. Therefore, if there are more than two levels, there is more than one identifier.

Table 9.2 Example of multilevel data where students are nested within classes which are then nested within schools

School (level 3)	Class (level 2)	Student (level 1)	Y (level 1)	X_1 (level 1)	X_2 (level 2)
1	1	1	12	33	1
1	1	2	16	25	1
1	1	3	14	35	1
1	1	4	15	40	1
1	2	1	22	93	0
1	2	2	23	64	0
1	2	3	26	86	0
1	2	4	26	86	0
1	3	1	18	58	1
1	3	2	20	53	1

The explanatory variables included in the model are situated at the different levels (although it is not necessary to include X-variables at each level), and their coefficients are estimated in an appropriate manner. However, the dependent variable is situated at the lowest level, and can be a function of lower- and higher-level factors. In Table 9.3 we have listed some examples of hierarchical structures often encountered in the social sciences.

Table 9.3 Different types of hierarchical data structures

Level 3			Schools	Countries	Countries
Level 2	Firms	Students	Classes	Regions	Years
Level 1	Employees	Tests	Students	Respondents	Respondents

9●1●1 Statistical reasons for using multilevel analysis

The objective of a multilevel analysis is to account for variance in a dependent variable measured at the lowest level by analysing information from all levels of analysis. As already mentioned, one statistical reason for employing multilevel modelling is the fact that respondents in hierarchical data share a context or frame of reference. For example, respondents from the same country possess more similarities than with respondents from other countries, due, among other things, to shared history, experiences, and environment. Ordinary regression analysis becomes problematic due to the shared dependency of individuals belonging to the same group (Bartels, 1996).

Such a shared context is a cause of dependency among observations. This intra-unit correlation changes the error variance of ordinary least-squares regression models, which represents the effect of the omitted variables *plus* the measurement errors, assuming that these errors are unrelated (Kreft and de Leeuw, 1998). It is this complex error structure that invalidates OLS regression as an estimation procedure. To compensate for this, multilevel modelling allows for the estimation of errors at all levels simultaneously with the linear coefficients (Ringdal, 1992).

If the level-1 dependent variable is influenced by level-2 variables, the observations at the lowest level are not independent; that is, they are clustered. If one violates the assumption that errors are independent, this will cause the estimated standard errors to be too low and the *t*-statistics to be too high (Steenbergen and Jones, 2002). By ignoring that there is a contextual level one could underestimate the standard errors and thus get invalid statistical test results. In multilevel regression the standard errors of level-2 (and also level-3, etc.) variables are estimated based on the *N* for the corresponding level. In an ordinary regression these would be calculated based on the level-1 *N*, resulting in standard errors that are too small and thus the risk of a Type I error. Hox (2010) also warns about the danger of interpreting aggregated data from the individual level, which leads to the ecological fallacy.[2]

For some sorts of structured data (such as panel data) it is common to use a *fixed effects model* (see Chapter 10, p. 240). However, this model has one drawback which makes it inferior to a multilevel model: one cannot model variables that are situated at level 2 (Jones, 2008).

Multilevel modelling is also called mixed modelling. It is a compromise between the two extremes of complete pooling and no pooling. The former means ignoring differences between groups and running a single regression, while the latter means running a regression on each group separately. It is defined as *partial pooling* (Gelman and Hill, 2007).

If we investigated all the level-2 units together (complete pooling) we would overstate the variation among these units. But if we ran separate regressions (no pooling) we would overfit the data within each level-2 unit, as it could be fitted with a small number of data points.

9.2 EMPTY OR INTERCEPT-ONLY MODEL

Multilevel models are usually estimated using maximum likelihood, restricted maximum likelihood or iterative generalized least-squares algorithms. In our examples we will use the most common type of calculation for our models, namely maximum likelihood, which is also used in logistic regression. In brief, maximum likelihood estimation finds the coefficients that make the data most likely. The maximum likelihood estimate is the hypothetical population value that is more likely than any other to generate the sample we actually observed (Wonnacott and Wonnacott, 1990: 568).

To understand the basics of multilevel modelling we start with an ordinary OLS regression equation for an empty model:

$$Y_i = \beta_0 + e_i . \tag{9.1}$$

Here *Y* is the value of the dependent variable for individual *i*, while β_0 is the regression intercept (the same as the mean), and e_i is the error term (or residual) for individual *i*. In an empty model the intercept approximately equals the mean value of the sample. Here we assume that the mean is the same for all individuals regardless of which group (school, firm, country) they belong to. The residuals are the individual deviations from the mean (as illustrated in Figure 9.6).

---

[2] When inferences about individuals are deduced from the group they belong to.

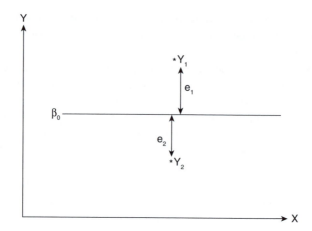

Figure 9.6 Level-1 residuals

However, if we have hierarchical data we would obtain more realistic estimates by employing a multilevel model. The two-level version of the empty model is given by:

$$Y_{ij} = \beta_{0j} + e_{ij} . \tag{9.2}$$

Though similar in certain respects, there are some important differences between equations (9.1) and (9.2). Y_{ij} is the value for an individual i from country (or school, firm, etc.) j. On the right-hand side of the equation, β_{0j} is the mean value of the dependent variable in country j (and not the mean for individuals in all countries). The error term e_{ij} is the difference between the observed value of our dependent variable for an individual i from country j, and the country mean of the dependent variable (as seen in Figure 9.7).

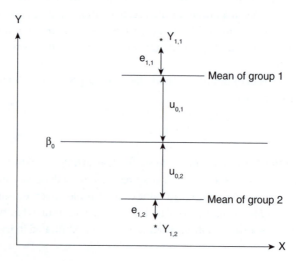

Figure 9.7 Level-1 and level-2 residuals

The mean value of the dependent variable for the countries in our sample can further be defined as

$$\beta_{0j} = \beta_0 + u_{0j}.$$ (9.3)

Here β_0 is the overall mean of the dependent variable, while u_{0j} is the error term, which is the difference between the group mean for country j and the total mean. Substituting equation (9.3) into equation (9.2) gives

$$Y_{ij} = \beta_0 + u_{0j} + e_{ij},$$ (9.4)

which essentially means:

$$dependent\_variable = total\_mean + error\_term\_level\_2 + error\_term\_level\_1.$$

There are two error terms: one for the country level and one for the individual level. We are now concerned with three coefficients: the total mean, the variance of the level-2 error term, and the variance of the level-1 error term. We can call these var(u_0) and var(e), respectively. This multilevel estimate for a given country j is a weighted average of the mean of the observations in the country $\bar{Y}_j$ and the mean of all countries $\bar{Y}_{all}$ (Gelman and Hill, 2007).

9•2•1 Example in Stata

Here we use individual-level data from the European Social Survey,[3] and open the dataset called *Lab1_ESS5.dta*. The dependent variable in our example is called *political trust* (0–30), which is a scale made by collapsing three related variables. High values indicate that the respondents have a great deal of trust in their country's institutions. This measure has an N of 46,341 and a mean of 10.256. There are 25 countries in our dataset.

We can use Stata to test the empty model. We use the `mixed` command for this. Since we argue that there are two levels in our model (individual and country) we need to find a variable that identifies level 2 (countries). We code this from the original variable called `cntry` (see Figure 9.8):

```
. tab cntry
```

Then we create our new variable by transforming our string variable *cntry* to the numerical variable *country*:[4]

```
. encode cntry, g(country)
```

We now have a level-2 identifier variable called `country`:

```
. mixed political_trust || country:, ml variance
```

---

[3] We use data from ESS (2004, 2006, 2008, 2010).

[4] It is also possible to use the variable *cntry* as an identifier variable. The variable *country* is included in the dataset. To generate it you must first write: `drop country`.

Country	Freq.	Percent	Cum.
BE	1,704	3.51	3.51
BG	2,434	5.02	8.53
CH	1,506	3.11	11.64
CY	1,083	2.23	13.87
CZ	2,386	4.92	18.79
DE	3,031	6.25	25.05
DK	1,576	3.25	28.30
EE	1,793	3.70	31.99
ES	1,885	3.89	35.88
FI	1,878	3.87	39.75
FR	1,728	3.56	43.32
GB	2,422	5.00	48.31
GR	2,715	5.60	53.91
HR	1,649	3.40	57.31
HU	1,561	3.22	60.53
IE	2,576	5.31	65.85
NL	1,829	3.77	69.62
NO	1,548	3.19	72.81
PL	1,751	3.61	76.42
PT	2,150	4.43	80.86
RU	2,595	5.35	86.21
SE	1,497	3.09	89.30
SI	1,403	2.89	92.19
SK	1,856	3.83	96.02
UA	1,931	3.98	100.00
Total	48,487	100.00	

Figure 9.8 Descriptive statistics of countries

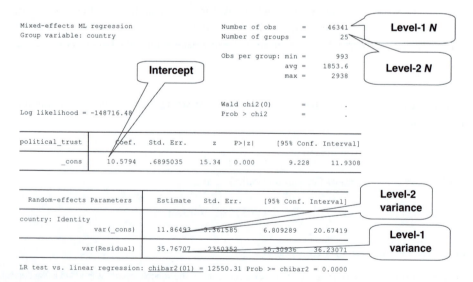

Figure 9.9 Empty random intercept model

Note the use of `ml` in the command. This is to specify that we fit the model using maximum likelihood. However, if we leave it out the model will still be calculated using maximum likelihood since this is the default option. The same is the case for `variance`, which tells us to display the variance components.

Figure 9.9 tells us that for level 1 we have $N = 46{,}341$ and for level 2 we have $N = 25$. We can also see that the mean N within each country is 1853.6. Here it is important to state that we do not need to have the same N for each country, nor is there any need to weight our level-1 units to achieve equal N. From a purely statistical point of view, one of the strengths of multilevel analysis is that one does not require the same number of units. However, from a substantive view we might want to weight them. For example, the size of the samples in each group may be a result of chance. Later, we will see how we can use the design weight to correct for this.

In the final table of the output we get var(e) in the second row (marked 'Residual'), and var(u_0) in the first row (marked '_cons'). This shows how much of the variance in our dependent variable (which is measured at level 1) can be explained by the individual and country level, respectively. The total variance is the sum of these two.

9.3 VARIANCE PARTITION OR INTRACLASS CORRELATION

We can find the amount of level-2 variance by calculating the *variance partition coefficient* (also known as the *intraclass correlation coefficient*). The VPC/ICC represents the proportion of the total variability in the outcome that is attributable to the second level:

$$\text{VPC} = \frac{\text{var}(u_0)}{\text{var}(e) + \text{var}(u_0)} \tag{9.5}$$

$$= \frac{11.865}{35.767 + 11.865} = 0.249.$$

Thus 24.9 per cent of the variance in the dependent variable is at level 2,[5] and thus $100 - 24.9 = 75.1$ per cent of the variance is at level 1. In the social sciences the norm is that the lion's share of the variance is at the individual level. A rule of thumb here is that if the VPC/ICC is 5 per cent or more it should not be ignored. If it is smaller, one can consider single-level models with robust estimation of standard errors (see Chapter 10).

The variance components can be explained by looking at our data. We have more than 46,000 individuals, all of whom have a score between 0 and 30 on *political trust*. Some people have a lot of trust (high scores), while others have little trust (low scores). Thus, we have variation in the values of *political trust*. This variation is measured by the variance, and is proportional to the sum of squared distance between the observed values of *political trust* and the mean value for the whole sample.

In multilevel modelling one divides the component into two parts. The first component (level 1) consists of the sum of the squared distances between each respondent within a country (e.g., Sweden) and the mean value of *political trust* for that particular country. The sums for each country are then totalled to give var(e). This variance component is also called the *within* component.

---

[5] You can also get this quantity by writing `estat icc` after running your model.

Our second variance component, the var(u_0) is proportional to the sum of the squared distances between the countries' mean values of *political trust* and the mean value for the whole sample. This is also called the *between* component. When running more advanced models the VPC/ICC is used as a baseline for estimating the variances at the different levels.

9.4 RANDOM INTERCEPT MODEL

In the social sciences the researcher is often interested in causal relationships, and thus wishes to see if there are any explanatory variables that exert influence on our dependent measure. The procedure when it comes to individual-level *X*-variables is similar to that of ordinary least-squares regression.

We now expand our model and introduce four independent variables measured at the individual level, namely *woman* (1=woman), *age*, *unemployed* (1=unemployed), and *years of education*:

$$Y_{ij} = \beta_0 + \beta_1 X_{1ij} + \beta_2 X_{2ij} + \beta_3 X_{3ij} + \beta_4 X_{4ij} + u_{0j} + e_{ij} ,$$ (9.6)

where the *ij* suffix on our *X*-variables means that they denote the value on *X* for individual *i* in country *j*. The following command produces the output in Figure 9.10:

```
. mixed political_trust woman age unemployed eduyrs || country:, ml variance
```

The fixed effect coefficients (Marked Effect of Variables) we see in the output are the average effects of the entire sample of countries. As such, it is of no major concern if some countries

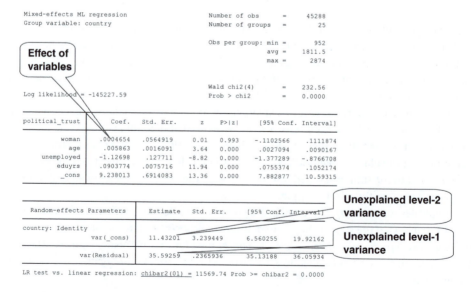

Figure 9.10 Stata output for random intercept model

have fewer or more units at level 1 than others.[6] We see that there is no significant effect of gender. Older persons have more trust than younger ones. Being unemployed is associated with lower trust levels. More education means more trust. The variance components have also been reduced by under 4 per cent (compared to the empty model). For the individual-level variance, var(e), the explanation is the same as in linear regression. Our new model (with the three independent variables) gives a better representation of the data, and thus less distance between the observed and predicted values. In other words, some of the variation in political trust can be explained by the X-variables included in our model.

The reduction in the unexplained level-2 variance, var(u_0), is due to the random intercept. That is, we take into account in the model that different countries have different means of the dependent variable.[7]

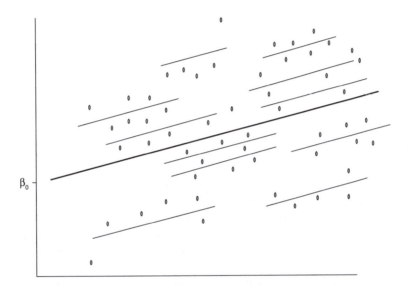

Figure 9.11 Random intercept model

In our random intercept model each country has a different intercept, and we get the mean intercept (constant) presented in the output (Figure 9.11). The regression lines are fixed and are interpreted in the same way as in ordinary linear regression. So β_1 is the increase in the response for a one-unit increase in X_1. For dummy variables, the starting points will be different, but the effect of having the value 1 is the same for each country (Figure 9.12).

---

[6] Only a small sample size at a higher level (2, 3, …) leads to biased estimates of the standard errors at the same level (Maas and Hox, 2005).

[7] It should be noted that a multilevel model is not the same as a fixed effects model. In the former, the level-2 error term is assumed to be normally distributed and independent of the other variables in the model as well as the level-1 error term. In the latter, this error term is treated as a set of fixed numbers which are estimated in the model. To visualize multilevel regression we can think of it as a regression with dummies for each level-2 unit, thus giving them different starting points on the Y-axis.

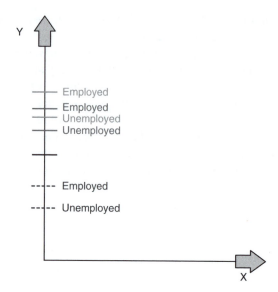

Figure 9.12   Random intercept, dummy explanatory variable

9 ● 5   LEVEL-2 EXPLANATORY VARIABLES

We now expand our model to include variables at the country level. There are only 25 level-2 units in our dataset, so we can easily download or code in the data for these in a separate dataset with countries as units. Here, we need to make sure that we have an identifier variable that has the same values in both datasets (in our case *country*).

We have reason to believe that how rich a society is will influence individual attitudes. Therefore we want to include *per capita GDP* in our analysis. It is a good idea to divide it by 1000 for easier interpretation (to avoid a coefficient of 0.000), which will not change the substantive results. When using country data it is common to use data from the year prior to the survey (because of causality). Remember that we need to include a similar identifier variable in both datasets before we merge them:[8]

```
. merge m:1 country using GDPcapita.dta
```

In regression there is a rule of thumb that there should be at the very least 10 observations for each independent variable. If we have less than 15–20 level-2 units this leads to confidence intervals that are unreliable (Stegmueller, 2013). It is important to stress that we only have 25 units at level 2, and thus should not include more than two level-2 variables in our model. Stata will identify which variables vary only between countries (and not between individuals) and calculate the standard errors for their coefficient based on the level-2 *N*.

---

[8] Before the file name, you need to enter the location of the dataset on your computer, for example c:\stata\GDP capita.dta. For more on merging, see Chapter 2, pp. 37–38. We have included *GDPcapita1000* in the working data, so in order to test the merge function you must first drop this variable: drop GDPcapita1000.

As such, it is more difficult to produce significant results (since a small N leads to a large standard error), but it is the correct way of doing it. A result at level 2 needs to be strong in order to be significant, so the researcher might consider also discussing results that are significant at the 0.10 level (in addition to the 0.05 and 0.01 levels).[9]

If we include *per capita GDP* our model can formally be written as

$$Y_{ij} = \beta_0 + \beta_1 X_{1ij} + \beta_2 X_{2ij} + \beta_3 X_{3ij} + \beta_4 X_{4ij} + \beta_5 X_{5j} + e_{ij} + u_{0j}. \tag{9.7}$$

We note that our new variable, X_{5j}, has subscript j rather than ij. This tells us that it is a level-2 variable that only varies between countries. We can now run our model:

```
. mixed political_trust woman age unemployed eduyrs GDPcapita1000 || country:,
ml variance
```

Mixed-effects ML regression Number of obs = 45288
Group variable: country Number of groups = 25

Obs per group: min = 952
avg = 1811.5
max = 2874

Level-2 variable

Log likelihood = -145215.39 Wald chi2(5) = 275.58
Prob > chi2 = 0.0000

political_trust	Coef.	Std. Err.	z	P>|z|	[95% Conf. Interval]
woman	.0009456	.0564918	0.02	0.987	-.1097762	.1116674
age	.0058665	.001609	3.65	0.000	.0027129	.0090201
unemployed	-1.127754	.1277087	-8.83	0.000	-1.378059	-.8774497
eduyrs	.0904258	.0075707	11.94	0.000	.0755874	.1052641
GDPcapita1000	.1409978	.0219212	6.43	0.000	.0980331	.1839626
_cons	4.839403	.8118732	5.96	0.000	3.248161	6.430645

SE calculated based on level-2 N

Random-effects Parameters	Estimate	Std. Err.	[95% Conf. Interval]
country: Identity			
var(_cons)	4.293036	1.219944	2.459689	7.492881
var(Residual)	35.59258	.2365935	35.13188	36.05933

LR test vs. linear regression: chibar2(01) = 5176.31 Prob >= chibar2 = 0.0000

Figure 9.13 Random intercept model, including level-2 variable

We notice from Figure 9.13 that the unexplained variance at level-2 has decreased (which could be expected since we included a country-level variable). We also see that the level-1 variance is the same as in the previous model (which could also be expected since we did not include any new variables at this level).

---

[9] The inclusion of clusters using the `vce(cluster clustvar)` option in OLS regression also helps in calculating the standard errors using the correct N. However, multilevel modelling is a safer alternative to clustering when it comes to over-rejection of the null hypothesis. A study by Bertrand et al. (2004) found substantial over-rejection also when correcting for clustering.

The interpretation of the effect of level-2 variables is somewhat different from that for level-1 variables. For each one-unit (1000-dollar) increase in per capita GDP, the country's mean for political trust increases by 0.141 points.

9•5•1 How much of the dependent variable is explained?

In ordinary regression R^2 tells us how much of the variation in the dependent variable is explained by the entire model. In hierarchically structured data we can calculate an analogous measure by estimating both an empty model (as in Figure 9.9) and a full model (as in Figure 9.10); see Bryk and Raudenbush (2002) and Hox (2010). We need to calculate how much of the level-1 and level-2 variance is explained by the independent variables which are included. The equation for level 1 is

$$R^2 = \frac{\text{var}(e)_b - \text{var}(e)_m}{\text{var}(e)_b}, \tag{9.8}$$

where $\text{var}(e)_b$ is the level-1 residual variance for the baseline model (Figure 9.7) and $\text{var}(e)_m$ is the level-1 variance for our model presented in Figure 9.11. We calculate

$$R^2 = \left(\frac{35.76707 - 35.59258}{35.76707} \right) = 0.0049,$$

which means that only 0.5 per cent of the variance at the individual level is explained by our model. For the level-2 variance the formula is

$$R^2 = \frac{\text{var}(u_0)_b - \text{var}(u_0)_m}{\text{var}(u_0)_b}, \tag{9.9}$$

where $\text{var}(u_0)_b$ is the level-2 residual variance for the baseline model (Figure 9.7) and $\text{var}(u_0)_m$ is the level-2 variance for our model presented in Figure 9.11. We calculate

$$R^2 = \left(\frac{11.86493 - 4.293036}{11.86493} \right) = 0.6382,$$

which means that 63.82 per cent of the variance at the country level is explained by our model (or by *per capita GDP*).

However, these measures are not unproblematic. Under some circumstances a variable can actually make a negative contribution to the explained variance, and these calculations are less valuable when it comes to models that include one or more random slopes.

9●6 LOGISTIC MULTILEVEL MODEL

The parameters of logistic models are estimated using maximum likelihood estimation. Multilevel models are also usually estimated using maximum likelihood. When combining logistic and multilevel modelling, the result is very complex calculations with large data requirements. The more units and variables there are in the model, the more complex the calculations are.

We use an example from Round 5 of the European Social Survey. This dataset is called *Lab2_ESS.dta*. The dependent variable is a dummy (0–1) denoting whether the respondent voted in the last national election, and we include explanatory variables at both the individual level and country level to explain the outcome. The level-2 variable is a dummy variable denoting whether a given country is Nordic or not (*Nordic*):

$$L_{ij} = \beta_0 + \beta_1 X_{1ij} + \beta_2 X_{2ij} + \beta_3 X_{3j} + e_{ij} + u_{0j}. \tag{9.10}$$

Equation (9.10) states that our dependent variable is a proportion and that we use a logit link function (the natural logarithm of the odds of the probability of $Y = 1$, expressed as $\log(p/(1-p))$). We also assume that, dependent on our explanatory variables, our Y-variable has a binomial distribution of errors. From the equation we read that we have two level-1 explanatory variables and one from level 2 (country). To run this model in Stata we type

```
. melogit vote age woman Nordic || Level2:,
```

```
Mixed-effects logistic regression              Number of obs      =      44,470
Group variable:              Level2             Number of groups   =          25

                                                Obs per group:
                                                              min =       1,010
                                                              avg =     1,778.8
                                                              max =       2,724

Integration method: mvaghermite                 Integration pts.   =           7

                                                Wald chi2(3)       =     1402.33
Log likelihood = -22689.865                     Prob > chi2        =      0.0000
```

vote	Coef.	Std. Err.	z	P>|z|	[95% Conf. Interval]	
age	.0253489	.0006827	37.13	0.000	.0240107	.026687
woman	.0326152	.0233816	1.39	0.163	-.0132118	.0784423
Nordic	.9549393	.2255426	4.23	0.000	.512884	1.396995
_cons	-.1003013	.0953848	-1.05	0.293	-.2872521	.0866496
Level2						
var(_cons)	.1638142	.0478219			.0924405	.290296

```
LR test vs. logistic model: chibar2(01) = 909.96     Prob >= chibar2 = 0.0000
```

Figure 9.14 Logistic multilevel model

We obtain the output in Figure 9.14. For the logistic multilevel model the same rules regarding transformations from logit to probability apply as in ordinary logit regression. We see that we have 44,470 level-1 and 25 level-2 units.

The computation time of a logistic multilevel model is a function of the number of parameters, the level-1 N, the number of quadrature points (the default option of `melogit` is *adaptive Gaussian quadrature*) and the total dimension of random effects. Thus, with large datasets and/ or a complex model, `melogit` can be time-consuming. If it proves to be difficult to produce the results of the logistic multilevel regression, then we have other options available. One is to run the `laplace` option. Then Stata will use the *Laplacian* approximation for calculating the results, which sets the number of quadrature points to one. However, we must keep in mind that the Laplacian approximation can produce biased parameter estimates, and should primarily be used before running your final model:

```
. melogit vote age woman Nordic || Level2:, intmethod(laplace)
```

Note that we can also do multilevel ordered logistic regression using the `meologit` command. There is no command for multilevel multinomial logistic regression; however, such models can be fitted using `gsem` (for more on these topics, see Chapter 8).

9 7 RANDOM COEFFICIENT (SLOPE) MODEL

In the previous models we assumed that all the level-1 dependent variables had the same effects in all countries included, and that the effects were fixed. However, often this is not the case in real life. For example, it could be that the effect of education was very different from one country to another. To take this into account we can use *random coefficient* models which allow variation in the regression coefficients between countries (Figure 9.15). Such models permit both the intercept and coefficients to vary, and both fixed and random coefficients can be included.

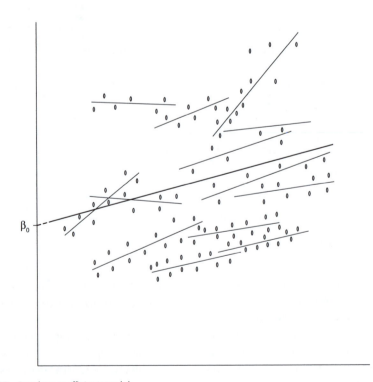

Figure 9.15 Random coefficient model

The effects of an independent variable will always differ from one country to another, and by modelling some variables as having a random slope we make the model more complex. To justify the use of random coefficients we need to have good reason to believe that the effects should vary substantially from one level-2 unit to another. We should only allow for random slope if it leads to a statistically significant improvement of the model. The reason for this is that the number of parameters to be estimated becomes too large and the model may not converge.

Here we use the dataset *Lab1_ESS5.dta*. Let us assume that we wish to set the variable *education years* as a random coefficient; that is, we will allow the effect to vary between level-2 units. We then make a small adjustment to equation (9.7), and get the following definition of a random coefficient model:

$$Y_{ij} = \beta_0 + \beta_1 X_{1ij} + \beta_2 X_{2ij} + \beta_3 X_{3ij} + \beta_4 X_{4ij} + \beta_5 X_{5j} + u_{0j} + u_{1j} X_{4ij} + e_{ij}, \qquad (9.11)$$

where it is seen that $u_{1j} X_{4ij}$ has been added. This is a new error term (or we could call it a random effect) that represents the difference between the effect of education in a given level-2 unit and the expected effect for all level-2 units, which is called β_4. We now estimate the expected coefficient of education as well as the residuals around this expected value for the different countries in our sample. There are now three types of residuals in our model. We can run the random coefficient model in Stata by including the variable(s) we wish to vary after the level-2 identifier:

`. mixed political_trust woman age unemployed eduyrs GDPcapita1000 || country: eduyrs, ml variance`

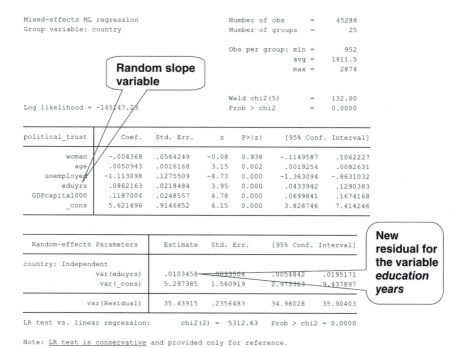

Figure 9.16 Random slope model

There are some minor changes in the coefficients, as we now have a better model fit. What is new is that we now have the output for the residual variance of *education years* which we call $Var(u_{1j})$.[10]

In the output in Figure 9.16 we get the mean coefficient for education years reported. In order to see the coefficient estimates for each country, we can run the following syntax after running the model:

```
. predict ebs ebi, reffects
. replace ebs = _b[political_trust:eduyrs] + ebs
. graph dot (mean) ebs, over (country, sort(ebs)) scheme(s1mono) plotregion
(style(none)) ytitle(Estimated coefficients [EB])
```

Going back to the point about whether or not we should model a variable as having a random slope, we should only do so if it constitutes a significant improvement of our model. Here, we should undertake a test based on the size of the log likelihood. We call this procedure a –2 log-likelihood test:

$$\chi^2_H = -2(LL_{K-H} - LL_K), \qquad (9.12)$$

where χ^2_H has a chi-squared distribution, LL_K is the large model (in this case where the variable is modelled as a random coefficient), and LL_{K-H} is the small model (where the variable in question is modelled as a fixed coefficient). We find the log-likelihood value for our small model (see Figure 9.13) to be –145,215.39 and the log-likelihood for our large model (Figure 9.16) to be –145,147.23. Then

$$\chi^2_H = -2(-145,215.39 - (-145,147.23)) = 136.32.$$

The degrees of freedom are given by the difference in the number of parameters (H), which in our case is only the single parameter u_{1j}. We then check the critical values in a chi-squared distribution with one degree of freedom ($df = 1$). Our χ^2_H value is highly significant – much larger than the corresponding critical value at the .001 level (which is 10.830).

The lrtest command may also be used to determine if a model is a significant improvement on another model. This provides us with the chi-squared distribution difference between the difference between each model and a linear regression. This number is found at the bottom of the output of Figures 9.11 and 9.14; the numbers are 5176.31 and 5312.63, respectively. The difference between these numbers is 136.31, so this is just another way of performing exactly the same test.[11]

---

[10] The default option in Stata is that the random slope and the random intercept are independent of one another. It is recommended that you include the cov (unstructured) option to get results that are translation-invariant (to avoid different results if you, for example, centre the variables). The model would then be written mixed political_trust woman age unemployed eduyrs GDPcapita1000 || country: eduyrs, cov(unstructured) ml variance.

[11] Difference of 0.01 is due to rounding up of decimals.

For the `lrtest` we need to run both models and save their estimates:

```
. qui mixed political_trust woman age unemployed eduyrs GDPcapita1000 ||
country:, ml variance
. estimates store ri
. qui mixed political_trust woman age unemployed eduyrs GDPcapita1000 ||
country: eduyrs, ml variance
. estimates store rc
. lrtest ri rc
```

```
     Likelihood-ratio test                     LR chi2(1)   =     136.31
     (Assumption: ri nested in rc)             Prob > chi2 =     0.0000
```

9.8 INTERACTION EFFECTS

Interaction effects between two variables at level 1 or between two variables at level 2 are interpreted in the same manner as regular interactions (see Chapter 6). There is no new error term in the equation when the variables in the interaction are situated at the same level. The standard error for the interaction term is calculated using the corresponding N (level-1 N if it is a level-1 interaction, level-2 N if it is a level-2 interaction). We devote the rest of this section to cross-level interaction.

We have a dummy variable, *Nordic*, denoting whether a level-2 unit is a Nordic country (Norway, Sweden, Denmark or Finland) or not. There is reason to believe that the effect of *age* (level 1) differs between Nordic and other European countries. In other words, that the variation between countries in the effect of education (as modelled in our random coefficient model) is not coincidental, but rather follows a pattern that we can model through what we call a *cross-level interaction term*.[12]

Such interaction terms between variables at different levels are often of interest when it comes to hierarchical modelling. The interpretation of such cross-level interaction terms is not different from that of an ordinary interaction term. It is formally described as:

$$Y_{ij} = \beta_0 + \beta_1 X_{1ij} + \beta_2 X_{2ij} + \beta_3 X_{3ij} + \beta_4 X_{4ij} + \beta_5 X_{5j} + \beta_6 X_{6j} + \beta_7 X_{2ij} X_{6j} + e_{ij} + u_{0j} + u_{1j} X_{2ij}, \quad (9.13)$$

where we have included a cross-level interaction term[13] $\beta_7 X_{2ij} X_{6j}$ and an extra error term for the level-1 variable $u_{1j} X_{2ij}$. We then type the following command in Stata:

```
. mixed political_trust woman age unemployed eduyrs GDPcapita1000 Nordic
Nordicage || country:, ml variance
```

The output is presented in Figure 9.17.

---

[12] Contrary to our example, Hox (2010) recommends that models including cross-level interactions should have at least 50 units at level 2.

[13] Cross-level interaction terms can be created by multiplying two variables (`generate Nordicage = Nordic*age`) or by using the `margins` option `##`. For more on interaction terms, see Chapter 6.

```
Mixed-effects ML regression                    Number of obs      =      45288
Group variable: country                        Number of groups   =         25

                                               Obs per group: min =        952
                                                              avg =     1811.5
                                                              max =       2874

                                               Wald chi2(7)       =     325.14
Log likelihood = -145195.14                    Prob > chi2        =     0.0000
```

political_trust	Coef.	Std. Err.	z	P>|z|	[95% Conf. Interval]
woman	-.0033925	.0564739	-0.06	0.952	-.1140793 .1072942
age	.0097856	.0017361	5.64	0.000	.0063829 .0131882
unemployed	-1.106167	.1277087	-8.66	0.000	-1.356471 -.8558625
eduyrs	.0923733	.0075745	12.20	0.000	.0775275 .1072191
GDPcapita1000	.1107031	.0242622	4.56	0.000	.0631501 .1582561
Nordic	4.041632	1.272009	3.18	0.001	1.548541 6.534723
Nordicage	-.0262395	.0043725	-6.00	0.000	-.0348094 -.0176695
_cons	5.126396	.7794626	6.58	0.000	3.598677 6.654114

Interaction effect

Random-effects Parameters	Estimate	Std. Err.	[95% Conf. Interval]
country: Identity			
var(_cons)	3.596747	1.023085	2.059624 6.281045
var(Residual)	35.56422	.236405	35.10388 36.0306

LR test vs. linear regression: chibar2(01) = 4315.98 Prob >= chibar2 = 0.0000

Figure 9.17 Model including cross-level interaction term

This interaction effect is relatively easy to interpret. We see that the effect of age is positive for non-Nordic countries (as they only get the positive effect of the *age* variable) and negative for Nordic countries (as they get the positive effect of *age*, and the larger negative effect of *Nordicage*). This can be graphed quite easily. First we can find the mean value of *political trust* in our sample by using the e(sample) command (see Figure 9.18):

. sum political_trust if e(sample)

Variable	Obs	Mean	Std. Dev.	Min	Max
political_~t	45288	10.27438	6.861295	0	30

Figure 9.18 Descriptive statistics for political trust

We then use the mean as the basis for our graph, and enter the appropriate values for the variables that constitute our cross-level interaction term. First, we predict the effect of age for the Nordic countries, and then do the same for the non-Nordic countries (see Figure 9.19):

. gen L1=10.27438+0.0097856*age+4.041631*1-0.0262395*1*age
. gen L2=10.27438+0.0097856*age+4.041631*0-0.0262395*0*age
. graph twoway mspline L1 age || mspline L2 age

It should be noted that the standard error for this cross-level interaction is calculated using the *N* of the lowest level (in our case 45,288). We can also use the margins command to

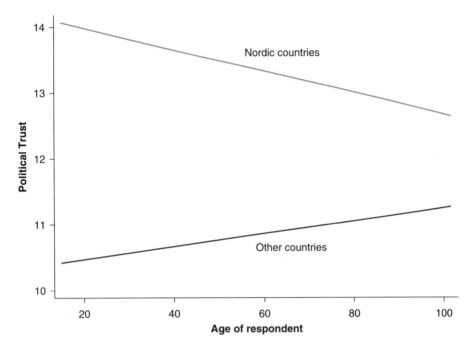

Figure 9.19 Cross-level interaction effect, *age* and *Nordic* on *political trust*

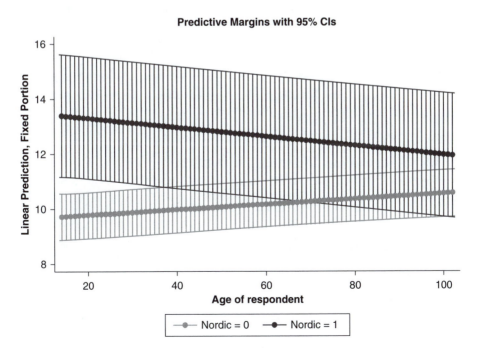

Figure 9.20 Marginsplot of *age* and *Nordic* on *political trust*

produce the same plot with confidence intervals (Figure 9.20). All the other variables are set at their mean values (so we get a different and more correct starting point at the Y-axis):[14]

```
. quietly mixed political_trust woman unemployed eduyrs GDPcapita1000
i.Nordic##c.age || country:, ml variance
. margins, at(age=(14(1)102) Nordic=( 0 1))
. marginsplot
```

9●9 THREE-LEVEL MODELS

As previously mentioned, there is no theoretical limit to how many levels one can model; this will depend on the data structure at hand. For the two-level model predicting *political trust* we used individuals as level-1 units and countries as level-2 units. The survey was conducted at approximately the same time in all countries.

Now we use data from four waves of the ESS (2004, 2006, 2008, 2010) in the dataset *Lab3_ESS.dta*. We now have countries (level 3), country survey years (e.g., France 2004, France 2006, etc.) and individual respondents. This means that we can also include independent variables on all three levels. As shown in Table 9.4, the variable *per capita GDP* varies from one country year to another, while the dummy variable *Nordic* (denoting whether it is a Nordic country or not) varies at the country level.

Table 9.4 Structure of three-level data

Country (level-3)	Country year (level-2)	Per capita GDP 1000	Nordic
Germany (6)	2004 (18)	29.36741	0
Germany (6)	2006 (19)	33.54278	0
Germany (6)	2008 (20)	50.27525	0
Germany (6)	2010 (21)	40.40299	0
Ireland (16)	2004 (55)	39.81493	0
Ireland (16)	2006 (56)	45.87319	0
Ireland (16)	2008 (57)	48.86639	0
Ireland (16)	2010 (58)	59.57357	0
Norway (18)	2004 (63)	49.26351	1
Norway (18)	2006 (64)	65.76702	1
Norway (18)	2008 (65)	77.61002	1
Norway (18)	2010 (66)	83.55625	1

The numbers alongside the country names and years in Table 9.4 are their values on our two identifier variables *Level-2* and *Level-3*. We can use *Level-3* and a time variable (in our case

---

[14] Since these are straight lines, it is not necessary to produce a predictive margin at every year. We could also have written: at (age= (14 102). The margins can take some time to compute if the dataset is large.

we have a variable denoting which survey the respondent answered) and create our level-2 identifier variable:

```
. egen Level2 = group(Level3 essround)
```

Then we can code or download explanatory variables:[15]

```
. merge m:1 Level2 using GDPcapitaLevel3.dta
```

Our three-level random intercept model can be defined as

$$Y_{ijk} = \beta_0 + e_{ijk} + u_{0jk} + v_{0k}, \tag{9.14}$$

where i stands for individuals (as previously), but j now denotes country years, and k represents countries. The level-3 error term is denoted by v_{0k}. We can now run an empty (or intercept) model in Stata:

```
. mixed political_trust || Level3:, || Level2:, ml variance
```

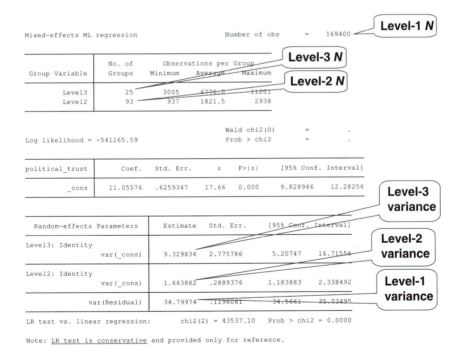

Figure 9.21 Empty three-level model

---

[15] Before the file name, you need to enter the location of the dataset on your computer, for example c:\stata\GDP capitaLevel3.dta. We have included *GDPcapita1000* in the working data, so in order to test the merge function you must first drop this variable: drop GDPcapita1000.

From the output in Figure 9.21 we see that we have 25 level-3 units, 93 level-2 units, and 169,400 level-1 units. We also see an extra residual variance, namely that for level 3. We call this var(v_0). We can now calculate how much of the variance in our dependent variable can be explained at each level by expanding the variance partition coefficient:

$$\text{VPC} = \frac{\text{var}(v_0)}{\text{var}(e) + \text{var}(u_0)\,\text{var}(v_0)}. \tag{9.15}$$

First, we calculate how much of the variance is situated at the country level (level-3):

$$\text{VPC} = \frac{9.329834}{34.79974 + 1.663882 + 9.329834} = 0.20374.$$

This means that 20.37 per cent of the variance in the dependent variable is situated at level 3. To calculate the two other percentages we just change the numerator: for level 2, we have

$$\text{VPC} = \frac{1.663882}{34.79974 + 1.663882 + 9.329834} = 0.03634;$$

and for level 1,

$$\text{VPC} = \frac{34.79974}{34.79974 + 1.663882 + 9.329834} = 0.75993.$$

We can now expand our model and include explanatory variables at all three levels:

$$Y_{ijk} = \beta_0 + \beta_1 X_{1ijk} + \beta_2 X_{2ijk} + \beta_3 X_{3ijk} + \beta_4 X_{4ijk} + \beta_5 X_{5jk} + \beta_6 X_{1k} + e_{ijk} + u_{0jk} + v_{0k}. \tag{9.16}$$

In Stata we run the following command:

```
. mixed political_trust woman age unemployed eduyrs GDPcapita1000 Nordic ||
Level3:, || Level2:, ml variance
```

which yields Figure 9.22.

We can also run a logistic three-level model (using the dataset Lab4_ESS.dta),

$$L_{ijk} = \beta_0 + \beta_1 X_{1ijk} + \beta_2 X_{2ijk} + \beta_3 X_{3jk} + \beta_4 X_{4k} + e_{ijk} + u_{0jk} + v_{0k}, \tag{9.17}$$

where we use the following Stata command:

```
. melogit vote age woman GDPcapita1000 Nordic || Level3:, || Level2:,
intmethod(laplace)
```

yielding Figure 9.23.

```
Mixed-effects ML regression                    Number of obs    =   165248
```

Group Variable	No. of Groups	Observations per Group		
		Minimum	Average	Maximum
Level3	25	2864	6609.9	10900
Level2	93	875	1776.9	2878

```
                                               Wald chi2(6)     =    906.35
Log likelihood = -527384.74                    Prob > chi2      =    0.0000
```

political_trust	Coef.	Std. Err.	z	P>|z|	[95% Conf. Interval]	
woman	-.032056	.0291062	-1.10	0.271	-.0891031	.0249912
age	-.0004964	.0002661	-1.87	0.062	-.0010179	.0000252
unemployed	-1.153537	.0743182	-15.52	0.000	-1.299198	-1.007876
eduyrs	.0932651	.0037984	24.55	0.000	.0858204	.1007097
GDPcapita1000	.0574774	.018314	3.14	0.002	.0215826	.0933721
Nordic	3.868901	1.09139	3.54	0.000	1.729816	6.007986
_cons	7.795171	.5921869	13.16	0.000	6.634506	8.955836

Random-effects Parameters	Estimate	Std. Err.	[95% Conf. Interval]	
Level3: Identity				
var(_cons)	2.732824	1.142645	1.204227	6.201761
Level2: Identity				
var(_cons)	1.866953	.3508267	1.291757	2.698274
var(Residual)	34.5439	.12021	34.30909	34.78031

```
LR test vs. linear regression:       chi2(2) = 17028.64   Prob > chi2 = 0.0000
```

Figure 9.22 Three-level model

Note that we have had to use the Laplacian estimation, as this is a very large and complicated model to run. Though it is not an optimal solution, the coefficients and their standard errors are well approximated by Laplace, and the same holds for model log-likelihoods and –2LL tests. The downside of this approach is that the variance components are less trustworthy than when using mvaghermite as the integration method. However, if your main concern is with the coefficient estimates, the Laplace approximation is an alternative when modelling large and/or complex models.

9•9•1 Cross-classified multilevel model

We can also encounter cases where there are three levels, but there is no strict hierarchical structure to the data. For example, you could be investigating data where the municipality of birth constitutes one level and the municipality of residence constitutes another. Here we have a cross-classification, as the level-1 units can be members of more than one higher-level unit simultaneously (Figure 9.24).

```
Mixed-effects logistic regression                    Number of obs      =    163508
```

Group Variable	No. of Groups	Observations per Group		
		Minimum	Average	Maximum
Level3	25	2971	6540.3	10499
Level2	93	941	1758.2	2838

```
Integration method:      laplace
```

```
                                              Wald chi2(4)       =    290.65
Log likelihood = -83323.428                   Prob > chi2        =    0.0000
```

vote	Coef.	Std. Err.	z	P>|z|	[95% Conf. Interval]	
age	.0053732	.0003224	16.67	0.000	.0047413	.0060051
woman	.0048666	.0122341	0.40	0.691	-.0191119	.028845
GDPcapita1000	.0043404	.0035056	1.24	0.216	-.0025305	.0112112
Nordic	.7119507	.2782361	2.56	0.011	.1666181	1.257283
_cons	.8294195	.1353104	6.13	0.000	.564216	1.094623
Level3						
var(_cons)	.2194085	.0657356			.1219636	.3947086
Level3>Level2						
var(_cons)	.0397811	.0076744			.0272563	.0580612

```
LR test vs. logistic regression:      chi2(2) =   5519.17    Prob > chi2 = 0.0000
```

Figure 9.23 Logistic three-level model

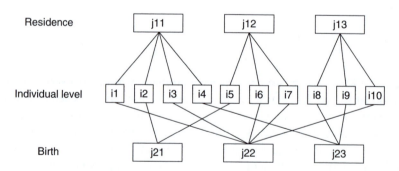

Figure 9.24 Cross-classified multilevel model

The equation for such a model would be

$$y_{i(j_1j_2)} = \beta_0 + u_{1j_1} + u_{2j_2} + e_{i(j_1j_2)}. \tag{9.18}$$

The Stata syntax for such a model is

```
. xtmixed y || _all: R.birth || residence:, ml var
```

where _all sets up an artificial supercluster, and the R. prefix creates annual indicators. Such a model is complex to run, and because of the nature of the _all supercluster it is not possible to run Laplacian approximation. If the model should prove difficult to run, you could set a maximum number of iterations:

```
. xtmixed y || _all: R.birth || residence:, ml var iterate(30)
```

Cross-classification enables us to take into account influences on the dependent variable coming from two different contexts, and to evaluate the importance of these two levels in explaining our level-1 outcome variable.

9 ● 10 WEIGHTING

Stata's mixed/melogit commands allow the units to be weighted. This enables a more appropriate analysis of survey data. We must keep in mind that in multilevel modelling group size matters for the effects of level-1 variables. For example, if one group has 50 respondents, these will have more influence over the level-1 effects than the 25 respondents in another group. This is unproblematic if the group's N makes theoretical sense (if the population of the first group was twice the size of the population of the second group). However, if the group N is random one should consider weighting.[16]

Regular statistical software (which is not designed for survey data) analyses data as if the data were collected using simple random sampling. When surveys are conducted, a simple random sample is not always collected. Simple random sampling is not only difficult to do, but also not as efficient as other sampling methods. When any sampling method other than simple random sampling is used, we usually need to use commands designed for survey data to take into account the differences between the design that was used and simple random sampling.

This is because the sampling design affects the calculation of the standard errors of the estimates. If the sampling design is ignored (e.g., simple random sampling was assumed when another type of sampling design was used), the standard errors are likely to be underestimated, possibly leading to results that seem to be statistically significant, when in fact they are not. While it is possible to achieve reasonably accurate results using non-survey software, there is no practical way to know beforehand how imprecise the results from non-survey software will be.

A weight is a mathematical device used to give some elements more 'weight' or influence on the result than other elements in the same set. In this example we use our two-level data from Round 5 of the European Social Survey. We open the datafile *Lab1_ESS.dta*.

Here there are two types of weights needed. The first is a design weight used when it has not been possible for all individuals in any given country to have the same chance of being selected in the survey (in our case the ESS). We thus have a variable called dweight which denotes the inverse probability that the observation is included because of the sampling design. However, the sample size is not the same in each country, so a variable has to be calculated to take this into account.

We assume that each unit (country) should have the same number of respondents: we need to adjust for this. The mean N is 48,487/25 = 1939.48. We now divide the mean by the N for each country and get the value for persons from that country on our *sample weight*:

---

[16] For more on weighting, see Chapter 13. With Stata14 it is now possible to use the svy: prefix to fit multilevel models.

```
. quietly levelsof cntry
. local numctry: word count `r(levels)'
. quietly count if missing(cntry)
. local cntpercntry = (_N-r(N))/`numctry'
. bys cntry: gen sample_weight = `cntpercntry' / _N if !missing(cntry)
```

We then multiply the design weight with our new sample weight:

```
. gen designsample=dweight*sample_weight
```

By using `designsample` we have a representative sample from each country, and each Pole, Norwegian, and Russian counts equally in our model. It is also possible to use the same procedure with a weight that takes into account population size (e.g., the fact that there are more Germans in Europe than there are Danes), and the ESS has its own pre-coded variable for this purpose.

We can now run the random intercept model with weights by using Stata's weighting for the model we previously ran (Figure 9.13):

```
. mixed political_trust woman age unemployed eduyrs GDPcapita1000
[pw=designsample] || country:, ml variance
```

```
Computing standard errors:

Mixed-effects regression                    Number of obs      =      45288
Group variable: country                     Number of groups   =         25

                                            Obs per group: min =        952
                                                           avg =     1811.5
                                                           max =       2874

                                            Wald chi2(5)       =     160.81
Log pseudolikelihood = -144891.89           Prob > chi2        =     0.0000
```

(Std. Err. adjusted for 25 clusters in country)

political_trust	Coef.	Robust Std. Err.	z	P>|z|	[95% Conf. Interval]	
woman	-.0006585	.0971511	-0.01	0.995	-.1910712	.1897541
age	.0020566	.0045654	0.45	0.652	-.0068913	.0110046
unemployed	-1.136354	.1695796	-6.70	0.000	-1.468724	-.8039838
eduyrs	.0872595	.0211611	4.12	0.000	.0457844	.1287346
GDPcapita1000	.1432531	.0180121	7.95	0.000	.10795	.1785562
_cons	4.986082	.7403535	6.73	0.000	3.535016	6.437148

Random-effects Parameters	Estimate	Robust Std. Err.	[95% Conf. Interval]	
country: Identity				
var(_cons)	4.241488	1.141435	2.502936	7.187648
var(Residual)	35.18935	1.21025	32.89549	37.64317

Figure 9.25 Weighted multilevel model

We see that the results in Figure 9.25 differ somewhat from those in Figure 9.13 (which was unweighted).

9 ● 11 CONCLUSION

Multilevel modelling should in many instances be the method of choice for a student or researcher dealing with nested data. Many kinds of data do not met the OLS regression requirement of independent units, as they have a hierarchical structure. This is where multilevel modelling becomes useful. It also allows us to test variables at the higher levels in a correct way, and we can calculate slopes that describe the population as a whole, as well as slopes for subgroups of the sample. Multilevel modelling allows for residual components at each level in the nested data structure. It can also be used to study units measured at different time points, thus being an alternative to repeated measures ANOVA.

 key terms

Cross-level interaction This is an interaction term composed of two variables situated at different levels.

Fixed effects This denotes regression lines that are the same for the whole sample.

Hierarchical/multilevel data Names for data that are nested within different levels.

Random coefficient This means slopes that differ between different subgroups of the sample.

Variance partition/intraclass correlation coefficient A measure of the variability in the dependent that is attributable to the second level.

QUESTIONS

1 What are the main statistical reasons for using multilevel modelling?
2 What is the difference between a random intercept and random coefficient model? Under what circumstances should we use the latter?
3 Why is it an advantage to have many level-2 (and level-3) units?

FURTHER READING

Bryk, A.S. and Raudenbush, S.W. (2002) *Hierarchical Linear Models: Applications and Data Analysis Methods* (2nd edn). Newbury Park, CA: Sage.

This book introduces the reader to multilevel modelling and issues around its application. The authors make good use of examples to illustrate the methods.

Goldstein, H. (2011) *Multilevel Statistical Models* (4th edn). London: Arnold.

This book provides step-by-step guidance on multilevel modelling, starting with the basic ideas and moving on to more complex models.

Hox, J. (2010) *Multilevel Analysis: Techniques and Applications* (2nd edn). New York: Routledge.

One of the classics of multilevel modelling, Hox presents an accessible introduction to the topic and includes advanced extensions. An invaluable reference work for students and researchers.

Kreft, I. and de Leeuw, J. (1998) *Introducing Multilevel Modeling*. London: Sage.

This book is an accessible and practical guide to using multilevel models in social research. The authors look especially at practical issues and potential problems of multilevel modelling.

REFERENCES

Bartels, L.M. (1996) Pooling disparate observations. *American Journal of Political Science*, 40(3), 905–942.

Bertrand, M., Duflo, E. and Mullainathan, S. (2004) How much should we trust differences-in-differences estimates? *Quarterly Journal of Economics*, 119(1), 249–275.

Bryk, A.S. and Raudenbush, S.W. (2002) *Hierarchical Linear Models: Applications and Data Analysis Methods* (2nd edn). Newbury Park, CA: Sage.

ESS Round 2: European Social Survey Round 2 Data (2004) Data file edition 3.3. Norwegian Social Science Data Services, Norway – Data Archive and distributor of ESS data.

ESS Round 3: European Social Survey Round 3 Data (2006) Data file edition 3.4. Norwegian Social Science Data Services, Norway – Data Archive and distributor of ESS data.

ESS Round 4: European Social Survey Round 4 Data (2008) Data file edition 4.2. Norwegian Social Science Data Services, Norway – Data Archive and distributor of ESS data.

ESS Round 5: European Social Survey Round 5 Data (2010) Data file edition 3.1. Norwegian Social Science Data Services, Norway – Data Archive and distributor of ESS data.

Gelman, A. and Hill, J. (2007) *Data Analysis Using Regression and Multilevel/Hierarchical Models*. Cambridge: Cambridge University Press.

Goldstein, H. (1986) Multilevel mixed linear model analysis using iterative generalized least squares. *Biometrika*, 74(1), 43–56.

Hox, J.J. (2010) *Multilevel Analysis: Techniques and Applications* (2nd edn). New York: Routledge.

Jones, B.S. (2008) Multilevel models. In J. M. Box-Steffensmeier, Brady, H. E. and Collier, D. (eds), *The Oxford Handbook of Political Methodology* (pp. 605–623). Oxford: Oxford University Press.

Kreft, I. and de Leeuw, J. (1998) *Introducing Multilevel Modeling*. London: Sage.

Maas, C.J.M. and Hox, J.J. (2005) Sufficient sample sizes for multilevel modeling. *Methodology*, 1(3), 86–92.

Ringdal, K. (1992) Recent developments in methods for multilevel analysis. *Acta Sociologica*, 35(3), 235–243.

Steenbergen, M.C. and Jones, B.S. (2002) Modeling multilevel data structures. *American Journal of Political Science*, 46(1), 218–237.

Stegmueller, D. (2013) How many countries for multilevel modeling? A comparison of frequentist and Bayesian approaches. *American Journal of Political Science*, 57(3), 748–761.

Wonnacott, T.H. and Wonnacott, R.J. (1990) *Introductory Statistics* (5th edn). New York: Wiley.

PANEL DATA
ANALYSIS

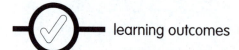

learning outcomes

○ Understand the structure of panel data
○ Understand between effects, fixed effects and random effects models

○ Use Stata to examine different forms of panel data models
○ Get an introduction to time-series cross-section methods

Panel data analysis[1] is the investigation of the development of variables over time. It is usually associated with a sample of respondents being interviewed at two or more time points. We call this sample a panel. However, panel data can also encompass units other than respondents, for example countries, firms or organizations. In this chapter the reader will learn how to treat panel data, and is guided through examples of random intercept and fixed effects models. We also take a closer look at a variant of panel data that has a somewhat different data structure than the classic panel studies, namely time-series cross-section data.

Panel data differs from pure cross-section data, as we have now added a longitudinal dimension. Each unit is measured at more than one point in time. The classic panel consists of a large number of units, indexed by i, observed over a small number of observations (or waves, or interviews), indexed by t. This means that each unit has two or more observations and the data is thus nested as the observations are not independent of each other. This is a breach of one of the assumptions of ordinary least-squares regression and gives us one of the hallmarks of panel data analysis, namely *intraclass correlation*.

The correlation between two (or more) classes of measurement was treated by Ronald A. Fisher (1925) when he laid the groundwork for what would later become the random effects model. In his examples, taken from the field of eugenics, he made the argument for data consisting of pairs of brothers (whose values one could assume to have an intraclass correlation).[2] The same logic also applies to observations of the same individual (or country, or firm) over time; these observations will also have an intraclass correlation (the class being the unit in question).

 ## PANEL DATA

The classic design for panel data is a large probability sample (e.g., 1000 respondents) with few (but more than one) measuring points. Here the sample is recorded at the same time, often by way of a survey. Ideally, the data collection should be performed in a similar fashion at each time point. What makes panel data different from time series is that it is the individual (or firm, organization, etc.) that is the unit of analysis rather than the time points.

---

[1] Panel data is known under other names in other fields, for example repeated measures or longitudinal data.

[2] In his example, Fisher presented two methods for taking into account the problem of investigating measurement of a given pair of brothers.

The units are measured usually at 2–4 time points (regular intervals). We do have panel data with more than four time points, but as the number of time points increases the risk of systematic drop-out from the study increases (see Figure 10.1).[3]

An advantage of such a design is that the same units of analysis are recorded over time, which makes causal analysis more trustworthy than when investigating cross-section data. Just as in cross-section studies, the dependent variable can be either continuous or categorical. Change is incorporated into the design, as we can observe changes in a variable within the same unit. We can say that there are primarily two important ways in which we can use panel data compared to cross-section data.

First, we can control for unobserved explanatory variables. This includes, for example, cultural factors, differences in business practices across companies; or variables that change over time but not across units, such as national policies or international agreements. Panel data suggests that our units are heterogeneous, and not controlling for this means a risk of getting biased results. With repeated observations on each individual, one is in a better position to account for unmeasured variables. We call this controlling for *individual heterogeneity*.

Second, we are able to analyse change over time, thus getting a truer estimate of the effect of an explanatory variable. We can, for example, see how people's income or attitudes change between panel dates, thus identifying effects that are not detectable in cross-section (or time-series) data.

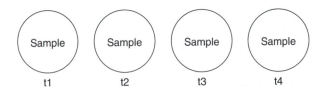

Figure 10.1 Panel data survey design with four waves

There are different types of panel data. If we have an equal number of time periods per individual it is called a *balanced panel* (as shown in Table 10.1). We note that the data in Table 10.1 are in long format.[4] If we have an unequal number of time periods per individual (e.g., due to missing observations) we call it an *unbalanced panel* (this is the most common type; see the example in Table 10.2). Though we would ideally like to operate with a balanced panel, it is possible to use the same statistical procedures regardless of whether the data is balanced or unbalanced. Unbalanced panels become problematic when the attrition rate is high (i.e., when many individuals or units drop out of the study).[5]

---

[3] Panel data analysis differs from multilevel analysis, as described in Chapter 9, and also from repeated cross-section data, which has the same structure but a new sample each time.

[4] See Chapter 2, p. 38 for the difference between wide and long data format.

[5] If missing data is infrequent and you can argue that data points are missing at random, you lose little efficiency in estimating your models. The larger the amount of missing data you have, the greater the loss of efficiency in your models. If the missing data are not missing at random, you get a biased sample (Cameron and Trivedi, 2010). There are ways of handling missing data, for example by using multiple imputation (see Chapter 13).

Table 10.1 Example of balanced panel data

Survey	Name	Woman	Age	Higher Education	Income
1990	Bob	0	20	0	54,000
1995	Bob	0	25	1	73,000
2000	Bob	0	30	1	72,000
2005	Bob	0	35	1	85,000
1990	Sarah	1	18	0	44,000
1995	Sarah	1	23	0	48,000
2000	Sarah	1	28	1	62,000
2005	Sarah	1	33	1	64,000
1990	Peter	0	26	1	63,000
1995	Peter	0	31	1	65,000
2000	Peter	0	36	1	67,000
2005	Peter	0	41	1	78,000
1990	Nicole	1	22	0	36,000
1995	Nicole	1	27	0	38,000
2000	Nicole	1	32	0	39,000
2005	Nicole	1	37	0	42,000

Table 10.2 Example of unbalanced panel data

Survey	Name	Woman	Age	Higher Education	Income
1990	Bob	0	20	0	54,000
1995	Bob	0	25	1	73,000
2005	Bob	0	35	1	85,000
1990	Sarah	1	18	0	44,000
1995	Sarah	1	23	0	48,000
2000	Sarah	1	28	1	62,000
2005	Sarah	1	33	1	64,000
1990	Peter	0	26	1	63,000
1995	Peter	0	31	1	65,000
1990	Nicole	1	22	0	36,000
1995	Nicole	1	27	0	38,000
2000	Nicole	1	32	0	39,000
2005	Nicole	1	37	0	42,000

There are some drawbacks associated with panel data. One is that they are rarely available, which is mainly due to data collection issues. However, with the coming of internet surveys this problem could be solved in the years to come. Non-response, which is also a problem in cross-sectional studies, carries an additional problem in panels, namely that of attrition. Respondents might fall out of the study (due to death, or cost of participation). The overall rates of attrition usually increase from one wave to another, and it is often not random who falls out of a study, which again causes biased results.[6]

10●2 POOLED OLS

A hallmark of panel data is that the number of observations is given by multiplying i (units) by t (time points). We are now able to model time and space as well as to generalize across them. However, to get valid results one needs to control for the correlation of the error terms for each unit i. This means that regular OLS regression usually underestimates the standard errors, thus inflating the t- and F-statistics. In other words, we risk producing statistically significant results that are not necessarily significant.

In OLS regression we assume that we are investigating a fully pooled model – that is, all units obey the same specification with the same parameter values:

$$y_{it} = \beta_0 + \beta x_{it} + \varepsilon_{it} . \tag{10.1}$$

Panel data can be consistently estimated using pooled OLS if the model is correctly specified and the explanatory (X) variables are uncorrelated with the error term. However, in panel data the error term will in most cases be correlated over time for a given unit (Cameron and Trivedi, 2010). This autocorrelation (or serial correlation) leads to inefficiency of the least-squares estimates and we will get biased estimates of the standard error. The standard errors are usually too small and thus our t- and F-statistics will be too large, and we may end up with false positive findings. Autocorrelated errors can also lead to a correlation between the X-variables and the error term, which among other things causes heteroscedasticity. If the mean between classes differs, the variance may differ proportionally.

For our first examples we will use data from the British Household Panel Survey (1991–2005),[7] where we can investigate the effect of marital status on mental distress. First we open the Stata file called *BritishHouseholdPanel.dta*. The Stata command to run panel data models is `xtreg` (the default of `xtreg` is a random effects model, see pages 250ff.). Before using this command we can tell Stata that we are dealing with panel data by using the command `xtset`, which makes Stata's time-series operators (`L.` and `F.`) work.[8] If you save the dataset afterwards Stata will remember

---

[6] For more on the advantages and disadvantages of panel data, see Baltagi (2013).

[7] The British Household Panel Survey is made available by the Institute for Social and Economic Research, University of Essex. See *British Household Panel Survey: Waves 1–11, 1991–2002: Teaching Dataset (Work, Family and Health)* [computer file], 2nd edition, http://dx. doi.org/10.5255/UKDA-SN-4901-2. The data has been prepared for use by Morten Blekesaune, University of Agder.

[8] As panel data contain data over time (e.g., t, $t-1$, $t-2$, ...) it is possible to use information about previous as well as current values of the variables. This allows us to better estimate the causal effect of X on Y by investigating the effect of X_{t-1} on Y, or to calculate changes in a variable. See pp. 253ff for more details on lagging and leading a variable.

this setting when you reopen the dataset. We use our group (id) and time (year) identification variables to sort the data:

```
. xtset id year

        panel variable:   id (unbalanced)
         time variable:   year, 1991 to 2005, but with gaps
                 delta:   1 unit
```

The output tells that the data are unbalanced (i.e., we do not have records for every unit for each time point). This can be illustrated further by writing:

```
. tabulate year
```

Year of interview	Freq.	Percent	Cum.
1991	4,019	6.35	6.35
1992	4,018	6.35	12.70
1993	4,042	6.39	19.09
1994	4,134	6.53	25.62
1995	4,066	6.42	32.04
1996	4,402	6.96	39.00
1997	4,502	7.11	46.11
1998	4,552	7.19	53.31
1999	4,175	6.60	59.90
2000	4,162	6.58	66.48
2001	4,427	7.00	73.48
2002	4,312	6.81	80.29
2003	4,247	6.71	87.00
2004	4,189	6.62	93.62
2005	4,038	6.38	100.00
Total	63,285	100.00	

Figure 10.2 Frequencies of *year*

We see from Figure 10.2 that the number of participants varies from year to year. We can also use the command xtdescribe to see the variation in observations per individual and what pattern of observations appear in the dataset.

The variable *id* is an identification variable for each individual participating in the study, and the variable *year* shows the time point of the recordings. We can now run a pooled OLS regression with *mental distress*[9] as the dependent variable, and the predictors *age, woman,*[10] *couple, separated, divorced,* and *never married.*[11] The equation for this model is as follows:

$$Y_{it} = \beta_0 + x_{1it}\beta_1 + x_{2i}\beta_2 + x_{3it}\beta_3 + x_{4it}\beta_4 + x_{5it}\beta_5 + x_{6it}\beta_6 + \varepsilon_{it} \qquad (10.2)$$

---

[9] This is a measure of mental distress which counts the number of psychiatric symptoms indicated by the two worst out of four response categories for 12 items. The variable has a mean of 0, and the higher the value the more mental stress the respondent has reported (Blekesaune, 2008).

[10] A dummy variable where *woman* = 1 means that the respondent is a woman.

[11] The latter four are dummy variables denoting marital status with the category *married* as reference.

We note that x_{2i} (*woman*) is time-invariant and does not have the subscript t. We run the model in Stata as follows:

```
. regress mental age woman couple separated divorced never_married
```

Source	SS	df	MS		Number of obs =	62549
					F(6, 62542) =	208.54
Model	1067.66694	6	177.944491		Prob > F =	0.0000
Residual	53366.0332	62542	.853283125		R-squared =	0.0196
					Adj R-squared =	0.0195
Total	54433.7002	62548	.870270835		Root MSE =	.92373

mental	Coef.	Std. Err.	t	P>|t|	[95% Conf. Interval]	
age	.0024708	.0003504	7.05	0.000	.001784	.0031576
woman	.2023694	.0074189	27.28	0.000	.1878285	.2169104
couple	.0075139	.0105725	0.71	0.477	-.0132083	.0282361
separated	.5583078	.0312398	17.87	0.000	.4970777	.6195378
divorced	.2241774	.0239372	9.37	0.000	.1772605	.2710943
never_married	.2236556	.0315205	7.10	0.000	.1618755	.2854358
_cons	-.2346901	.01642	-14.29	0.000	-.2668732	-.202507

Figure 10.3 OLS regression on panel data

The output is shown in Figure 10.3.

The pooled OLS model treats the data as if the observations were independent of each other. Our results show that people who do not live with a partner are generally more prone to mental distress than those who do. We also note that women are more distressed than men, and that older people report more mental distress than younger people.

There are, however, two problems associated with these results. The first is, as previously mentioned, with regard to autocorrelation and heteroscedasticity, and as an effect of this, inefficient coefficients and underestimated standard errors.[12]

First, we can test for autocorrelation after running our regression. We could have used the Durbin–Watson (Durbin and Watson, 1950, 1951) test to detect the presence of autocorrelation (the command is `estat dwatson`, as described in Chapter 7); however, it is not compatible with panel data. Instead we can install a program for testing serial correlation in linear panel-data models created by Drukker (2003).[13] To install the program we type the following:

```
. net sj 3-2 st0039
. net install st0039
```

---

[12] We should note that autocorrelation can be a symptom of an incorrectly specified model, which may produce incorrect coefficient estimates.

[13] This program implements a test for serial correlation in the errors of a linear panel data as described by Wooldridge (2010).

Then we run the test:

```
. xtserial mental age woman couple separated divorced never_married
```

```
        Wooldridge test for autocorrelation in panel data
        H0: no first-order autocorrelation
            F(  1,     6151) =    108.684
                     Prob > F =      0.0000
```

We see that the null hypothesis of no autocorrelation is firmly rejected, meaning that we do have a problem with autocorrelation in our model.

Recall that the presence of autocorrelation could lead to heteroscedasticity, which means that the model predicts some values of the dependent more precisely than others. First we can plot the residuals against the fitted values:

```
. quietly regress mental age woman couple separated divorced never_married
. predict Pmental
. gen Rmental=mental-Pmental (you can also write predict Rmental, resid)
. scatter Rmental Pmental
```

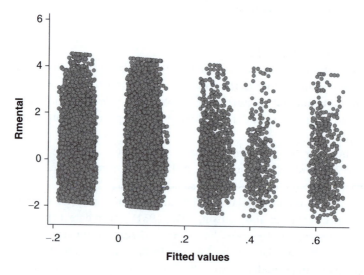

Figure 10.4 Predicted values vs. residuals

In a well-fitting model there should be no pattern to the residuals plotted against the fitted values. We see that there is a certain pattern (Figure 10.4); our model has more precise prediction for those with a high score on *mental distress* than for those with a low score (i.e., the model gives a better estimate of the person's true value). This can also be tested statistically, namely with the Breusch–Pagan/Cook–Weisberg test for heteroscedasticity (Breusch and Pagan, 1979; Cook and Weisberg, 1983) which has the command hettest:

```
. hettest

            Breusch-Pagan / Cook-Weisberg test for heteroskedasticity
                Ho: Constant variance
                Variables: fitted values of mental

            chi2(1)      =   1243.72
            Prob > chi2  =    0.0000
```

A significant value means that there is presence of heteroscedasticity. As we see, this is also the case for our model.[14]

OLS regression assumes that errors are both independent of each other (absence of auto-correlation) and normally distributed. Using robust standard errors relaxes either or both of those assumptions. Following from this, when heteroscedasticity is present, robust standard errors tend to be more trustworthy. We can use the Huber–White robust standard errors, also called heteroscedasticity-consistent standard errors (Huber, 1967; White, 1980). The use of robust standard errors does not change coefficient estimates, but (because the standard errors are changed) the test statistics will give reasonably accurate *p*-values.[15] The robust option relaxes the assumption that the errors are identically distributed, while cluster[16] relaxes the assumption that the error terms are independent of each other. The robust standard errors are implied when using the cluster option. By using the vce(cluster clustvar) option the observations are independent across groups (clusters) but not necessarily within groups. This also implies that variables that do not change within a unit do not have their standard errors calculated based on all the observations, but rather, similar to level-2 variables in mul-tilevel regression (see also Chapter 9, p. 206), are calculated based on the number of groups:

```
. regress mental age woman couple separated divorced never_married,
vce(cluster id)
```

We notice from the output in Figure 10.5 that the coefficients are the same as in our previous model, but the standard errors are larger (and more correct), and the standard error of *woman* is calculated based on the number of clusters rather than the number of total observations.

However, the second problem and the main argument for not choosing pooled OLS for panel data analysis is that when investigating the results we are not able to separate selection effects from real effects. Using the example of mental distress and divorce, it is reasonable

---

[14] To perform the Breusch–Pagan test after a random effects model, we must use the command xttest0.

[15] Heteroscedasticity resulting from misspecification of the model is always a problem, and should be corrected. Some important variables could have been left out of the model, curvilinear relationships could have been modelled as linear, and relevant conditional relationships could have been left out.

[16] The cluster option keeps the assumption of zero correlation between groups, but allows for within group correlation. In our data, each person is a group (with several observations at different years). It is also recommended to use the robust and cluster options when using the fixed and random effects estimators for linear regression. We can also use robust standard errors in combination with the fixed effects and random effects models.

```
Linear regression                                        Number of obs  =    62549
                                                         F(  6,  7583)  =    51.97
                                                         Prob > F       =   0.0000
                                                         R-squared      =   0.0196
                                                         Root MSE       =   .92373

                            (Std. Err. adjusted for 7584 clusters in id)
```

mental	Coef.	Robust Std. Err.	t	P>|t|	[95% Conf. Interval]	
age	.0024708	.0006718	3.68	0.000	.0011539	.0037877
woman	.2023694	.015618	12.96	0.000	.1717538	.2329851
couple	.0075139	.0178959	0.42	0.675	-.027567	.0425948
separated	.5583078	.0559887	9.97	0.000	.4485543	.6680612
divorced	.2241774	.0481785	4.65	0.000	.1297343	.3186205
never_married	.2236556	.0561824	3.98	0.000	.1135226	.3337886
_cons	-.2346901	.0305801	-7.67	0.000	-.2946356	-.1747446

Huber–White robust SE

Figure 10.5 OLS regression with robust standard errors

to assume that there could have been other underlying variables affecting both who has a successful marriage (and who does not) as well as people's mental health. A person with a certain illness or appearance could be more prone to mental problems as well as less prone to becoming married, or more prone to divorce if married.

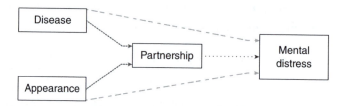

Figure 10.6 Spurious relationship

This is called a spurious relationship (Figure 10.6), as another variable can be said to be (at least part of) the cause of both our independent and dependent variable. Our problem here is that we do not know what part of the relationship depicted by the dotted line (the significant relationship we found in our regression model) is due to partnership status or other variables. There are two main ways we can solve this problem. First, we can introduce the relevant variables (disease and appearance). However, this is a difficult task. We do not necessarily have data on the relevant variables, and it could be that we do not know what these variables are. Second, and the most common option in the analysis of panel data (and a great advantage of having panel data), we can run a fixed effects model (see p. 240) where we can identify the *within unit variation*, an issue we will treat in detail later in the chapter.

 BETWEEN EFFECTS

Between effects modelling allows you to use the variation between the units to estimate the effect of the omitted independent variables on your Y-variable. In other words, regression with between effects is employed when you want to control for omitted variables that change over time, but are constant between units. Running a between effects model is the same as taking the mean of each variable for each unit across time, and then running a simple regression on the collapsed dataset of means:

$$\bar{y}_i = \beta_{0B} + \beta_{1B}\bar{x}_{1i} + \beta_{2B}x_{2i} + \varepsilon_i. \tag{10.3}$$

As such, this estimator makes comparisons between units in their average outcomes. As this estimator is referred to as the *between estimator*, we use the subscript B (Petersen, 2004). We note that $\bar{x}_{1i}$ is the average value of x_{1it} and x_{2i} is a time-invariant variable.

In such a model it is not possible to include variables that are the same for all individuals in a given year, but vary between time points (e.g., macroeconomic conditions). Also, by collapsing values and taking the mean for each unit (see Table 10.3, income column) for each variable you also lose a lot of information. Because of this, between effects are not used much in practice. However, the between effects estimator is important to understand because it constitutes a part of the random effects estimator.

Table 10.3   Example of balanced panel data with only between variation

Survey Year	Name	Woman	Higher Education	Income
1990	Bob	0	1	71,000
1995	Bob	0	1	71,000
2000	Bob	0	1	71,000
2005	Bob	0	1	71,000
1990	Sarah	1	0	54,500
1995	Sarah	1	0	54,500
2000	Sarah	1	0	54,500
2005	Sarah	1	0	54,500
1990	Peter	0	1	68,250
1995	Peter	0	1	68,250
2000	Peter	0	1	68,250
2005	Peter	0	1	68,250
1990	Nicole	1	0	38,750
1995	Nicole	1	0	38,750
2000	Nicole	1	0	38,750
2005	Nicole	1	0	38,750

There are two ways of running a between effects model in Stata. First, we can do it manually by aggregating (collapsing, taking the mean for each person over years) data by our person identifier variable id. Remember to save the dataset under a new name (if you wish to save it), as this changes the data structure (which you can check by viewing the Data editor window before and after; see Figures 10.7 and 10.8).

Several observations for each person

	id	age	mastat	year	mental	woman	married	couple	separated	divorced	never_marr~d
1	10014578	54	married	1991	-.5502676	1	1	0	0	0	0
2	10014578	55	married	1992	.1431346	1	1	0	0	0	0
3	10014578	56	married	1993	-.0310326	1	1	0	0	0	0
4	10014578	59	married	1996	.1431346	1	1	0	0	0	0
5	10014578	61	married	1998	-.434826	1	1	0	0	0	0
6	10014578	62	married	1999	-.434826	1	1	0	0	0	0
7	10014578	63	married	2000	-.2305806	1	1	0	0	0	0
8	10014608	57	married	1991	-1.563305	0	1	0	0	0	0
9	10014608	58	married	1992	-1.587	0	1	0	0	0	0
10	10014608	59	married	1993	-.864336	0	1	0	0	0	0
11	10014608	62	married	1996	-.9067082	0	1	0	0	0	0
12	10014608	64	married	1998	-.864336	0	1	0	0	0	0
13	10016813	37	married	1992	1.887546	0	1	0	0	0	0
14	10016813	39	married	1994	-.4449705	0	1	0	0	0	0
15	10016813	44	divorced	1999	.0435938	0	0	0	0	1	0

Figure 10.7 Data before collapsing

One observation for each person

Mean of all observations in Figure 10.7

	id	mental	age	woman	couple	separated	divorced	never_marr~d
1	10014578	-.1993234	58.5714	1	0	0	0	0
2	10014608	-1.157137	60	0	0	0	0	0
3	10016813	.4953898	40	0	0	0	.3333333	0
4	10016848	.3100214	41	1	.6666667	0	0	0
5	10017933	-.7896879	55	1	0	.0909091	.5454546	0
6	10017968	.5231872	47.25	0	0	0	0	0
7	10025804	-.3505359	36.6	0	0	0	0	0
8	10047069	.8330157	34	0	0	.125	0	0

Figure 10.8 Data after collapsing (mean for each person over years)

We note that by manually creating means using the collapse command we will not automatically exclude missing values from our model. We also need to do this manually by using the e(sample) command which only includes the observations that were included in the last run model:

- quietly regress mental age woman couple separated divorced never_married
- collapse (mean) mental age woman couple separated divorced never_married if e(sample), by(id)
- regress mental age woman couple separated divorced never_married

The output is in Figure 10.9.

Source	SS	df	MS			
Model	125.183024	6	20.8638373			
Residual	3312.90297	7577	.437231486			
Total	3438.08599	7583	.453393906			

Number of obs = 7584
F(6, 7577) = 47.72
Prob > F = 0.0000
R-squared = 0.0364
Adj R-squared = 0.0356
Root MSE = .66123

mental	Coef.	Std. Err.	t	P>|t|	[95% Conf. Interval]	
age	.002414	.0007231	3.34	0.001	.0009965	.0038315
woman	.1949775	.015271	12.77	0.000	.1650422	.2249129
couple	.0357703	.0225018	1.59	0.112	-.0083394	.07988
separated	.7931771	.1325742	5.98	0.000	.5332951	1.053059
divorced	.5139704	.0847859	6.06	0.000	.3477666	.6801743
never_married	.3309017	.0819682	4.04	0.000	.1702214	.4915821
_cons	-.2518096	.0346075	-7.28	0.000	-.3196499	-.1839692

Figure 10.9 Between effects regression

The equation for our model would now be:

$$\bar{y}_i = \beta_{0B} + \beta_{1B}\bar{x}_{1i} + \beta_{2B}x_{2i} + \beta_{3B}\bar{x}_{3i} + \beta_{4B}\bar{x}_{4i} + \beta_{5B}\bar{x}_{5i} + \beta_{6B}\bar{x}_{6i} + \varepsilon_i \qquad (10.4)$$

and we note that our second variable (*woman*) is time-invariant. We can go back to the original data file and use the between effects command be (which does not alter the data structure):

. xtreg mental age woman couple separated divorced never_married, be

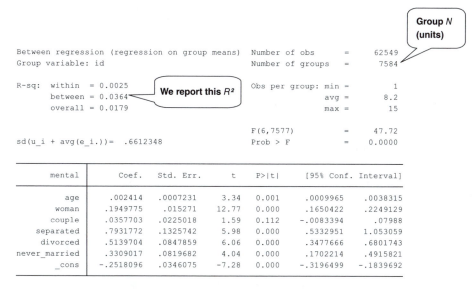

Between regression (regression on group means) Number of obs = 62549
Group variable: id   Number of groups = 7584

Group *N* (units)

R-sq: within = 0.0025   Obs per group: min = 1
        between = 0.0364   We report this *R²*   avg = 8.2
        overall = 0.0179   max = 15

                                    F(6,7577)   = 47.72
sd(u_i + avg(e_i.))= .6612348   Prob > F   = 0.0000

mental	Coef.	Std. Err.	t	P>|t|	[95% Conf. Interval]	
age	.002414	.0007231	3.34	0.001	.0009965	.0038315
woman	.1949775	.015271	12.77	0.000	.1650422	.2249129
couple	.0357703	.0225018	1.59	0.112	-.0083394	.07988
separated	.7931772	.1325742	5.98	0.000	.5332951	1.053059
divorced	.5139704	.0847859	6.06	0.000	.3477666	.6801743
never_married	.3309017	.0819682	4.04	0.000	.1702214	.4915821
_cons	-.2518096	.0346075	-7.28	0.000	-.3196499	-.1839692

Figure 10.10 Between effects regression, using be command

From the output in Figure 10.10 we notice that three R-squared values are presented. The one we should be concerned with for a between effects model is the *between* one (0.0364). This is the same as the R-squared in the regression model with the collapsed means. In both cases it shows us the explained variance as a proportion of the total variance for the unit means of the variables included in the model. When we compare the two last models we see that the results are identical.

10.4 FIXED EFFECTS (WITHIN ESTIMATOR)

One of the main worries when it comes to panel data is whether or not the error term is correlated with one or more of our X-variables. Suppose, for example, we were investigating *wage* (Y) as a function of education (X_1) and experience (X_2), but we had a suspicion that an unmeasured variable called *ability* (C) was influencing our model:

$$y_{it} = \beta_0 + \beta_1 x_{1it} + \beta_2 x_{2it} + (c_i + e_{it})$$ (10.5)

Here c_i together with e_{it} (the within variation) constitutes our error term (unexplained variance). Our worry is that $\text{cov}(x_1, c_i) \neq 0$, that is, that some unmeasured variable is correlated with one (or more) of our explanatory variables causing the coefficient(s) to be biased (see the illustration in Figure 10.11). Even if only one variable is endogenous all parameters can be biased.

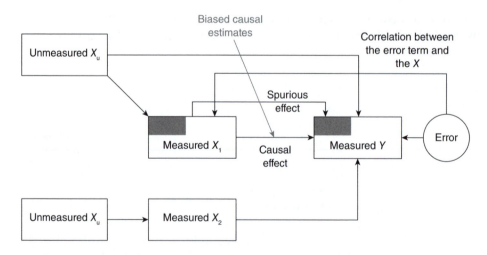

Figure 10.11 The assumption of no correlation between the error term and X-variables

The rule of thumb is as follows: if $\text{cov}(x_1, c_i) = 0$ then you may choose the random effects estimator,[17] while if $\text{cov}(x_1, c_i) \neq 0$ then you should choose the fixed effects estimator.

The generally accepted way of determining which model to choose is by running a Hausman (1978) test. This test checks a more consistent model (fixed effects) against a more efficient model (random effects) in order to make sure the more efficient model also gives

---

[17] In practice this means if $\text{cov}(x_1, c_i) = $ approximately zero.

consistent results. In order to run the Hausman test we need to estimate both a fixed and a random effects model and save their coefficients:

- `quietly xtreg mental age woman couple separated divorced never_married, fe`
- `estimates store fixed`
- `quietly xtreg mental age woman couple separated divorced never_married, re`
- `estimates store random`
- `hausman fixed random`

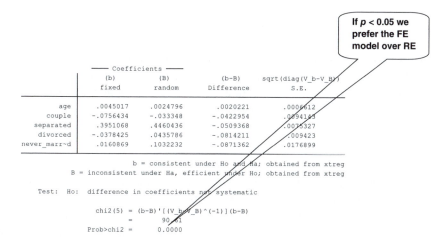

Figure 10.12 Hausman test

For our *BritishHouseholdPanel.dta* dataset we see that the `Prob>chi2` is significant (the value is below 0.05; Figure 10.12). This means that we should use fixed effects. If this value were above 0.05 we could use random effects.[18]

10●4●1 Explaining fixed effects

When we have repeated observations on each unit (e.g., persons), we can elaborate on the regression equation by including unit-specific dummy variables D_i. One thus includes a dummy variable for each unit (except the reference category) and estimates its effect (Petersen, 2004). The fixed effects (within) estimator takes into account the measured time-varying independent variables we have (x_{it}) but also accounts for both the time-invariant independent variables (x_i) that cannot be included in our model (as they are being captured by the unit dummy variables) and the unmeasured time-invariant variables (x_i^u) (also captured by the dummy variables):

$$y_{it} = \beta_{0w} + \beta_{1w}x_{1it} + \beta_{2w}x_{2i} + \beta_{3w}x_{3i}^u + \varepsilon_{it}. \qquad (10.6)$$

---

[18] However, there are also other reasons for choosing one model over another, such as identifying the right effects and being able to model theoretically important time-invariant variables. This is discussed throughout this chapter. It is also possible to use the Hausman test on other pairs of estimators, such as first differences versus pooled OLS.

We introduce the dummy variables for each unit D_i as well as their effects α_i which capture the effects of measured time-invariant independent variables and unmeasured time-invariant variables as the units are given different starting values on the Y-axis. This enables us to investigate how the time-dependent explanatory variables influence the time-dependent Y-variable. It is common to suppress the dummy variable D_i in the equation, so we get

$$y_{it} = \beta_{0w} + \beta_{1w}x_{1it} + \beta_{2w}x_{2i} + \beta_{3w}x_{3i}^u + \varepsilon_{it}$$ (10.7)
$$y_{it} = \beta_{0w} + \beta_{1w}x_{1it} + \alpha_i D_i + \varepsilon_{it}$$
$$y_{it} = \beta_{0w} + \beta_{1w}x_{1it} + \alpha_i + \varepsilon_{it},$$

where $\alpha_i = \beta_{2w}x_i + \beta_{3w}x_i^u$ as the effect of the dummy variables captures all the time-constant variation (the fixed effects). What actually happens and the reason why we can only investigate what changes over time is that (because we introduce the dummy variables) we are in fact looking at changes from the mean in each unit:

$$(y_{it} - \bar{y}_i) = \beta_1(x_{1it} - \bar{x}_{1i}) + \beta_2(x_{2it} - \bar{x}_{2i}) + \dots + \beta_n(x_{nit} - \bar{x}_{ni}) + (\varepsilon_{it} - \bar{\varepsilon}_i)$$ (10.8)

When performing OLS regression we face the problem that we cannot be certain what type of effect we are measuring. Open the dataset called *Happiness.dta*. Suppose that we are investigating the effect of *income* on *happiness* on four individuals (Bob, Sarah, Peter, and Nicole); see Table 10.4. We can write label list id. If Bob (who has the highest income) has some mental issue (an unobserved time-invariant variable) that makes him generally more unhappy than others, the OLS regression would be biased as the *income* variable also catches the effect of this variable (as illustrated in Figure 10.11). This is where fixed effects become useful. We are now only comparing Bob's *income* values against his own *happiness* values. As shown in equation (10.7), by including the unit dummy variables we are in fact modelling

$$(y_{it} - \bar{y}_i) = \beta_1(x_{1it} - \bar{x}_{1i}) + (\varepsilon_{it} - \bar{\varepsilon}_i)$$ (10.9)

or

$$\left(happy_{it} - \overline{happy}_i\right) = \beta\left(income_{it} - \overline{income}_i\right) + (\varepsilon_{it} - \bar{\varepsilon}_i).$$

In other words, we use fixed effects whenever we are only interested in the impact of variables that vary over time. This estimator helps us explore the relationship between the dependent and the explanatory variables within a unit (person, company, country, etc.) Each unit has its own individual characteristics that may or may not influence the predictor variables.

Figures 10.13 and 10.14 illustrate how the fixed effects estimator can change our results. In Figure 10.13 (OLS regression) the effect of *income* on *happiness* is negative, as Bob's illness skews the results. But by estimating within each case we get the true effect (controlled for every x_i and x_i^u) which in fact is positive (see Figure 10.14).

Figure 10.13 shows us the regression line for *income* on *happiness*. We could do the fixed effects regression manually by creating dummy variables for each of the four persons.

Table 10.4 Example of fixed effects calculation

Survey	Name	Income	Mean income	$(x_{it} - \bar{x}_{1i})$	Happiness	Mean happiness	$(y_{it} - \bar{y}_i)$
1990	Bob	54,000	71,000	−17,000	1	1.75	−0.75
1995	Bob	73,000	71,000	2,000	1	1.75	−0.75
2000	Bob	72,000	71,000	1,000	2	1.75	0.25
2005	Bob	85,000	71,000	14,000	3	1.75	1.25
1990	Sarah	44,000	54,500	−10,500	5	5.5	−0.5
1995	Sarah	48,000	54,500	−6,500	5	5.5	−0.5
2000	Sarah	62,000	54,500	7,500	5	5.5	−0.5
2005	Sarah	64,000	54,500	9,500	7	5.5	1.5
1990	Peter	63,000	68,250	−5,250	4	5.75	−1.75
1995	Peter	65,000	68,250	−3,250	5	5.75	−0.75
2000	Peter	67,000	68,250	−1,250	7	5.75	1.25
2005	Peter	78,000	68,250	9,750	7	5.75	1.25
1990	Nicole	36,000	38,750	−2,750	8	8.5	−0.5
1995	Nicole	38,000	38,750	−750	7	8.5	−1.5
2000	Nicole	39,000	38,750	250	9	8.5	0.5
2005	Nicole	42,000	38,750	3,250	10	8.5	1.5

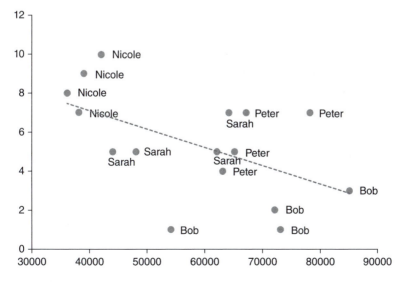

Figure 10.13 Trend line for *income* (X) against *happiness* (Y)

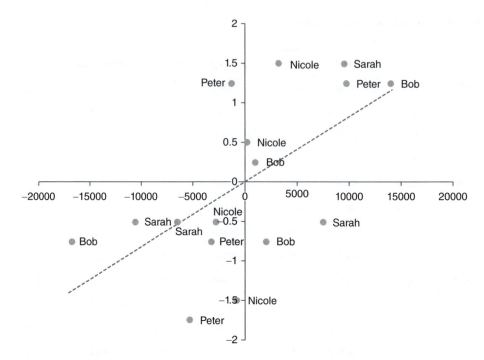

Figure 10.14 Trend line for $(x_{it} - \bar{x}_i)$ against $(y_{it} - \bar{y})$

We continue to use the dataset *Happiness.dta*. First we create dummy variables for each of the four persons (who are numbered 1–4 on the *id* variable):[19]

```
. generate Dbob=id==1 if !missing(id)
. generate Dsarah=id==2 if !missing(id)
. generate Dpeter=id==3 if !missing(id)
. generate Dnicole=id==4 if !missing(id)
```

We leave Dbob out of our model as he functions as the reference category (and is represented by the intercept). We use a new income variable which shows the salary in thousands for easy interpretation:

```
. regress happiness Dsarah Dpeter Dnicole income1000
```

This produces the output in Figure 10.15, which we use in the next step:

```
. gen Bob = -4.107029 + 0.0824934 * income1000
. gen Sarah = -4.107029 + 5.111141 + 0.0824934 * income1000
. gen Peter = -4.107029 + 4.226857 + 0.0824934 * income1000
. gen Nicole = -4.107029 + 9.410411 + 0.0824934 * income1000
```

---

[19] It is also possible to generate the dummies via `tabulate id, gen(D)`.

Source	SS	df	MS		Number of obs =	16
					F(4, 11) =	24.47
Model	98.6638594	4	24.6659649		Prob > F =	0.0000
Residual	11.0861406	11	1.00783096		R-squared =	0.8990
					Adj R-squared =	0.8623
Total	109.75	15	7.31666667		Root MSE =	1.0039

happiness	Coef.	Std. Err.	t	P>|t|	[95% Conf. Interval]	
Dsarah	5.111141	.8916484	5.73	0.000	3.148636	7.073646
Dpeter	4.226857	.7155433	5.91	0.000	2.651957	5.801757
Dnicole	9.410411	1.271248	7.40	0.000	6.612413	12.20841
income1000	.0824934	.0327004	2.52	0.028	.0105203	.1544665
_cons	-4.107029	2.37537	-1.73	0.112	-9.335184	1.121125

Figure 10.15 Fixed effects using manually made dummies

We can now graph the results, to get a more correct picture of how a fixed effects regression is done (Figure 10.16):[20]

```
. graph twoway line Bob income1000 || line Sarah income1000 || line Peter
income1000 || line Nicole income1000
```

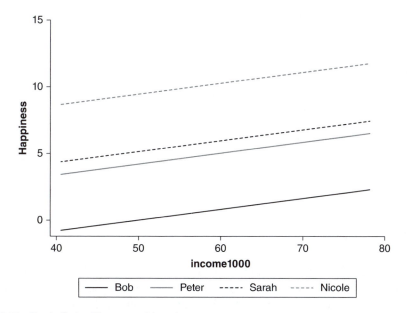

Figure 10.16 Fixed effects of *income* and *happiness*

---

[20] Another way of producing the plot would be:

```
. quietly regress happiness i.id c.income1000

. quietly margins id, at(income1000=(40 80))

. marginsplot, noci legend(row(1))
```

Figure 10.16 shows the same positive effect as in Figure 10.14 (the scales are different). We can double-check this by running a regression using $(x_{1it} - \bar{x}_{1i})$ and $(y_{it} - \bar{y}_i)$:

. regress happinessDM income1000DM

Source	SS	df	MS		Number of obs =	16
					F(1, 14) =	8.10
Model	6.41385942	1	6.41385942		Prob > F =	0.0130
Residual	11.0861406	14	.791867185		R-squared =	0.3665
					Adj R-squared =	0.3213
Total	17.5	15	1.16666667		Root MSE =	.88987

happinessDM	Coef.	Std. Err.	t	P>|t|	[95% Conf. Interval]	
income1000DM	.0824934	.0289858	2.85	0.013	.020325	.1446618
_cons	0	.2224673	0.00	1.000	-.4771449	.4771449

Figure 10.17 Fixed effects using differences from mean

This model (Figure 10.17) is the same as running a fixed effects model. If we run the model as an OLS regression we get the negative coefficient as illustrated in Figure 10.18.

. regress happiness income1000

Source	SS	df	MS		Number of obs =	16
					F(1, 14) =	5.75
Model	31.9560368	1	31.9560368		Prob > F =	0.0310
Residual	77.7939632	14	5.55671165		R-squared =	0.2912
					Adj R-squared =	0.2405
Total	109.75	15	7.31666667		Root MSE =	2.3573

happiness	Coef.	Std. Err.	t	P>|t|	[95% Conf. Interval]	
income1000	-.0946145	.0394539	-2.40	0.031	-.1792347	-.0099943
_cons	10.87447	2.367769	4.59	0.000	5.796107	15.95282

Figure 10.18 OLS regression

There is also a command in Stata for running a fixed effects model (fe) which does the same as in our model with dummies. The effects of the dummy variables are not reported in this model. First we need to tell Stata what our unit identifier variable is:

. xtset id
. xtreg happiness income1000, fe

From the Stata output in Figure 10.19 we see that our coefficient for *income* (0.0824934) is the same as in the previous models (except for the simple regression). In our model with

```
Fixed-effects (within) regression          Number of obs      =        16
Group variable: id                         Number of groups   =         4

R-sq:                                       Obs per group:
     within  = 0.3665                                        min =         4
     between = 0.7123                                        avg =       4.0
     overall = 0.2912                                        max =         4

                                            F(1,11)            =      6.36
corr(u_i, Xb)   = -0.7916                   Prob > F           =    0.0283
```

happiness	Coef.	Std. Err.	t	P>|t|	[95% Conf. Interval]
income1000	.0824934	.0327004	2.52	0.028	.0105203 .1544665
_cons	.5800729	1.91721	0.30	0.768	-3.639677 4.799823

sigma_u	3.8587653	
sigma_e	1.0039078	
rho	.93660603	(fraction of variance due to u_i)

```
F test that all u_i=0: F(3, 11) = 22.06                   Prob > F = 0.0001
```

Figure 10.19 Fixed effects regression, using `fe` command

the dummy variables the intercept represented Bob (–4.107). We see now that we have a new intercept. This intercept is the average value of the fixed effects.[21] What we should be concerned with from the output is the coefficient of *income* as well as the within R-squared (0.3665). The rho value (ρ = 0.93660603) tells us that 93.7 per cent of the variance is due to differences across time (within units), `sigma_u` (σ_u) is the standard deviation of residuals within groups and `sigma_e` (σ_e) is the standard deviation of residuals overall. The rho is also known as the interclass correlation, and tells us how strongly the observations within each unit resemble each other. It is calculated from the variances of the residuals as follows:

$$\rho = \frac{\sigma_u^2}{\sigma_u^2 + \sigma_e^2}.$$ (10.10)

Let us open *BritishHouseholdPanel.dta* and try to model a person's mental state using fixed effects. Recall from p. 233 that when doing an OLS regression we found that those who were not living with a partner had more mental distress than those in a relationship. However, we had reason to believe that we had the problem of a selection effect in our data. In order to get an unbiased estimate of marital status on mental health, we now run the same model using the fixed effects estimator:

```
. xtset id
. xtreg mental age woman couple separated divorced never_married, fe
```

---

[21] For a more thorough discussion on the estimation of the intercept presented in Stata, see http://www.stata.com/support/faqs/statistics/intercept-in-fixed-effects-model/

```
Fixed-effects (within) regression          Number of obs     =     62,549
Group variable: id                         Number of groups  =      7,584

R-sq:                                       Obs per group:
    within  = 0.0051      ┌──────────────┐         min =          1
    between = 0.0014      │ Omitted      │          avg =        8.2
    overall = 0.0032      │ because time-│          max =         15
                          │ invariant    │
                          └──────┬───────┘     F(5,54960)         =      56.33
corr(u_i, Xb)   = -0.0459        │ │          Prob > F           =     0.0000
                                 │ │
```

mental	Coef.	Std. Err.	t	P>|t|	[95% Conf. Interval]
age	.0045017	.0008475	5.31	0.000	.0028406	.0061628
woman	0	(omitted)				
couple	-.0756434	.0159661	-4.74	0.000	-.1069371	-.0443497
separated	.3951068	.0293305	13.47	0.000	.3376188	.4525947
divorced	-.0378425	.0263161	-1.44	0.150	-.0894224	.0137373
never_married	.0160869	.0378081	0.43	0.670	-.0580171	.090191
_cons	-.1891764	.035558	-5.32	0.000	-.2588704	-.1194825

sigma_u	.6746844					
sigma_e	.74201635					
rho	.45257982	(fraction of variance due to u_i)				

```
F test that all u_i=0: F(7583, 54960) = 5.69              Prob > F = 0.0000
```

Figure 10.20 Fixed effects model on mental distress

We notice from the output in Figure 10.20 that the variable *woman* is omitted (as this is time-invariant) and that we do have a substantive difference in our results juxtaposed with the output from the OLS regression.

We see from Figure 10.21 that mental distress is higher for those who are separated, but actually a bit lower for divorcees than for those who are married. This is calculated by looking at the within variation (changes in persons going through different categories) and tells us that the end of a marriage (usually in the form of separation) is stressful, but that people get over the distress (later, when divorced).

10•4•2 Summary of fixed effects

There are both advantages and drawbacks associated with the fixed effects model. The big advantage is that since it is able to control for all time-invariant variables (which we can denote by x_i and x_i^u or c_i) we are able to get rid of much of the problem with spurious relationships, as we get a purer relationship between x_{it} and y_{it} in our regression output. It is the best and most consistent mode to use if you suspect that $\text{cov}(x_1, c_i) \neq 0$.

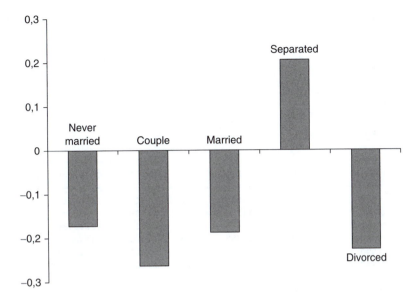

Figure 10.21 The effect of marital status on mental distress[22]

The big drawback of fixed effects modelling is that we are only able to estimate the effects of variables that vary over time (x_{it}) and the time-invariant ones (x_i) are omitted from the model. It can also be a problem estimating variables that seldom change. This is a challenge within the social sciences as we are often interested in the effect of time-invariant variables (e.g., gender, political institutions, and geographic variables). Ideally we would like to be able to state the substantive reason why Norway was better able to cope with the financial crisis than other countries, and not simply conclude that it did so because it was Norway (as we would in a fixed effects model). Also, if the conditions are right (e.g., that $\text{cov}(x_1, c_i) \neq 0$), fixed effects may not be the most efficient model to run, and will not produce the most correct estimates. It is also possible to perform a fixed effects logistic regression using the `xtlogit` command. However, this model will only investigate the units that have switched status on the dependent variable.

10•4•3 Time-fixed effects

It is possible to assume that there are unobserved effects that vary across time rather than across units that have an impact on the dependent variable. We can do so as follows:

```
. xtset year
. xtreg mental age woman couple separated divorced never_married, fe
```

---

[22] These are graphed predictions based on Figure 10.20.

```
Fixed-effects (within) regression          Number of obs      =    62,549
Group variable: year                       Number of groups   =        15

R-sq:                                      Obs per group:
     within  = 0.0193                                    min =     3,949
     between = 0.4014                                    avg =   4,169.9
     overall = 0.0196                                    max =     4,509

                                           F(6,62528)         =    204.95
corr(u_i, Xb)   = 0.0279                    Prob > F           =    0.0000
```

mental	Coef.	Std. Err.	t	P>|t|	[95% Conf. Interval]	
age	.0024107	.0003529	6.83	0.000	.001719	.0031024
woman	.2023145	.0074176	27.27	0.000	.187776	.216853
couple	.0041996	.0106624	0.39	0.694	-.0166988	.0250979
separated	.551324	.0312857	17.62	0.000	.490004	.6126441
divorced	.2191748	.024074	9.10	0.000	.1719897	.26636
never_married	.2171943	.0316373	6.87	0.000	.1551851	.2792036
_cons	-.2313118	.0165575	-13.97	0.000	-.2637645	-.1988592

```
sigma_u  |  .02701765
sigma_e  |  .92347916
    rho  |  .0008552   (fraction of variance due to u_i)
```

```
F test that all u_i=0: F(14, 62528) = 3.46              Prob > F = 0.0000
```

Figure 10.22 Time fixed effects

The result of this regression (Figure 10.22) is similar (but not identical) to an OLS regression. The intercept (we have included a dummy variable for each year) includes the variation between years rather than the variation between units (persons). In some cases a phenomenon (Y) will vary between time points (years/months/weeks) for reasons not captured by the X-variables in our model. If this is the case, we risk getting omitted variable bias by not including time dummies. An example of such a variable could be the financial climate (affecting people's mental distress in the same manner, but differently from time to time).

10.5 RANDOM EFFECTS

A random effects model can be used if there is no (or little) covariation between the error term and the explanatory variables, that is, if $cov(x_1,c_i) = 0$. We can perform a Hausman test, as described on p. 240, which tests if both the fixed and random effects are consistent estimators. If this holds, the random effects model is more efficient, and its standard errors should be smaller than those of the fixed effects model. But even if the test should be statistically significant (i.e., Prob>chi < 0.05, which means that the fixed effects model is more consistent than the random effects model) it is still possible to use a random effects model. If the correlation between the error term and the X-variables is caused by omitted variables we can add further explanatory variables (both time-varying and time-invariant) and run the test again (Cameron and Trivedi, 2010). Or, if we have time-invariant explanatory variables that are of great theoretical importance, we may be forced to choose random effects, as these will be absorbed by the intercept in the fixed effects model.

The random effects estimator is to be used if you believe that both variations within units (fixed effects) and between units (between effects) have some influence (also theoretically) on your dependent variable. This estimator is a combination of the between and within estimators:

$$y_{it} = \beta_{0RE} + \beta_{1RE}x_{1it} + \beta_{2RE}x_{2i} + v_i + e_{it} \,. \tag{10.11}$$

Here we have two error terms in the random effects equation. v_i is a unit-specific (rather than time-specific) error term, assumed to be independent of the observed variables x_{it} and x_i, as well as within variation error term e_{it}. The model is calculated using *generalized least squares*. This estimation technique is used in the presence of heteroscedasticity and/or autocorrelation, as OLS regression may be inefficient and can give misleading estimates.[23] We note that we are inflating the N of the time-invariant variables. In reality they have the same N as the number of units in our model, but are now multiplied by t.

The random effects estimator presents a weighted average of the within and between estimators. Units that are only observed at one data point are included, but they only contribute through the between effects estimator (Petersen, 2004). If you believe that some of your omitted variables are constant over time but vary between units, and others are fixed between units but vary over time, then you would include both by using random effects.

We can now run a random effects model on our British Household Panel Survey data. One difference from the fixed effects model is that we can now include the variable *woman*:

$$y_{it} = \beta_{0RE} + \beta_{1RE}x_{1it} + \beta_{2RE}x_{2i} + \beta_{3RE}x_{3it} + \beta_{4RE}x_{4it} + \beta_{5RE}x_{5it} + \beta_{6RE}x_{6it} + v_i + e_{it} \tag{10.12}$$

In Stata we can insert re after the comma when running xtreg, or we can just leave it blank (as random effects is the default of xtreg):[24]

```
. xtset id
. xtreg mental age woman couple separated divorced never_married, re
```

When we compare the results in Figure 10.23 to our fixed effects model in Figure 10.22, we see that the coefficient for *divorced* has changed sign and that the effect of *never married* has become significant. We also notice that we now have the output for the effect of our time-invariant variable *woman*. Here we should be most concerned with the overall R-squared, as the random effects estimator includes both between and within effects.

---

[23] Generalized least squares is a regression on a transformed version of the data. The standardization of the error term reduces the problem of autocorrelation and heteroscedasticity.

[24] For a random effects logit model the derivation of maximum likelihood (which is used instead of generalized least squares) involves bivariate numerical integration (Baltagi, 2013). This model can be run in Stata by using the following command:

```
xtlogit Y X X X, re
```

```
Random-effects GLS regression                  Number of obs        =       62549
Group variable: id                             Number of groups     =        7584

R-sq:   within  = 0.0047      We report        Obs per group: min =           1
        between = 0.0284      this R²                         avg =         8.2
        overall = 0.0182                                      max =          15

                                               Wald chi2(6)         =      501.47
corr(u_i, X)   = 0 (assumed)                   Prob > chi2          =      0.0000
```

mental	Coef.	Std. Err.	z	P>|z|	[95% Conf. Interval]	
age	.0024796	.0005302	4.68	0.000	.0014404	.0035187
woman	.2013067	.0147352	13.66	0.000	.1724261	.2301872
couple	-.033348	.0128953	-2.59	0.010	-.0586223	-.0080738
separated	.4460436	.0283467	15.74	0.000	.3904851	.5016021
divorced	.0435786	.0245713	1.77	0.076	-.0045802	.0917374
never_married	.1032232	.0334143	3.09	0.002	.0377323	.168714
_cons	-.2229397	.0252407	-8.83	0.000	-.2724107	-.1734688
sigma_u	.55640445					
sigma_e	.74201635					
rho	.35991072	(fraction of variance due to u_i)				

Figure 10.23 Random effects model

The major issue with random effects estimation is the assumption that $cov(x_1, c_i) = 0$ (which is not the case in our example). If breached it leads to inconsistent estimates of β_{RE}. Compared to fixed effects, the drawback of random effects is that we cannot be sure of what we are measuring. In the fixed effects example we asked what the changes in mental distress were if one unit (person) went from one marital state to another. In random effects modelling we ask this question together with an additional one: what are the differences in mental distress between people belonging to different marital statuses? Thus, in the presence of omitted variable bias, we cannot be sure what exactly we are measuring.

10.6 TIME-SERIES CROSS-SECTION METHODS

Time-series cross-section (TSCS) data can be seen as a subgroup of panel data. Whereas classic panel data consists of a large number of units recorded at relatively few time points (large i, small t), TSCS data has a different structure. Here one analyses a small or moderate number of units recorded at several time points (small or moderate i, large t). An example might be economic data for all countries in the world for the period 1970–2010 (around 190 countries and 40 time points). TSCS data has the advantage that the researcher is able to increase the number of observations by multiplying i by t.

TSCS data is characterized by the same problems as panel data, namely heteroscedasticity and autocorrelation. Because of the time-series dimension we get the additional issue of *non-stationarity*. This is because we are investigating time series for each unit.

Stationary data[25] means that parameters of our data (such as the mean and variance) do not change over time (though we can and should have fluctuations from time point to time point). For an example, see Figure 10.24.

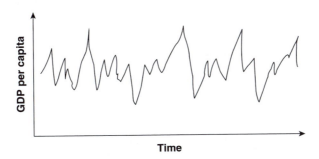

Figure 10.24 A stationary time series

If non-stationarity is present (as illustrated in Figure 10.25) it can cause problems in our statistical inference. Two unrelated series that both have the same time trend will produce a false significant relationship, that is, we can get misleading results due to spurious relationships.

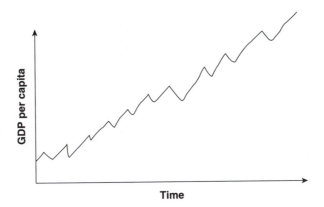

Figure 10.25 A non-stationary time series

When running regressions on time-series data it is common to include lagged values of the dependent variable as an independent variable ('lagged' means using past values of a variable; see the example in Table 10.5).[26] Such a regression is called a *vector autoregression*. It makes sense to include, for example, Y_{t-1} (the value of the dependent variable for the previous time

---

[25] For most uses the formal definition of stationarity is too strict. In this chapter we use the word 'stationary' for second-order stationarity, which means a series that has a constant mean, a constant variance, and an autocovariance that does not depend on time.

[26] For more on lagging of variables, see Finkel (1995).

point) on the right-hand side of the regression equation if you expect that the current value of the dependent variable is heavily influenced by last year's value.[27]

By employing a lagged dependent variable one takes into account historical factors that may cause current differences in the endogenous variable that can be difficult to operationalize otherwise. However, it must be noted that this is not a perfect solution to the problem of controlling for unobserved variables (Wooldridge, 2013).

Table 10.5 Lagged values of tax revenue as a percentage of GDP

Country	Year	Tax revenue	Lagged tax revenue
Canada	1992	14.65	14.70
Canada	1993	14.00	14.65
Canada	1994	13.39	14.00
Canada	1995	13.62	13.39
Canada	1996	14.24	13.62
Canada	1997	14.94	14.24
Canada	1998	15.05	14.94
Canada	1999	15.06	15.05
Canada	2000	15.24	15.06
Canada	2001	14.62	15.24
Canada	2002	13.82	14.62

It is also common practice to lag the independent variables. In a non-lagged model the Y-variable and the X-variables are observed at the same point in time. In a lagged model we use previous values of the independent variables. The main reason for this is that X should come before Y in time. For example, it would take some time for the effects of an economic policy to show in the form of an increase or reduction in foreign direct investment. A vector autoregression model with a lagged independent variable would be written as

$$y_{it} = \beta_0 + y_{i,t-1} + \beta x_{i,t-1} + \varepsilon_{it}.$$ (10.13)

X-variables that are time-invariant cannot of course be lagged, and if we include such a variable (such as *sea border*) the equation looks like this:

$$y_{it} = \beta_0 + y_{i,t-1} + \beta x_{i,t-1} + \beta x_i + \varepsilon_{it}.$$ (10.14)

As with regular panel data, TSCS data is often plagued with heteroscedasticity and autocorrelation. Here too the use of Huber–White robust standard errors (Huber, 1967; White, 1980) is recommended. An additional concern comes with the study of geographical data

---

[27] You can also choose a lag other than one time unit, though a one-year lag is the most commonly used.

(countries, regions, communes) where it is reasonable to assume correlations across panels. For example, Alabama in 1995 could be correlated with Mississippi in 1995. To correct for this it is possible to use Beck and Katz's (1995) panel-corrected standard errors which will correct the underestimated standard errors that result from this type of serial dependence. The command for this is xtpcse. This method requires that there are time points in the data with observations for all countries in the model.

Let us open the data file *TimeSeriesCrossSection.dta*. Here the data are structured on the variable *cow* ('correlates of war'), which is the Gleditsch and Ward (1999) country number, as well as the time variable *year*. The units of analysis are countries, with data on civil war and control variables for 1985–2011. The first thing we do is time-set the data:

```
. tsset cow year

        panel variable:  cow (unbalanced)
         time variable:  year, 1985 to 2011
                 delta:  1 unit
```

Then we can check that the data is in order:

```
. tabulate cow
```

No unit should have more than 27 observations. Some countries have fewer observations (e.g., newly independent states) which makes the panel unbalanced. If there should be duplicates in the data (two or more observations for the same country-year) we need to address it. To find duplicates we can type the following:

```
. duplicates report cow year

        Duplicates in terms of cow year
```

copies	observations	surplus
1	5198	0

Figure 10.26 Looking for duplicates: none found

The output in Figure 10.26 shows that in our data there are no duplicates. Checking for duplicates is relevant for all panel data, but the larger the time series the greater the risk of problems with the data. If we had duplicates it would have been reported as in Figure 10.27.

copies	observations	surplus
1	5197	0
2	2	1

Figure 10.27 Duplicates found

In such a case type

```
. duplicates list cow year
```

to get an output like Figure 10.28, then

```
. duplicates tag cow year, gen(isdup)
. edit if isdup
```

Then we can manually delete the unit(s) that are duplicates.

```
           Duplicates in terms of cow year

           obs:    cow    year

            43      20     2000
          5199      20     2000
```

Figure 10.28   Specifying duplicates

10•6•1 Testing for non-stationarity

We choose to use *fdi* (foreign direct investment) as our dependent variable. First we examine this variable:

```
. sum FDI, detail
```

```
                                  FDI

              Percentiles       Smallest
      1%       -4.82e+08        -8.47e+10
      5%        -7100000        -3.17e+10
     10%          470000        -2.53e+10     Obs                 4618
     25%        1.70e+07        -2.49e+10     Sum of Wgt.         4618

     50%        1.54e+08                      Mean            4.19e+09
                                 Largest      Std. Dev.       1.93e+10
     75%        1.30e+09         2.94e+11
     90%        7.21e+09         3.21e+11     Variance        3.71e+20
     95%        1.95e+10         3.33e+11     Skewness         10.18312
     99%        6.83e+10         3.40e+11     Kurtosis         134.7067
```

Figure 10.29   Summary statistics for *fdi*

We note from the output in Figure 10.29 that the distribution is skewed and very pointed which we see from the skewness and kurtosis values.[28] A common way of dealing with this is

---

[28] In a normal distribution the skewness value is 0 and kurtosis value is 3 (in Stata). A kurtosis value of more than 3 means a pointy distribution, a value below 3 means flat. Negative skewness means the data points are skewed to the left, positive means to the right. For more on this, see Chapter 13, p. 326ff.

to log-transform the variable. Note that when log-transforming a variable with zeros and/or negative values, these will be removed in the new variable (for more on this, see Chapter 13, pp. 329ff.). Log transformation is used to make a highly skewed distribution more normal:

```
. generate lnFDI=ln(FDI)
. sum lnFDI, detail
```

```
                              lnFDI

            Percentiles      Smallest
     1%       11.77529       2.374347
     5%       14.16868       4.60517
    10%       15.44881       4.60517       Obs                 4266
    25%       17.26875       6.907755      Sum of Wgt.         4266

    50%       19.17433                     Mean            19.13451
                             Largest       Std. Dev.       2.917849
    75%       21.18511      26.40783
    90%       22.81647      26.49556       Variance        8.513841
    95%       23.75934      26.53061       Skewness       -.3715863
    99%       25.04065      26.5524        Kurtosis         3.56363
```

Figure 10.30 Summary statistics for log-transformed foreign direct investment

The output in Figure 10.30 shows that the transformed variable is much closer to normal.[29]

To test if this variable (*lnFDI*) is non-stationary (presence of a unit root) we may use the augmented[30] Dickey–Fuller test (Dickey and Fuller, 1979). The null hypothesis of this test is that the variable contains a unit root, and the alternative is that the variable was generated by a stationary process. It is common to include a lag of one interval (in this case one year) to test if the dependent variable is non-stationary (that Y_{t-1} provides relevant information in predicting the change in Y_t). By including more lags we test if the dependent variable is predicted by Y_{t-2}, Y_{t-3}, ... This test does not allow the use of panel data, so we must look at each unit (country) individually (Table 10.6).

Table 10.6 List of some countries by *cow* number

cow	Country
2	United States
20	Canada
70	Mexico
200	United Kingdom
210	Netherlands
255	Germany

---

[29] Such a transformation can be done both to the *Y*- and *X*-variables. This gives a more correct statistical model, but it also complicates the direct interpretation of the coefficients.

[30] The test is 'augmented' because we include lags.

By graphing the variable over time we see that there is a tendency for foreign direct investment to increase:

```
. graph twoway line lnFDI year if cow<100
. graph twoway line lnFDI year if cow>=100 & cow<200
. graph twoway line lnFDI year if cow>=200 & cow<300
. graph twoway line lnFDI year if cow>=300 & cow<400
. graph twoway line lnFDI year if cow>=400 & cow<500
. graph twoway line lnFDI year if cow>=500 & cow<600
. graph twoway line lnFDI year if cow>=600 & cow<700
. graph twoway line lnFDI year if cow>=700
```

As we have now established that there is a trend in the data, we need to include a trend term when performing our test for the presence of non-stationarity:

```
. dfuller lnFDI if cow==20, trend lags(1)
```

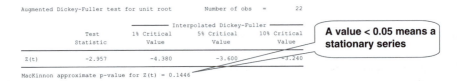

Figure 10.31 Dickey–Fuller test for unit root

We can also add `regress` to the command to get the regression output:

```
. dfuller lnFDI if cow==20, trend lags(1) regress
```

We see from Figure 10.31 that the test statistic is not significant (0.1446), which means that we cannot reject the hypothesis that the series is non-stationary (that there is a time trend). Then we repeat the operation, replacing the *cow* number to get a picture of the problem of non-stationarity in our data.[31] Another drawback with the Dickey–Fuller test (and others) is that they have low statistical power, that is, there is a real probability of not rejecting the null hypothesis when the null hypothesis is false (Enders, 2010). This leads to researchers concluding that there is a unit root present more often than they should.

10•6•2 Lag selection

If we have determined that a unit root is present, then we should apply what is known as the lagged dependent variable to the series. A rule of thumb when it comes to lagging variables is to use the time unit present in our data (one year for yearly data, one month for monthly data).

---

[31] There is also a unit root test for panel data called `xtunitroot`. However, this test is significant if only one of the units is stationary, the null hypothesis being that all panels contain unit roots.

It could also be that values in the past (beyond one unit) affect today's values, and in this case a different lag (or more lags) may be necessary.

The most intuitive way to determine which lag to use is to explore a correlogram to determine the correlation between our dependent variable and its previous values. Unfortunately, the corrgram command does not work with panel data, but we can test each unit individually. We set the lags at 10, as it is unrealistic for values further back than 10 years to have substantial statistical influence on our dependent variable:

```
. corrgram lnFDI if cow==20, lags(10)
```

					-1	0	1 -1	0	1
LAG	AC	PAC	Q	Prob>Q	[Autocorrelation]		[Partial Autocor]		
1	0.7022	0.7419	14.36	0.0002					
2	0.4548	-0.1155	20.635	0.0000					
3	0.3243	0.0211	23.963	0.0000					
4	0.2710	0.4243	26.393	0.0000					
5	0.2780	0.2844	29.072	0.0000					
6	0.3383	0.2604	33.238	0.0000					
7	0.2353	-0.4199	35.358	0.0000					
8	0.1422	0.0195	36.176	0.0000					
9	0.0202	.	36.193	0.0000					
10	-0.0002	.	36.193	0.0001					

Figure 10.32 Autocorrelation for Canada

For Canada (*cow* = 20) we see from Figure 10.32 that a one-year lag is best, as this has the highest correlation with our variable. The partial autocorrelation is the autocorrelation that is not accounted for by lags 1 to $k - 1$. We carry out the same procedure for the other units (countries) in our sample to get an overall picture of which lag we should include in our model. To view the same correlogram graphically we can write:

```
. ac lnFDI if cow==20, lags(10)
```

The output in Figure 10.33 includes a 95 per cent confidence interval (the shaded area), and correlations outside this area are significant. We see that this is the case for Y_{t-1}. To employ a one-year lagged dependent variable we include 1.lnFDI in the syntax (we could also write 11.lnFDI). If we wanted to produce a two-year lag we would write 12.lnFDI (and similarly for longer lags).[32]

Due to causality issues we lag independent variables whenever the theory indicates that it takes time for them to influence our dependent variable. We choose to do this with *gdppercapita*, *incidence* (presence of war in a given country-year), and *gdpgrowth*.[33] Remember that it is not necessary to lag variables that do not vary over time.

---

[32] It is also possible to lead the variable (put it one time unit ahead), by replacing the 1 with f.

[33] *gdppercapita* and *gdpgrowth* are from World Bank (2014) and *incidence* is from Gleditsch et al. (2002).

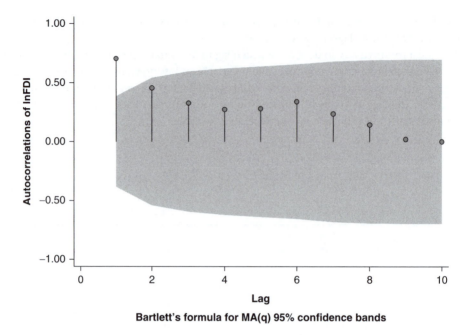

Figure 10.33   Graph of autocorrelation

10•6•3 The TSCS model

We can now use the same approach as with the classic panel data, namely the pooled OLS, between effects, fixed effects,[34] and random effects models. The X-variables included would now be *gdppercapita*, *gdpgrowth*, *ethfrac* (ethnolinguistic fractionalization index),[35] and *incidence*. The equation for a pooled OLS model is:

$$y_{it} = \beta_0 + \beta_1 y_{i,t-1} + \beta_2 x_{1i,t-1} + \beta_3 x_{2i,t-1} + \beta_4 x_{3i} + \beta_5 x_{4t-1} + \varepsilon_{it} . \tag{10.15}$$

Note that X_3 is time-invariant and that the other X-variables are all lagged one year. We should also remember to deal with autocorrelation and heteroscedasticity by including the vce and `cluster` options (Figure 10.34):[36]

```
. regress lnFDI l.lnFDI l.GDPperCapita l.GDPGrowth ethfrac l.incidence,
vce(cluster cow)
```

---

[34] Note that including a lagged dependent variable leads to bias in a fixed effect model, as described by Nickell (1981). However, this problem is reduced by increasing *t*. The same bias also affects random effects models.

[35] This variable is taken from Fearon and Laitin (1996).

[36] Even though we have included Y_{t-1} in our equation we might still have a problem with autocorrelation. This can be tested on panel data by using `xtserial` (as described on p. 234).

```
Linear regression                                  Number of obs =      3129
                                                   F(  5,    150) = 1964.10
                                                   Prob > F       =   0.0000
                          Lagged Y                 R-squared      =   0.8459
                                                   Root MSE       =   1.0527

                                      (Std. Err. adjusted for 151 clusters in cow)
```

lnFDI	Coef.	Robust Std. Err.	t	P>|t|	[95% Conf. Interval]	
lnFDI						
L1.	.8697302	.0116164	74.87	0.000	.8467773	.8926831
GDPperCapita						
L1.	.0000124	2.57e-06	4.82	0.000	7.30e-06	.0000174
GDPGrowth						
L1.	.01117	.0043547	2.57	0.011	.0025656	.0197744
ethfrac	-.1037323	.0998098	-1.04	0.300	-.3009469	.0934823
incidence						
L1.	-.01008	.0602551	-0.17	0.867	-.1291384	.1089784
_cons	2.643636	.2261663	11.69	0.000	2.196753	3.090519

Figure 10.34 Regression with a lagged dependent and lagged independent variables

10.7 BINARY DEPENDENT VARIABLES

There are some additional problems associated with binary TSCS (BTSCS).[37] The most pronounced is the lack of a simple residual. This makes it harder to model either the time series or the cross-sectional property of the error process (Beck, 2008). When performing an analysis on BTSCS data the estimator used is the maximum likelihood and one uses the logit (as in ordinary logistic regression) to estimate the data. One can use either the logit or the xtlogit command. Note that the default of xtlogit is a random effects model, and that a fixed effect model will exclude units with only ones or only zeros on the dependent variable.

You can use the Huber–White robust standard errors even when your dependent variable is dichotomous. But here, as in linear regression, you should make sure your model is correctly specified. If not, you will only get consistent estimates of the standard errors for incorrect parameters (logits). Also note that you cannot use robust and cluster options with the xtlogit command.

In our example we will use the onset of civil war, *onset2*, as our dependent variable,[38] and the one-year lagged *gdpgrowth* and *gdppercapita*, as well as the time-invariant *ethfrac* variable:

$$L_{it} = \beta_0 + \beta_1 x_{1i,t-1} + \beta_2 x_{2i,t-1} + \beta_3 x_{3i,t-1} + \varepsilon_{it} .$$ (10.16)

[37] When the dependent variable can only take two values: 0 and 1.

[38] The variable is based on the Uppsala Armed Conflict Dataset (Gleditsch et al., 2002). *onset2* assigns the code 1 for the country-years where a conflicted started in which there were more than 25 battle-related deaths per year.

First we look at our dependent variable (Figure 10.35):

. tab onset2

onset2v412	Freq.	Percent	Cum.
0	4,307	96.61	96.61
1	151	3.39	100.00
Total	4,458	100.00	

Figure 10.35 Frequencies of *onset2*

Then we can run the regression, output of which is shown in Figure 10.36.

. logit onset2 l.GDPGrowth l.GDPperCapita ethfrac, vce(cluster cow)

```
Logistic regression                          Number of obs   =      3623
                                             Wald chi2(3)    =     21.20
                                             Prob > chi2     =    0.0001
Log pseudolikelihood =  -484.3116            Pseudo R2       =    0.0628
```

(Std. Err. adjusted for 151 clusters in cow)

onset2	Coef.	Robust Std. Err.	z	P>|z|	[95% Conf. Interval]	
GDPGrowth						
L1.	-.0047944	.0130362	-0.37	0.713	-.0303449	.0207561
GDPperCapita						
L1.	-.0000692	.0000327	-2.12	0.034	-.0001332	-5.12e-06
ethfrac	1.983527	.5937031	3.34	0.001	.8198901	3.147164
_cons	-4.14326	.3522623	-11.76	0.000	-4.833682	-3.452839

Figure 10.36 Logistic regression with lagged independent variables

We can also run a random effects logit model (Figure 10.37):

. xtlogit onset2 l.GDPGrowth l.GDPperCapita ethfrac

Then we can look at the dependent variable for those units that were included in the last model (Figure 10.38):

. tab onset2 if e(sample)

It is also possible to account for temporal dependence in BTSCS data. Obviously we cannot lag the dependent variable as there is not enough information in the 0/1 properties of $t - 1$

```
Random-effects logistic regression              Number of obs      =        3623
Group variable: cow                             Number of groups   =         151

Random effects u_i ~ Gaussian                   Obs per group: min =           6
                                                               avg =        24.0
                                                               max =          26

Integration method: mvaghermite                 Integration points =          12

                                                Wald chi2(3)       =       26.43
Log likelihood   = -468.4484                    Prob > chi2        =      0.0000
```

onset2	Coef.	Std. Err.	z	P>|z|	[95% Conf. Interval]	
GDPGrowth						
L1.	-.0064479	.0137044	-0.47	0.638	-.033308	.0204122
GDPperCapita						
L1.	-.0000693	.0000272	-2.55	0.011	-.0001226	-.000016
ethfrac	1.950461	.5595827	3.49	0.000	.8536994	3.047223
_cons	-4.535469	.3763273	-12.05	0.000	-5.273057	-3.797881
/lnsig2u	-.0501848	.3404252			-.7174059	.6170362
sigma_u	.9752198	.1659947			.6985818	1.361406
rho	.2242563	.0592222			.1291772	.3603579

```
Likelihood-ratio test of rho=0: chibar2(01) =   31.73 Prob >= chibar2 = 0.000
```

Figure 10.37 Random effects logistic model

onset2v412	Freq.	Percent	Cum.
0	3,506	96.77	96.77
1	117	3.23	100.00
Total	3,623	100.00	

Figure 10.38 Frequencies of *onset2* for observations included in last run model

to inform *t* (Beck, 2008). One way of solving this is to use another variable named *incidence*,[39] which counts if there is a civil war present in a given country-year. We use the lagged value of this variable (Figure 10.39):

. logit onset2 l.incidence l.GDPGrowth l.GDPperCapita ethfrac, vce(cluster cow)

Alternatively, we can use another method to account for temporal dependence. We can create a variable that counts the time (year) since the presence of the last event (in this case, the last year in a given country that was engaged in war, before the next onset of war). Then we have to create a set of smoothing variables for this temporal count variable, called a natural

---

[39] Not to be confused with civil war onset.

```
Logistic regression                              Number of obs   =      3622
                                                 Wald chi2(4)    =     24.63
                                                 Prob > chi2     =    0.0001
Log pseudolikelihood = -481.74779                Pseudo R2       =    0.0677
```

(Std. Err. adjusted for 151 clusters in cow)

onset2	Coef.	Robust Std. Err.	z	P>|z|	[95% Conf. Interval]	
incidence L1.	.4788901	.3208178	1.49	0.136	-.1499013	1.107682
GDPGrowth L1.	-.0035738	.0124777	-0.29	0.775	-.0280296	.020882
GDPperCapita L1.	-.0000642	.0000316	-2.03	0.042	-.0001261	-2.34e-06
ethfrac	1.855374	.5274327	3.52	0.000	.8216249	2.889123
_cons	-4.217128	.3587312	-11.76	0.000	-4.920228	-3.514028

Figure 10.39 Logistic regression with time control

cubic spline, with a given number of knots.[40] The reason for including the latter is that there is no *a priori* reason to expect a linear impact of time on the probability of conflict. We would assume that in the first years after a war the chance of a new civil war onset drops rapidly, but then the effect would slow down (see Figure 10.40).

We now open the ado-file called *btscs.ado*, mark all the text and run it.[41] Then we write:

```
. btscs incidence year cow, generate(peaceyears) nspline(3)
```

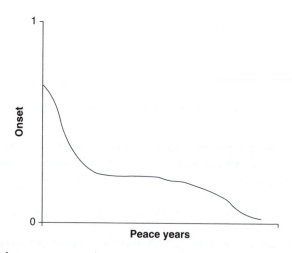

Figure 10.40 Effect of *peace years* on *civil war onset*

---

[40] The estimated spline coefficients can be used to trace out the path of duration dependence (Beck et al., 1998).

[41] This ado-file can be downloaded from http://www.prio.org/Data/Stata-Tools/. An ado-file is a way to define a Stata command.

We write the variable we want to use as a basis for the temporal dependence, followed by the time variable and the unit identifier. After the comma we generate and give the name of the new variable, and define how many splines we want. Now we can replace lagged incidence with *peaceyears* and the three splines:

```
. logit onset2 peaceyears _spline1 _spline2 _spline3 1.GDPGrowth 1.GDPperCapita
ethfrac, vce(cluster cow)
```

```
Logistic regression                              Number of obs    =        3623
                                                 Wald chi2(7)     =       42.51
                                                 Prob > chi2      =      0.0000
Log pseudolikelihood = -472.63305                Pseudo R2        =      0.0854
```

(Std. Err. adjusted for 151 clusters in cow)

onset2	Coef.	Robust Std. Err.	z	P>|z|	[95% Conf. Interval]	
peaceyears	-.0023897	.2035633	-0.01	0.991	-.4013663	.396587
_spline1	-.003038	.0196465	-0.15	0.877	-.0415445	.0354684
_spline2	.0027273	.0049825	0.55	0.584	-.0070383	.0124928
_spline3	-.001817	.0019315	-0.94	0.347	-.0056027	.0019688
GDPGrowth						
L1.	-.0010486	.0108698	-0.10	0.923	-.022353	.0202558
GDPperCapita						
L1.	-.0000462	.0000285	-1.62	0.105	-.000102	9.61e-06
ethfrac	1.896907	.5171279	3.67	0.000	.8833552	2.910459
_cons	-3.866036	.3445227	-11.22	0.000	-4.541288	-3.190784

Figure 10.41 Logistic regression with *peaceyears* and splines

This model, as with the models including a lagged dependent variable, gives us a better representation of the relationship between the explanatory variables and our dependent variable (Figure 10.41), given that the latter is a function of its previous values. It is more often than not a good strategy to take time dependence into account, as this in most cases produces a better model than when ignoring it.

10●8 CONCLUSION

Nested data such as panel data do not meet the OLS regression requirement of independent units. In this chapter we have shown the nature of this type of data, as well as describing the logic behind different models and how to run these in Stata. Special attention was given to data where *i* is moderate and *t* is large, which carries some additional statistical challenges. Treatment of panel data is a complicated matter, and this chapter is intended to function as an introduction to this topic that students and researchers can build on when developing more advanced models. This is especially the case for the time-series cross-section part of the chapter, where we recommend that readers also consult Beck and Katz (1995) and Beck et al. (1998).

key terms

Between effects A regression model taking the mean of each variable for each unit across time, and then running a regression on the collapsed dataset of means.

Fixed effects A regression including a dummy variable for each unit.

Random effects A regression model using a weighted average of between effects and fixed effects.

Spurious relationship This denotes the incorrect conclusion that two variables have a direct causal connection, when in reality they do not.

Time-series cross-section data This describes panel data with a small or moderate *i* and a large *t*.

Non-stationarity This means that mean and variance either decreases or increases over time.

Lagged dependent This means including Y_{t-1}, or a longer lag, on the right-hand side of the regression equation.

QUESTIONS

1   What are the main advantages of the fixed effects estimator compared to pooled OLS and random effects?
2   What are the main advantages of the random effects estimator compared to fixed effects?
3   What is the main additional concern with time-series cross-section data compared to more classic panel data?

FURTHER READING

Baltagi, B.H. (2013) *Econometric Analysis of Panel Data*. Chichester: Wiley.

This book is regarded as a leading textbook for postgraduate courses in panel data. It provides a practical introduction to panel data analysis, as well as a thorough discussion of its underlying principles.

Markus, G.B. (1979) *Analyzing Panel Data*. Beverly Hills, CA: Sage.

A part of the Sage series on quantitative applications in the Social Sciences, this book gives the reader an introduction to panel data analysis.

Petersen, T. (2004) Analyzing panel data: Fixed- and random-effects models. In M. A. Hardy and A. Bryman (eds), *Handbook of Data Analysis* (pp. 332–346). London: Sage.

This book chapter gives a thorough explanation of the logic of fixed and random effects modelling.

REFERENCES

Baltagi, B.H. (2013) *Econometric Analysis of Panel Data*. Chichester: Wiley.
Beck, N. (2008) Time-series cross-section methods. In J.M. Box-Steffensmeier, H.E. Brady and D. Collier (eds), *The Oxford Handbook of Political Methodology* (pp. 456–493). Oxford: Oxford University Press.

Beck, N. and Katz, J.N. (1995). What to do (and not to do) with time-series cross-section data. *American Political Science Review*, 89(3), 634–647.

Beck, N., Katz, J.N. and Tucker, R. (1998). Taking time seriously: Time-series-cross-section analysis with a binary dependent variable. *American Journal of Political Science*, 42(4), 1260–1288.

Blekesaune, M. (2008) Partnership transitions and mental distress: Investigating temporal order. *Journal of Marriage and Family*, 70(4), 879–890.

Breusch, T.S. and Pagan, A.R. (1979) A simple test for heteroskedasticity and random coefficient variation. *Econometrica*, 47, 1287–1294.

Cameron, A.C. and Trivedi, P.K. (2010) *Microeconomics Using Stata*. College Station, TX: Stata Press.

Cook, R.D. and Weisberg, S. (1983) Diagnostics for heteroskedasticity in regression. *Biometrika*, 70, 1–10.

Dickey, D.A. and Fuller, W.A. (1979) Distribution of the estimators for autoregressive time series with a unit root. *Journal of the American Statistical Association*, 74(366), 427–431.

Drukker, J.M. (2003). Testing for serial correlation in linear panel-data models. *Stata Journal*, 3(2), 1–10.

Durbin, J. and Watson, G.S. (1950) Testing for serial correlation in least squares regression, I. *Biometrika*, 37(3–4), 409–428.

Durbin, J. and Watson, G.S. (1951) Testing for serial correlation in least squares regression, II. *Biometrika*, 38(1–2), 159–179.

Enders, W. (2010) *Applied Econometric Time Series* (3rd edn). Hoboken, NJ: Wiley.

Fearon, J.D. and Laitin, D.D. (1996) Explaining interethnic cooperation. *American Political Science Review*, 90(4), 715–735.

Finkel, S. E. (1995). *Causal Analysis with Panel Data*. Thousand Oaks, CA: Sage.

Fisher, R.A. (1925) *Statistical Method for Research Workers*. Edinburgh: Oliver and Boyd.

Gleditsch, K.S. and Ward, M. D. (1999). Interstate system membership: A revised list of the independent states since 1816. *International Interactions*, 25(4), 393–413.

Gleditsch, N.P., Wallensteen, P., Eriksson, M., Sollenberg, M. and Strand, H. (2002) Armed conflict 1946–2001: A new dataset. *Journal of Peace Research*, 39(5), 615–637.

Hausman, J.A. (1978) Specification tests in econometrics. *Econometrica*, 46(6), 1251–1271.

Huber, P.J. (1967) The behavior of maximum likelihood estimates under nonstandard conditions. In L. LeCam and J. Neyman (eds), *Proceedings of the Fifth Berkeley Symposium on Mathematical Statistics and Probability* (Vol. 1, pp. 221–233). Berkeley: University of California Press.

Nickell, S. (1981). Biases in dynamic models with fixed effects. *Econometrica*, 49(6), 1417–1426.

Petersen, T. (2004) Analyzing panel data: Fixed- and random-effects models. In M. A. Hardy and A. Bryman (eds), *Handbook of Data Analysis* (pp. 332–346). London: Sage.

White, H. (1980) A heteroskedasticity-consistent covariance matrix estimator and a direct test for heteroskedasticity. *Econometrica*, 48(4), 817–830.

Wooldridge, J.M. (2010) *Econometric Analysis of Cross Section and Panel Data* (2nd edn). Cambridge, MA: MIT Press.

Wooldridge, J.M. (2013) *Introductory Econometrics: A Modern Approach* (5th edn). Mason, OH: South-Western.

World Bank (2014) *World Development Indicators*. http://data.worldbank.org/data-catalog/world-development-indicators.

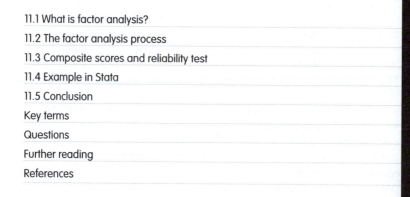

11

EXPLORATORY
FACTOR ANALYSIS

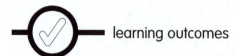

learning outcomes

- ○ Understand the purpose of factor analysis
- ○ Explain the stages of factor analysis
- ○ Know the difference between principal component analysis and other factor extraction methods

- ○ Understand and interpret factor analysis using Stata
- ○ Obtain estimated and generated factor scores and perform reliability tests

In this chapter, we explain exploratory factor analysis,[1] or just factor analysis, a technique which in practice is often used for data reduction purposes in the social sciences. In doing so, where appropriate, we also clarify the major differences between factor analysis and principal component analysis (another statistical technique used for data reduction). Having explained the details (extraction, loadings, rotation, etc.) of factor analysis, we illustrate how we can apply it to a real-life dataset using Stata. As reduced data (factors representing different subsets of variables) are often used as dependent or independent variables in subsequent analyses (regression analysis, analysis of variance, etc.) in much social science work, we also explain the procedures (factor score computation, reliability tests, etc.) necessary prior to the subsequent use of these factors/components.

 WHAT IS FACTOR ANALYSIS?

Factor analysis is a statistical technique used to detect a smaller set of underlying factors[2] that explain the covariance/correlation among a larger set of observed variables.[3] Conceptually put, then, each factor would correspond to a subset of observed variables that are relatively highly correlated. To further clarify the notion of factor analysis, let us use a hypothetical example. Suppose that a random sample of people have responded to the following statements (on a scale from 1 = totally disagree to 5 = totally agree) included in a questionnaire distributed by an environmental psychologist.

Var1 – Most of my friends think I should use environmentally friendly products

Var2 – Most of my neighbours think I should use environmentally friendly products

Var3 – Most of my colleagues think I should use environmentally friendly products

Var4 – I feel a moral obligation to buy environmentally friendly products

---

[1] In this chapter, we focus solely on exploratory factor analysis. We will, however, present confirmatory factor analysis in the next chapter as a special case of structural equation modelling.

[2] Alternative terms for factors are unobserved variables, hypothetical variables, latent variables and constructs.

[3] Alternative terms for observed variables are items, indicators, manifest variables and measured variables.

Var5 – I feel a moral obligation to recycle household waste

Var6 – I feel a moral obligation to buy products made with recycled ingredients

In this case, responses given to each of these statements would represent observed variables (also called items) represented by *Var1–Var6* in the researcher's dataset. Suppose further that we discover that *Var1*, *Var2* and *Var3* are highly correlated and that *Var4*, *Var5* and *Var6* are correlated (see Table 11.1). Let us assume here that there are two unobservable hypothetical concepts out there, say, SOCIAL NORMS and PERSONAL NORMS that are the reasons for the high correlations among *Var1–Var3* and *Var4–Var6*, respectively. Put differently, it is these hypothetical concepts that are influencing people to respond to each of the statements above in a specific manner.

Table 11.1 Initial correlation matrix with communalities in the diagonal

	Var1	**Var2**	**Var3**	**Var4**	**Var5**	**Var6**
Var1	**0.6844**					
Var2	0.8219	**0.8115**				
Var3	0.7391	0.8555	**0.7392**			
Var4	0.2295	0.1975	0.2194	**0.3440**		
Var5	0.1645	0.1658	0.1906	0.5492	**0.3677**	
Var6	0.1315	0.1331	0.1631	0.3826	0.4427	**0.2275**

Schematically, the above example factor model can be drawn as in Figure 11.1 in which SOCIAL NORMS and PERSONAL NORMS are the two factors assumed to account for the variance in all six items (*Var1–Var6*).

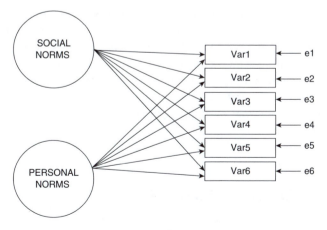

Figure 11.1 Schematic representation of a factor model[4]

---

[4] In this example, we do not assume correlation between the two factors (i.e., factors are orthogonal to each other). However, it we had assumed correlation between the factors, there would then be a curve linking the two factors visually.

However, as can be seen in Figure 11.1, since the two factors would not be able to account for all the variance in the six items, there will be other causes (besides the factors) of the variance (in each item) which are represented by the error term. This implies that factor analysis can simply be presented in the form of a regression equation as well. To illustrate this idea, we simply rewrite *Var1*, ..., *Var6* as Y_1, ..., Y_6 and the two factors as X_1, X_2, since these are respectively the dependent and independent variables as also depicted in Figure 11.1. The resulting equation will, as expected, resemble a multiple regression equation (generalized below) including two predictors for any of the six observed variables:

$$Y_i = \beta_0 + \beta_1 X_{1i} + \beta_2 X_{2i} + \varepsilon_i .$$

Since we normally work with standardized variables in factor analysis, the constant/intercept will be 0, thus our equation should be rewritten as:

$$Y_{ij} = \beta_{1i} X_{1ij} + \beta_{2i} X_{2ij} + \varepsilon_{ij} . \tag{11.1}$$

The value of each of the observed variables is estimated by (11.1) where the influence of the two factors on each observed variable is determined by their respective weights represented by the regression coefficients as well as the error term. Regression coefficients and error term have their corresponding names (loadings and uniqueness) in the realm of factor analysis which we will come back to later in the chapter.

11•1•1 What is factor analysis used for?

As the definition of the factor analysis provided above indicates, factor analysis is, firstly, used to reduce a large number of variables down to a meaningful and manageable number of factors that can reflect most of these variables' contents. Secondly, factor analysis is used to examine the dimensionality of a set of variables. Here, the researcher would be interested in finding out whether there exists one or more than one dimension in the variables. If the latter is the case, then the factor analysis would reveal how many and which variables belong to which dimensions. Thirdly, factor analysis is used to assess some of the psychometric properties of a multidimensional scale. Fourthly and relatedly, factor analysis is used in the early stages of a scale development. The just-mentioned uses of factor analysis are somewhat overlapping as factor analysis can serve several purposes in a single study.

11•2 THE FACTOR ANALYSIS PROCESS

Regardless of the purpose, the factor analysis process involves four main steps: extracting the factors, determining the number of factors, rotating the factors, and refining and interpreting the factors. Figure 11.2 depicts factor analysis as a circular process. The reason for this is that many researchers in practice move back and forth between the four main steps in an attempt to find the best factor solution.

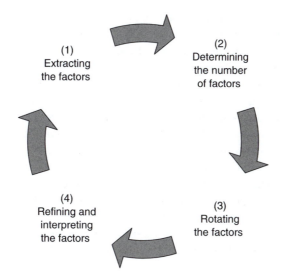

Figure 11.2 Circular process of factor analysis

11•2•1 Extracting the factors

Factor extraction is the first step in the factor analysis process, starting with a correlation matrix including all the correlations among the observed variables to be factor-analysed. The values put in the diagonals of the correlation matrix constitute essentially, at least mathematically, the only difference among many of the factor extraction methods[5] adopted. These factor extraction methods are mainly principal (axis) factor (PF), iterated principal (axis) factor (IPF), principal component factor (PCF) and maximum likelihood factor (ML). We will in this chapter focus on PF, IPF and PCF, and we will present ML in the next chapter when we come to confirmatory factor analysis.

The *principal factor* extraction method inserts estimates of the common/shared variance (also called communality) in the diagonals[6] of the starting correlation matrix instead of 1s (see Table 11.1). Communality values are obtained by estimating the squared multiple correlation[7] of each variable with all the other variables in the matrix. The reason why PF uses communalities in the diagonals is that it assumes that some of the variance in the variables is caused by some other unique sources[8] which ideally should be removed from the analysis. This is also the main difference between all of the factor analysis extraction methods (PF, IPF

---

[5] Maximum likelihood extraction manipulates off-diagonal elements rather than values in the diagonals (Tabachnick and Fidell, 2014: 688).

[6] A correlation matrix would generally have 1s in the diagonals, suggesting that each observed variable contributes 100 per cent variance to the trace. So, if you have four variables, the total variance will be 4. This is, however, not the case in PF.

[7] These are easily obtained by regressing each variable on the remaining variables.

[8] All the factor analysis methods (apart from principal component analysis) make this assumption.

and ML) and the principal component method in that the principal component method uses 1s in the starting diagonals in the correlation matrix without sorting out the variance caused by other sources than the factors themselves. Following this, we can briefly assert that PCF method analyses variance (1s in the diagonals) whereas the PF, IPF and ML methods analyse covariance (communalities in the diagonals) (see Tabachnick and Fidell, 2014).

Furthermore, the unique variance is in theory further divided between specific/systematic variance and measurement error/random variance. The specific variance can be caused by biased wording that may affect the responses of a person consistently were the item to be completed at two points in time, but they are specific to that item in that the biased wording would not necessarily influence responses to other items in the battery (Fabrigar and Wegener, 2011). The measurement error variance, on the other hand, can be caused by ambiguous wording that can be interpreted differently at two points in time by the same person depending on the person's psychological state (Fabrigar and Wegener, 2011). Having said that, factor analysis in practice does not distinguish between specific variance and measurement error variance, which in tandem are encompassed by the term 'unique variance' in the computations.

Estimating and then inserting the communalities in the diagonals of the correlation matrix was the first task in factor extraction. The next task is to compute eigenvalues and eigenvectors from this correlation matrix which are then used to compute factor loadings (see Kline, 1994). Eigenvectors are simply sets of weights (w) that generate factors with the largest possible eigenvalues, while eigenvalues (e) are variances captured by these factors. The factor extraction proceeds as follows (see Kline, 1994):[9]

1 A series of eigenvectors (and their corresponding eigenvalues) are computed[10] repeatedly from the initial correlation matrix (with communalities in the diagonals) until the solution converges (i.e., additional vectors are nearly identical to the last one); this last vector and its eigenvalue are the basis of the first factor.
2 The common variance that the first factor explains/captures is then subtracted from the initial correlation matrix, resulting in a residual matrix (i.e., diagonals are now less than those in the initial matrix).
3 To extract the second factor, the same computation procedure described in step 1 takes place once again, but this time based on the residual matrix instead of the initial correlation matrix,
4 The variance that the second factor explains/captures is also subtracted from the residual matrix, resulting in another reduced residual matrix.
5 To extract a further factor, the same procedure as in step 1 takes place again using this reduced residual matrix.
6 And so on.

Based on the correlation matrix in Table 11.1, Stata, by adopting the PF extraction method, can easily compute the necessary eigenvectors and eigenvalues. Figure 11.3, for instance,

---

[9] This procedure applies exactly in the same way to the PCF method. In fact, Kline (1994) actually explains the whole procedure based on the PCF method.

[10] Kline (1994) explains how eigenvectors and eigenvalues are computed manually, observing also that statistical software uses matrix algebra for these computations.

Eigenvectors (w)	
Factor 1	**Factor 2**
0.5127617	−0.1951717
0.5592738	−0.2552949
0.5344650	−0.1897104
0.2399653	0.5371445
0.2218162	0.5926331
0.1784647	0.4701110

Eigenvalues (e)	
Factor 1	2.575541
Factor 2	1.030058

$$l = w\sqrt{e}$$

$$= 0.513\sqrt{2.576} = -0.196\sqrt{1.030}$$
$$= 0.560\sqrt{2.576} = -0.255\sqrt{1.030}$$

etc.

	Factor loadings (l)	
	Factor1	**Factor2**
Var1	0.8229093	−0.1980738
Var2	0.8975704	−0.2590631
Var3	0.8577443	−0.1925387
Var4	0.3850864	0.5451761
Var5	0.3559512	0.6014738
Var6	0.2863748	0.4771296

Figure 11.3 Overview of eigenvectors, eigenvalues and unrotated factor loadings

shows eigenvectors associated with the first two factors with the largest eigenvalues.[11] It also shows the formula used to compute the factor loadings. Here, each eigenvector for a variable is multiplied by the square root of the factor eigenvalue to obtain the factor loading for the variable. The complete overview of the factor loadings shown in Figure 11.3 was generated by Stata.

As can be seen, the sum of the two eigenvalues (2.576 + 1.030 = 3.606) is the total amount of common variance (communality) these two factors explain together. This figure should optimally be the same as the sum of the diagonals in the correlation matrix (in Table 11.1) that we started with. The sum of the diagonals (3.1743) of the initial matrix is, however, somewhat less[12] than the sum of the eigenvalues.[13] As this situation occurs often using principal factors, factor analysts prefer to use an iterative procedure, the *iterated principal factor* method. While PF starts and completes the factor extraction process (steps 1–6 above) with one set of estimated communalities (squared multiple correlations), IPF replaces these estimated communalities by new estimates (h^2) emerging from the factor extraction process each time until the difference between the two communalities (last inserted and last estimated) is

---

[11] There will be eigenvectors and eigenvalues computed for each factor. However, here and generally, the common practice is to be concerned with only those that capture most variance.

[12] The reason why this (not unusual) difference occurs in factor analysis is the fact that the squared multiple correlations that we inserted in the diagonals in the initial matrix as the estimates of the communalities were not perfectly accurate (Hatcher, 2006).

[13] This explains also why the two factors together would apparently explain more than 100 per cent. In Stata, the variance explained by each factor is provided under the column named 'proportions' in the factor analysis output which we will interpret in more detail later in the chapter.

minimized (Lattin et al., 2003: 136). In a nutshell, PF is a factor extraction process run only once, while IPF is run several (usually at least 25) times.

Regardless of the factor solution from PF, PCF or IPF, factor loadings (unless factors are correlated)[14] would reflect correlations between observed variables and their respective factors. As a result, if we square these correlations, the results will show us how much variance of each observed variable each factor explains. For instance, take the factor loading of Var5 on factor 1, from the PF solution above, which is 0.3560. Squaring this gives 0.1267. This means that factor 1 explains 12.67 per cent of the variance in Var5. Further, we also see that the factor loading of Var5 on factor 2 is 0.6015. Squaring this gives 0.3618, meaning that factor 2 explains 36.18 per cent of the variance in Var5. Summing 12.67 and 36.18, we find that 48.85 per cent of the variance in Var5 is accounted for by factor 1 and factor 2 together, represented by h^2. We can thus compute the unique variance,[15] which is $100 - 48.85 = 51.15$ per cent, including both specific and measurement error variance:

$$\text{uniqueness} = 1 - h^2, \text{ where } h^2 = \Sigma l^2. \tag{11.2}$$

11●2●2 Determining the number of factors

Having computed the eigenvectors and eigenvalues, we now, in the second step of the factor analysis process, have to make a decision as to the number of factors to retain. There is unfortunately no clear-cut answer to this question in the multivariate statistics literature. There are, however, some good reasons for using a combination of the following criteria when deciding the number of factors: eigenvalue rule, scree test, parallel analysis, and theoretical reasoning.

Eigenvalue rule ·

In principal component analysis, factors associated with eigenvalues greater than 1 are generally recommended to be retained for interpretation. The idea here is that the factor retained should explain at least as much variance as one observed variable contributes, a situation represented by 1s in the diagonal. Since we insert communalities (which are less than 1) instead of 1s in the diagonal for factor analysis (PF or IPF), the rule of eigenvalues greater than 1 should accordingly be adjusted. One such rule is to choose eigenvalues greater than the average of the initial communalities (Afifi et al., 2012).

Scree test

The scree test is about examining a plot/curve, produced after factor extraction, containing the eigenvalues on the Y-axis and the factors on the X-axis. The idea of the scree test is that

---

[14] Factors can be assumed correlated when rotating the factor solution using a type of oblique rotation such as promax. Otherwise, PF, like PCF, assumes and produces orthogonal (no correlation between factors) solution initially.

[15] Unique variances are provided under the column titled 'Uniqueness' in Stata output.

factors along the tail of the curve represent mostly random error variance (trivial eigenvalues), and consequently, the factor solution just before the levelling of the curve should be chosen (Kachigan, 1991).

Parallel analysis

Parallel analysis is about estimating the same factor model as the original one using randomly simulated data, resembling the original data in terms of both the number of variables and observations. Eigenvalues obtained from the simulated data (e.g., 25 times) are subsequently averaged and contrasted with their counterparts from the original data. If the eigenvalue of a factor from the original data proves to be larger than the average[16] of the eigenvalues from the simulated data, the factor can be retained. Otherwise, the factor would be considered no more substantial than a random factor and thus discarded (see Matsunaga, 2010). Although parallel analysis is generally considered the best procedure for deciding the number of factors, there are still, as noted by Fabrigar and Wegener (2011), many conditions under which its performance is untested. Thus, we recommend that parallel analysis is used in tandem with the other criteria treated here.

Theoretical sensitivity

Despite the exploratory nature of factor analysis, the researcher should still employ theoretical sensitivity (subject knowledge as well as common sense) when examining the number of factors to retain. In an exploratory factor analysis, different factor solutions (two factors, three factors, etc.) may be considered. The most salient point is that the competing factor solutions should make theoretical/conceptual sense. Depending solely on statistical criteria may in some cases be misleading.

11•2•3 Rotating the factors

Having decided on the number of factors, the next task in the factor analysis process is, as depicted in Figure 11.4, to rotate the initial factor solution (the black axis) in order to obtain a more easily interpretable factor solution (the dashed axis). An easily interpretable factor solution is associated with an output that contains a factor loading (pattern) matrix with variables with the maximum possible loading (close to 1) on one factor and the minimum possible loading (close to 0) on the remaining factor(s), a situation often referred to as a 'simple structure' in the literature, as first described by Thurstone (1947).

In the unrotated solution, as presented in Figure 11.3 and further visualized in Figure 11.4, three of the variables (*Var4–Var6*) load heavily on (are close to) both factors.[17] Geometrically, this means that the distance between *Var4–Var6* and factor 2 (d_2) when compared to the

---

[16] Some suggest the 95th percentile be used instead.

[17] This is in fact a normal occurrence in an unrotated solution in factor analysis.

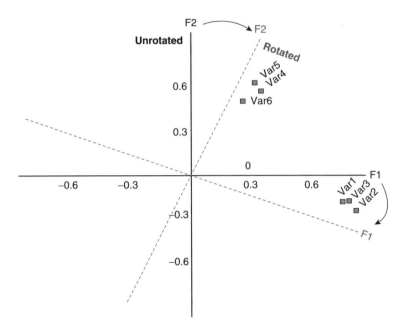

Figure 11.4 Geometrical representation of an orthogonal rotation

distance between *Var4–Var6* and factor 1 (d_1) which is also not substantial. After rotation, however, this distance $(d_2 - d_1)$ becomes more apparent in that *Var4–Var6* get closer to factor 2 but more distant from factor 1. That is, in the rotated solution, we obtain new coordinates showing that *Var4–Var6* load more strongly on factor 2 while loading more weakly on factor 1. Incidentally, the strong and weak loadings of *Var1–Var3* on factor 1 and factor 2, respectively, do not change substantially. Geometrically the closer the variables are to each other or factors, the higher the correlations are and vice versa.

The new coordinates above are estimated using the most widely used orthogonal rotation technique, namely *varimax* rotation. Varimax maximizes the variance of the squared loadings for each factor, thus polarizing loadings so that they are either high or low, making it easier to identify factors with specific variables (Hamilton, 1992: 261). As also shown in Figure 11.4, varimax, at the same time, keeps the angle between the axis of factor 1 and factor 2 at 90 degrees (cos(90) indicating zero correlation between the two factors). If it were not for this restriction, the rotated axes would go right through the cloud of variables in Figure 11.4.

It should further be noted that rotation does not influence (increase or decrease) the *total variance explained* by the factors. However, the total variance explained gets distributed differently among the factors (i.e., *eigenvalues* change). Suppose that two factors explain 75 per cent variance together, with 48 per cent and 27 per cent of the variance attributable to the first and second factor, respectively. After rotation, the factors would together still explain 75 per cent variance, but now with, say, 44 per cent and 31 per cent of the total variance attributed to the first and second factor, respectively. Relatedly, the total amount of variance of each variable explained by the factors (i.e., *communality*) would also stay the same but the *factor loadings* would change after rotation. In addition to varimax, there are several other orthogonal rotation techniques such as quartimax, equamax, and parsimax which are less commonly encountered in the social science research.

As an alternative to orthogonal rotation, oblique rotation can be used. The idea of oblique rotation is that the restriction of a 90 degree angle between the factor axes (imposed by orthogonal rotation) is relaxed when rotating (see Figure 11.5). There is general support for this relaxation among social scientists as it is more realistic that factors (latent variables) measuring behavioural phenomena are somewhat correlated. As such, it is widely recommended that one by default employs an oblique rotation to be able to take this correlation into account in the factor model estimation.[18] Even if the factors are not correlated or only weakly correlated, an oblique rotation would still produce a similar solution to that provided by an orthogonal rotation (Harman, 1976).

The most common oblique rotation technique is *promax*. Promax starts with an orthogonal rotation (varimax) in which the loadings are, first, raised to a specific[19] power (2, 3 or 4) and then the solution is rotated to allow for correlations among the factors (Pett et al., 2003). Raising varimax loadings/coefficients to a given power makes all the resulting loadings/coefficients closer to zero, but the effect differs across original values that are larger in magnitude (e.g., $0.87^3 = 0.66$) as opposed to smaller in magnitude (e.g., $0.25^3 = 0.016$) (Thompson, 2004). The goal here is to obtain a factor solution containing the best structure using the lowest possible power loadings and thus with the lowest correlation among the factors (Pett et al., 2003). Thus, power values

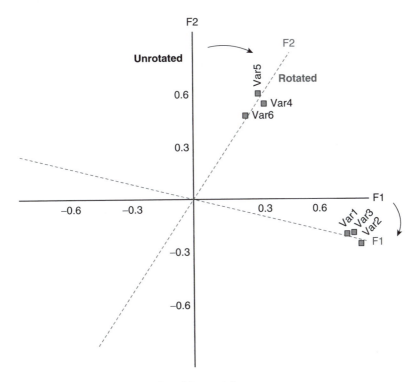

Figure 11.5 Geometrical representation of an oblique rotation

---

[18] What this means is that oblique rotation estimates the correlation between the factors and then generates a solution (Harman, 1976).

[19] The default power value used for promax in Stata is 3.

larger than 4 are generally not recommended (StataCorp, 2015: 662). In addition to promax, there are several other oblique rotations, among which direct oblimin, oblimax and quartimin which are less commonly used in the literature.

11•2•4 Refining and interpreting the factors

After rotating the factors, the next step is to refine and interpret them using both quantitative criteria and qualitative judgement. Qualitative judgement is about examining the factor solution on theoretical and/or conceptual grounds. One salient quantitative criterion is the examination of factor loadings. A factor loading is a quantity measuring the strength of the relationship between an observed variable and a factor. In an orthogonal solution,[20] a factor loading corresponds directly to the standardized coefficient (or correlation) in a bivariate/ simple regression model. In an oblique solution, however, a factor loading corresponds to the partial standardized coefficient (or partial correlation) in a multiple regression model. This is because, in the oblique solution, the relationship (loading) between an observed variable and a factor is estimated having controlled for the other factor(s), as visualized in Figure 11.6.

In line with the above explanation, the interpretation of the *factor loading matrix (factor pattern matrix)* produced by orthogonal or oblique rotation will be different. In the orthogonal case (see Figure 11.6), we would interpret, for instance, a loading of 0.8 of *Var1* on factor 1 as 'for every unit increase in factor 1, there will be an average increase of 0.8 in *Var1*'. This interpretation would slightly change in the oblique case. Here, we would instead say 'for every unit increase in factor 1, there will be an average increase of 0.8 in *Var1*, *having controlled for factor 2*'.

In addition to the pattern matrix, oblique rotation generates two other matrices: a factor correlation matrix and a factor structure matrix. The *factor correlation matrix* shows simple correlations between the factors. The *factor structure matrix* contains loadings which are actually zero-order correlations of the observed variables with the factors. Since these loadings are not adjusted for the correlation between the factors, there is little use in interpreting these. We should thus examine and report the results from the factor pattern matrix instead of those from the factor structure matrix.

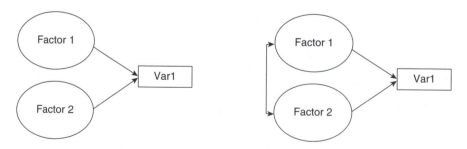

Figure 11.6 Orthogonally (left) and obliquely (right) rotated factor solutions

---

[20] Principal component analysis applies orthogonal rotation by default, whereas in factor analysis this is optional and scholars mostly opt for oblique rotation.

When examining the factor pattern matrix, regardless of orthogonal or oblique rotation, and based on a general consensus found in the literature (e.g., Brown, 2015; Hatcher, 2006), we suggest 0.4 be used as a threshold[21] to distinguish between practically significant and non-significant loadings. This means that loadings below 0.4 would indicate a weak relationship between an observed variable and a factor. As such, variables loading weakly on all of the factors in a solution should generally be removed from the analysis. This general rule applies also to variables loading strongly on at least two factors, as this situation would cause problems for establishing discriminant validity of the factors. Removal of the observed variables must be done sequentially, meaning that after deletion of each variable, the factor model should be re-estimated and examined before possibly removing another variable. Removal of variables must be considered after having tried out different extraction methods as well as rotation techniques.

We further suggest that removal (as well as inclusion, for that matter) of variables should be guided by the theoretical sensitivity of the researcher. The researcher should examine whether variables loading strongly on a factor can actually be represented by the factor conceptually as well. While examining each variable's content and loading[22] on different factors, the researcher can also start labelling the factors. These labels would usually be inspired by the relevant theory as well as common sense.

Labelling the factors actually completes the circular factor analysis process. Nevertheless, many social scientists wish to use the resulting factors in further analyses. That is, the resulting factors are often used as predictors (and sometimes as outcomes) in a statistical model. To do so, the factors must be given a metric and their reliabilities must be assessed.

11 ● 3   COMPOSITE SCORES AND RELIABILITY TEST

There are two main ways of computing a metric (or a composite score) for a factor: estimating a factor score and generating a factor score (i.e., summated scale). *Estimated factor scores* are standardized and weighted values showing the standing of each individual on the factor. As shown in Figure 11.7, an individual's estimated factor score is computed by summing the products of the standardized factor score coefficients (weights) and the standardized scores (i.e., z-scores) of the individual on all of the variables, a similar procedure to that used for prediction purposes in multiple regression analysis.

The above method is therefore referred to as the *regression method*[23] for estimating factor scores in the literature. Technically, factor score coefficients (weights) are computed by multiplying the inverse of the sample correlation matrix by the factor loading (pattern) matrix.[24]

---

[21] In principal component analysis, however, the threshold should be 0.7. The reason is that the loadings would usually be lower in factor analysis than in principal component analysis as a result of lower values than 1 occurring on the diagonals in factor analysis.

[22] The sign of the loadings is also important to examine. We recommend that variables loading negatively on factors be reversed to make the interpretation easier.

[23] Here we will only present the regression method. However, in addition to the regression method, there is also the Bartlett method and Anderson–Rubin method (see Pett et al., 2003).

[24] This can be easily done using Stata.

Factor score coefficients

Scoring coefficients

Variable	Factor1	Factor2
Var1	0.20845	0.04980
Var2	0.53094	-0.01758
Var3	0.26327	0.08672
Var4	0.01966	0.33599
Var5	0.00944	0.38687
Var6	0.00627	0.23817

Standardized (z-scores) values

z_Var1	z_Var2	z_Var3	z_Var4	z_Var5	z_Var6
.96042038	.9582161	1.0439712	.72305588	.76442534	.04416852

$$Y_i = \beta_1 X_{1i} + \beta_2 X_{2i} + \ldots + \beta_k X_{ki}$$

Factor score of individual 1 on factor 1

$= .20845 \times .96042 + .53094 \times .95821 + .26327 \times 1.04397$
$+ .01966 \times .72305 + .00944 \times .76442 + .00627 \times .04416$
$= 1.005$

Factor score of individual 1 on factor 2

$= .04980 \times .96042 + (-.01758) \times .95821 + .08672 \times 1.04397$
$+ .33599 \times .72305 + .38687 \times .76442 + .23817 \times .04416$
$= .6707$

Figure 11.7 Estimated factor scores

The advantage of the estimated factor score is that it represents all of the variables load-ing on the factor, while its disadvantage is that the scores obtained are not unique values (i.e., factor indeterminacy)[25] and thus not easily replicable across studies (Hair et al., 2013; Pett et al., 2003). Consequently, it has been suggested that the factor determinacy coefficient (see Beauducel, 2011) be examined before using estimated factors scores as variables in sub-sequent analyses. According to Gorsuch (1983), such a coefficient should be at least 0.90 if the factor score is to be used as a substitute for the observed variables.

Generated factor scores are raw and unweighted values obtained for each individual either by summing or averaging only those variables loading most strongly on a factor. As opposed to their standardized and weighted counterpart, generated factor scores exclude those vari-ables that load weakly on the factor in the computation. While this can be viewed as a drawback, the main advantage of generated factor scores is that they are replicable across studies (Hair et al., 2013).

The reliability of any generated factor score should be examined (Hair et al., 2013) as the final step prior to its use in subsequent analysis. The *reliability* of a scale is estimated as 1 minus the proportion of error variance (Kline, 2011). *Cronbach's alpha*, given by

$$\alpha = \frac{K}{K-1} \frac{s_T^2 - \sum_{i=1}^{K} s_i^2}{s_T^2}, \tag{11.3}$$

where K is the number of variables, s_i^2 is the variance of each variable and s_T^2 is the variance of the summated score, is commonly computed to assess the reliability of generated factor scores. It ranges from 0 to 1. A coefficient of 0.7 or greater is usually considered satisfactory; a coefficient of 0.7 would mean that 70 per cent of this scale is reliable or alternatively 30 per cent of the variance is due to error.

---

[25] The factor solution is not unique due to the problems of factor rotation and communality estimation (see Sharma, 1996).

11●4 EXAMPLE IN STATA

In this section, we will estimate an exploratory factor model using Stata based on a real-life dataset (entitled *workout3.dta*). Our data was collected from members of a training/fitness centre in 2014 in a medium-sized city in Norway. The members were asked, using an ordinal scale (from 1 = not at all important, to 6 = very important), to indicate how important each of the following reasons was for working out:

Var1 – to help manage stress

Var2 – to release tension

Var3 – to mentally relax

Var4 – to have a good body

Var5 – to improve my appearance

Var6 – to look more attractive

Our aim here is simply to reduce the data, that is, extract a small number of factors that can capture most of the covariance in the correlation matrix.

Recall from Figure 11.2 that the first step in the factor analysis is to decide on the extraction method. Stata lets you estimate a factor model using the four methods discussed in this chapter: PCF, PF, IPF and ML. We also know that PCF is distinctively different from the remaining methods in that it explains the variance in the initial correlation matrix. However, we want to estimate a pure factor model, thus we must decide between PF, IPF and ML. As PF is the most widely used factor extraction method, we estimate our factor model using PF in this section. This is the default model in Stata.

To estimate the factor model, it will suffice to write the main command `factor` followed by the variables to be factor-analysed (see Figure 11.8) without adding `pf` at the end. However, if you want to use any of the other methods, you must add `ipf`, `ml` or `pcf` depending on your choice (e.g., `factor Var1 Var2 Var3, ml`).

The second step is to determine the number of factors to retain. One criterion that we can use is to locate those factors with eigenvalues greater than the average of the initial communalities (squared multiple correlations). We can obtain the initial communalities inserted in the diagonal by using the command `estat smc` after factor estimation. This will give us the results shown in Figure 11.9, which shows that the average of these communalities is about 0.725. When we look at our factor solution in Figure 11.8, we observe that the first factor (2.34) and second factor (2.28) are associated with eigenvalues clearly above 0.725.

Although the eigenvalue rule alone lends support to a two-factor solution, we can further perform the parallel analysis and scree test discussed in Section 11.2.2. Since we can use the plot produced by the parallel test command to also undertake the scree test, we can directly use the user-written command `fapara`[26] to get the details of both parallel analysis and scree plot. Typing `fapara` after factor estimation yields Figure 11.10.

---

[26] This is a user-written command. To install it, just type `findit fapara` and follow the installing advice.

```
. factor Var1 Var2 Var3 Var4 Var5 Var6
(obs=194)
```

Factor analysis/correlation	Number of obs	=	194
Method: principal factors	Retained factors	=	2
Rotation: (unrotated)	Number of params	=	11

Factor	Eigenvalue	Difference	Proportion	Cumulative
Factor1	2.34378	0.06348	0.5390	0.5390
Factor2	2.28031	2.28404	0.5244	1.0635
Factor3	-0.00373	0.06681	-0.0009	1.0626
Factor4	-0.07054	0.00915	-0.0162	1.0464
Factor5	-0.07969	0.04239	-0.0183	1.0281
Factor6	-0.12208	.	-0.0281	1.0000

```
LR test: independent vs. saturated:  chi2(15) =  889.42 Prob>chi2 = 0.0000
```

Factor loadings (pattern matrix) and unique variances

Variable	Factor1	Factor2	Uniqueness
Var1	0.8581	0.0814	0.2571
Var2	0.9194	0.0710	0.1498
Var3	0.8518	0.1563	0.2501
Var4	-0.0451	0.8020	0.3547
Var5	-0.1092	0.9141	0.1524
Var6	-0.1511	0.8748	0.2119

Figure 11.8   Factor model estimated using principal factors (unrotated solution)

```
. estat smc
```

Squared multiple correlations of variables with all other variables

Variable	smc
Var1	0.7020
Var2	0.7900
Var3	0.7098
Var4	0.6125
Var5	0.7872
Var6	0.7465

```
. di (0.7020+0.7900+0.7098+0.6125+0.7872+0.7465 )/6
.72466667
```

Figure 11.9   Initial communalities (squared multiple correlations)

As far as the scree test is concerned, in Figure 11.10 we see that there are two obvious factors before the curve levels off – a finding confirming the two-factor solution supported by the eigenvalue rule.

As for parallel analysis, first, when we look at Figure 11.10 we see that the parallel analysis line (i.e., dashed line) crosses the factor analysis line (i.e., bold line) before reaching the third factor. This observation indicates that we should retain the first two factors. The parallel analysis command produces the following numerical findings as well.

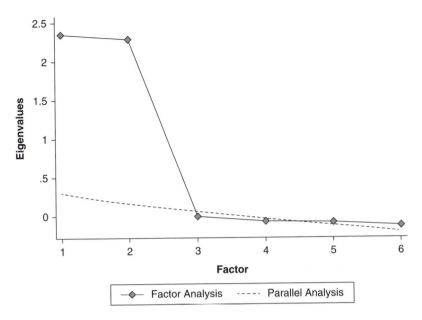

Figure 11.10 Parallel analysis and scree plot

```
. fapara, reps(25)

PA -- Parallel Analysis for Factor Analysis -- N = 194
PA Eigenvalues Averaged Over 25 Replications
          FA          PA          Dif
    1.  2.343784    .2955685    2.048216
    2.  2.280308    .1595826    2.120726
    3. -.0037325    .0625588   -.0662913
    4.  -.070543   -.0306946   -.0398484
    5. -.0796921   -.1174139    .0377218
    6. -.1220786   -.1968631    .0747844
```

Here too, we see clear support for a two-factor solution in that only the eigenvalues of the first two factors (FA) are larger than the average of the eigenvalues from the simulated data (PA).

In addition to the quantitative evidence provided by the above criteria, we can also justify the two-factor solution based using our theoretical sensitivity. Looking at the content of the first three variables (*Var1–Var3*), we see that they all are about relaxation whereas the remaining three variables (*Var4–Var6*) revolve around appearance.

Although the unrotated solution shown in Figure 11.7 is already relatively easily interpretable, we still can rotate it to be able to further polarize the loadings. Since our two factors represent two different phenomena (relaxation and appearance) we do not assume a strong correlation[27] between the factors. Thus, we go ahead and rotate the factors orthogonally using the default varimax rotation procedure. To do so in Stata, we simply type `rotate` after factor estimation. As Figure 11.11 shows, the first three variables (*Var1–Var3*) load more strongly on

---

[27] You can also find out the correlation between the factors by first rotating the factor solution obliquely by typing `rotate, oblique promax` and then `estat common`.

```
. rotate //or rotate, orthogonal v arimax
```

```
Factor analysis/correlation                    Number of obs    =      194
    Method: principal factors                  Retained factors =        2
    Rotation: orthogonal varimax (Kaiser off)  Number of params =       11
```

Factor	Variance	Difference	Proportion	Cumulative
Factor1	2.34290	0.06171	0.5388	0.5388
Factor2	2.28119	.	0.5246	1.0635

```
    LR test: independent vs. saturated:   chi2(15)  =   889.42 Prob>chi2 = 0.0000
```

Rotated factor loadings (pattern matrix) and unique variances

Variable	Factor1	Factor2	Uniqueness
Var1	0.8617	-0.0204	0.2571
Var2	0.9213	-0.0380	0.1498
Var3	0.8643	0.0547	0.2501
Var4	0.0498	0.8018	0.3547
Var5	-0.0006	0.9206	0.1524
Var6	-0.0469	0.8865	0.2119

Figure 11.11   Factor model estimated using principal factors (orthogonally rotated solution)

factor 1 and more weakly on factor 2, whereas the remaining variables (*Var4–Var6*) load more strongly on factor 2 and more weakly on factor 1.

If we want to show the relationship between the variables and factors geometrically, we just type `loadingplot` in Stata. This command yields Figure 11.12.

Rotating the factors does not change the total variance explained. The total variance will be equal to the sum of the item (variable) communalities.[28] We can obtain the communalities

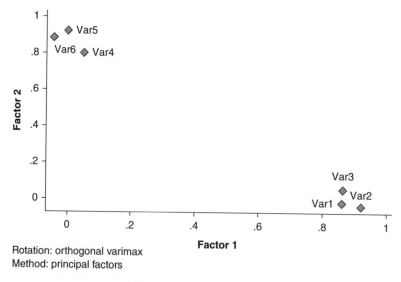

Rotation: orthogonal varimax
Method: principal factors

Figure 11.12   Plot of factor loadings after rotation

---

[28] Instead of squared multiple correlations (usually not very good estimates) we use communalities after estimation to obtain the total variance.

by typing `facom`[29] after factor estimation. It appears that the sum of these communalities is 4.624. Remember, if we adopted the PCF method, the total would be 6. To be able to find out the proportion of the total variance that each of our factors explains, we would simply divide the final eigenvalues by the total variance. As such, we see that factor 1 and factor 2 explain about 50 per cent of the variance each.

As far as the factor loading matrix (Figure 11.11) is concerned, we suggest that one goes about it vertically and horizontally. When we interpret the matrix vertically, we locate the correlations[30] between a factor and all the observed variables. For instance, the loading of *Var1* on factor 1 is 0.8617. This means that nearly (0.8617^2) 74 per cent of the variance of *Var1* is explained by factor 1. We interpret the remaining loadings in the same manner. When we interpret the matrix horizontally, we obtain item communalities. For instance, we see that the loadings of *Var3* on factor 1 and factor 2 are 0.8643 and 0.0547, respectively. Squaring and adding these two values together would show us the proportion (about 75 per cent) of the total variance of *Var3* that is explained by factor 1 and factor 2 in tandem. What is left (about 25 per cent) represents the unique variance. Since all the loadings are clearly above our threshold of 0.4, we would go along with the current factor solution. There are no variables loading equally strongly on both of the factors either. The final step of the factor analysis process is labelling the factors that we decide to retain. As we mentioned earlier, having studied the content of the items and loadings, we choose to label factor 1 as *relaxation* and factor 2 as *appearance*.

If the purpose of our factor analysis were to examine only the factor structure (which variables can be underlined by which factors) we would stop the process here. However, we know that many social science studies use factors in subsequent analysis. To go down this path, we first need a metric for the two hypothetical constructs. As you know, we can choose between the estimated factor score and generated factor score. Since the loadings are clearly polarized, we choose to generate factor scores. This can be done by taking either the sum or average of the variables expressing each factor. We will choose to take the average to keep the factor metric on the same scale (1–6) as the original observed variables. Next, we also need to test the reliability of this summated scale based on Cronbach's alpha coefficient. For both generating factor score (average) and reliability test, we will use a user-written command[31] called `sumscale` as below:

```
. sumscale, f1(Var1 Var2 Var3) f2(Var4 Var5 Var6)
```

Factor (Items)	N	Mean	Std	Min	Max	Cronbach Alpha
Factor1 (Var1 Var2 Var3)	210	4.12	1.44	1.00	6.00	0.92
Factor2 (Var4 Var5 Var6)	206	3.50	1.50	1.00	6.00	0.92

New factor-average variable/s are generated in your data set!

Figure 11.13 The `sumscale` command

---

[29] This is a user-written command. To install it, just type `findit facom` and follow the instructions.

[30] In orthogonally rotated solutions loadings are simply correlations.

[31] Just type `ssc install sumscale` in Stata to install this package.

This command will provide us with the generated factor scores, their Cronbach's alpha coefficient and some descriptive statistics as shown in Figure 11.13. You can then rename f1 as relaxation and f2 as appearance in your dataset for use as independent or dependent variables in subsequent analyses.

11.5 CONCLUSION

Exploratory factor analysis is a useful statistical technique that has a wide range of uses in social sciences. Understanding exploratory factor analysis lays a very good foundation for learning confirmatory factor analysis, a special case of structural equation modelling, which is the topic of the next chapter. We have also learnt that factor analysis is a more subjective statistical technique than traditional techniques such as linear regression. This feature of factor analysis thus requires more of the analyst in an attempt to ascertain the optimal factor solution. In this chapter we have also presented some of the most commonly used factor-related commands in Stata. Stata offers many more features that can be explored using help factor.

 key terms

Factor extraction A method used to explain the variance in the correlation matrix.

Eigenvectors Sets of weights that generate factors with the largest possible eigenvalues.

Eigenvalue The amount of variance captured/explained by a factor.

Factor loading The correlation (bivariate or partial) between the observed variable and factor.

Communality The squared multiple correlation of each variable with all the other variables in the correlation matrix.

Uniqueness The amount of variance not captured/explained by the factor(s).

Parallel analysis A technique used to decide the number of factors to retain.

Orthogonal rotation A factor rotation technique assuming no correlation between factors when extracting the factors.

Varimax A type of orthogonal rotation technique.

Oblique rotation A factor rotation technique allowing for correlation between factors when extracting the factors.

Promax A type of oblique rotation technique.

Reliability The consistency between the items or observed variables.

Cronbach's alpha A measure of reliability.

Factor score Value of a factor computed for each observation.

QUESTIONS

1   What is the difference between principal component and principal factor extraction methods?
2   What is the rationale behind rotating factors?
3   How do you go about determining the number of factors to retain?

4   What is a factor score?
5   Explain what Cronbach's alpha is used for and how it is used.

FURTHER READING

Fabrigar, L.R. and Wegener, D.T. (2011) *Exploratory Factor Analysis*. Oxford: Oxford
   University Press.

This is a good short introduction to exploratory factor analysis. The authors explain mainly
in a non-technical manner the different steps of the factor analysis process with some
example factor models estimated at the end of the book.

Hair, J.F., Black, W.C., Babin, B.J. and Anderson, R.E. (2013) *Multivariate Data Analysis* (7th edn).
   Harlow: Pearson.

This comprehensive multivariate statistics book includes a relatively lengthy chapter
on factor analysis. The authors explain the salient aspects of factor analysis without
mathematical details, leading the reader through an example factor analysis study.

Kline, P. (1994) *An Easy Guide to Factor Analysis*. New York: Routledge.

This book explains first principal component analysis with mathematical formulas before
covering the typical common factor analysis methods (principal factor analysis, maximum
likelihood factor analysis). The author's approach really does help one understand the logic
behind and difference between PCA and factor analysis.

Pett, M.A., Lackey, N.R. and Sullivan, J.J. (2003) *Making Sense of Factor Analysis: The Use
   of Factor Analysis for Instrument Development in Health Care Research*. Thousand Oaks,
   CA: Sage.

Of the four books in this list, this provides the most comprehensive coverage of factor
analysis. The book explains not only the factor analysis technique but also the stage before,
namely designing an instrument. The authors provide a short but useful introduction to
matrices as well. The authors explain the different stages with examples and interpretation
of software output.

REFERENCES

Afifi, A.A., May, S. and Clark, V.A. (2012) *Practical Multivariate Analysis*. Boca Raton, FL:
   Chapman and Hall/CRC.
Beauducel, A. (2011) Indeterminacy of factor score estimates in slightly misspecified
   confirmatory factor models. *Journal of Modern Applied Statistical Methods*, 10(2), 583–598.
Brown, T.A. (2015) *Confirmatory Factor Analysis for Applied Research*. New York: Guilford
   Press.
Fabrigar, L.R. and Wegener, D.T. (2011) *Exploratory Factor Analysis*. Oxford: Oxford
   University Press.
Gorsuch, R.L. (1983). *Factor Analysis*. Hillsdale, NJ: Lawrence Erlbaum Associates.
Hair, J.F., Black, W.C., Babin, B.J. and Anderson, R.E. (2013) *Multivariate Data Analysis* (7th edn).
   Harlow: Pearson.

Hamilton, L.C. (1992) *Regression with Graphics – A Second Course in Applied Statistics*. Belmont, CA: Duxbury Press.

Harman, H.H. (1976) *Modern Factor Analysis*. Chicago: University of Chicago Press.

Hatcher, L. (2006) *A Step-by-Step Approach to Using SAS for Factor Analysis and Structural Equation Modeling* (8th edn). Cary, NC: SAS Institute.

Kachigan, S.K. (1991) *Multivariate Statistical Analysis: A Conceptual Introduction*. New York: Radius Press.

Kline, P. (1994) *An Easy Guide to Factor Analysis*. New York: Routledge.

Kline, R.B. (2011) *Principles and Practice of Structural Equation Modeling* (3rd edn). New York: Guilford.

Lattin, J.M., Carroll, J.D. and Green, P.E. (2003) *Analyzing Multivariate Data*. Pacific Grove, CA: Thomson Brooks/Cole.

Matsunaga, M. (2010) How to factor-analyze your data right: do's, don'ts, and how-to's. *International Journal of Psychological Research*, 3(1), 97–110.

Pett, M.A., Lackey, N.R. and Sullivan, J.J. (2003) *Making Sense of Factor Analysis: The Use of Factor Analysis for Instrument Development in Health Care Research*. Thousand Oaks, CA: Sage.

Sharma, S. (ed.) (1996) *Applied Multivariate Techniques*. New York: Wiley.

StataCorp (2015) *Stata Multivariate Statistics Reference Manual: Release 14*. College Station, TX: Stata Press.

Tabachnick, B.G. and Fidell, L.S. (2014) *Using Multivariate Statistics* (6th edn). Harlow: Pearson.

Thompson, B. (2004) *Exploratory and Confirmatory Factor Analysis: Understanding Concepts and Applications*. Washington, DC: American Psychological Association.

Thurstone, L.L. (1947) *Multiple-Factor Analysis: A Development and Expansion of The Vectors of the Mind*. Chicago: University of Chicago Press.

12

STRUCTURAL EQUATION MODELLING AND CONFIRMATORY FACTOR ANALYSIS

learning outcomes

- Understand the scope of structural equation modelling
- Explain structural equation modelling through confirmatory factor analysis
- Learn to specify, identify and estimate a structural equation model

- Learn to assess measurement and structural parts of a structural equation model
- Understand and interpret structural equation models using Stata

In this chapter, we first define what structural equation modelling (SEM) is. We then present several types of SEM, including confirmatory factor analysis (CFA). Since the CFA model is a very commonly used type of structural equation model, we explain the issues of model specification, model identification, model estimation, model fit measures and model modification with the help of some simple CFA models. In doing so, we also explicate how CFA compares with the exploratory factor analysis that we dealt with in the previous chapter. We then go through the SEM process using a latent path model (also called a full/complete SEM or structural model) using Stata. In this review, we focus more on the interpretation of the model parameters.

12.1 WHAT IS STRUCTURAL EQUATION MODELLING?

In the previous chapters we have presented some of the more traditional statistical techniques (linear regression, logistic regression, multilevel regression, etc.) that are used to examine the relationship between one or more independent variables and *only one dependent variable*. The independent and dependent variables in the above-mentioned models are observed[1] ones such as income, height, weight, years of education and so on. Following this reasoning, we can refer to these traditional statistical approaches as single-equation techniques with observed variables both on the left-hand side (dependent) and right-hand side (independent) of the equation.

Like any of the traditional techniques, SEM too can be used for explanation and/or prediction purposes in the social sciences. The difference and thus the advantage of SEM (as opposed to single-equation techniques) is that it allows one to estimate the relationship between a number of independent variables and *more than one dependent variable* at the same time. Furthermore, while traditional techniques such as regression analysis let one only use observed variables, SEM includes latent[2] independent and dependent variables. As such, in a strict sense, we can refer to SEM[3] as a simultaneous multiple-equation technique including latent variables on both sides of the equations,[4] as graphically portrayed in Figure 12.1.

---

[1] Alternative terms are indicator, manifest and measured variables.

[2] Alternative terms are factor, construct, hypothetical, and unobservable.

[3] SEM is also referred to as latent variable modelling, covariance structure analysis, and linear structural relationships (LISREL).

[4] In a broader sense, SEM as a framework allows one to model observed and latent variables as independent and/or dependent variables. However, we will confine ourselves to the strict sense definition of SEM in this chapter.

KSI (ξ) = exogenous (latent independent) variable

ETA (η) = endogenous (latent dependent) variable

x = indicator of exogenous variable

y = indicator of endogenous variable

DELTA (δ) = measurement error for x indicator

EPSILON (ε) = measurement error for y indicator

PHI (ϕ) = correlation between exogenous variables

GAMMA (γ) = coefficient between an exogenous and an endogenous variable

BETA (β) = coefficient between two endogenous variables

ZETA (ζ) = unexplained variance in an endogenous variable

LAMBDA (λ) = coefficient (loading) between indicators and latent variables

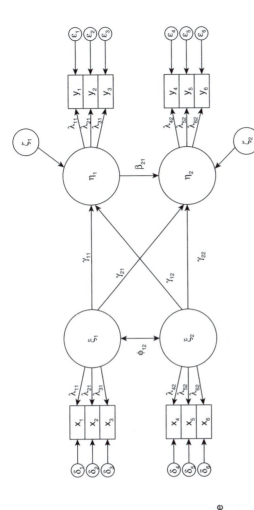

for instance,

λ_{42}, for exogenous variable, shows the loading of x_4 on the second exogenous variable

λ_{21}, for exogenous variable, shows the loading of y_2 on the first endogenous variable

ϕ_{12} represents the correlation between the first and second exogenous variable

γ_{21} shows the effect of the first exogenous variable on the second endogenous variable

γ_{12} shows the effect of the second exogenous variable on the first endogenous variable

β_{21} shows the effect of the first endogenous variable on the second endogenous variable

Figure 12.1 A structural equation model with LISREL notation

As we can see in Figure 12.1, in the SEM framework, latent variables are represented by large circles while observed variables are shown by rectangles. One-way arrows (→) represent direct effects, while two-way arrows (↔) represent covariances/correlations. Errors are exhibited by small circles. The notation depicted in Figure 12.1 is known as LISREL[5] notation, which is typically used to graphically portray and mathematically specify all types of structural equation models.[6]

12•1•1 Types of structural equation modelling

SEM can be used to estimate any kind of model including latent variables. This is particularly due to advances in specialized computer software. Most models estimated using SEM will fall into one of the following categories:

1 *Confirmatory factor analysis* is used to assess a hypothesized latent factor structure containing a set of indicators and one or more latent variables. For instance, we could use CFA to inquire whether the well-known 'Big Five' personality trait factor structure (extraversion, agreeableness, conscientiousness, neuroticism and openness to experience) would emerge in a particular dataset.

2 *Latent path analysis* (LPA)[7] is used not only to examine a factor structure but also to test hypothesized structural relationships among the latent variables. For instance, we could, by using LPA, examine whether customer satisfaction is a two-dimensional construct reflecting 'happiness with the product' and 'willingness to recommend the product' as well as assessing whether the former dimension influences the latter.

3 *Latent mean analysis* (LMA) is used to statistically test mean differences between two (or more) groups on latent variable(s). LMA, like LPA, would also include a CFA. We could use LMA to test whether men and women differ in terms of their mean scores on a latent variable such as the 'extraversion' personality trait. LMA is the direct latent equivalent of traditional ANOVA (Kline, 2011).

4 *Latent change/growth analysis* (LGA) is used to test whether there is change in a latent variable over time. LGA would also include a CFA. For instance, we may, by using LGA, try to find out if a particular organizational intervention (e.g., reward scheme) has been successful in improving employees' job satisfaction (latent variable), which may have been measured at two different time points (see Raykov and Marcoulides, 2006: 5–6, for details of such an example).

5 *Latent class analysis* (LCA) is a model-based approach to clustering individuals into segments (i.e. latent classes) based on their responses to a set of observed variables (Wang and Wang, 2012). LCA would include a CFA too. For instance, we may in a LCA find out that there are two latent classes (quality-sensitive and price-sensitive customers) emerging from a particular dataset.[8]

---

[5] LISREL is a SEM program developed by Jöreskog and Sörbom (1989).

[6] Since most of the literature uses the LISREL notation, it is useful to get accustomed to it.

[7] LPA is also referred to as structural regression modelling, full/complete SEM or combined SEM in the literature.

[8] LCA is not necessarily readily available in all standard SEM software. In Stata, there are user-written plugins and packages developed for LCA.

The above list can certainly be extended. The first two (CFA and LPA) are, however, the most commonly used SEM techniques in the social sciences. Further, we believe that learning CFA and LPA will lay a sound foundation for understanding the remaining and more advanced SEM techniques. We will therefore in this chapter focus on CFA and LPA.

We further suggest that one starts learning SEM through CFA. One reason for this is that it is after all the CFA part of all types of SEM that makes SEM a distinctively special statistical technique as compared to its traditional counterparts (regression, ANOVA, etc.). A second reason is that understanding CFA is an important prerequisite for developing and estimating complex structural equation models adequately, as problems encountered in SEM stem usually from poorly specified CFA (Bowen and Guo, 2012). A third reason is that all the SEM issues (identification, estimation, etc.) are basically the same for CFA and any other SEM technique. Finally, a standard CFA is a relatively simple case of SEM which may help one understand some of the complex issues more easily.

12.2 CONFIRMATORY FACTOR ANALYSIS

CFA is an alternative to or an extension of the exploratory factor analysis (EFA) that we treated in Chapter 11. Both CFA and EFA belong to the so-called common factor model family which partitions the variance of an indicator into common/shared variance and unique variance including measurement error (Brown, 2015). In other words, in CFA measurement error (unreliability) of indicators is removed during the model estimation. This specific feature of CFA (embedded in SEM) contributes to making structural equation model estimates less biased compared to traditional techniques like regression which assume no measurement error at all (Harlow, 2014). This is the main reason for the increasing popularity and application of SEM techniques in social science research publications.

If EFA removes the measurement error just as CFA does, why do we need CFA? The answer to this question is that CFA is a confirmatory statistical technique which *a priori* imposes restrictions on the factor model to be estimated (Brown, 2015). In CFA, we specify the number of factors and pattern of indicator-factor loadings beforehand, as well as other model parameters such as those bearing on the independence or covariance of the factors and indicator error variances (Brown, 2015). Specification is only, as seen below, the first step of the entire CFA/SEM process, and is followed by model identification, model estimation, model assessment and model modification.

Let us now explain these five steps using a real-life data[9] example. The data that we use here is obtained from a survey of 1004 Norwegian individuals. In this survey, the respondents were asked to indicate (on an ordinal scale[10] from 1 = not at all important, to 5 = very important) how important each of the following personal values was as a guiding principle in their lives: being well respected by others (x_1), a sense of security (x_2), a sense of accomplishment (x_3), self-fulfilment (x_4), and self-respect (x_5).

---

[9] The name of the dataset that we use is *values.dta*.

[10] Here, we treat ordinal data as if they are continuous and thus fit a linear model using the sem command. However, if we wanted to fit a model for ordinal data, we would then use the gsem command.

12•2•1 Model specification

Using the just-mentioned data, based on the relevant theory, we specify a two-dimensional factor structure including two personal value types (factors): collectivistic values (which x_1 and x_2 load on) and individualistic values (which x_3, x_4 and x_5 load on). We further assume a covariance/correlation between these two factors. No other specification is chosen for our model, which is graphically depicted in Figure 12.2.

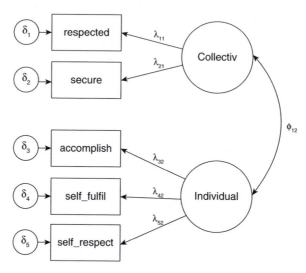

Figure 12.2 Graphical representation[11] of our CFA model

Using the LISREL notation presented earlier (see Figure 12.1), we can readily transform our graphically depicted model (Figure 12.2) into regression equations as follows:

$$
\begin{aligned}
x_1 &= \lambda_{11}\xi_1 + \delta_1, \\
x_2 &= \lambda_{21}\xi_1 + \delta_2, \\
x_3 &= \lambda_{32}\xi_2 + \delta_3, \\
x_4 &= \lambda_{42}\xi_2 + \delta_4, \\
x_5 &= \lambda_{52}\xi_2 + \delta_5.
\end{aligned}
\tag{12.1}
$$

Thus, there are five regression models estimated at one go while also taking into account the correlation between the two factors. This is the reason why we referred to SEM earlier as a simultaneous multiple-equation technique. Listing these equations helps us to understand how SEM works computationally; however, in practice, SEM software does the computation (much faster) using a compact matrix language which encompasses all the regression equations. For instance, our model with the five regression models can be presented in one single matrix equation as follows:

$$
x = \lambda_x \xi + \delta.
\tag{12.2}
$$

---

[11] This model was drawn using the SEM Builder in Stata: choose SEM from the Statistics pull-down menu in Stata. In the SEM Builder, by default all errors are represented by epsilon (ε) unless you customize them.

This matrix equation for our model states that the vector of values for a variable x in a raw dataset is a product of the variable's factor loading (Λ) on the latent variable (ε) and the vector of scores for cases on that latent variable, plus a vector of error terms (δ) (Bowen and Guo, 2012) as follows:

$$\begin{bmatrix} x_1 \\ x_2 \\ x_3 \\ x_4 \\ x_5 \end{bmatrix} = \begin{bmatrix} \lambda_{11} & 0 \\ \lambda_{21} & 0 \\ 0 & \lambda_{32} \\ 0 & \lambda_{42} \\ 0 & \lambda_{52} \end{bmatrix} \begin{bmatrix} \xi_1 \\ \xi_2 \end{bmatrix} + \begin{bmatrix} \delta_1 \\ \delta_2 \\ \delta_3 \\ \delta_4 \\ \delta_5 \end{bmatrix}. \tag{12.3}$$

In (12.3), the zero values indicate that x_1 and x_2 do not load on factor 2 (individual values) and x_3, x_4 and x_5 do not load on factor 1 (collectivist values).

12•2•2 Model identification

To facilitate parameter estimation and model testing in CFA/SEM, first, the number of freely estimated parameters (unknowns) must not exceed the number of elements (knowns) in the sample variance–covariance matrix denoted **S** (Brown, 2015). The difference between the number of knowns (k) and the number of unknowns (u) is equal to the number of degrees of freedom of the model ($df = k - u$). When $df < 0$ the model is said to be under-identified, when $df = 0$ the model is considered just-identified, and finally, when $df > 0$ the model is referred to as over-identified. Due to the fact that we cannot estimate model parameters for under-identified models and that we cannot test the fit of just-identified models,[12] we would in CFA/SEM opt for over-identification (Kline, 2005).

Let us now examine our model in Figure 12.2. We can obtain the number of knowns (k) from the formula $p(p + 1)/2$ where p denotes the number of indicators (Raykov and Marcoulides, 2006). Since we have five indicators, for our model $k = 5(5 + 1)/2 = 15$. As for the number of unknowns (parameters to estimate), we have three factor loadings (λ_{21}, λ_{42}, λ_{52}), five error variances (δ_1, δ_2, δ_3, δ_4 and δ_5), one covariance (Φ_{12}) and two factor variances (Φ_{11} and Φ_{22}), so that $u = 11$. Then $df = 15 - 11 = 4 > 0$.[13] Thus, we can consider our model identifiable, a condition necessary for estimating parameters and testing model fit. Stata provides this df automatically at the bottom of its estimation output (see Figure 12.3).

In addition to the condition $df > 0$, latent variables must be assigned a scale/metric for model identification (Kline, 2011) since they do not have any metric prior to estimation. There are two main approaches to assigning a metric to a latent variable.

The first approach is to pass the marker/reference indicator's metric on to the latent variable (Brown, 2015). In Stata (and in other SEM software, for that matter), the first indicator is by

---

[12] The reason is that, in just-identified cases, the model fit would by default be perfect (see Raykov & Marcoulides, 2006).

[13] Although the $df > 0$ rule works fine for CFA/SEM in most instances, in the case of so-called empirical under-identification, this rule will not be a sufficient criterion to judge the identifiability of a model. Empirical under-identification typically occurs when the covariances in the sample variance–covariance matrix equal 0 (see Brown, 2015, for further details).

The annotation callouts read:

- This is the command estimating CFA/SEM in Stata

- ML converges after 3 iterations. This is the log of the maximized likelihood of the parameters given the data

- Since our model is a CFA, the results are reported under the heading 'Measurement'. The indicator *respected* is used as the marker indicator of the latent variable *Collectiv* as its factor loading is fixed to 1. The same applies to *accomplish* which is used as the marker indicator of the latent variable *Individual*

- These are the error variances of the indicators and variances of the latent variables

- This is the covariance between the two latent variables

- Since there is an arrow pointing to these in Figure 12.2, this means that the latent variables are predicting these indicators which are then the endogenous (dependent) variables

- Since there is an arrow departing from the latent variables in Figure 12.2, they are the exogenous (independent) variables

- The sample size is 1004, but since ML uses listwise deletion, the sample size is reduced to 976.

- This is the unstandardized factor loading of the indicator *secure* on the latent variable *Collectiv*

- This is the unstandardized factor loading of the indicator *self_fulfil* on the latent variable *Individual*

- This is the unstandardized factor loading of the indicator *self_respect* on the latent variable *Individual*

```
. sem (Collectiv -> respected secure) (Individual -> accomplish self_fulfil self_respect)
(28 observations with missing values excluded)

Endogenous variables

Measurement:    respected secure accomplish self_fulfil self_respect

Exogenous variables

Latent:         Collectiv Individual

Fitting target model:

Iteration 0:   log likelihood = -4709.3064
Iteration 1:   log likelihood = -4708.8674
Iteration 2:   log likelihood = -4708.8659
Iteration 3:   log likelihood = -4708.8659

Structural equation model                       Number of obs    =       976
Estimation method  = ml
Log likelihood     = -4708.8659

 ( 1)  [respected]Collectiv = 1
 ( 2)  [accomplish]Individual = 1
```

	Coef.	OIM Std. Err.	z	P>|z|	[95% Conf. Interval]
Measurement					
respected <-					
Collectiv	1.0000	(constrained)			
_cons	4.4580	0.0227	196.50	0.000	4.4135 4.5025
secure <-					
Collectiv	0.9058	0.0546	16.59	0.000	0.7988 1.0128
_cons	4.5461	0.0217	209.18	0.000	4.5035 4.5887
accomplish <-					
Individual	1.0000	(constrained)			
_cons	4.1680	0.0278	149.90	0.000	4.1135 4.2225
self_fulfil <-					
Individual	1.0678	0.0424	25.18	0.000	0.9847 1.1509
_cons	4.1434	0.0282	146.70	0.000	4.0881 4.1988
self_respect <-					
Individual	0.6968	0.0344	20.28	0.000	0.6295 0.7642
_cons	4.4631	0.0232	192.38	0.000	4.4176 4.5086
var(e.respected)	0.1710	0.0190			0.1375 0.2127
var(e.secure)	0.1892	0.0166			0.1592 0.2248
var(e.accomplish)	0.2619	0.0188			0.2275 0.3014
var(e.self_fulfil)	0.2169	0.0192			0.1824 0.2580
var(e.self_resp-t)	0.2861	0.0154			0.2575 0.3179
var(Collectiv)	0.3313	0.0276			0.2815 0.3900
var(Individual)	0.4926	0.0352			0.4283 0.5666
cov(Collectiv, Individual)	0.2578	0.0203	12.69	0.000	0.2179 0.2976

```
LR test of model vs. saturated: chi2(4)    =    30.49, Prob > chi2 = 0.0000
```

Figure 12.3 Stata output from ML estimation with the unstandardized solution

default selected as the marker indicator and its unstandardized factor loading is fixed to 1. In our example model, the marker indicators are *respected* and *accomplish* for the latent variables *Collectiv* and *Individual*, respectively (see Figure 12.3). Both of these indicators are measured using an ordinal scale (from 1 to 5) which will also be the scale/metric of the two latent variables. This does not mean that the latent variables will themselves be ordinal. The latent variables will be assumed to have a metric following a normal distribution with mean 0. What we *can* say about the metric of the latent variables is that the variance of the latent variables will be a portion of the variance of the corresponding marker indicator.

The second approach is that the variance of the latent variable is fixed to 1, meaning that the latent variable is standardized (Brown, 2015), while allowing all the unstandardized factor loadings to be freely estimated. This approach provides semi-standardized coefficients[14] in the solution which are generally of less interest for researchers. Thus, the marker indicator approach, which provides both unstandardized and completely standardized estimates, appears to have been more commonly used in social science publications. This is probably also the reason why the marker indicator approach is the default procedure in the SEM module of Stata.

Speaking of fixing a variable, there are three types of parameters we can make use of in CFA/SEM. A *fixed* parameter is a parameter (loading, variance, etc.) that is fixed to a specified value. A *free* parameter is an unknown element that needs to be model estimated. Finally, a *constrained*[15] parameter is a parameter that is unknown but is constrained to equal one or more other parameters in the model (Wang and Wang, 2012). The difference between a fixed and a constrained parameter is that the former is not estimated while the latter is estimated but kept equal for more than one parameter (e.g., factor loadings).

12•2•3 Parameter estimation

The objective of CFA/SEM is to obtain estimates for each parameter of the model (factor loadings, factor variances, etc.) to produce a predicted variance–covariance matrix (denoted by Σ) that resembles the sample variance–covariance matrix (**S**) as closely as possible (Brown, 2015: 62). In other words, as in ordinary least-squares regression (see Chapter 3), the aim here is also to minimize the difference between the predicted (Σ) and the observed sample values (**S**). This minimization is measured using a fitting function (*F*). Each estimation method has its own fitting function. The most common estimation method used in CFA/SEM is maximum likelihood, which applies the fitting function

$$F_{ML} = \ln |\mathbf{S}| - \ln |\Sigma| + \text{trace } (\mathbf{S}\Sigma^{-1}) - p,$$

where $\ln |\mathbf{S}|$ is the natural log of the determinant[16] of **S**, $\ln |\Sigma|$ is the natural log of the determinant of Σ, Σ^{-1} is the inverse of Σ, and p is the number of indicators.

---

[14] Shows the change in *Y* (i.e., indicator) in its original units caused by one standard deviation increase in *X* (latent variable)

[15] In Stata, anything that is constrained to a fixed value will be denoted as constrained.

[16] The determinant shows the non-overlapping variance in a matrix.

When $F_{ML} = 0$, the model fits the data perfectly. However, there is always some gap between **S** and **Σ**. Maximum likelihood uses an iterative procedure to try to find the estimate that minimizes this gap. The smaller the gap, the better the model fit to the data.

In addition to maximum likelihood (ML), in CFA/SEM estimation can be done using weighted least squares (WLS/ADF), robust weighted least squares (WLSMV), unweighted least squares (ULS), or generalized least squares (GLS). Stata provides the following four estimation methods (see also Acock, 2013: 15), three of which are essentially ML estimations while one is asymptotically distribution-free (ADF) estimation:

1 Maximum likelihood (ML) is the default and commonly used option when there is no severe departure from multivariate normality.
2 Quasi-maximum likelihood (QML) is a method combining ML with Huber–White (`robust`) or Satorra–Bentler standard errors (`sbentler`) not assuming multivariate normality.
3 Asymptotically distribution-free (ADF) is a form of weighted least squares not assuming multivariate normality.
4 Maximum likelihood with missing values (MLMV) is also referred to as full-information maximum likelihood and is recommended for use when you have missing data in that it uses all the information available (whereas the three methods above use listwise deletion). This method assumes multivariate normality.

We estimate our model using ML[17] and provide the resulting Stata output in Figure 12.3.

12•2•4 Model assessment

Model assessment entails the interpretation of parameter estimates and the evaluation of the model fit measures.

Interpreting parameter estimates

It is more common to interpret and report CFA/SEM results based on the standardized solution/output. Thus, in addition to the unstandardized solution in Figure 12.3, in Stata we can easily ask for the standardized solution for our model by typing sem, standardized after our initial (SEM) estimation. The standardized solution is provided in Figure 12.4.

Let us now interpret the standardized factor loadings in Figure 12.4. As you can see, none of the factor loadings is fixed to 1 but instead they all are freely estimated. The reason is that when we ask for the completely standardized solution, the variance of the latent variable is fixed to 1 as in the case of using the factor variance approach to assign a metric to a latent variable.[18] For instance, the standardized loading of the indicator *respected*

---

[17] The sem command by default assumes latent variables are capitalized and indicators are in lower case.

[18] While in the factor variance approach we standardize only the latent variable, here we standardize both the latent variable and the indicator, giving us the so-called completely standardized estimates.

```
. sem, stand

Structural equation model                         Number of obs      =        976
Estimation method   = ml
Log likelihood      = -4708.8659

 ( 1)  [respected]Collectiv = 1
 ( 2)  [accomplish]Individual = 1
```

Standardized	Coef.	OIM Std. Err.	z	P>|z|	[95% Conf. Interval]	
Measurement						
respected <-						
Collectiv	0.8121	0.0240	33.91	0.000	0.7652	0.8591
_cons	6.2899	0.1459	43.11	0.000	6.0039	6.5759
secure <-						
Collectiv	0.7679	0.0241	31.90	0.000	0.7207	0.8150
_cons	6.6957	0.1549	43.23	0.000	6.3921	6.9993
accomplish <-						
Individual	0.8080	0.0163	49.56	0.000	0.7761	0.8400
_cons	4.7983	0.1132	42.38	0.000	4.5764	5.0202
self_fulfil <-						
Individual	0.8493	0.0153	55.44	0.000	0.8193	0.8794
_cons	4.6957	0.1110	42.30	0.000	4.4782	4.9133
self_respect <-						
Individual	0.6748	0.0210	32.14	0.000	0.6337	0.7160
_cons	6.1580	0.1430	43.06	0.000	5.8778	6.4383
var(e.respected)	0.3404	0.0389			0.2721	0.4259
var(e.secure)	0.4104	0.0370			0.3440	0.4896
var(e.accomplish)	0.3471	0.0263			0.2991	0.4028
var(e.self_fulfil)	0.2786	0.0260			0.2320	0.3346
var(e.self_resp~t)	0.5446	0.0283			0.4918	0.6031
var(Collectiv)	1.0000	.			.	.
var(Individual)	1.0000	.			.	.
cov(Collectiv,						
Individual)	0.6380	0.0281	22.67	0.000	0.5829	0.6932

```
LR test of model vs. saturated: chi2(4)    =    30.49, Prob > chi2 = 0.0000
```

Figure 12.4 Stata output from ML estimation with the standardized solution

on the latent variable *Collectiv* is 0.8121 which is statistically significant ($p<0.001$). The standardized factor loading of 0.8121 can be interpreted as the correlation between the indicator and the latent variable as long as there are no cross-loading indicators in the model[19] (Brown, 2015: 115). As such, the squared factor loading of 0.8121 is 0.6595 indicating that nearly 66% of the variance in the indicator 'respected' is explained by the latent variable *Collectiv*. We can interpret the remaining standardized loadings in the same manner. We would generally opt for standardized factor loadings equal to or above 0.4 in CFA/SEM. In Figure 12.4, we observe that all of the standardized loadings are clearly above the threshold of 0.4, lending support to our model.

By the way, the amount of the variance in an indicator explained by a latent variable can also be considered as *indicator reliability* (Brown, 2015). By typing estat eqgof after our SEM estimation in Stata, you would obtain the complete overview of indicator reliabilities. Further down in Figure 12.4, we also observe the amount of variance in each indicator not accounted

---

[19] For indicators loading on more than one latent variable, standardized loadings would resemble standardized beta coefficients in a multiple regression. This is the same as saying that one latent variable is predicting the indicator while holding the other latent variable constant (Brown, 2015: 131).

for by its latent variable. For instance, var(e.respected) shows that about 34 per cent of the variance in the indicator *respected* is not explained by the latent variable *Collectiv*. This confirms our interpretation above that 66 per cent of the variance of this indicator is explained.

Having examined the indicator reliabilities, we can further examine the factor/scale reliabilities. *Factor/scale reliability* refers to the proportion of the total variation in a scale formed by our indicators that is attributed to the true score (i.e., latent variable) (Acock, 2013: 20). To examine the reliability of our scales, we will compute and report Raykov's (1997) reliability coefficient (RRC), a measure which is commonly seen as more accurate than Cronbach's alpha. In Stata there is a user-written command called relicoef[20] that computes factor reliability coefficients for CFA/SEM factors using Raykov's (1997) formulas: for factors without correlated errors (no error covariance), we have

$$RRC = \frac{\left(\sum \lambda_i\right)^2 \phi}{\left(\sum \lambda_i\right)^2 \phi + \sum \theta_{ii}} \tag{12.4}$$

where the λ_i are the unstandardized loadings, ϕ is the factor variance, and θ_{ii} are the unstandardized error variances; while for factors with correlated errors (at least one error covariance), we have

$$RRC = \frac{\left(\sum \lambda_i\right)^2 \phi}{\left(\sum \lambda_i\right)^2 \phi + \sum \theta_{ii} + 2\theta_i} \tag{12.5}$$

where the θ_i are the unstandardized error covariances.

The reliability coefficients of our two latent variables are computed in Figure 12.5. As we observe from the results, both of the latent variables are associated with reliability coefficients above 0.7 which should be the minimum level of reliability for a CFA/SEM factor/scale.

In addition to indicator reliability and scale reliability, we should also examine the *construct validity* of the latent variables in CFA/SEM. A latent variable can be claimed to be valid when both convergent and discriminant validity are demonstrated. Convergent validity is the extent to which a set of indicators reflecting the same latent variable are positively correlated. Convergent validity is established when a latent variable has (at least) an average correlation (standardized loading) of 0.7 with its corresponding indicators. Squaring this

```
.  relicoef

Raykov's factor reliability coefficient
```

Factor	Coefficient
Collectiv	0.770
Individual	0.831

```
Note:  We seek coefficients >= 0.7
```

Figure 12.5 The relicoef command

---

[20] Type ssc install relicoef to install this user-written package.

average correlation (0.7^2) would provide us with the average variance extracted (AVE, here 0.5) by the latent variable, meaning that the latent variable should explain (at least) an average of 50% variance in its associated indicators.

Discriminant validity is about the distinctiveness of latent variables. The higher the correlation between a latent variable and its indicators as compared to its correlation with the other indicators in the model, the more distinct the latent variable is. As we have just seen, the AVE is a function of the correlation between a latent variable and its indicators. Further, the squared correlation between two different latent variables indicates how much variance the latent variables share with each other's indicators. As such, we should expect each of the latent variables' AVE to be larger than the squared correlation between them (Fornell and Larcker, 1981) to establish discriminant validity.

To compute the AVE for each latent variable as well as squared correlation between latent variables can be a tedious task. There is, however, a user-written command called `condisc`[21] that we can run in Stata right after our SEM estimation as we do in Figure 12.6. According to these results, we can first claim that convergent validity is present in that both AVE values are above the suggested minimum level of 0.5. Secondly, discriminant validity can also be claimed to be exhibited since the AVEs (0.625 and 0.610) are clearly larger than the squared correlation (0.407) between the two latent variables.

```
. condisc

              Convergent and Discriminant Validity Assessment
_____
Squared  correlations (SC) among  latent  variables
_____

               Collectiv  Individual
  Collectiv      1.000
  Individual     0.407       1.000

_____
Average variance extracted (AVE) by latent variables
_____

  AVE_Collec~v          0.625          No problem with discriminant validity
                                       No problem with convergent validity

  AVE_Indivi~l          0.610          No problem with discriminant validity
                                       No problem with convergent validity
_____

  Note: when AVE values >= SC values there is no problem with discriminant validity
        when AVE values >= 0.5 there is no problem with convergent validity
```

Figure 12.6 The `condisc` command

Model fit indices

Model fit is in a way the extent to which our model predicts the sample variance–covariance matrix. The way we can measure the model fit is to compare the model-predicted variance–covariance matrix (Σ) to the sample variance–covariance matrix (**S**). The smaller the difference between Σ and **S,** the better our model fits the data. There are many kinds of model fit

---

[21] Type `ssc install condisc` to install this user-written package.

indices proposed in the literature (see West et al., 2012: 212–213) each of which essentially measures the difference between the two matrices (Σ – **S**) in different ways (Bollen, 1989). In the following we will treat some of the most commonly reported model fit indices which are also provided by Stata: the chi-squared (x^2) test, the standardized root mean squared residual (SRMR), root mean squared error of approximation (RMSEA), comparative fit index (CFI), Tucker–Lewis index (TLI).

Chi-squared (x^2) test

The x^2 test works quite like the *F*-test used for comparing nested models in multiple regression. Since the aim of our hypothesized CFA/structural equation model (HM) is to reproduce **S**, one way of assessing our HM's performance is to compare our model's log-likelihood (LL)[22] with that of a model that already reproduces **S**. One such model is the so-called saturated model (SM), fitting the data perfectly (*df* = 0). An SM includes only variances and covariances/correlations. The x^2 test for the comparison of the two models (HM and SM) would assess the following:

H_0: HM fits no worse than SM (i.e., Σ = **S**),

H_1: HM fits worse than SM (i.e., $\Sigma \neq$ **S**).

Having already estimated our HM, we know that its log-likelihood (LL_{HM}) is –4708.8659 (see Figure 12.3). We can also estimate the SM by typing

```
. sem (<-respected secure accomplish self_fulfil self_respect)
```

This will yield a log-likelihood LL_{SM} = –4693.6228. The difference between LL_{HM} – LL_{SM} is –15.2431. Multiplying this difference by –2 makes the resulting figure (30.4862) follow the x^2 distribution. We also know that the HM has *df* = 4 and the SM has *df* = 0. We can then get the probability of falsely rejecting our null hypothesis above by typing di chi-2tail(4,30.4862) in Stata, which gives us the *p*-value of 0.000. This means that we reject the null hypothesis that our HM fits no worse than the SM, and conclude that our HM fits worse than the SM.[23] These results are identical to those readily provided by Stata shown in Figure 12.7.[24]

---

[22] This is the log of the maximized likelihood of the parameters given the data.

[23] Briefly, then, we would want a non-significant x^2 to be able to claim that a CFA/structural equation model fits the data well.

[24] You just type estat gof, stats(all) after our SEM estimation to obtain the *chi-square test* results as well as the remaining default fit indices supplied by Stata.

```
. estat gof, stats(all)
```

Fit statistic	Value	Description
Likelihood ratio		
chi2_ms(4)	30.486	model vs. saturated
p > chi2	0.000	
chi2_bs(10)	1886.339	baseline vs. saturated
p > chi2	0.000	
Population error		
RMSEA	0.082	Root mean squared error of approximation
90% CI, lower bound	0.057	
upper bound	0.111	
pclose	0.021	Probability RMSEA <= 0.05
Information criteria		
AIC	9449.732	Akaike's information criterion
BIC	9527.867	Bayesian information criterion
Baseline comparison		
CFI	0.986	Comparative fit index
TLI	0.965	Tucker-Lewis index
Size of residuals		
SRMR	0.024	Standardized root mean squared residual
CD	0.951	Coefficient of determination

Figure 12.7 Model fit indices[25]

There is a general consensus in the literature that the χ^2 test is highly sensitive to sample sizes in that the χ^2 statistic tends to be statistically significant in large samples.[26] On the other hand, small samples may obscure poor fit and yield less precise estimates of the parameters in CFA/SEM (West et al., 2012). Thus, it is generally recommended to also examine the following model fit indices.

Standardized root mean squared residual (SRMR)

The difference between the predicted and the sample variance–covariance matrix is the residual variance–covariance matrix.[27] The residual matrix indicates how well our hypothesized model is actually doing in terms of prediction. One omnibus way of quantifying the residual matrix is to take the average[28] of all its elements (i.e., variances and covariances). This quantity

---

[25] The Akaike information criterion (AIC) and Bayesian information criterion (BIC) are less commonly reported in SEM-based publications. They are two alternative comparative fit measures. A model with lower AIC/BIC value can be claimed to have a better fit.

[26] Large samples make it possible to detect very small differences.

[27] In Stata we can ask for this (unstandardized) residual matrix by typing `estat residuals` after estimating our structural equation model.

[28] Technically, this is the square root of the average of the squared residuals.

is referred to as the root mean squared residual (RMR). However, the RMR is computed based on the covariances (i.e., raw units) of Σ and $\mathbf{S}$. As there are often indicators with different units of measurement in CFA/SEM, it will be difficult to interpret a given RMR (Kline, 2005), precluding comparisons across datasets (West et al., 2012).

One way of overcoming these drawbacks is simply to take the average (see footnote 28) of all the elements in the residual matrix, which is arrived at by subtracting predicted and sample correlation (and not covariance) matrices. The resulting quantity is referred to as the standardized root mean square residual (SRMR). It simply shows the average difference between the correlations in Σ and $\mathbf{S}$ (Brown, 2015). This index can be used for comparison purposes in CFA/SEM. The smaller the SRMR, the better the model. The SRMR ranges from 0 (best fit) to 1 (worst fit). SRMR < 0.1 is generally associated with acceptable fit in CFA/SEM (Wang and Wang, 2012). When we look at the SRMR of our hypothesized model in Figure 12.7, it certainly provides support for a good fit.

Root mean squared error of approximation (RMSEA)

As opposed to the so-called *absolute fit* indices like x^2 and the SRMR, the root mean squared error of approximation (RMSEA) takes the model complexity and sample size into consideration in that it penalizes models with too many parameters to estimate (i.e., with low *df*) and accordingly favours simpler models (i.e., with higher *df*). More specifically, RMSEA compensates for the effect of model complexity by conveying discrepancy in fit ($\Sigma - \mathbf{S}$) per degree of freedom in the model using the following formula (Brown, 2015):

$$\text{RMSEA} = \sqrt{\frac{d}{df_{\text{HM}}}}, \text{ where } d = \frac{\left(x^2 - df\right)_{\text{HM}}}{N_{\text{HM}}}. \tag{12.6}$$

Let us apply this formula to our model. We have $d = (30.486 - 4)/976 = 0.0271373$, so

$$\text{RMSEA} = \sqrt{\frac{0.0271373}{4}} = 0.08236701. \tag{12.7}$$

As can be seen from this formula, as we decrease the *df* (i.e., include more parameters to estimate in our model), the RMSEA value increases. High RMSEA values will be a sign of poor model fit. RMSEA values ≥ 0.10 indicate poor model fit (Browne and Cudeck, cited in Bowen and Guo, 2012: 145). As shown in Figure 12.7, our model is associated with an RMSEA value of 0.082 which incidentally is same as the value that we calculated in (12.7). Since our RMSEA < 0.10 we can claim that our model fit is acceptable.

Comparative fit index (CFI)

When performing the x^2 test we essentially compare our HM with the saturated model (perfect fit). Here, we compare our HM with the baseline model (BM, poorest fit) so as to find out the relative improvement in the fit of our HM over that of the BM (Kline, 2011). The default BM (in Stata) is a model that assumes zero covariances/correlations among the indicators. As we have already estimated our HM, we know that its *df* and x^2 values of are 4 and 30.49, respectively (see Figure 12.3). We can also estimate BM by typing

```
. sem (<- respected secure accomplish self_fulfil self_respect), ///
covstr(respected secure accomplish self_fulfil self_respect, diagonal)
```

in Stata to obtain its $df = 10$ and $\chi^2 = 1886.34$. Using the formula below we get the CFI of our estimation:

$$\text{CFI} = 1 - \frac{\left(\chi^2 \ df\right)_{\text{HM}}}{\left(\chi^2 - df\right)_{\text{BM}}} . \tag{12.8}$$

Let us now apply this formula to our model:

$$\text{CFI} = 1 - \frac{30.49 - 4}{1886.34 - 10} = 0.986 . \tag{12.9}$$

Observe that this value (0.986) is same as the CFI provided by Stata in Figure 12.7. The CFI generally ranges from 0 to 1. CFI values ≥ 0.90 are generally associated with acceptable model fit (Acock, 2013). A CFI value of 0.986 indicates that our model does 98.6 per cent better than the worst-fitting model that assumes no correlations among the indicators (Acock, 2013). As such, based on the CFI value of 0.986, we can claim that our model's fit is acceptable (in fact, very good).

Tucker–Lewis index (TLI)

The TLI is another way of comparing our HM with the BM, defined (Wang and Wang, 2012: 19) as

$$\text{TLI} = \frac{\left(\chi^2/df\right)_{\text{HM}} - \left(\chi^2/df\right)_{\text{BM}}}{\left(\chi^2 - df\right)_{\text{BM}} - 1} \tag{12.10}$$

Let us now apply this formula to our model:

$$\text{TLI} = \frac{(30.49/4) - (1886.34/10)}{(1886.34/10) - 1} = 0.965 . \tag{12.11}$$

As (12.8) shows, the TLI imposes a penalty for model complexity as the more parameters to estimate the smaller the value of df_{HM}, thus the larger is $\left(\chi^2/df\right)_{\text{HM}}$, leading to smaller TLI (Wang and Wang, 2012). Notice that the value computed in (12.11) is identical to the TLI computed by Stata in Figure 12.7. The TLI also generally ranges from 0 to 1. TLI values ≥ 0.90 are generally associated with acceptable model fit (Acock, 2013). Based on our large TLI (0.965), we can conclude that our model fit is a good one.

12•2•5 Model modification

Model modification is about respecifying a poorly fitting initial CFA/structural equation model in an exploratory manner. Researchers respecify their initial models with the help of the so-called modification indices (MIs) computed by the software. MIs represent the predicted decrease in model χ^2 if a fixed or constrained parameter is freely estimated (Kline, 2005: 145). MIs are like a cost–benefit analysis in that the cost of letting one parameter be freely estimated is one degree of freedom, and the benefit is the reduction that we get in χ^2.

One way of finding out whether the benefit outweighs the cost is to consider the size of the reduction in x^2. If this reduction is (considerably) larger than 3.84, we can claim that the benefit outweighs the cost. The value of 3.84 is the critical x^2 value for $df = 1$. As such, for each modification index larger than 3.84, we would significantly improve the fit of the model by reducing x^2 significantly (Acock, 2013: 26).

Although the fit of our model is not poor and thus there is no need to try to improve its fit, for pedagogical purposes we will still use our model as an example here to show how to go about using modification indices. In Stata, we obtain the MIs for our model by typing estat mindices after our structural equation model estimation, a procedure that yields the results shown in Figure 12.8.

We see that the MI for the suggested correlation between the errors of the indicators *accomplish* and *self_respect* is 21.568. This means that we would reduce x^2 by 21.568 for 1 *df*, which is considerably larger than 3.84. We then decide to include this correlation in our model in Stata by typing the following:

```
. sem (Collectiv -> respected secure) (Individual -> accomplish ///
self_fulfil self_respect), cov(e.accomplish*e.self_respect)
```

To see the model fit after this modification, we simply ask for the model fit indices (as we did earlier) by typing estat gof, stats(all). Figure 12.9 shows the model fit results before and after modification. As we can see, including the suggested correlation has indeed improved all of the model fit indices (e.g., RMSEA goes down from 0.082 to 0.036).

Modifying a model based on the MI should be assisted by theoretical insights, an approach which has been shown to increase the chances of discovering the true model (Kline, 2005). A second suggestion is that modifications should be made one at a time, beginning with

```
. estat mindices
```

Modification indices

	MI	df	P>MI	EPC	Standard EPC
Measurement self_fulfil <- Collectiv	21.568	1	0.00	-.3299606	-.215241
self_respect <- Collectiv	15.798	1	0.00	.2204734	.1750985
cov(e.secure, e.self_fulfil)	10.401	1	0.00	-.0357749	-.1765986
cov(e.secure, e.self_respect)	4.495	1	0.03	.0206079	.0885852
cov(e.accomplish, e.self_fulfil)	15.798	1	0.00	.1268317	.5320919
cov(e.accomplish, e.self_respect)	21.568	1	0.00	-.0808387	-.2953228

EPC = expected parameter change

Figure 12.8 Modification indices

Before modification

Fit statistic	Value
Likelihood ratio	
chi2_ms(4)	30.486
p > chi2	0.000
chi2_bs(10)	1886.339
p > chi2	0.000
Population error	
RMSEA	0.082
90% CI, lower bound	0.057
upper bound	0.111
pclose	0.021
Information criteria	
AIC	9449.732
BIC	9527.867
Baseline comparison	
CFI	0.986
TLI	0.965
Size of residuals	
SRMR	0.024
CD	0.951

After modification

Fit statistic	Value
Likelihood ratio	
chi2_ms(3)	6.701
p > chi2	0.082
chi2_bs(10)	1886.339
p > chi2	0.000
Population error	
RMSEA	0.036
90% CI, lower bound	0.000
upper bound	0.072
pclose	0.693
Information criteria	
AIC	9427.947
BIC	9510.965
Baseline comparison	
CFI	0.998
TLI	0.993
Size of residuals	
SRMR	0.011
CD	0.969

Figure 12.9 Fit indices before and after modification

the largest, because a single change can affect other parts of the solution (Raykov and Marcoulides, 2006). Finally, as it is highly likely that the modification improvements apply to the particular dataset (Raykov and Marcoulides, 2006), modified models should be replicated with independent samples where possible (Chou and Huh, 2012).

12.3 LATENT PATH ANALYSIS

We have in the previous section covered the SEM process using CFA. In doing so, we have explained the SEM issues (from identification to modification) from a theoretical/conceptual perspective and given applications using Stata. Since the SEM issues treated in our discussion of CFA in Section 12.2 apply directly to any kind of SEM in general, there is no need to treat these again in this section. Instead, we present an additional application of SEM using latent path analysis (LPA) which is probably the most commonly applied technique in the social sciences. LPA is used to examine a factor structure as well as testing hypothesized structural relationships. The factor structure is concerned with the relationships between indicators and latent variables, whereas the structural relationships concern links between latent variables. The former is referred to as the measurement part, while the latter is named the structural part; together they comprise LPA.

Let us now first present the real-life dataset that we use to build up our LPA model. Our dataset (entitled *workout2.dta*) was collected from members of a training/fitness centre in 2014 in a medium-sized city in Norway. The members were asked to indicate how well certain features (x_1 and x_2 in Table 12.1) described them as a person, using an ordinal scale (1 = very badly, to 6 = very well). Using a similar scale (1 = not at all important, to 6 = very important), the members were also asked to indicate how important various factors (y_1, ..., y_9 in Table 12.1) were for working out.

Table 12.1 Overview of the indicators and latent variables for our model

Indicators	Latent variables
x_1 – attractive face x_2 – sexy	Attractive
y_1 – to have a good body y_2 – to improve my appearance y_3 – to look more attractive	Appearance
y_4 – to develop my muscles y_5 – to get stronger y_6 – to increase my endurance	Muscle
y_7 – to lose weight y_8 – to burn calories y_9 – to control my weight	Weight

12●3●1 Specification of the LPA model

Based on relevant evolutionary psychology theories, we propose the following hypotheses:

H_1: The more attractive a person perceives her/himself the more the person wants to work out to improve her/his physical appearance (i.e., *Attractive → Appearance*)

H_2: The more the person wants to work out to improve her/his physical appearance, the more s/he wants to work out to build up muscles (i.e., *Appearance → Muscle*)

H_3: The more the person wants to work out to improve her/his physical appearance, the more s/he wants to work out to lose weight (i.e., *Appearance → Weight*)

H_4: The more attractive the person perceives her/himself, the more this will indirectly influence her/him to want to work out more to build up muscles (i.e., *Attractive → Appearance → Muscle*)

H_5: The more attractive the person perceives her/himself, the more this will indirectly influence her/him to want to work out more to lose weight (i.e., *Attractive → Appearance → Weight*).

It is usual in SEM-based publications and in fact quite useful to put together these hypotheses in a path diagram (as done in Figure 12.10) to ease the understanding of the relationships as well as providing a basis for equation-based formulations of these hypotheses.

Using the LISREL notation presented earlier (see Figure 12.1), we can transform our graphical model (Figure 12.10) into regression equations as shown in Table 12.2. As you can see, we give the equations for both the measurement and structural parts.

Our structural model can be represented in a single matrix equation as follows:

$$\boldsymbol{\eta} = \mathbf{B}\boldsymbol{\eta} + \boldsymbol{\Gamma}\boldsymbol{\xi} + \boldsymbol{\zeta}. \tag{12.12}$$

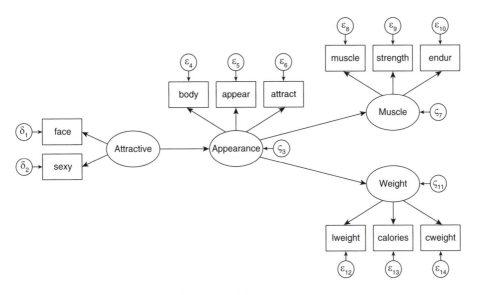

Figure 12.10 Graphical representation of our LPA model

Table 12.2 Equations for the measurement and structural model

Measurement part		Structural part	
Attractive	$x_1 = \lambda_{11}\xi_1 + \delta_1$ $x_2 = \lambda_{21}\xi_1 + \delta_2$	Appearance ← Attractive	$\eta_1 = \gamma_{11}\xi_1 + \zeta_3$
Appearance	$y_1 = \lambda_{11}\eta_1 + \varepsilon_4$ $y_2 = \lambda_{21}\eta_1 + \varepsilon_5$ $y_3 = \lambda_{31}\eta_1 + \varepsilon_6$	Muscle ← Appearance	$\eta_2 = \beta_{21}\eta_1 + \zeta_7$
Muscle	$y_4 = \lambda_{42}\eta_2 + \varepsilon_8$ $y_5 = \lambda_{52}\eta_2 + \varepsilon_9$ $y_6 = \lambda_{62}\eta_2 + \varepsilon_{10}$	Weight ← Appearance	$\eta_3 = \beta_{31}\eta_1 + \zeta_{11}$
Weight	$y_7 = \lambda_{73}\eta_3 + \varepsilon_{12}$ $y_8 = \lambda_{83}\eta_3 + \varepsilon_{13}$ $y_9 = \lambda_{93}\eta_3 + \varepsilon_{14}$		

12•3•2 Measurement part

Estimation of our LPA model proceeds in two steps, in that we first establish a psychometrically sound (i.e., valid and reliable) measurement model and subsequently test the structural model (see Anderson and Gerbing, 1988). The measurement part of the LPA model includes the relationship between each of our four latent variables (*Attractive*, *Appearance*, *Muscle* and *Weight*) and its respective indicators shown in Figure 12.10. As such, we estimate the measurement model (which essentially is a standard CFA) and ask for its fit indices using the commands below in Stata:

```
. sem (Attractive->face sexy) (Appearance->body appear attract) ///
(Muscle->muscle strength endur) (Weight-> lweight calories ///
cweight), stand
. estat gof, stats(all)
```

We do not show the results (factor loadings, error variances etc.) obtained from the estimation of the measurement model here. Instead, we present only the model fit indices since our purpose is first to obtain a good fit for the measurement model (Bowen and Guo, 2012: 127) prior to examining its psychometric properties. As can be seen in Figure 12.11a, several of our model fit indices (RMSEA > 0.1, TLI < 0.9, etc.) are not acceptable. In order to improve the fit of the measurement model, we ask for the modification indices (by typing estat mindices)[29] and find that correlating the error variances of two different pairs of indicators (*muscle* and *endur*, *lweigh* and *body*) would improve the model fit. Making this modification to the measurement model, we re-estimate our respecified/modified model using the following commands:[30]

```
. sem (Attractive->face sexy) (Appearance->body appear attract) ///
(Muscle->muscle strength endur) (Weight-> lweight calories cweight) ///
, stand cov(e.muscle*e.endur e.lweight*e.body)
. estat gof, stats(all)
```

As we can see in Figure 12.11b, the fit indices of our modified model are improved to acceptable levels.[31]

Since we have established an acceptable fit for our modified measurement model, we can now go on to examine its psychometric properties (validity and reliability). Thus, we now present the estimation results of our modified model (i.e., Figure 12.11b). To save space, we show only those parts of the results (i.e., standardized loadings) which are of most interest to us here. As can be seen in Figure 12.12, all of the standardized loadings are above the minimum acceptable level of 0.4 and they are all statistically significant.

What is even more important here is to check the convergent and discriminant validity of this modified model. This is easily done in Stata with the condisc command, which yields the output in Figure 12.13. This shows that our model exhibits both convergent and discriminant validity. As far as convergent validity is concerned, all of the AVEs are above the suggested level of 0.5. When it comes to discriminant validity, all of the AVEs are considerably larger than all of the squared correlations among the latent variables.

---

[29] For space reasons, we have omitted the output of modification indices.

[30] In fact, we estimate the model by adding the first correlation between the error variance of *muscle* and *endur*, and then we estimate the extended model by adding the second correlation between the error variances of *lweigh* and *body*.

[31] For this illustrative example, we accept the RMSEA value of 0.107 in the modified model. However, in reality we would want RMSEA lower than 0.10.

(a) Before modification

Fit statistic	Value
Likelihood ratio	
chi2_ms(38)	155.981
p > chi2	0.000
chi2_bs(55)	1308.679
p > chi2	0.000
Population error	
RMSEA	0.129
90% CI, lower bound	0.108
upper bound	0.150
pclose	0.000
Information criteria	
AIC	6152.926
BIC	6278.939
Baseline comparison	
CFI	0.906
TLI	0.864
Size of residuals	
SRMR	0.076
CD	1.000

(b) After modification

Fit statistic	Value
Likelihood ratio	
chi2_ms(36)	113.576
p > chi2	0.000
chi2_bs(55)	1308.679
p > chi2	0.000
Population error	
RMSEA	0.107
90% CI, lower bound	0.085
upper bound	0.130
pclose	0.000
Information criteria	
AIC	6114.520
BIC	6246.996
Baseline comparison	
CFI	0.938
TLI	0.905
Size of residuals	
SRMR	0.069
CD	1.000

Figure 12.11 Fit indices of the measurement part of LPA model

Standardized	Coef.	OIM Std. Err.	z	P>|z|	[95% Conf. Interval]	
Measurement						
face <-						
Attractive	0.7243	0.1028	7.04	0.000	0.5228	0.9258
_cons	3.3455	0.1878	17.81	0.000	2.9774	3.7136
sexy <-						
Attractive	0.9223	0.1237	7.46	0.000	0.6799	1.1647
_cons	2.3863	0.1434	16.64	0.000	2.1052	2.6675
body <-						
Appearance	0.8143	0.0269	30.27	0.000	0.7615	0.8670
_cons	2.7082	0.1590	17.03	0.000	2.3966	3.0198
appear <-						
Appearance	0.9637	0.0136	70.76	0.000	0.9370	0.9904
_cons	2.0328	0.1280	15.88	0.000	1.7818	2.2838
attract <-						
Appearance	0.8916	0.0187	47.69	0.000	0.8550	0.9282
_cons	1.7830	0.1177	15.15	0.000	1.5524	2.0137
muscle <-						
Muscle	0.9546	0.0800	11.93	0.000	0.7977	1.1114
_cons	2.4720	0.1473	16.79	0.000	2.1834	2.7606
strength <-						
Muscle	0.6730	0.0651	10.33	0.000	0.5453	0.8007
_cons	4.0214	0.2204	18.24	0.000	3.5893	4.4534
endur <-						
Muscle	0.7280	0.0873	8.34	0.000	0.5569	0.8990
_cons	4.7513	0.2563	18.54	0.000	4.2489	5.2537
lweight <-						
Weight	0.8512	0.0250	34.03	0.000	0.8021	0.9002
_cons	2.0914	0.1294	16.16	0.000	1.8379	2.3450
calories <-						
Weight	0.9109	0.0194	46.95	0.000	0.8729	0.9490
_cons	2.5121	0.1491	16.85	0.000	2.2199	2.8042
cweight <-						
Weight	0.8849	0.0212	41.76	0.000	0.8434	0.9264
_cons	2.4957	0.1483	16.83	0.000	2.2050	2.7865

Figure 12.12 Result of the modified measurement model

```
. condisc
```

Convergent and Discriminant Validity Assessment

Squared correlations (SC) among latent variables

	Attractive	Appearance	Muscle	Weight
Attractive	1.000			
Appearance	0.063	1.000		
Muscle	0.013	0.208	1.000	
Weight	0.001	0.213	0.069	1.000

Average variance extracted (AVE) by latent variables

AVE_Attrac~e	0.688	No problem with discriminant validity No problem with convergent validity
AVE_Appear~e	0.796	No problem with discriminant validity No problem with convergent validity
AVE_Muscle	0.631	No problem with discriminant validity No problem with convergent validity
AVE_Weight	0.779	No problem with discriminant validity No problem with convergent validity

Note: when AVE values >= SC values there is no problem with discriminant validity
      when AVE values >= 0.5 there is no problem with convergent validity

Figure 12.13 Convergent and discriminant validity

Finally, we examine the scale reliabilities of the latent variables of our modified measurement model. To compute the reliability coefficients, we just type `relicoef` in Stata, yielding the results in Figure 12.14. The results indicate that all of the reliability coefficients are clearly above the recommended threshold of 0.7.

```
. relicoef
```

Raykov's factor reliability coefficient

Factor	Coefficient
Attractive	0.823
Appearance	0.952
Muscle	0.982
Weight	0.912

Note: We seek coefficients >= 0.7

Figure 12.14 Reliability coefficients

12•3•3 Structural part

Given that we have established a sound measurement model, we can now go on to assess the structural part of our model. Thus, we need to estimate the full LPA model. In other words, we extend our measurement (modified) with the hypothesized relationships among the latent variables and then estimate the resulting model (i.e., Figure 12.10 plus the correlations among the error variances) using the following commands in Stata, yielding the output shown in Figure 12.15.

```
. sem (Attractive->face sexy) (Appearance->body appear attract) ///
(Muscle->muscle strength endur) (Weight-> lweight calories cweight) ///
(Appearance<-Attractive) (Muscle Weight <-Appearance) ///
, stand cov(e.muscle*e.endur e.lweight*e.body)
. estat gof, stats(all)
```

The first step is to examine the fit of the LPA model. Due to sample size sensitivity, we do not base our evaluation of the model fit on the chi-squared test. As can be seen in Figure 12.15, RMSEA is just on the edge of being acceptable. Given that the CFI and TLI are both above 0.9 and the SRMR is less than 0.1 we would conclude that the fit of our LPA model is satisfactory, a condition which is generally necessary if we want to go on to examine and interpret the estimates.

The assessment of the structural part is similar to that when examining a statistical model tested using linear regression analysis (see Chapters 3 and 4). First, the sign, significance and size (3S) of path coefficients should be considered. Path coefficients are estimates that help us to assess the hypothesized relationships in the structural part. These path coefficients are typically presented in a standardized form (as in Figure 12.15), which is equivalent to standardized betas in linear regression. Standardized coefficients range generally between −1 and 1. The closer a path coefficient is to ±1 the stronger the relationship (positive/negative) is. And naturally, the closer a path coefficient is to 0, the weaker the relationship is. Standardized beta coefficients equal to or less than 0.09 indicate a small effect, coefficients between 0.09 and 0.2 indicate a moderate effect, and coefficients larger than 0.2 indicate large effect (see Chapter 4).

Turning to the standardized beta coefficients of our model in Figure 12.15, we observe that all the signs of the coefficients are in the hypothesized direction. That is, *Attractive* has a large and positive effect on *Appearance*, and *Appearance* has a large and positive effect on both *Muscle* and *Weight*. Finally, all of the standardized coefficients are statistically significant at 0.01. All these findings provide clear support for the first three of our study hypotheses (H_1, H_2, and H_3). Further, we can also ask for the R-squared values for the dependent/endogenous variables of our model. This is done by typing estat eqgof in Stata, yielding the results in Figure 12.16. Here, we see that *Attractive* alone explains about 7 per cent of the variance in *Appearance* whereas *Appearance* solely explains about 22 per cent and 21 per cent of the variance in *Muscle* and *Weight*, respectively.

Turning to the last two hypotheses (H_4 and H_5), we need to estimate the indirect effect of *Attractive* (via *Appearance*) on *Muscle* and *Weight*. To do so in Stata, we simply type estat

Figure 12.15 The estimation results of the LPA model

[output omitted]

Standardized	Coef.	OIM Std. Err.	z	P>|z|	[95% Conf. Interval]	
Structural						
Appearance <-						
Attractive	0.2543	0.0803	3.17	0.002	0.0970	0.4116
Muscle <-						
Appearance	0.4662	0.0688	6.77	0.000	0.3313	0.6011
Weight <-						
Appearance	0.4609	0.0634	7.27	0.000	0.3367	0.5851
Measurement						
face <-						
Attractive	0.7674	0.1155	6.65	0.000	0.5411	0.9937
_cons	3.3455	0.1878	17.81	0.000	2.9774	3.7136
sexy <-						
Attractive	0.8705	0.1277	6.82	0.000	0.6202	1.1207
_cons	2.3863	0.1434	16.64	0.000	2.1052	2.6675
body <-						
Appearance	0.8136	0.0269	30.23	0.000	0.7608	0.8664
_cons	2.7061	0.1589	17.03	0.000	2.3947	3.0176
appear <-						
Appearance	0.9647	0.0135	71.48	0.000	0.9383	0.9912
_cons	2.0328	0.1280	15.88	0.000	1.7818	2.2838
attract <-						
Appearance	0.8908	0.0188	47.48	0.000	0.8541	0.9276
_cons	1.7830	0.1177	15.15	0.000	1.5524	2.0137
muscle <-						
Muscle	0.9554	0.0788	12.12	0.000	0.8009	1.1099
_cons	2.4720	0.1473	16.79	0.000	2.1834	2.7606
strength <-						
Muscle	0.6787	0.0640	10.60	0.000	0.5533	0.8042
_cons	4.0214	0.2204	18.24	0.000	3.5893	4.4534
endur <-						
Muscle	0.7025	0.0800	8.79	0.000	0.5458	0.8593
_cons	4.7513	0.2563	18.54	0.000	4.2489	5.2537
lweight <-						
Weight	0.8469	0.0253	33.51	0.000	0.7974	0.8964
_cons	2.0898	0.1293	16.16	0.000	1.8364	2.3432
calories <-						
Weight	0.9150	0.0192	47.76	0.000	0.8774	0.9525
_cons	2.5121	0.1491	16.85	0.000	2.2199	2.8042
cweight <-						
Weight	0.8840	0.0213	41.45	0.000	0.8422	0.9258
_cons	2.4957	0.1483	16.83	0.000	2.2050	2.7865

	Coef.	Std. Err.	z	P>|z|	[95% Conf. Interval]	
var(e.face)	0.4111	0.1772			0.1766	0.9569
var(e.sexy)	0.2423	0.2223			0.0401	1.4632
var(e.body)	0.3381	0.0438			0.2622	0.4358
var(e.appear)	0.0693	0.0260			0.0332	0.1447
var(e.attract)	0.2064	0.0334			0.1503	0.2835
var(e.muscle)	0.0873	0.1506			0.0030	2.5702
var(e.strength)	0.5393	0.0869			0.3933	0.7396
var(e.endur)	0.5064	0.1124			0.3278	0.7823
var(e.lweight)	0.2828	0.0428			0.2102	0.3805
var(e.calories)	0.1628	0.0351			0.1067	0.2483
var(e.cweight)	0.2185	0.0377			0.1558	0.3065
var(e.Appeara~e)	0.9353	0.0408			0.8586	1.0189
var(e.Muscle)	0.7826	0.0642			0.6664	0.9191
var(e.Weight)	0.7876	0.0584			0.6810	0.9108
var(Attractive)	1.0000	.				
cov(e.body,						
e.lweight)	-0.3752	0.0787	-4.77	0.000	-0.5293	-0.2210
cov(e.muscle,						
e.endur)	-1.7979	2.0396	-0.88	0.378	-5.7956	2.1997

LR test of model vs. saturated: chi2(39) = 118.36, Prob > chi2 = 0.0000

Fit statistic	Value
Likelihood ratio	
chi2_ms(39)	118.363
p > chi2	0.000
chi2_bs(55)	1308.679
p > chi2	0.000
Population error	
RMSEA	0.104
90% CI, lower bound	0.083
upper bound	0.126
pclose	0.000
Information criteria	
AIC	6113.308
BIC	6236.090
Baseline comparison	
CFI	0.937
TLI	0.911
Size of residuals	
SRMR	0.077
CD	0.822

Callouts:
- This is the structural part of the LPA model
- These are the standardized beta coefficients
- This is the measurement part of the LPA model
- These are the standardized factor loadings
- These are the standardized error variances of the indicators and latent variables
- These are the correlations between the error variances of the indicators
- These are the fit indices of the LPA model

```
. estat eqgof
```

Equation-level goodness of fit

depvars	fitted	Variance predicted	residual	R-squared	mc	mc2

[output omitted]

latent						
Appearance	1.493021	.0965595	1.396461	.0646739	.2543107	.0646739
Muscle	2.27	.4933958	1.776605	.217355	.4662134	.217355
Weight	2.197208	.4667143	1.730494	.2124124	.4608822	.2124124
overall				.8223466		

```
mc  = correlation between depvar and its prediction
mc2 = mc^2 is the Bentler-Raykov squared multiple correlation coefficient
```

Figure 12.16 *R*-squared values associated with the endogenous variables

`teffects, stand nodirect nototal compact`, a procedure which yields the results (both unstandardized and standardized) in Figure 12.17. Here, we observe that *Attractive* has a moderate and positive indirect effect on both *Muscle* and *Weight*, and that these indirect effects are statistically significant at the 0.01 level.

```
. estat teffects, stand nodirect nototal compact
```

Indirect effects

	Coef.	OIM Std. Err.	z	P>|z|	Std. Coef.

[output omitted]

Structural Appearance <-						
Muscle <-						
Attractive	0.238	0.088	2.7130	0.007		0.119
Weight <-						
Attractive	0.231	0.086	2.6950	0.007		0.117

Figure 12.17 The indirect effects

12.4 CONCLUSION

We have in this chapter provided a compact introduction to SEM through two of its most commonly applied techniques, CFA and LPA. In a broader sense, however, SEM should be seen as a statistical framework (rather than a single technique) that can replace most of the traditional statistical techniques (regression, ANOVA, logistic regression, etc.) as well as their extensions (seemingly unrelated regression, MANOVA, multinomial logistic regression, etc). In other words, SEM can be used to estimate any model that includes any number of independent and dependent variables of only observed or of only latent nature as well as a combination of these. This statement is particularly feasible/testable through Stata's powerful SEM commands `sem` and `gsem`. The latter, briefly put, can be used with non-continuous dependent/endogenous variables (binary, count etc.) as well as multilevel data.[32]

 **key terms**

Indicator variable A measured variable regressed on the latent variable.

Latent variable An unmeasured variable predicting the indicator variable.

Exogenous variable A predictor variable.

Endogenous variable An outcome variable.

CFA A model examining the relationship between indicator and latent variables.

Measurement error Represents an unreliable portion of variance of an indicator variable.

Under-identified model Associated with *df* less than 0.

Just-identified model Associated with *df* equal to 0.

Over-identified model Associated with *df* larger than 0.

Indicator reliability The amount of variance in an indicator explained by a latent variable.

Scale reliability The proportion of the total variation in a scale formed by our indicators that is attributed to the true score (i.e., latent variable).

Convergent validity The extent to which a set of indicators reflecting the same latent variable are positively correlated.

Discriminant validity The extent to which a latent variable is correlated with its indicators as opposed to the indicators of another latent variable.

Measurement model Includes the relationship between latent variables and their indicators.

Structural model Includes the relationship between latent variables.

Indirect effect The effect of a variable (via another variable) on a dependent variable.

QUESTIONS

1   Explain the criteria for assessing the performance of a confirmatory factor analysis as well as a latent path analysis.
2   Try to build and estimate alternative CFA models to the one that we estimate early in this chapter using the same dataset.

---

[32] We have left out the treatment of `gsem` in this chapter. You can, however, type `help gsem` in Stata to get to know this command and its further capabilities. We suggest you to do this particularly after reading the chapter on logistic regression as well as the chapter on multilevel analysis.

3 Explain why structural equation modelling can be used as a substitute for traditional analyses such as the *t*-test, analysis of variance and linear regression.
4 Use the `sem` command to estimate a standard regression model and compare its results with what you obtain by estimating the same model using the `regress` command.
5 Find and evaluate an article in your field that has applied a CFA or an LPA model.

FURTHER READING

Acock, A.C. (2013) *Discovering Structural Equation Modeling Using Stata*. College Station, TX: Stata Press.

This book gives a treatment of structural equation modelling from an applied perspective. It functions as an extension of this chapter in that the author goes into detail about the multi-group analysis as well as latent growth analysis. The author shows also how to estimate models using the SEM Builder in Stata.

Bowen, N.K. and Guo, S. (2012) *Structural Equation Modeling*. New York: Oxford University Press.

This book provides a matrix-based explanation of SEM using several applied examples. The book also has a brief chapter on preparation for SEM analyses that nicely supplements this chapter.

Brown, T.A. (2015) *Confirmatory Factor Analysis for Applied Research*. New York: Guilford Press.

Despite the fact that this is a book solely on confirmatory factor analysis, a thorough reading of it will enable you to understand SEM in depth. Working through the examples in the book using Stata would provide useful practice. The book treats some further advanced topics in SEM as well.

StataCorp (2014). *Stata Structural Equation Modeling Reference Manual Release 14*. Texas: Stata Press.

This is the official Stata manual, which gives comprehensive and detailed explanations of Stata's `sem` and `gsem` commands. You can also type `help sem` or `help gsem` in Stata.

REFERENCES

Acock, A.C. (2013) *Discovering Structural Equation Modeling Using Stata*. College Station, TX: Stata Press.

Anderson, J.C. and Gerbing, D.W. (1988) Structural equation modeling in practice: A review and recommended two-step approach. *Psychological Bulletin*, 103(3), 411–423.

Bollen, K.A. (1989) *Structural Equations with Latent Variables*. New York: Wiley.

Bowen, N.K. and Guo, S. (2012) *Structural Equation Modeling*. New York: Oxford University Press.

Brown, T.A. (2015) *Confirmatory Factor Analysis for Applied Research*. New York: Guilford Press.

Chou, C.-P. and Huh, J. (2012) Model modification in structural equation modeling. In R.H. Hoyle (Ed.), *Handbook of Structural Equation Modeling* (pp. 232–246). New York: Guilford Press.

Fornell, C. and Larcker, D. F. (1981) Evaluating structural equation models with unobservable variables and measurement errors. *Journal of Marketing Research*, 18, 39–50.

Harlow, L.L. (2014) *The Essence of Multivariate Thinking: Basic Themes and Methods*. New York: Routledge.

Jöreskog, K.G. and Sörbom, D. (1989) *LISREL 7: A Guide to the Program and Applications*. Chicago: SPSS Inc.

Kline, R.B. (2005) *Principles and Practice of Structural Equation Modeling*. New York: Guilford Press.

Kline, R.B. (2011) *Principles and Practice of Structural Equation Modeling* (3rd edn). New York: Guilford Press.

Raykov, T. (1997) Estimation of composite reliability for congeneric measures. *Applied Psychological Measurement*, 21, 173–184.

Raykov, T. and Marcoulides, G.A. (2006) *A First Course in Structural Equation Modeling*. Mahwah, NJ: Lawrence Erlbaum.

Wang, J. and Wang, X. (2012) *Structural Equation Modeling: Applications Using Mplus*. Chichester: Wiley.

West, S.G., Taylor, A.B. and Wu, W. (2012) Model fit and model selection in structural equation modeling. In R.H. Hoyle (Ed.), *Handbook of Structural Equation Modeling* (pp. 209–231). New York: Guilford Press.

13

CRITICAL ISSUES

learning outcomes

o Learn how to transform skewed or pointy variables

o Be able to perform robust regression

o Be able to treat missing data using different techniques

In this chapter we take a look at how to treat regression when conditions are not ideal. This could be because of skewed variable distributions, when the assumption of normally distributed errors is not met or when we have a problem with missing data. Too much skewness and/or kurtosis can cause problems with regression assumptions and the influence of outliers, and can to a certain degree be sorted out through power transformations. Robust regression may be a solution when the conditions for OLS are not ideal. Finally, there are various ways of approaching the problem of missing data.

TRANSFORMATION OF VARIABLES

Skewness, kurtosis and outliers can create problems for regression analysis, and can even create problems for a simple statistic like the mean. For example, if we have a sample of 20 persons and we are investigating their income, the mean can be a good measure of central tendency given that we do not have any severe outliers. However, if one of the persons is a football star playing for Real Madrid, his income will heavily influence the mean, and we might be better off using the median as our measure of central tendency. Just as such an outlier can influence the mean, it can also influence our regression coefficients and our error term. However, we can prevent problems by dealing with these distributions beforehand.

13•1•1 Skewness and kurtosis

A normal distribution is important in statistics as it plays a role in statistical generalization and the central limit theorem. A normal distribution is bell-shaped and symmetric about the mean; approximately 68 per cent of all observations lie within one standard deviation of the mean, and 95 per cent lie within 1.96 standard deviations. Normal distributions can come in different forms as long as they possess these characteristics. Figure 13.1 shows a standard normal distribution where the mean is 0 and the standard deviation is 1.

Skewness can be defined as the lack of symmetry in a distribution. A normal distribution has a skewness value of 0. If a distribution has a longer tail to the left (and the median is usually greater than the mean) it is said to have negative skewness. If the distribution has a longer tail to the right (and the median is usually smaller than the mean) it is said to have positive skewness. This is illustrated in Figure 13.2.

Kurtosis, on the other hand, is a measure of the pointiness of a distribution and was introduced by Pearson (1905). In Stata a normal distribution has a kurtosis value of 3 (be aware that SPSS and other statistical programs use methods that give a kurtosis value of

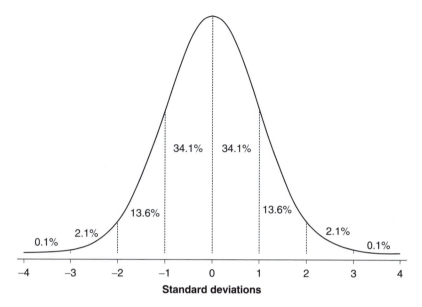

Figure 13.1 Standardized normal distribution

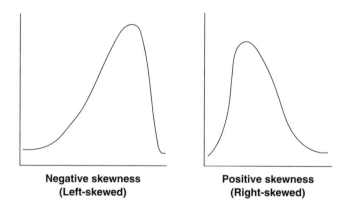

Figure 13.2 Negative and positive skewness

0 for a normal distribution;). If a distribution has too many observations close to the mean it has high kurtosis (greater than 3) and is described as leptokurtic. If a distribution has too few observations close to the mean it has low kurtosis (less than 3) and is described as platykurtic. This is illustrated in Figure 13.3.

There are three ways in Stata to determine whether a distribution is skewed or pointy. First, we can plot a histogram including the normal curve and visually inspect the distribution. Second, we can obtain the skewness and kurtosis values by summarizing the variable, using the detail option. Let us open the dataset *Critical_issues.dta*. Here we investigate country-year data for the period 1985–2011 gathered from World Bank (2014). We will take a closer look at the variable *GDPperCapita*:

```
. histogram GDPperCapita, normal
```

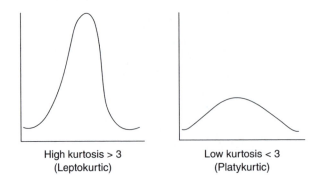

High kurtosis > 3   Low kurtosis < 3
(Leptokurtic)   (Platykurtic)

Figure 13.3 High and low kurtosis

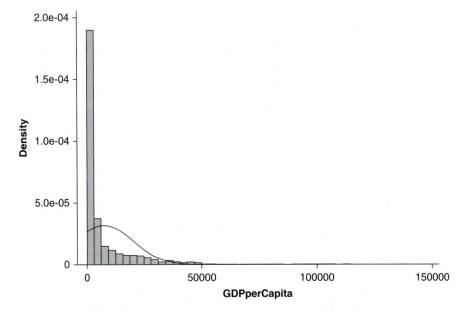

Figure 13.4 Histogram by *GDPperCapita*

. summarize GDPperCapita, detail

```
                              GDPperCapita

             Percentiles      Smallest
      1%       137.5107        64.35624
      5%       213.6175        64.8064
     10%       287.6725        69.05118      Obs                4285
     25%       579.0612        72.32932      Sum of Wgt.        4285

     50%      1936.696                       Mean           7493.085
                                Largest      Std. Dev.      12566.91
     75%      7929.696        103574.2
     90%      24075.09        106919.5       Variance       1.58e+08
     95%      35087.89        112028.5       Skewness        2.90578
     99%       54140.5        114508.4       Kurtosis       14.41547
```

Figure 13.5 Summary statistics for *GDPperCapita*

We see from Figures 13.4 and 13.5 that this variable is right-skewed (has positive skewness) and has a very high kurtosis. Third, as mentioned in Chapter 7, (p. 152) we can also perform the `sktest` to see if the distribution is significantly different from a normal distribution.

13•1•2 Transformations

As a skewed or pointy distribution can create problems for regression analysis, it is common practice to use transformations to pull in outliers and make the distribution more symmetrical. A negative consequence of transformations is that the direct interpretation of the regression results becomes more difficult. You can still look at the direction of the coefficient and whether the result is statistically significant, but the coefficient now represents a one-unit change in the transformed variable. In addition to helping us meet the assumptions of inferential statistics, transformations are used to make the data more interpretable. By transforming the data we change the form of relationships between variables, but the relative differences between observations for a given variable stay the same. Note that for a skewed variable any confidence interval is likely to have the wrong coverage probability; transforming the variable can correct this.

We can use power transformations to change the distributional shape of our variables. If we raise a variable to a power $p > 1$, we will reduce negative skew. If $p = 1$ the data stays the same, and if $p < 1$ (you can also use negative values) we will reduce positive skew. The further p is from 0, the stronger the effect of the transformation. For our dataset,

```
. generate transformedGDP = GDPperCapita^2
```

which usually reduces negative skew, does not work well, as GDP is positively skewed. However,

```
. generate transformedGDP = GDPperCapita^-1
```

which reduces positive skew, will give us a somewhat better distribution.

Another common way of reducing positive skew is to log-transform (using the natural logarithm) the variable (it does not work well with negative skew):

```
. generate lnGDP = ln(GDPperCapita)
. summarize lnGDP, detail
```

Figure 13.6 shows that we now have a better distribution than in the original variable (compare Figure 13.5).

However, we must remember that the logarithm of zero or a negative number is undefined. If our variable has either zeros or negative numbers, we need to add a constant to the data before we do the transformation. In our dataset we have a skewed variable *FDI* (foreign direct investment) where we have negative values (the lowest being –84,662,791,822). We thus add a constant which is the lowest value + 1:

```
. generate FDItest = FDI + 84662791823
. generate lnFDI = ln(FDItest)
```

lnGDP

	Percentiles	Smallest		
1%	4.923702	4.164434		
5%	5.364187	4.171404		
10%	5.661823	4.234848	Obs	4,285
25%	6.361408	4.281229	Sum of Wgt.	4,285
50%	7.568739		Mean	7.708129
		Largest	Std. Dev.	1.624449
75%	8.97837	11.54804		
90%	10.08893	11.57983	Variance	2.638834
95%	10.46561	11.62651	Skewness	.2389481
99%	10.89934	11.6484	Kurtosis	2.027544

Figure 13.6 Summary statistics for log-transformed *GDPperCapita*

Keep in mind that the syntax is just for the sake of example, and that log-transforming this particular variable does not improve its distribution.

It is possible to correct negatively skewed data using log transformation. In order to do this we have to reverse the score (don't forget about the reverse transformation when you interpret the results). The highest value of our *FDI* variable is 340,065,000,000. We can reverse this by subtracting each score from this value + 1 (so our lowest score on the reversed variable becomes 1):

```
. generate FDIreverse = 340065000001 - FDI
```

Now we can log-transform the reversed variable.

An easy way to get an overview over what type of transformation comes closest to a normal distribution is to use the gladder[1] command:

```
. gladder GDPperCapita
```

Compared to our original distribution (Figure 13.4) we see that log transformation would be the preferable option here (see Figure 13.7).

When it comes to dependent variables we can also use the glm command instead of transforming our *Y*. This has the advantage of avoiding the problem of negative or zero values when log-transforming the variable. A generalized linear model[2] (GLM) allows our dependent variable to have a distribution other than normal. This is taken care of by way

---

[1] One can also use the ladder or qladder command for different types of statistics and visual statistics.

[2] For more on generalized linear models, see Hardin and Hilbe (2012).

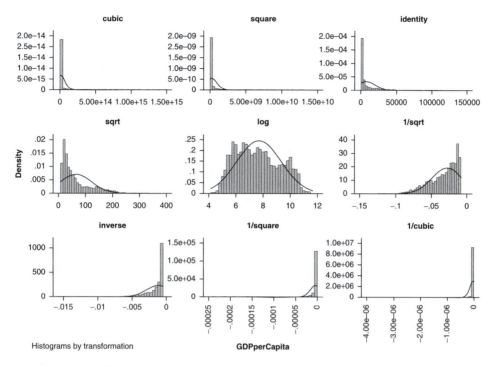

Figure 13.7 Output of transformations using `gladder` command

of a link function, where we define how our covariates (*X*-variables) are linked to our out-come variable:

```
. glm FDI GDPperCapita ethfrac incidence, link(log)
```

13●2 WEIGHTING CASES

Stata allows us to weight cases in regression analysis. We might be investigating survey data, where the researchers have either not been able to gather a random sample of the population, or chosen to oversample certain groups that might be of special interest or so as to get the most power for the least expenditure.[3] In either case, if we want to generalize to the total population we are required to weight the data. Such datasets will often include a weighting variable. Also, if we are investigating countries we can choose to treat each country as one unit, or we might want to weight them according to their size (this might be their population, area, or GDP). Stata

---

[3] Most survey designs do not sample individuals independently, and instead use clustering (for example, by county or municipality). The clusters of the first level of sampling are called *primary sampling units*, and individuals are sampled from the clusters. This results in larger sample-to-sample variability than sampling individuals directly. Sampling weights will thus help us get the regression coefficients correct, yet we must consider weighting, clustering, and stratification to get correct standard errors (which will often be too small if not taking this into account). For more on this, see StataCorp (2013a).

allows us to use four types of weights: `aweight`, `iweight`, `pweight` and `fweight`... We briefly describe each type of weight, but will only focus on the first and the third in our examples.

`aweight`: Analytic weights which can be used in weighted least-squares regression (a variant of robust regression; see next section) and similar procedures. These weights are commonly employed with data containing averages.

`iweight`: Importance weights which reflect the importance of the observations. The commands that support this weight will define how such weights are treated. These weights are mostly used by programmers.

`pweight`: Probability or sampling weights are what you use when you have a weight variable with weights that are proportional to the inverse of the probability that an observation is included due to sampling strategy. A case with a weight greater than 1 will count more in the analysis than a case with a weight less than 1.

`fweight`: Frequency weights which count the number of duplicated observations and indicate replicated data. If you use a weight together with this command, the weight will tell you how many observations each observation really represents. Frequency weights must be integers. They allow us to operate with smaller datasets that can be enlarged by the use of this option.

Let us open the dataset *WeightingP.dta*, which is taken from the European Social Survey (ESS, 2010). Here we investigate individual-level survey data from the United Kingdom; more specifically, we look at people's trust in political institutions (*Political_Trust*), which we will explain using the explanatory variables *woman*, *age*, *unemployed* and *eduyrs* (years of education). As already mentioned, many datasets operate with what is known as a weighted sample. In this case, this means that the European Social Survey has not drawn a true representative sample of the population of each country (including the UK). This is adjusted for by including a weight variable denoting the inverse probability of being drawn in the sample. This has been coded after comparing the drawn sample with population statistics (on certain parameters) to adjust for, for example, too few women being drawn or too many with higher education. In this dataset the weight variable is called `dweight` (design weight; see the output in Figure 13.8):

```
. tab dweight
```

Design weight	Freq.	Percent	Cum.
.5291676	675	27.87	27.87
.5291676	147	6.07	33.94
1.058335	992	40.96	74.90
1.058335	221	9.12	84.02
1.587503	257	10.61	94.63
2.11667	105	4.34	98.97
2.645838	14	0.58	99.55
3.175005	8	0.33	99.88
3.175005	1	0.04	99.92
3.704173	2	0.08	100.00
Total	2,422	100.00	

Figure 13.8 Frequencies of weight variable

We can use this weight to get a representative sample when running our analysis:

```
. regress Political_Trust woman age unemployed eduyrs [pweight=dweight]
```

Table 13.1 Unweighted and weighted coefficients

Variables	Coefficients	Weighted coeff.
Constant	7.314	8.233
Woman	–0.255	–0.149
Age	0.011	0.002
Unemployed	–3.282	–2.984
Education	0.255	0.222

Table 13.1 shows the difference in estimates in our unweighted and weighted regression models.

Using the `pweight` command is especially relevant for social scientists analysing survey datasets. This command is also central in the `survey` command option in Stata, which centres around the `svy` prefix:[4]

```
. svyset _n [pweight = dweight]
. svy: regress Political_Trust woman age unemployed eduyrs
```

In other instances, we might want to look at data that summarizes individual observations, or to weight units differently according to some measure of size. Let us now open the dataset *WeightingA.dta* which contains data on different countries in 2010. Here we will look at per capita GDP (*GDPperCapita*) and *population* taken from World Bank (2014) and democracy (*polity2*). The latter variable ranges from –10 to 10, where large values indicate a high score on democracy (Marshall and Jaggers, 2004). First, we will show descriptive statistics for *GDPperCapita*, weighting the units according to their population size. This means that the United States will count more than 300,000,000 and St. Lucia will count 174,000 when calculating the mean:

```
. summarize GDPperCapita [aweight = population]
```

In the output we get summary statistics where the countries are weighted according to their population size. We can also perform a regression using analytic weights:

```
. regress GDPperCapita polity2 [aweight=population]
```

---

[4] For more on the `survey` command, see Hamilton (2013, Chapter 4). The reader should also note that significance testing changes when performing analysis with `svy` (StataCorp, 2013a: 91).

13 3 ROBUST REGRESSION

As we have seen in previous chapters, OLS regression performs better than other regression methods when conditions are ideal. In real-life data we often encounter problems with skewed variables, heavy outliers, heteroscedasticity and non-normally distributed residuals. In OLS regression outliers are calculated with the same weight as any other observation, but can exert too much influence on the parameters. As was shown in Chapter 7, a solution is to run one model including and one excluding the most problematic outliers. However, another approach is to employ robust regression. This method will give a weight to each unit based on their total influence on the model (some observations will be given weight 0, and thus be dropped from the model). Robust regression is a quick and easy way to see how outliers influence the regression line as it will counter the influence of outliers (Hamilton, 1992: 223).

For this purpose, we can use the `rreg` command. This performs a version of robust regression. It starts by fitting an OLS regression, calculating the Cook's distance value for each observation, and excluding any observation with a Cook's distance greater than 1. Further, it calculates weights for each observation based on the residuals, then runs another regression based on the new weights, calculating new weights based on the new residuals, and so on (for more on this method, see Hamilton 1992).[5]

Let us open the dataset *Robust_regression.dta* which consists of economic data for the countries of the world in 2011. First, we will perform an OLS regression with *GDPperCapita* as our dependent variable and log-transformed foreign direct investment (*lnFDI*) as our independent variable (Figure 13.9):

```
. regress GDPperCapita lnFDI
```

Source	SS	df	MS		Number of obs =	156
					F(1, 154) =	43.24
Model	1.3276e+10	1	1.3276e+10		Prob > F =	0.0000
Residual	4.7281e+10	154	307022712		R-squared =	0.2192
					Adj R-squared =	0.2142
Total	6.0557e+10	155	390692806		Root MSE =	17522

GDPperCapita	Coef.	Std. Err.	t	P>|t|	[95% Conf. Interval]	
lnFDI	4316.25	656.3871	6.58	0.000	3019.565	5612.935
_cons	-77199.77	13886.64	-5.56	0.000	-104632.7	-49766.88

Figure 13.9 OLS regression

```
. predict GDPhat1 (this is for later use, see Figure 13.15)
. label variable GDPhat1 "OLS regression"
. predict res, residual
. histogram res
```

---

[5] The `rreg` command deals with outliers and long tales, which makes it different from the robust option (vce) which gives standard errors that are robust to heteroscedasticity.

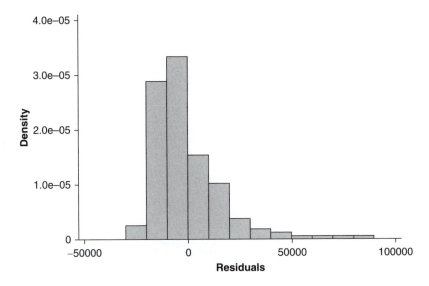

Figure 13.10 Histogram of residuals

We see from Figure 13.10 that the residuals of our variable are positively skewed with a high kurtosis (you can also check this by writing `sum res, detail`). We can use the `rvfplot` command to test for heteroscedasticity, and the output in Figure 13.11 shows that we have a problem with our model.

```
. rvfplot
```

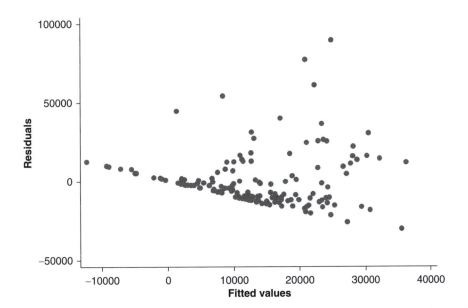

Figure 13.11 Graph of residuals vs. fitted values

We can also find the countries that exert most influence on our model (see Figure 13.12):

```
. graph twoway (scatter GDPperCapita lnFDI, mlabel(ccode)) (lfit GDPperCapita
lnFDI, mlabel(ccode))
```

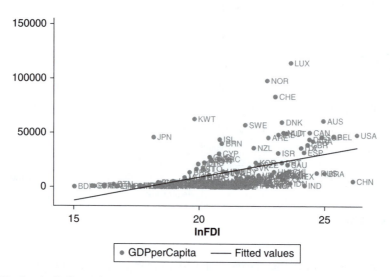

Figure 13.12 Graph of influential countries

Alternatively we can produce the Cook's distance values (Figure 13.13):[6]

```
. predict cooksd, cooksd
. sort cooksd
. browse ccode cooksd
```

150	KWT	.041992
151	AUS	.0444108
152	JPN	.0601535
153	CHN	.0682895
154	CHE	.074531
155	NOR	.1020857
156	LUX	.2136348

Figure 13.13 List of Cook's distance values

---

[6] Alternatively, we could write:

```
. predict cooksd, cooksd
. gsort -cooksd
. list in 1/10
```

In any case, we see that our largest outliers are Luxembourg, Norway and Switzerland.

As our model has non-normally distributed residuals, a problem with heteroscedasticity and obvious outliers, we can now run a robust regression on the same data:

```
. rreg GDPperCapita lnFDI
```

```
    Robust regression                        Number of obs =      156
                                             F(  1,    154) =    38.94
                                             Prob > F       =   0.0000
```

GDPperCapita	Coef.	Std. Err.	t	P>|t|	[95% Conf. Interval]
lnFDI	1250.73	200.4367	6.24	0.000	854.7698	1646.69
_cons	-20761.27	4240.474	-4.90	0.000	-29138.27	-12384.26

Figure 13.14 Robust regression model

We note from Figure 13.14 that we have a smaller coefficient for *lnFDI* than in the OLS model.[7] To compare the two models, we type the following:

```
. predict GDPhat2
. label variable GDPhat2 "robust regression"
. graph twoway scatter GDPperCapita GDPhat1 GDPhat2 lnFDI, mlabel(ccode)
```

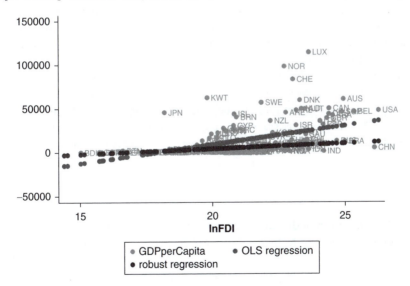

Figure 13.15 Comparison of OLS regression and robust regression

In Figure 13.15 we see the lighter grey line representing the OLS regression and the darker grey line is for the robust regression. Robust regression is a good way to see the effect of outliers

---

[7] To produce the weights used, you can type: `rreg GDPperCapita lnFDI, genwt(w)`

on our model, but should be treated with caution, as should OLS in the presence of outliers. There are also other Stata programs available for robust regression, such as Veradi and Croux's (2009) mmregress. This package can be installed by writing:

```
. ssc install mm_regress.pkg
. mmregress GDPperCapita lnFDI
```

 ## 13.4 MISSING DATA

In an ideal statistical world we would operate with complete datasets. However, in the real world we will often encounter missing data. There are several reasons why data are missing: refusal to answer a question, forgetting to ask (in the case of an interviewer) or answer (in the case of a respondent) a question, not knowing the answer to a question, lack of information about (say) a country, or loss of some document or other. Such missing data can lead to problems. Such problems are both practical (as most statistical procedures presuppose complete data matrices) and analytical (as missing data often gives biased estimates of the parameters).

We can classify different types of missing data according to their severity. The least problematic is what we call data that are *missing completely at random* (MCAR). This is the case if the probability of missing data on a given variable X is unrelated to the value of X or the values of any other variables in the dataset. If this is the case, we can view the observations that are present in the dataset (for X) as a random subsample from the original set of observations (Allison, 2002). MCAR can be regarded as a very strong assumption which is seldom the case in real-life survey data. We can test this assumption by checking the mean on other variables for persons with and without missing on X.

Let us open the dataset *Missing_data.dta*, which is the sample for the UK from the European Social Survey (ESS, 2012). We will look at the variable *trstep* (trust in the European Parliament) which ranges from 0 to 10, with high values indicating a high degree of trust. This variable has an N of 1928, which means 355 missing data points out of a total of 2286. First we generate a new variable where those with missing values on *trstep* get the value 1, and all others get the value 0.

```
. generate trstep_miss = missing(trstep)
```

Then we check the mean of the two subsamples on the variables *woman, age* and *lrscale* (self-placement on a left–right scale, high values meaning rightist attitudes):

```
. summarize age woman trstprl lrscale if trstep_miss==0
. summarize age woman trstprl lrscale if trstep_miss==1
```

We discover that the means differ somewhat, and those with missing values tend to be younger, female and more rightist than those with values present on *trstep*. Thus, we cannot assume that the MCAR assumption holds.

Another categorization is *missing at random* (MAR). This is the case when the probability of missing data on X is unrelated to the value of X, after controlling for other variables in the our model (Allison, 2002). In other words, the missingness can depend on other variables, but within each category of another variable, the probability of missingness on X is unrelated to the value on X. It is not possible to test whether this assumption holds. For practical purposes, we can say that missing data is non-ignorable if it is not MAR (or MCAR). If this is the case we should approach the problem as is prescribed in the following sections in order to get good estimates of our parameters.

13•4•1 Traditional methods for handling missing data

In this section we guide the reader through some of the traditional methods for handling missing data. These methods have flaws and can produce biased results, but are intended as background to understanding multiple imputation (Section 13.4.2).

Listwise deletion

Listwise deletion is the default option in Stata. This option means that for a given analysis, any observation that has missing data on one or more of the variables in our model is removed. Listwise deletion can be used for any type of analysis and does not require any special computation methods. If data are MCAR, this will only result in a reduced (but still random) sample of the original data. Our results will thus be unbiased, but with somewhat larger standard errors (due to the reduced N). However, if the data are not MCAR, this option can lead to biased estimates. Even so, many researchers employ listwise deletion if the degree of missingness is not too large. But ideally we should be concerned if we cannot show that the data are MCAR (MAR would be problematic with listwise deletion). Listwise deletion has been employed in the previous examples in this book.

Pairwise deletion

This means that all calculations are based on all available data pairwise for all pairs of variables that are included in the analysis. Pairwise deletion implies that different parameters are calculated based on different samples (as there is a variation in N from pair to pair). As such, all variance estimates and the t- and F-tests are biased, and our advice is not to employ pairwise deletion. There are some Stata commands available for pairwise deletion, such as `pwcorr`, `pwmean` and `pwcompare`. To sum up, for simple comparisons of pairs of variables, pairwise deletion can be used.

Missing data in a categorical variable

If we want to use a categorical variable with more than two values in a regression analysis our approach would be to dummy-code this variable. This means that we include all the dummy variables in our analysis, except for one, which we call the reference category (see Chapter 5). Take the variable *prtvtgb* (party voted for in last national election). Writing

```
. tab prtvtgb, missing
```

Party voted for in last national election, United Kingdom	Freq.	Percent	Cum.
Conservative	496	21.70	21.70
Labour	516	22.57	44.27
Liberal Democrat	255	11.15	55.42
Scottish National Party	37	1.62	57.04
Plaid Cymru	21	0.92	57.96
Green Party	19	0.83	58.79
Other	57	2.49	61.29
Ulster Unionist Party (nir)	10	0.44	61.72
Democratic Unionist Party (nir)	10	0.44	62.16
Sinn Fein (nir)	5	0.22	62.38
Social Democratic and Labour Party (nir	7	0.31	62.69
Alliance Party (nir)	3	0.13	62.82
Other (nir)	2	0.09	62.90
.	848	37.10	100.00
Total	2,286	100.00	

Figure 13.16 Frequencies of party voted for in last national election

We see from Figure 13.16 that this variable has 848 missing values which we might not want dropped from our analysis (but at the same time we wish to include this variable in the regression). The solution is simple. We code dummy variables for each category (and use either Conservative or Labour as reference). For Liberal Democrat one way to do the coding is as follows:

```
. generate dummy_LibDem=0
. replace dummy_LibDem=1 if prtvtgb==3
```

We do the same for all the categories we want (we might want to collapse some of the smaller ones). To avoid missing data we also code an additional dummy variable for those that did not answer this question:

```
. generate dummy_miss=0
. replace dummy_miss=1 if prtvtgb==.
```

We should be careful when interpreting *dummy_miss* as we are not sure which individuals are present in this category. This method, though intuitively appealing, has been proven to be biased even when data are MCAR (Allison, 2002), but when using listwise deletion the inclusion of this dummy means that we will not lose these 848 persons from the rest of the analysis.

Dummy variable adjustment

This approach is proposed by Cohen and Cohen (1985) and implies that we should insert a new value for all missing observations in a variable (e.g., 0 or the mean of the variable).

In addition, we should include a dummy variable coded 1 if the data in the original variable is missing, and 0 if present:

```
. generate new_trstep = trstep
. summarize trstep
. replace new_trstep = 3.297199 if trstep==.
```

Now we can run a regression including both *new_trstep* and *trstep_miss* (which we coded earlier, denoting whether or not the respondent has missing values on *trstep*). We perform a regression explaining how happy the respondent is (0–10):

```
. regress happy woman age new_trstep trstep_miss
```

Even though this approach lets us keep observations that would otherwise be deleted, it produces biased estimates of the coefficients (Allison, 2002). But this method can be used in cases where the missing value is non-existent ('not applicable' for the respondent). An example could be the question 'how long have you been married', which would not be applicable for unmarried respondents. However, we would still recommend not using the dummy-variable adjustment.

Single imputation

With single imputation we mean that we impute (put in) a reasonable guess where we have missing observations. The easiest method is mean imputation. That is, we impute the mean for those with data present where the variable has missing values (same as in above example):

```
. sum trstep
. generate mean_trstep = trstep
. replace mean_trstep = 3.297199 if trstep==.
```

This method will produce biased estimators and should be avoided. A better method is to use what we call regression imputation. Here, we use the information from other variables to get better guesses for our missing values. That is, we perform a regression analysis with our missing-ridden variable as the dependent, then predict the *Y*-values and replace the missing values with the predictions from the regression analysis. In our regression we include the variables *ppltrst* (most people can be trusted), *freehms* (gays and lesbians free to live as they wish) and *imsmetn* (allow many/few immigrants of same race as majority) in addition to *woman* and *age*:

```
. regress trstep ppltrst freehms imsmetn woman age
. predict Y
. generate predict_trstep = trstep
. replace predict_trstep = Y if trstep==.
```

However, this is a flawed solution to the problem of missing values. If we analyse models where we use imputed variables the standard errors will be underestimated and the test statistics overestimated. The reason is that our models do not adjust for the uncertainty that the missing values represent (we interpret it as a complete dataset). The general advice is that if data are missing, one should either use listwise deletion or multiple imputation (if possible).

13•4•2 Multiple imputation

This is a statistical technique for analysing incomplete datasets. Here one uses information from all values from other variables where data are available to predict values on the variable(s) with a low N in order to fill in the blanks. The objective of multiple imputation is not to predict the values as closely as possible to the true ones, but rather to enable us to handle missing data in a way that can provide us with valid statistical inference (Rubin, 1996). This method starts from the idea of regression imputation, but adds some further steps to achieve more realistic estimates. Multiple imputation is similar to regression imputation in the sense that we are using the observed variables from other variables in the model to predict the missing values. In addition, we can use the dependent variable and other variables in our prediction equations and we add several steps in the process to account for the uncertainty in our imputation procedure. Multiple imputation is a broad term that encompasses a collection of techniques. Typically, we need to assume that the data are MAR, however, in practice multiple imputation can help us get more reliable results even when missing is not MAR. Its strength is that it can restore observations and statistical power, and at the same time reduce the likelihood of biased coefficients. Its weakness is that the imputed values will on average have lower variance than the non-missing ones, thus leading to too low standard errors and the risk of Type I error.

Multiple imputation is a three-step process, as shown in Figure 13.17. We start with our incomplete data (where we have missing values on one or more variables). Then we start imputing, that is, we fill in the missing values using data from other variables in our model (including the dependent, the other explanatory variables, and other variables outside our model that might help explain our missing values). We do this not once, but m times (where typically m is set between 5 and 20). This results in m complete datasets. The imputations are generated by imposing a probability model on the complete data (observed and missing values).[8]

Next, each of the m datasets is analysed separately (e.g., m regression models). The result of this are m analyses. Finally, the m results are pooled so that the parameter estimates are the mean of their corresponding values in the m datasets. The standard errors from the m models

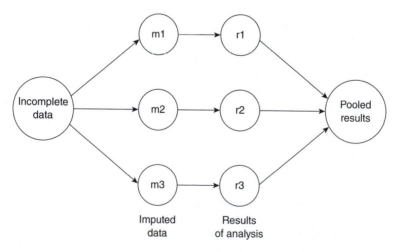

Figure 13.17 Multiple imputation

---

[8] For more details on multiple imputation, see StataCorp (2013b).

are also combined. If the models differ, an uncertainty term is added to the standard errors. If these steps are followed, the resulting inferences will be statistically valid (Rubin, 1987).

We will now look at how to perform multiple imputation in Stata, still using the dataset *Missing_data.dta*. First, we perform a regression analysis, explaining people's feeling of happiness (*happy*) based on how much trust they have in the EU Parliament (*trstep*), how much television they watch (*tvtot*), how much trust they have in people (*ppltrst*), how they feel about homosexuals (*freehms*), their views on immigration (*imsmetn*), as well as *woman* and *age*:

```
. regress happy trstep tvtot ppltrst freehms imsmetn woman age
```

Source	SS	df	MS		Number of obs =	1845
					F(7, 1837) =	22.72
Model	542.275993	7	77.467999		Prob > F =	0.0000
Residual	6264.78851	1837	3.41033669		R-squared =	0.0797
					Adj R-squared =	0.0762
Total	6807.0645	1844	3.69146665		Root MSE =	1.8467

happy	Coef.	Std. Err.	t	P>|t|	[95% Conf. Interval]	
trstep	.0816988	.0204805	3.99	0.000	.0415312	.1218664
tvtot	-.0451925	.0223711	-2.02	0.044	-.0890679	-.001317
ppltrst	.1654352	.0217794	7.60	0.000	.1227201	.2081502
freehms	-.1751684	.0525257	-3.33	0.001	-.2781847	-.0721521
imsmetn	-.1144462	.0559683	-2.04	0.041	-.2242143	-.0046781
woman	.0508997	.0873274	0.58	0.560	-.1203716	.222171
age	.0151377	.0025844	5.86	0.000	.010069	.0202063
_cons	6.341493	.2588148	24.50	0.000	5.83389	6.849095

Figure 13.18 OLS regression with missing values

Figure 13.18 shows our regression results, where we notice that *N* is 1845 (and we know the dataset has 2286 respondents). Since Stata uses listwise deletion, we know there must be a problem with missing values on one or more variables. Therefore, we investigate the whole dataset:

```
. misstable summarize
```

			Obs<.			
Variable	Obs=.	Obs>.	Obs<.	Unique values	Min	Max
ppltrst	10		2,276	11	0	10
pplfair	18		2,268	11	0	10
trstprl	67		2,219	11	0	10
trstep	358		1,928	11	0	10
prtvtgb	848		1,438	13	1	22
lrscale	373		1,913	11	0	10
freehms	37		2,249	5	1	5
imsmetn	69		2,217	4	1	4
imdfetn	56		2,230	4	1	4
happy	9		2,277	11	0	10
age	15		2,271	80	15	94

Figure 13.19 Reporting counts of missing data

One of the variables in our regression (*trstep*) stands out with only 1928 observations (see Figure 13.19). Therefore, we will impute the missing values of this variable in order to increase the *N* of our regression model. Our first step is to tell Stata that we want to use the data in the marginal long style (`mlong`) as this is memory-efficient (for more on this, see StataCorp, 2013b: 333):[9]

```
. mi set mlong
```

Our next step is to register which variable(s) we want to impute and also which variables will help us in imputing. As already mentioned, for the latter we should include all relevant variables: the dependent variable from our regression model, the other *X*-variables as well as additional variables that can predict a person's score on the variable with missing values.[10] In this case, we will include *pplfair* (most people try to take advantage of you), *trstprl* (trust in parliament) and *imdfetn* (allow many/few immigrants of different race/ethnic group as majority):

```
. mi register imputed trstep
. mi register regular happy tvtot ppltrst freehms imsmetn woman age
ppl. fair trstprl imdfetn
```

We are now ready to use multiple imputation. Here, we need to set the number of imputations (`add()`), that is, we generate 20 new imputed datasets, as well as to specify the `rseed()`. The latter is used for reproducibility, that is, if you want to get the same results you should use the same `rseed` value. In practice, we can just insert a random number[11] (here, we chose 1234). Also, for our example, we need to add the `force` option. The reason is that our regular variables also contain some missing values, and this option means that we proceed with the imputation even if missing imputed values are encountered. If all these variables had complete data there would be no need to use `force`. After the `impute` command we choose `regress`. This means that we fill in missing values of a continuous variable using the Gaussian normal regression imputation method (Stata Corp, 2013b: 253):

```
. mi impute regress trstep happy tvtot ppltrst freehms imsmetn woman age
pplfair trstprl imdfetn, add(20) rseed(1234) force
```

We see (Figure 13.20) that 265 of the 358 missing values of *trstep* were imputed. Not all were imputed due to there being missing values on the regular variables.

Now we want to compare our original data with the imputed data. This is always a good idea so that we can see if the imputed vales make sense. Here we set the numbers to 0, 1, and

---

[9] You could also look at the multiple imputation control panel by typing: `db mi`

[10] The imputation model and estimation model must be congenial (include the same variables). That is, all variables used in the estimation should be included in the imputation, together with the outcome (*Y*) variable and any auxiliary variables that may contain information about missing data.

[11] More specifically, it must be an arbitrary non-negative integer.

```
Univariate imputation                        Imputations =        20
Linear regression                                  added =        20
Imputed: m=1 through m=20                         updated =         0
```

	Observations per m			
Variable	Complete	Incomplete	Imputed	Total
trstep	1928	358	265	2286

```
(complete + incomplete = total; imputed is the minimum across m
 of the number of filled-in observations.)

Note: right-hand-side variables (or weights) have missing values;
      model parameters estimated using listwise deletion
```

Figure 13.20   Multiple imputation

20, where 0 means the original data, 1 means the first imputation and 20 means the last (we could of course include more numbers here):

```
. mi xeq 0 1 20: summarize trstep


m=0 data:
-> summarize trstep
```

Variable	Obs	Mean	Std. Dev.	Min	Max
trstep	1,928	3.297199	2.335696	0	10

```
m=1 data:
-> summarize trstep
```

Variable	Obs	Mean	Std. Dev.	Min	Max
trstep	2,193	3.28271	2.342886	−4.142136	10

```
m=20 data:
-> summarize trstep
```

Variable	Obs	Mean	Std. Dev.	Min	Max
trstep	2,193	3.273601	2.346516	−2.547195	10

Figure 13.21   Comparison of original and imputed data

As we can see from Figure 13.21, our imputed data falls below the range of *trstep* (which is 0–10). Ideally, we would like to restrict the imputed values of *trstep* to be within its observed range. Therefore we should instead use the pmm imputation method (instead of regress) in order to restrict the values. pmm stands for 'predictive mean matching' and is used on continuous variables. This option replaces a missing value with an observed value whose linear prediction is closest to that of the missing value.[12] It is recommended that we increase the number of nearest neighbours from which the imputed value is drawn. This is done by way of the knn() option. We need to reopen the data (without saving, as the data structure is altered), and run the procedure again, but this time using the pmm and knn() option:

```
. mi set mlong
. mi register imputed trstep
. mi register regular happy tvtot ppltrst freehms imsmetn woman age pplfair
trstprl imdfetn
. mi impute pmm trstep happy tvtot ppltrst freehms imsmetn woman age pplfair
trstprl imdfetn, add(20) rseed(1234) knn(10) force
. mi xeq 0 1 20: summarize trstep
```

m=0 data:
-> summarize trstep

Variable	Obs	Mean	Std. Dev.	Min	Max
trstep	1,928	3.297199	2.335696	0	10

m=1 data:
-> summarize trstep

Variable	Obs	Mean	Std. Dev.	Min	Max
trstep	2,193	3.299134	2.337782	0	10

m=20 data:
-> summarize trstep

Variable	Obs	Mean	Std. Dev.	Min	Max
trstep	2,193	3.29503	2.343273	0	10

Figure 13.22 Comparison of original and imputed data, using the pmm and knn() option

Now we see (Figure 13.22) that the values fall within the original range, and we are ready to do the regression (which in practice means that we are pooling the regression results for the 20 imputed datasets we created):

```
. mi estimate: regress happy trstep tvtot ppltrst freehms imsmetn woman age
```

We have increased the N of our model to 2110 (Figure 13.23) from 1845 when we first ran the model).

It is also possible to impute more than one variable. Let us clear our data, and open the dataset *Missing_data.dta* again (the reason is that we altered the data in our last procedure, so we want to start over again). Now we want to impute an additional variable called lrscale (people's self-placement on a left–right scale).

---

[12] For more on this, see Stata Corp (2013b: 241).

```
Multiple-imputation estimates          Imputations       =         20
Linear regression                      Number of obs     =      2,110
                                       Average RVI       =     0.0191
                                       Largest FMI       =     0.1304
                                       Complete DF       =       2102
DF adjustment:    Small sample         DF:      min      =     704.77
                                                avg      =   1,891.83
                                                max      =   2,099.18
Model F test:     Equal FMI            F(   7, 2084.0)   =      29.17
Within VCE type:       OLS             Prob > F          =     0.0000
```

happy	Coef.	Std. Err.	t	P>|t|	[95% Conf. Interval]	
trstep	.0748239	.0205258	3.65	0.000	.0345249	.1151229
tvtot	-.0615058	.0211062	-2.91	0.004	-.1028971	-.0201145
ppltrst	.1780047	.0202488	8.79	0.000	.1382944	.217715
freehms	-.1713068	.0494001	-3.47	0.001	-.2681851	-.0744285
imsmetn	-.1421843	.0527119	-2.70	0.007	-.2455578	-.0388109
woman	.0944893	.0824916	1.15	0.252	-.0672846	.2562631
age	.0163655	.0024112	6.79	0.000	.011637	.0210941
_cons	6.346202	.2417712	26.25	0.000	5.872045	6.82036

Figure 13.23 Result of regression using multiple imputation

```
. mi set mlong
. mi register imputed lrscale trstep
. mi register regular happy tvtot ppltrst freehms imsmetn woman age pplfair
trstprl imdfetn
```

For our next step we need to use the impute mvn option. This allows us to fill in values for one or more continuous variables using multivariate normal regression.[13] A drawback of this method is that we risk getting values that fall outside the variables' range:

```
. mi impute mvn trstep lrscale = happy tvtot ppltrst freehms imsmetn woman
age pplfair trstprl imdfetn, add(20) rseed(1234) force
. mi xeq 0 1 20: summarize lrscale trstep
```

Last, we add the variable *lrscale* to our previous regression model:

```
. mi estimate: regress happy lrscale trstep tvtot ppltrst freehms imsmetn
woman age
```

Multiple imputation can also be performed for logistic, multinomial, and ordered logit models (mi impute logit/ologit/mlogit and mi estimate: logit/ologit/mlogit). These options are further described in StataCorp (2013a).

---

[13] For more on this, see Stata Corp (2013b: 203).

13●5 CONCLUSION

In this final chapter, we have introduced some advanced topics relevant to regression analysis. First, we looked at how to transform variables in the presence of skewed or pointy/flat variable distributions. Then we moved on to the weighting of observations, where we focused on the `pweight` and `aweight` options in Stata. Finally, we guided you through the problem of missing data, presenting several ways to deal with it, with a special focus on multiple imputation.

 key terms

Skewness This is a measure of the lack of symmetry of a distribution. The skewness of a standard normal distribution is 0. If the skewness coefficient is negative, the distribution is left-skewed, and if it is positive, the distribution is right-skewed.

Kurtosis This is a measure of peakedness of a distribution. The kurtosis reported in Stata of a standard normal distribution is 3. A kurtosis coefficient greater than 3 means a pointy distribution, and less than 3 means a flat distribution.

Weights A weight function is a mathematical device used to give some observations more influence on the result than other observations in the same dataset.

Robust regression This method is an alternative to OLS regression if the data suffers from heavy outliers and/or influential observations.

Multiple imputation This term describes a statistical technique for analysing data in the presence of missing observations. It includes three steps: imputation, analysis and pooling.

QUESTIONS

1 Which statistical problems can skewed variable distributions lead to?
2 Name two situations where we should weight the cases in a regression analysis, and explain why weights are needed.
3 What makes multiple imputation a better method for handling missing data than other imputation methods?

FURTHER READING

Allison, P.D. (2002) *Missing Data*. London: Sage.

Part of the Sage series on quantitative applications in the Social Sciences, this book gives the reader an introduction to different ways to treat missing data.

Carpenter, J.R. and Kenward, M.G. (2013) *Multiple Imputation and its Application*. Chichester: Wiley.

This book focuses on the method of multiple imputation, and uses real-world examples from both medical and social statistics.

StataCorp (2013) *Stata Survey Data Reference Manual: Release 13*. College Station, TX: StataCorp LP.

This Stata manual provides an overview of the survey commands and background to topics like weighting, clustering, and stratification.

REFERENCES

Allison, P.D. (2002). *Missing Data*. London: Sage.

Cohen, J. and Cohen, P. (1985) *Applied Multiple Regression and Correlation Analysis for the Behavioral Sciences* (2nd edn). Hillsdale, NJ: Erlbaum.

ESS Round 5: European Social Survey Round 5 Data (2010) Data file edition 3.1. Norwegian Social Science Data Services, Norway – Data Archive and distributor of ESS data.

ESS Round 6: European Social Survey Round 6 Data (2012) Data file edition 3.1. Norwegian Social Science Data Services, Norway – Data Archive and distributor of ESS data.

Hamilton, L.C. (1992) *Regression with Graphics: A Second Course in Applied Statistics*. Pacific Grove, CA: Brooks/Cole.

Hamilton, L.C. (2013) *Statistics with Stata: Updated for Version 12*. Boston: Brooks/Cole.

Hardin, J.W. and Hilbe J.M. (2012) *Generalized Linear Models and Extensions* (3rd edn). College Station, TX: Stata Press.

Marshall, M.G. and Jaggers, K. (2004) *Polity IV Project: Political Regime Characteristics and Transitions, 1800–2004. Dataset Users' Manual*. Polity IV Project, Center for Global Policy, School of Public Policy, George Mason University.

Pearson, K. (1905) 'Das Fehlergesetz und seine Verallgemeinerungen durch Fechner und Pearson'. A rejoinder. *Biometrika*, 4(1/2), 169–212.

Rubin, D.B. (1987) *Multiple Imputation for Nonresponse in Surveys*. New York: Wiley.

Rubin, D.B. (1996) Multiple imputation after 18+ years. *Journal of the American Statistical Association*, 91(434), 473–489.

StataCorp (2013a) *Stata Survey Data Reference Manual: Release 13*. College Station, TX: StataCorp LP.

StataCorp (2013b) *Stata Multiple-Imputation Reference Manual: Release 13*. College Station, TX: StataCorp LP.

Verardi, V. and Croux, C. (2009) Robust regression in Stata. *Stata Journal*, 9(3), 439–453.

World Bank (2014) *World Development Indicators*. http://data.worldbank.org/data-catalog/world-development-indicators.

INDEX